FROM YOGA TO KABBALAH

Religious Exoticism and the Logics of Bricolage

VÉRONIQUE ALTGLAS

OXFORD
UNIVERSITY PRESS

OXFORD

UNIVERSITY PRESS

Oxford University Press is a department of the University of Oxford.
It furthers the University's objective of excellence in research, scholarship,
and education by publishing worldwide.

Oxford   New York
Auckland   Cape Town   Dar es Salaam   Hong Kong   Karachi
Kuala Lumpur   Madrid   Melbourne   Mexico City   Nairobi
New Delhi   Shanghai   Taipei   Toronto

With offices in
Argentina   Austria   Brazil   Chile   Czech Republic   France   Greece
Guatemala   Hungary   Italy   Japan   Poland   Portugal   Singapore
South Korea   Switzerland   Thailand   Turkey   Ukraine   Vietnam

Oxford is a registered trademark of Oxford University Press
in the UK and certain other countries.

Published in the United States of America by
Oxford University Press
198 Madison Avenue, New York, NY 10016

CIP data is on file at the Library of Congress

ISBN 978–0–19–999762–6 (hbk); 978–0–19–999763–3 (pbk)

1 3 5 7 9 8 6 4 2
Printed in the United States of America
on acid-free paper

Contents

Acknowledgments

THE SUCCESS OF academic work is not a single person's effort. It depends on the encouragement and contribution of many others. My greatest debts are to the many research participants who allowed me to "hang around" and agreed to tell me their life stories. This book would never have materialized without their contribution.

I take this opportunity to express my gratitude to Jim Beckford, Monique Bénard, Françoise Champion, Robert Fine, Roberte Hamayon, and David Lehmann, who have profoundly influenced me throughout the years of my education and early career. I hope they will feel the time and attention they spent on me has not been totally in vain.

I am particularly grateful to my colleagues of Queen's University Belfast for their willingness to read and comment on parts of this book: Nicola Carr, Lisa Smyth and, most of all, Matthew Wood. His boundless patience, intellectual interest, and critical reading have deeply stimulated and improved this work. The mistakes, omissions, and misconceptions are nonetheless mine alone.

From Yoga to Kabbalah

Introduction

"WHATEVER NEW THINGS come up, I'm up for trying," asserts Kim.[1] Kim is a 24-year-old artist. Dismissive about her Anglican education, she has been frequenting the Hindu-based movement Siddha Yoga in London for seven months. She has also experimented with yoga, hypnotherapy, and card reading, as well as alternative therapies such as acupuncture and chiropractic. Over the years, I have met numerous individuals who would endorse Kim's motto and who explore, successively or simultaneously, a vast array of religious teachings and alternative therapies originating from different cultural backgrounds.

By and large, the popularization of yoga and meditation, public curiosity about shamanism and Sufism, and the recent craze for Kabbalah all demonstrate the appeal of foreign religious traditions to a wide audience in advanced industrial societies. Strange and enticing, their perceived otherness seems to lend them authenticity and to nourish hopes for the discovery of mysteries and hidden truths. However, such popularization has not led to mass conversions to Buddhism, Hinduism, Islam, or Judaism. These traditions, as Kim's example suggests, are often explored as fragmented "resources" that are combined in seemingly eclectic assortments. This exoticism in the religious sphere, as such, has never been sociologically investigated: Why are individuals attracted to "foreign" religious traditions especially? Why are some of them appropriated and not others? Does their popularization entail their transformation and, if so, which ones? How do people engage with religious beliefs and practices that are initially foreign to them? By exploring a range of teachings and practices in different religious traditions, do individuals craft their personal religion? What roles do these appropriated religious teachings play in people's lives? Finally, what does this popularization of yoga, Sufism, meditation, or Kabbalah tell us about contemporary societies? These are the questions that this book addresses through cross-national research on three case studies: the Hindu-based Siddha Yoga and Sivananda Centres in France and Britain, and the Kabbalah Centre in France, Britain, Brazil, and Israel.

Bricolage and Religious Individualism

Sociologists of religion have not considered *religious exoticism*, the fascination for "foreign" religions, as an object of study in itself. Rather, they considered this fascination to be evidence of the fact that in contemporary society, individuals increasingly craft their religious life and identity by picking and mixing from a wide range of religious traditions. This has been called *bricolage*. *Bricolage* is a French common word that has no direct translation in the English language. It designates activities of fabricating, repairing, and installing—something like "DIY." It conveys the idea that this practice is amateurish or not serious—the verb *bricoler* in some contexts can be translated as "fiddling." Lévi-Strauss (1966) originally used the term as a metaphor to explain the ways in which mythological thought creates meaning and "fixes" myths by replacing missing or forgotten elements with residual components. In short,

> [f]or Levi-Strauss, mythical meaning-making bricoleurs combine their imagination with whatever knowledge tools they have at-hand in their repertoire (e.g., ritual, observation, social practices) and with whatever artifacts are available in their given context (i.e., discourses, institutions, and dominant knowledges) to meet diverse knowledge-production tasks. (Rogers 2012, 3)

Bastide developed the notion of bricolage to analyze syncretism with reference to Afro-Brazilian religions. He makes of bricolage a response to the "holes" of collective memory. It is about repairing what is already here (as such, bricolage is not pure invention but is organized) and, by doing so, it creates new meaning. Thus, Bastide's (1970) "sociology of bricolage" is an attempt to grasp the rules and logics that organize the manipulation, transformation, and making of symbolic resources.

Despite being originally used in the study of traditional societies, sociologists of religion started to refer to bricolage to describe the religious life in advanced industrial societies. Thus, "bricolage" was presented by Luckmann (1979) as an outcome of the privatization of religion. For Luckmann, because religious institutions lose their social control in the modern world, religion becomes a private matter, and hence individuals elaborate personally their beliefs and practices from diverse sources:

> The privatization of individual existence is linked to the privatization of religion in general. As for religious themes one is tempted to say with some exaggeration: *anything goes*. In the global interpenetration

of cultures, a vast—and by no means silent, although perhaps imagi-
nary—museum of values notions, enchantments, and practices has become *available*. It has become available "directly" but primarily through
the filter of mass media rather than social relations. The choice is determined rather *less by social conditions*—although evidently they continue to play a kind of screening role—*than by individual psychologies*.
(Luckmann 1979, 136, my emphases)

The assumptions being made here by Luckmann—an absolute eclecticism,
the unthought-of "availability" of undifferentiated symbolic resources, and extreme religious individualism—unfortunately remain within the sociology of
religion up to this day. As so often, here the reference to globalization is descriptive rather than explanatory.

Indeed, sociologists of religion have by and large understood bricolage
as the making of eclectic and personal religiosities within modern individualism. "Sheilaism," coined by one of Bellah et al.'s (1985, 221) interviewees
who named her religion after herself, also seemed to legitimate the idea that
belief has become unique to each individual. Like Luckmann, Hervieu-Léger's
seminal works on religion and modernity emphasize processes of individualization and subjectivization in the making of modern religious life: "in the domain of religion like elsewhere, we have observed the capacity of the individual
to elaborate his own universe of norms and values from his own singular
experience tends to impose itself beyond the regulatory endeavors of institutions" (Hervieu-Léger 1999, 69, my translation). Individualization and subjectivization are unsurprisingly emphasized in relation to the most heterodox
and unregulated religious spheres: Heelas (1996a, 23), for instance, believes
that "(much) of the New Age movement is beyond tradition, beyond established or codified ethicality, indeed beyond belief." Pushing the Luckmannian
theory of privatization to its extreme, Heelas and Woodhead (2005) evoke a
vibrant "spirituality" growing outside institutions and generated by a "subjective turn": as fewer and fewer people live according to "external expectations,"
"the subjectivities of each individual become a, if not the, unique source of
significance, meaning and authority" (Heelas and Woodhead 2005, 10, 3–4).
The authors do not address practices of bricolage, but their claim about the
primacy of "self-authority" over "external" constraints presupposes that the
"spiritual revolution" they predict is about the rise of a personal form of religiosity, which authorizes the free appropriation of various religious resources.

These assumptions about religious individualism and bricolage have been
reinforced by reference to theories developed outside the sociology of religion.
First, they echo the paradigm of individualization and detraditionalization

that Giddens, Beck and Beck-Gernsheim elaborated. This paradigm has remained significantly influential within the social sciences until today, despite growing criticisms (Atkinson 2007; Brannen and Nilsen 2005; Savage 2000; Skeggs 2004). By and large, Giddens (1991), Beck (1992), and Beck and Beck-Gernsheim (1996, 2002) contend that extrinsic, traditional authorities do not structure people's lives as they once did and that, in "reflexive" societies, individuals are left to produce their own biography and identity through personal choice. Therefore, in a reflexive society, it is believed that "we are, not what we are, but what we make of ourselves" (Giddens 1991, 75). According to this perspective, bricolage with exotic religious resources would be the result of individuals' liberation from collective norms and values. They now would be free to pursue the realization of themselves through diverse means chosen on the basis of unique, subjective experiences. Yet, sociologists of religion seem to forget that for Beck (in Atkinson 2007, 353), such reflexive constructions of personal biographies are relatively standardized, because individuals become more dependent on the dictates of various institutions and experts (including religious movements) to lead them on an increasingly important quest for self-fulfillment.

Like the individualization and detraditionalization paradigm itself, some of the depictions of religious individualism draw on postmodern theories. These theories presuppose that we have entered a new era, characterized by the death of tradition and great narratives. Instead, the postmodern world involves the fragmentation of information and knowledge, the collapse of boundaries between reality and representations, and the implosion of social classes and genders—by making such claims, postmodern theories clearly intended to challenge social theory (Kellner 1990). Postmodernity is thus the end of a single worldview; it celebrates the local and the heterogeneous, the plurality of voices and meanings, the patchwork, pick and mix, and the pastiche (Jencks 1992). Applied to religion, the postmodern stance makes of bricolage a playful individual practice that consecrates the breaking of boundaries between and within traditions, and even more if we follow Blain (2002, 3–4) about neo-shamanism in Europe: "Within Western 'post-modern society' an increasing number of people are turning to construct their own spiritual relationships with the earth, other people, and those with whom we share the earth: plants, animals, and various spirit-beings found in the mythologies of the world." The postmodern perspective is also illustrated below by Srinivas's (2010, 179) study of Sathya Sai Baba devotees:

> Devotees do not choose one religious system and reject another; they choose parts of different systems, putting them together individually

in a pastiche (similar to what Levi Strauss has called bricolage), the ways that citizens experience and craft a multiculturalist approach. In a sense then, the Sai devotees "craft" a religious structure and a religious identity for themselves. They self-consciously shape a devotional iden- tity by picking and choosing parts of the Sathya Sai system of belief for which they feel an affinity.... [Identity] becomes a space in which con- scious choice occurs not merely between preconstructed identities but also between parts of identities.

Srinivas completes this description by outlining "both the power and pleasure of agency" involved in bricolage. As a way to engage with a di- versity of religious traditions, bricolage is also, in her view, an empower- ing "skill of living in multicultural societies and in the postmodern world" (2010, 180, 179).

Finally, economic metaphors of the market are increasingly applied to reli- gion. These also emphasize both the freeing of religion from the control of institutions and individuals' ability to freely elaborate religions *à la carte*. In this perspective, practices of bricolage with foreign religious resources would suggest that religions have become objects of consumption chosen by empow- ered consumers (Carrette and King 2005; Hervieu-Léger 2001, 148–151; Lau 2000). For instance,

one can practice Chinese meditation while listening [to] Andean relax- ation music and burning Indian incense. One can go on a yoga retreat in the Caribbean, enjoy aromatherapy massages, and eat a strictly mac- robiotic diet based on Japanese foods. Through the very combination of the public sphere of alternative health and the global marketplace, the individual is *empowered* to create his or her *own unique strategy for living in the modern world*—at least according to an implicit code of con- sumption which suggests that buying into this *bricolage* is the first step toward responsibility. (Lau 2000, 13, my emphasis)

This short presentation of sociological discussions of bricolage emphasizes how the sociology of religion has approached the exploration of foreign reli- gious traditions: in short, as a characteristic of a social world that has broken with tradition and historicity. In such a world, emancipated individuals choose, consume, and combine religious resources of all kind in unique assortments, thereby elaborating personal, hence unique, religious identities and systems. This book suggests that this understanding of bricolage with foreign reli- gions largely overestimates its eclecticism, takes for granted the availability of religious resources, and misunderstands religious individualism. Overall, inflating the eclectic and personal nature of practices of bricolage has led to a neglect of their social and cultural logics.

I am certainly not the first to challenge sociology of religion's approach to bricolage. The first criticism concerns the distortion and misunderstanding of the metaphor once used by Lévi-Strauss and Bastide. For the anthropologist André Mary (1994, 1995, 2000, 2005), we cannot talk about "bricolage" anymore. For a start, bricolage as described by sociologists of religion does not imply a need to "repair" a culture's gaps and discontinuities. On the contrary, for Mary, in the modern or postmodern setting, fragmentations, paradoxes, and heterodoxies seem to be characteristically unproblematic for social actors. Mary also outlines that bricolage, as defined by Lévi-Strauss, implies "pre-constraints" relating to the meaning and content of resources that are being used, and which the bricoleur cannot ignore. Besides, the range of resources that can be used is finite and limited. Finally, bricolage is not free in the traditional societies to which it was originally applied. In African and South American syncretisms, the introduction of new resources in religious life was linked to colonial contexts. Power relations and cultural domination generated hierarchies in values and meanings which, in turn, affected the making of bricolage (Mary 1994, 93). All of these constraints make bricolage a process of tensions, negotiations, and compromises, leading to the elaboration of syncretic syntheses. Mary thus prefers to talk about "post-traditional" or "postmodern collages" in contemporary societies, to emphasize what he sees as their lack of constraints and tensions. In his view, collages are not creative of new religious syntheses; they indifferently patch together *any* religious resource from a seemingly unlimited stock and empty them of their original meanings. Contemporary society "praises the making of collages and resolutely inscribes itself in a conversion to the fragmentary, to a plural and imploded reality, consecrating the loss to any reference to foundational and unifying great narratives" (Mary 2000, 194, my translation). In other words, while making a valuable critique of the use of "bricolage" by sociologists of religion, Mary shares their understanding of radical religious individualism when it comes to "postmodern collages."

Other scholars express their doubts about this radical religious individualism and highlight the need to understand bricolage in social context. Campiche (1993, 2003, 2004) underscores the significance of socialization, by reminding us that individuals do not elaborate their religious identity in a social vacuum. Personal experience may have become determinant in religious life, but it is anchored in social contexts; a nexus of social relations and interactions enable social actors to authenticate it. Accordingly, bricolage is relative and entails beliefs that are, to a certain extent, collectively shared, a view endorsed by Obadia (1999) in his study of Tibetan Buddhism in France. Indeed, is not Sheila explaining that she believes in "God" and in fact "would be willing to endorse few more specific injunctions" (Bellah et al. 1985, 221)? Wood (2009, 241) actually underscores the Christian undertone of Sheila's depiction of her belief in his critique of "self-authority" within the sociology of spirituality. Indeed, even the most atomized religious milieus have common orientations and constitute a coherent system of meaning that are collectively shared; this is precisely what Champion established in her long-term study of the French "mystical-esoteric nebula." She presented its "psycho-religious orientations" as worldliness, the value of intimate experience, the quest for unity, individual responsibility, love as ethical basis, a form of humanistic ethics, confidence in one's journey, and the belief in the possibility of "non-ordinary" realities (Champion 1990). By and large, Champion (2004, 61) notes the lack of precise sociological analyses of bricolage's internal "organization."

Both Hervieu-Léger (2001, 127) and Mary (1994, 97; 2005, 286) acknowledge that self-realization, and more widely individualization, constitute an imperative that affects contemporary practices of bricolage. Yet this imperative is more presumed than investigated, and the authors do not seem to envisage that the necessity to make religious choices may grant bricolage a rather coherent and predictable social dimension. Indeed, Hervieu-Léger (2005, 300) insists on the "increasing eclecticism that characterize[s] individuals' productions in terms of belief," despite recognizing (without further developments) that the availability of religious resources is not boundless in a given social context and that people do not have the same predispositions to access these resources. Available resources are certainly limited in a given social environment, but what makes some of them (e.g., Buddhism, Hinduism, Kabbalah, or shamanism) "available"? As suggested by Hervieu-Léger, sociologists have observed that it is the urban educated middle classes that engage with these religious traditions in seemingly eclectic religious trajectories, but why is that so? What should this observation tell us about the meaning and role of bricolage as social practice?

In short, not only are scholars of religion prone to overestimate the individual and eclectic nature of bricolage, but their methodological individualism does not encourage them to ponder the social constraints, norms, and factors that they acknowledge and that might reveal its internal logics. Besides, none of them enquire into the prominent role played by foreign religious resources in bricolage, the uneven "availability" and appeal of these resources, and how, in practice, individuals engage with these "things foreign."

For a Critical Sociology of Religion

Beyond an understanding of religious exoticism and the logics of bricolage, this study is inscribed inside a larger effort to contribute to a critical sociology of religion (Wood and Altglas 2010; Altglas 2012). My stance is not new in this regard: Beckford (1989, 1–17) and Turner (1991, 3–4) regretted that the sociology of religion remains isolated from wider sociological debates; it privileges the detailed descriptions of religious experiences and beliefs to the detriment of consideration of social class, family organization, power, and authority. The current tendency to overestimate personal subjectivity, "choice," and "freedom" in the making of bricolage, or in the study of "spirituality" (Wood 2009, 2010), makes these flaws of the sociology of religion even more acute.

It is, however, not the only subfield affected by a propensity to inflate the role of agency and subjectivity while denying that of structure, or to simply imagine that these things are disjointed. There is in today's social sciences a "retreat of the social" as Kapferer (2005, 1–2) put it, "a shift away from a concern with social, relational and interactive structures, as well as institutional and organizational formations ... [t]he complexities of their internal dynamics, their structuring processes, and the forces of their effects on human action within and beyond them." Yet, sociology emerged as a new discipline through this epistemological break: it claims that the individual is, and cannot but be, social. Durkheim's study of suicide is foundational in that it demonstrates that even the most intimate and personal decision that seems to rest upon contingent and unique circumstances, is socially determined to the point that we can predict suicide rates and explain their variations in relation to identified social factors and trends. The "sociological imagination" is therefore an ability to understand the interplay between individual biographies and the wider social and historical context (Mills 1959). For that reason, opposing the individual and the social, making of the self a "natural" category unaffected by class, ethnicity, or gender, and assuming that individuals craft personal identities and religious systems all constitute a break from the epistemological foundations of sociology, if not a subversion of these.

It indeed becomes a subversion of sociology when one makes the most radical claims about religious individualism and individualization by rewriting the discipline's epistemological foundations. Heelas and Woodhead (2005, 1), for instance open their book *The Spiritual Revolution* with an abridged citation from Durkheim's *The Elementary Forms of the Religious Life*: "[truncated: There still remain] those contemporary aspirations towards a religion which would consist entirely in internal and subjective states, and which would be constructed freely by each of us." Presented as such, this quotation seems to suggest that Durkheim believes in the existence of the religious life described by Heelas and Woodhead in their book. However, the reader of the *Elementary Forms* (1971 [1915], 47) would see that for Durkheim, these aspirations "remain" to be considered and are then dismissed immediately by him as "uncertain possibilities." Therefore, Durkheim continues, they do not constitute a hindrance to defining religion as he famously did ("beliefs and practices which unite into one single moral community...all those who adhere to them") and to concluding that religion is "an eminently collective thing." In fact, this section of the *Elementary Forms* is very interesting: in the preceding paragraphs, Durkheim responds to thinkers of his time who wondered "if the day will not come when there will be no other cult than that which each man will freely perform within himself." The idea of an absolute religious individualism is therefore not new, and neither are its critiques. Durkheim (1971 [1915], 46) concedes that "individual cults" may exist in certain social contexts, yet nonetheless to him they are "simply aspects of the religion common to the church to which individuals belong" and not "distinct and autonomous religious systems." Therefore, "individual cults" still imply that "it is the church that teaches the individual the identity of his personal gods, what their role is, how we must enter into relationship with them, and how we must honour them." In other words, for Durkheim, individualized forms of religion would necessarily be shaped by socialization from religious institutions.

This subversion of sociology manifests itself in a repetition of the process: in the concluding sections of their book, Heelas and Woodhead (2005, 148) cite Durkheim (in Pickering 1975, 96–97) as distinguishing a "religion handed down by tradition" and a "free, private and optional religion, fashioned according to one's needs and understanding." They name other scholars as well, saying that they all believed that "spirituality" was growing, thereby confirming their own hypothesis—a "spiritual revolution" was occurring while institutional forms of religion declined. But Heelas and Woodhead omit to cite the paragraph that follows Durkheim's distinction, in which he explains that "public" and "private" religions "belong to the same family," that the practices and beliefs of the "individual" religion are insignificant, and again, that "it is obviously private belief which is derived from public belief." It might not be a bad idea indeed to refer to Durkheim's ideas about religious individualism. This would allow sociologists to consider the possibility for much more coherence and continuity in the religious life of "spiritual seekers" and bricoleurs. Indeed, previous regular churchgoing is a predicting factor for participation in "spiritual" milieus (Wood 2009, 245). Not only did I find that most of the individuals exploring Hindu or Kabbalistic teachings have had a religious education, but also that several claimed to rediscover the Christian faith they were raised in through this "detour." But such usage of sociology as described above rather demonstrates an impoverishment of the sociological way of thinking while still seeking its legitimacy in the authority of its founders.

A critical sociology of religion entails a reflexive approach. Some sociologists of religion attempt to address critically the subfield's normative penchant, which sometimes leads scholars to "defend" their object of study and hence to assume its positive social role (Bender et al. 2013), or its universality (Beaman 2013), as well as to misjudge its public significance through the flawed notion of "post-secularity" (Beckford 2012). It is also an ambivalent relationship with the object of study (religion) that informs assumptions about radical religious individualism. As illustrated by the writings of Luckmann, Hervieu-Léger, and Heelas and Woodhead, radical religious individualism is more often than not articulated with the idea that, outside declining religious institutions, there is an invisible, recomposed religious life and perhaps, an ongoing "spiritual revolution." Underlying this is the belief that religion may change shape but cannot decline. Luckmann (1990, 127) contends that "religion is not disappearing from the modern world: experiences of transcendence are a universal component of human life." By not conceiving the possibility of the decline of religion's influence, some scholars may tell us more about their own experience than about the social world they aim to describe. Yet these academic discourses are not socially innocuous: they authorize certain views of the social world and as such have practical consequences—there are, for example, questionable practical and regulative consequences of assumptions about religion's significance and universality (Beaman 2013).

Thus, a critical sociology of religion, as Bourdieu (2010 [1987]) advances in his address to sociologists of religion, requires them to reflect on the ways in which they might, in some instances, position themselves simultaneously in the academic and religious fields, and thus play a double play. Bourdieu contends that it is not possible to understand religion adequately *and* take part in religious contestations and stakes at the same time, simply because such involvement binds scholars to the beliefs and preconceptions associated with belonging to the religious field—for instance, assuming that religion is universal, or that it has a significant or positive social role.

Assuming that individuals are now free to make their own identity has the same epistemological weakness, in other words, reflecting and legitimizing academics' social experience. In her critique of the paradigm of individualization and detraditionalization, Skeggs underlines that the emphasis on fluidity, empowerment, mobility, and choice in fact reveals the habitus of those contributing to such a theoretical framework, that is to say, the social experience of a small upper middle-class minority that is far from being representative of society as a whole. "Their sociology," Skeggs (2004, 53) argues, "can thus be viewed as part of a symbolic struggle for the authorization of their experience and perspectives." Again, this is not without consequences: it is hardly difficult to catch a glimpse of the potential interplays between social theories that inflate the significance of agency and subjectivity, on the one hand, and forms of governance that encourage the formation of autonomous and self-managed individuals, on the other hand. Ultimately, reflecting on the conditions in which we produce sociological knowledge and on how this knowledge is affected by these conditions (Bourdieu 2013) is a core element of a critical sociology of religion.

Religious Exoticism as Framework

This book aims to provide an understanding of the ways in which certain foreign religious practices and beliefs, which I call "exotic religious resources," are disseminated and appropriated in contemporary practices of bricolage. These practices are understood as part of a "religious exoticism"; this notion draws attention to the processes that make "available" cultural and religious resources for their appropriation. It also addresses the type of engagement that individuals develop with the culturally and religiously foreign.

Two preliminary notes of caution are nonetheless necessary. First, there is nothing normative in the reference to "religious exoticism." By using this notion, I am not lamenting over the ways in which social actors engage with foreign religions, since I do not imply that this engagement is more superficial or less authentic than another. Every encounter with foreign cultures or religions implies an understanding from one's point of view and necessitates interpretations, translations, and selections. Authenticity, or authentic interest in other cultures, if such things existed, is not what I propose to discuss here. Ultimately, I do not believe that the role of academics is to be the "authorized guardians" of tradition (Huss 2007b). Second, "religious exoticism" addresses *one* way of engaging with foreign religions, among others. I do not pretend to describe within this framework every way in which social actors interact with various religions in the contemporary world. Alongside religious exoticism, other individuals, for instance, undertake a process of conversion, thereby adopting a new way of life and identity. In these cases, religious exoticism might (or might not) contribute to social actors' phases in the discovery of a new religion; it does not suggest a static relation. The relation that "religious exoticism" aims to capture is nonetheless significant. Indeed, while conversions to Buddhism, Hinduism, or Judaism are relatively small in number, certain fragments of these religions are widely explored by a large public, through literature, courses, conferences, and retreats, as well as short term-involvement in various religious movements. This is what religious exoticism focuses on.

Exoticism has mostly been discussed in cultural studies, in particular to explore the ways in which artists and intellectuals have used or depicted non-Western cultures in the knowledge or art that they produce. "Exoticism" is derived from the Greek *exōtikos*, "foreign," from *exō*, "outside." It suggests an attempt to grasp otherness, yet what is exotic is not an "inherent quality" of particular social groups, places, ideas or practices. Indeed, no one is intrinsically "other." Exoticism is instead relational; it is a "particular mode of aesthetic perception" that emphasizes, and to a certain extent elaborates, the otherness of groups, locations, ideas, and practices (Huggan 2001, 13). Moreover, the exotic is attractive *because* it is seen as being "different" (Todorov 1993, 264); exoticism makes otherness "strangely or unfamiliarly beautiful and enticing" (Figueira 1994, 1). Yet it is less about accounting for cultural differences than formulating an ideal, by dramatizing and even constructing differences. For example, the analysis of the popularization of Kabbalah and neo-Hinduism shows that these religious traditions are perceived—and appropriated—as primordial and mystical kernels of "spirituality."[2] This construction of otherness can involve a distance in time rather than in culture only: neo-pagans for example, by trying to reclaim ancestral European practices such as Druidism or witchcraft, exoticize pre-modern Europe. I thereby suggest that exoticism can manifest itself in one's relation with one's own religious tradition: partly secularized Jews can be attracted by Kabbalah as a primordial Jewish "spirituality," while ignoring or even rejecting contemporary Judaism as lived in its mainstream institutions (see Chapter 2). Similarly, a section of the bourgeoisie in Muslim countries who have a conflicted relation with Islam rediscover it through westernized forms of Sufism (Haenni and Voix 2006; Philippon 2014).

Through the construction of idealized others, exoticism often seeks to reclaim "'elsewhere' values 'lost' with the modernization of European society" (Bongie 1991, 5). In this regard, orientalism (a particular form of exoticism) offers a case in point. Said (1978) explains how the Orient was a European invention, a representation of otherness that, by contrast, enabled the affirmation of European culture and identity (as modern, rational, potent) when the East was deemed to be irrational, emotional, and mystical. Orientalism was precisely a way to think of the "East" as an absolute complement to the West where, writes Said (1978, 115), "what mattered was not Asia so much as Asia's use to modern Europe." For romantic orientalists, such a portrayal of the Orient was particularly potent: in the *fin de siècle* era, it captured what they believed modern Europe had left behind. Studying and knowing the "mystical East" would thus allow European culture to regenerate itself. These representations proved to be long-lasting. In fact, they are still shared by those whom I interviewed, who think that "the West has lost it," as one of them put it, and who look to yoga and meditation as authentic sources of personal regeneration. Overall, this book demonstrates that exotic religious resources are, indeed, constructed and disseminated on the terms of those who appropriate them—that is, as universal and flexible techniques for the realization of the self.

Furthermore, Todorov (1993, 265) argues that, to elaborate and maintain the representations of idealized others, it is necessary to ignore the "reality" of other peoples and cultures:

Knowledge is incompatible with exoticism, but lack of knowledge is in turn irreconcilable with praise of others; yet praise without knowledge is precisely what exoticism aspires to be. This is its constitutive paradox.

Exoticism's paradoxical ignorance is well illustrated in the Chapter 3 of this book by the representations of a spiritual and timeless India among those who traveled and even lived there, overlooking the modernity of contemporary Indian society. Similarly, students of Kabbalah who travel to Israel for festivals and pilgrimages, by their own account, seem to dip into biblical times.

Exoticism's ambivalence derives from specific cultural encounters and relations, in which discourses and representations about other people have been associated with their subjugation. This is why Arac and Ritvo (1991, 3) consider that exoticism conceals, by its aestheticization of otherness, asymmetrical power relations. This also suggests that there is nothing arbitrary in the selection of particular "others" to be exoticized, while some, deemed too "primitive," are rejected. For example, discourses about the "mystical East" that emerged in the nineteenth century were not independent from imperialist ideology and colonial practice in Asia. The ways in which Christian interpretations of Kabbalah extracted it from its Jewish context to confirm the truths of Christianity, and even to convert Jews, reflected Christian Europe's conflicted relations with its Jewry (Chapter 1 of this book develops these examples). Thus, contextualized, exoticism may be interpreted as a way to conquer culture "from the inside," through knowing, interpreting, and appropriating it; Root (1995), for instance, sees exoticism as a "cannibal culture." This terminology might seem slightly extreme regarding the contemporary popularization of yoga or Kabbalah, yet less so when one thinks of the non-Jewish Kabbalists, "white gurus," and "plastic shamans"[3] who became authorities in the religions of others.

Because of their foucauldian stance, postcolonial studies are prone to underline how power is exerted through knowledge when analyzing exoticism. However, as Said (1993) himself acknowledges, the subjects of exotic discourses are not passive; in fact they have often used these discourses to resist imperialism. Orientalist ideas about India's spiritual supremacy, for instance, have been appropriated in the elaboration of an anti-colonial Hindu nationalism, but also by gurus who came to Europe and North America in a "counter-mission" (Hummel 1988; King 1999; Kopf 1969). More recently, contemporary gurus and Kabbalists actively contribute to the making of idealized Eastern spiritualities and Kabbalistic mysteries, respectively. They also instrumentalize exotic representations with subtlety to add mystery and distinction to their teachings, as shown by Siddha Yoga's reference to Kashmir Shaivism and the Kabbalah Centre's identification with the Moroccan Kabbalistic tradition (see Chapter 3). Yet, it remains that exoticism, as a way to simultaneously think about and ignore others, reflects asymmetric relations. This is underscored by the fact that exotic representations and discourses are overwhelmingly elaborated by the observer, not the observed (Todorov 1993, 264). This presupposes the entitlement and the power to do so (Figueira 1994, 2). While I certainly do not make assumptions about the intentionality of religious exoticism, practicing yoga or meditation, joining Native Americans in a sweat lodge, studying Kabbalah while expressing disdain for Judaism (Chapter 2), are all contemporary practices that unavoidably presuppose a sense of entitlement.

Exoticism is accordingly fundamentally ambivalent about other cultures, which are viewed with a mixture of fascination and distaste. Nineteenth-century orientalists perceived contemporary India as a backward civilization and had no interest in its popular, contemporary religious life, which they believed was a degradation of Hinduism. Instead, they were looking for its "golden age," a pure Hinduism to be found in the Upanishads, believed to contain untouched mysticism and truths. Similarly, christianized Kabbalah had become a core element of European esoteric tradition, but some of the prominent figures of nineteenth-century esotericism refused to consider Kabbalah as Jewish; for them, it had to have nobler origins. Contemporary students of yoga, meditation, or Kabbalah idealize "Eastern spiritualities" and Kabbalah, respectively, but they certainly do not aspire to become Hindu or Jewish. In fact, when confronted with the Hindu or Jewish character of these teachings, they evoke feelings of discomfort and may display dismissive attitudes (Chapter 2).

This conflicted way of engaging with others' traditions requires selections, translations, and interpretations to deal with what triggers feelings of distaste. Exoticism entails a "domestication of the foreign and unpredictable," writes Foster (1982, 21), "so that once the labeling is imposed, the phenomena to which they then apply begin to be structured in a way which makes them comprehensible and possibly predictable, if predictably defiant of total familiarity." Exoticism is, therefore, relatively self-referential. Indeed, for Huggan (2001, 22),

> [exoticism] acts as the safety-net that supports these potentially dangerous transactions, as the regulating mechanism that attempts to manoeuvre difference back again to the same. Exoticism posits the lure of difference while protecting its practitioners from close involvement.

Finally, through this process of domestication, objects, ideas, and practices are somewhat removed from their original cultural context. Appadurai (1986, 28) illustrates what he calls the "aesthetics of decontextualization" with examples of tools and artifacts that are commoditized, consumed, and diverted from their original meaning, to be displayed in Western homes. This book emphasizes that popularized Hindu-based and Kabbalistic teachings are de-linked from their original religious and cultural frameworks to reach a non-Hindu or non-Jewish audience, and are significantly shaped by the therapy culture of advanced industrial society. Needless to say, the psychologization of Vedanta and Kabbalah makes them familiar and predictable.

Book Content

As an analytical framework, exoticism aptly captures the ways in which foreign religious beliefs and practices are disseminated and appropriated in advanced industrial societies. Chapter 1 provides an overview of the cultural and historical context of the popularization of Vedantic and Kabbalistic teachings. These religious beliefs and practices have been constructed, disseminated, and appropriated in ways which reflect desires and expectations that were, at first, external to traditional Hinduism and Judaism: perceived as pure, primordial, and mystical traditions (and subsequently presented as such by Hindu and Jewish leaders), they were hoped to revitalize Western contemporary religious and cultural life. Western expectations thus largely contributed to shape Hindu-based and Kabbalistic teachings before they were adopted in Euroamerican societies. The "availability" of exotic religious resources is therefore not a given, but the result of specific cultural encounters and historical contexts that made some of them (and not others) "available."

Chapter 2 explores neo-Hindu disciples' and Kabbalah students' outlooks on Hinduism and Judaism, respectively, as well as their religious identities and trajectories. While idealizing the "mystical East" and Kabbalistic mysteries, they explore yoga, meditation, or Kabbalah *despite* their Hindu or Jewish characters. Indeed, when confronted with the "reality" of otherness (through language, liturgy, or devotional practices), these prove to be a source of discomfort, if not of culture shock. Accordingly, the majority never envisage conversion; instead, they tend to adopt a selection of practices during peripheral and short-term involvement. Thus, another important finding of this research is that social actors rarely engage with otherness in a free, unproblematic, and playful manner.

Religious exoticism's ambivalence explains why Kabbalistic and Hindu-based teachings are appealing despite being strange and mysterious, at the same time as their particularisms are neutralized. This is the focus of Chapter 3. As they spread transnationally, neo-Hindu movements and the Kabbalah Centre refuse to be identified as Hindu or Jewish, but present their teachings as universal meta-religions that transcend national, religious, and cultural boundaries. This entails reinterpreting the significance of rituals and core tenets that make traditional Hinduism and Judaism ethnic religions, introducing new practices, engaging in endless interpretative discourses, and implementing organizational strategies. The domestication processes of exotic religious resources are plentiful, contradictory, and perilous for what were initially movements of revitalization. Scholars describe bricolage as fluid, playful, and unaffected by diversity; but there is a "backstage" that enables it and which reveals that otherness truly matters for the "producers" of exotic religious resources.

Ultimately, universalistic ambitions are also affected by constraints and opportunities at the local level. In particular, national responses to religious diversity and the characteristics of the religious landscape are decisive. By comparing neo-Hindu movements in France and Britain, on the one hand, and the Kabbalah Centre in these two countries, on the other hand, Chapter 4 shows that in certain contexts, these religious organizations sometimes think it is wiser to identify with Hinduism or Judaism respectively. Conversely, depending on the local context as well, the development of universalistic or particularistic strategies impacts locally on the potential for the dissemination of religious teachings. Once again, the availability of exotic religious resources results from a complex and conflicted process of negotiations and reinterpretations, in interaction with social environments and in which otherness tremendously matters, both for their public and their producers. In short, bricolage is also shaped by national contexts.

Exotic religious resources are popularized by being universalized, de-ethnicized, but also, as shown in Chapter 5, psychologized. Indeed, the main motivation of their audience is to find in these resources efficient means to improve their lives through the transformation of the self and its attitudes. The leaders of the studied religious movements present Vedanta and Kabbalah as an inner-worldly salvation, shaped by an ethos of self-realization. Therapy culture also shapes how the exotic religious resources are disseminated, that is, in courses, workshops, and retreats, through which "students" pay to access and take home techniques for self-improvement. Because therapy culture significantly standardizes religious teachings, the eclecticism of their students' religious trajectory is overstated by sociologists of religion. Furthermore, religious incursions in yoga, meditation, or Kabbalah tend to contribute to a rather unchanging quest, since individuals successively adopt practical methods for the realization of the self in a sort of "lifelong religious learning." In other words, rather than making successive different choices, they reiterate a coherent religious orientation.

The domestication and appropriation of exotic religious resources as tools for self-realization is at the core of religious exoticism; Chapter 6 therefore discusses the social significance of such aims. At this point, the book deepens its criticisms of the sociology of religion's methodological individualism. It shows that the quest for self-realization does not evidence "self-authority," but rather entails the conformity to a set of norms and values that actually reveals wider constraints exerted on individuals in advanced industrial societies. Flexible economies and the shrinking of the welfare state require from individuals that they become increasingly responsible for themselves, in a relatively unpredictable and insecure social environment. In this context, the self has become the locus of individuals' governance. Religion, even in its most privatized forms, does not escape from this social context, as shown by incentives to work on oneself, adopt appropriate practices, and constantly evaluate and control one's emotions. In short, bricolage with religious and therapeutic resources is significantly shaped by the neoliberal political, economic, and cultural perspective that requires individuals to be self-managed and autonomous.

The book's last two chapters underscore that social actors' participation in this self-making is largely affected by gender and class. Exotic religious resources may be used by women to perform gendered roles in their private and professional lives. Chapter 7 shows that they are also typically appropriated by middle-class individuals as techniques enhancing emotional competence.

Being flexible, "positive," managing one's reactions, coping with stress, developing harmonious relationships with others: these soft skills are transferable—and transferred—in the working life of professionals. Exoticism is also highly significant: those exploring exotic religious resources tend to belong to what Bourdieu called the "new petite bourgeoisie." Therapists, artists, or those working in marketing, advertising, public relations, fashion, and design, are traders of symbolic goods and services. Their predisposition to "cosmopolitanism," and hence their attraction to meditation, yoga, shamanism, or Kabbalah, reflect the fact that accessing symbolic resources and controlling their circulation are vital in relation to their socio-professional position. The analysis of particular individual trajectories indeed suggests that the use of exotic religious resources as cultural capital is particularly beneficial for those who are experts in personal growth, alternative therapies, or "spirituality," and who represent a significant proportion of students of neo-Hinduism and Kabbalah. In their case, practices of bricolage need to be understood as the continuous re-skilling of freelancers involved in competitive and unregulated markets of specific symbolic goods.

An Empirical Approach

The general understanding of religious exoticism and reassessment of bricolage presented in this book would not have been possible without an empirical and comparative approach. This work draws on two large-scale and cross-national studies that I have undertaken, first among Hindu-based movements in France and Britain, and more recently on the Kabbalah Centre in France, Britain, Brazil, and Israel.[4] When possible, references to works on the popularization of Tantrism, Sufism, shamanism, Buddhism, and Asian traditional medicines in Euroamerican societies are made to show that the notion of "religious exoticism" captures general trends beyond my case studies.

Fieldwork on Hindu-based religions focused on two movements: Siddha Yoga and the Sivananda Centres. This research involved two years of participant observation and the collection of 80 non-directive interviews with the leaders and members of these two groups, in London and Paris, between 1999 and 2005. This research was completed by a short study of the ways in which religious movements that refer to Hinduism are affected by national responses to religious diversity in France and Britain (2005–2006).[5] This entailed a new collection of data through visits to the International Society for Krishna Consciousness (ISKCON) and other neo-Hindu movements, and the Hindu Forum of Britain was contacted for documents and information on their activities and purposes. Semi-structured interviews were also conducted with the social players involved in the management of religious diversity in both countries.[6]

The study of the Kabbalah Centre took place between 2007 and 2010. It involved 13 months of participant observation and 80 interviews, mainly in Paris, London, Rio de Janeiro, and Tel Aviv.[7] Interviews were conducted with the Kabbalah Centre's teachers and students, former teachers and students, representatives of governmental bodies regulating religions, anti-cult movements, rabbis and spokespersons of Liberal and Orthodox Judaism, as well as other social actors interacting directly or indirectly with the Kabbalah Centre, such as journalists. I also attended various events and courses relating to Kabbalah in these four locations and interviewed individuals who teach Kabbalah, either within or outside a Jewish setting. Press articles, television programs, and official reports were also collected.

The reader might wonder why these case studies in particular have been selected. For a start, new religious movements (NRMs), as circumscribed groups with a specific teaching, represent good settings to investigate the production and appropriation of religious resources. These processes in less "formative" (Wood 2009) environments, such as those designated New Age, are more diffuse and therefore less easy to observe. There is no doubt that a solid and valuable study of religious esotericism could have been undertaken by analyzing the popularization of teachings referring to shamanism, Buddhism, or Sufism. The choice of Kabbalistic and Hindu-based teachings simply reflects my itinerary as a researcher. In my early years, I was encouraged to research movements referring to Hinduism, since at the time no such study had been undertaken in France. Thus, in the mid-1990s, I investigated the Sri Chinmoy Centre and Sahaja Yoga in Paris and explored the range of religious teaching referring to Hinduism in Paris—the present book sometimes refers to these preliminary studies (Altglas 1997, 1998, 2000). Starting my doctoral thesis, I decided to compare the transnational diffusion of Siddha Yoga and Sivananda Centres, and the ways in which their teachings are appropriated in France and Britain. I chose these two groups because, while some Hindu-based movements were often investigated (ISKCON, the Rajneesh movement, Transcendental Meditation), this was not so much the case with Siddha Yoga and the Sivananda Centres, despite the fact that they seemed to be relatively lively organizations in Paris when I first got to know them. This research's main argument was that the presence of Hindu teachings in Euroamerican societies did not demonstrate an easternization of the West, as suggested by Campbell (2007). Rather, their adaptive strategies and the way in which their disciples appropriated neo-Hindu practices and values entailed a westernization of Hindu teachings (Altglas 2005). The present book draws on the data collected for this in-depth research on Siddha Yoga and the Sivananda Centres. In any case, it seems a good idea for a study of religious exoticism to include a case relating to the "mystical East," since the dissemination of Asian beliefs and practices and the popularity of Buddhism have become prominent features of religious life in advanced industrial societies.

I also felt it was important to maintain a comparative approach to avoid generalizing the particularities of one case study and to be able, instead, to develop a larger reflection of higher significance. In other words, my aim was to work around a sociological problem, rather than being the expert of one specific case study. The Kabbalah Centre may have been an easy choice: it had been one of the most controversial NRMs of the early 2000s, subjected to intense media coverage because of the celebrities who joined the movement. More important, representations of both Hinduism and Judaism seemed symbolically powerful, as they refer to a golden age and a holy land, India or Israel, which mobilizes religious imagination. Just as modern gurus claim the Vedanta to be universal and to transcend all cultural boundaries, the founder of the Kabbalah Centre, Philip Berg, declared that the Torah was not transmitted to the Jews only, but to all, and part of the controversies raised by the movement was that he made an esoteric teaching available to anyone, whereas in mainstream Judaism, Kabbalah is usually supposed to be studied only by Jewish mature men. Thus, like neo-Hindu movements, the Kabbalah Centre seemed to be a fascinating example of the transformation of a non-proselytizing, ethnic religion into a global religious network. I suspected that as in neo-Hinduism, the universalization of Kabbalah would imply innovations to adapt it to a wider audience. This book underscores that the universalization, de-contextualization and psychologization of these teachings are very comparable. Despite their different origins, doctrines, and practices, they become very standardized and use similar techniques for self-realization and fulfillment.

The differences between these case studies were also potentially interesting. I was intrigued by the fact that, while Siddha Yoga and the Sivananda Centres in Euroamerican societies tend not to attract disciples of South Asian origin, the Kabbalah Centre attracted two different kinds of disciples: secular Jews who, I imagined, may wish to reconnect with their religious background, and others, non-Jews, who were probably engaged in another religious trajectory. How these different constituencies interact in the movement, and how its leaders reconcile their expectations, were fascinating issues. I had observed that some neo-Hindu gurus have a nationalistic discourse in India, but in the West successfully emphasize the therapeutic virtues of their teachings (giving them a non-ethnic, non-political aspect), which made me wonder how religious leaders strategically play the specific as well as the universal card in transnational religions. I knew that Berg had claimed that the Torah was given not only to the Jews, and was said to have subsequently lost Jewish disciples. By and large, these strategies would prove to be an issue of tremendous importance for the Kabbalah Centre's current crises and tensions (these issues are addressed in Chapters 2 and 3).

Cross-National Perspectives

The advantage of cross-national approaches is that they avoid generalizing what may be specific to a case study in one location. Beyond the British-French axis of the research on neo-Hindu movements, I widened the cross-national comparison for the study of the Kabbalah Centre by conducting research in Brazil and Israel. The limits of such an enterprise need to be acknowledged, and they have to do with the level of expertise a researcher can acquire in a lifetime. The sections of the book on the psychologization of religion, neo-liberalism, religious teaching and social classes heavily draw on the British and French contexts, which I know particularly well. A thorough comparative analysis of economic liberalism with the Israeli and Brazilian contexts would require a level of expertise which admittedly I do not have. Similarly, while I am confident to analyze in-depth responses to religious diversity and the religious landscape in Britain and France, it would be far too ambitious for me to attempt a similar thorough exercise for other national contexts.

Yet, while being clear about the limits of what one can solidly investigate, it is still worth trying: it has become obvious that transnational religious phenomena require cross-national investigations. It is the only way to identify constant features and local variations across branches, and to gauge the impact of national contexts on these transnational organizations. For instance, whereas the British state has been relatively liberal regarding "cults," the French state considers them a threat to the state and society. Comparison of responses to NRMs in France and Britain based on neo-Hindu case studies proved to be revealing. In Britain, neo-Hindus are torn between the institutional pressure to emphasize the reference to Hinduism and their universalistic ideology, which targets a Western audience. In contrast, it is crucial for NRMs in France to differentiate themselves from the so-called cults, insisting, for example, on their religious character or authenticity. Accordingly, a comparison of adaptive strategies to a very controversial movement with ambiguous relations to Judaism such as the Kabbalah Centre seemed very promising. And indeed, it proved to be so. In London, the movement flourished as a "universal wisdom" among a very mixed and cosmopolitan constituency. By contrast, in France, the Kabbalah Centre was relatively successful in the 1990s among the Jewish population. However, students who initially found in the Kabbalah Centre a way of strengthening their Jewish identity moved away, discouraged by the fierce opposition of French Jewish authorities and dissatisfied with the Kabbalah Centre's universalistic and psychologizing turn, leading to the Parisian Centre's closure. This double cross-national comparison (neo-Hindu movements in France and Britain versus the Kabbalah Centre in France and Britain) informs the Chapter 4.

Moreover, I would argue that comparing four national contexts, especially in qualitative research, does not need to be rigid by systematically granting the same status to each of these contexts included in the comparison, unless we decide that the comparison becomes an end in itself. Rather, my aim was to investigate the popularization of exotic religious resources through practices of bricolage; a flexible comparative approach, opportunistically driven by the research aims, seemed more useful. The book therefore addresses the peculiarities of each context in points in time in order to shed light on the subtleties, logics, and tensions in the making of religious teachings and identities. As such, the comparative perspective provides an understanding of the popularization of exotic religious resources that no singled-out, unique case could have done.

Israel seemed to be an obvious choice in the study of the Kabbalah Centre, because it started there. Moreover, in the only existing Jewish state, Judaism is strongly intertwined with Israeli national identity. I therefore wondered whether the strategy of universalizing Kabbalah was applied in the Israeli branch of the movement and, if so, how the audience responded to it. Indeed, I suspected that the involvement of Israeli members in the Kabbalah Centre could be slightly different and may involve the strengthening of their Jewish identity. The research proved that was the case and that the leaders' universalistic strategy had its discontents. The references to the Israeli case appear at different points in the book, for instance, in order to address its distinctiveness regarding religious identity. The predominance of Orthodox Judaism in Israel and its effects on the development of the Kabbalah Centre is also compared with the French, British, Brazilian, and American contexts.

While the Kabbalah Centre encounters the opposition of religious orthodoxy in Israel, it faces a very different situation in Brazil. Unsurprisingly, two of the seven Latin American Kabbalah Centre's branches are Brazilian. Indeed, Brazil represents an exceptional case of exuberant religious culture, which has generated numerous organizations that are now part of global religious networks. I thought that the Kabbalah Centre would contribute to the alternative religious scene that has grown up among the urban middle classes since the 1980s, including Eastern religions, esoteric organizations, and alternative therapies. The historical religious diversity that discouraged the formation of strong anti-cult networks and policies in Brazil seemed to be fascinating to compare with the other national contexts. Chapter 2 of this book discusses why, despite all these favorable conditions, the Kabbalah Centre has not been as successful in Brazil as I initially thought it would be. Data suggest that the Brazilian religious field, as diverse as it may be, represents a challenge for a movement anchored in the Jewish tradition, despite a form of prestige associated with the Jewish identity in Brazil. This would require further investigation, yet in the light of arguments being made in this book, the idea that Brazil's unusual capacity to assimilate and combine various traditions has its limits and logics should not surprise us.

TO SUMMARIZE, THIS study of religious exoticism sheds light on the following. First, bricolage is not independent from cultural and historical contexts that make available certain religious resources. The pool of resources is therefore neither unlimited not arbitrary. Second, contemporary bricoleurs are prone to break with the "pre-constraints" of the resources that they use, but not out of "freedom" and indifference for their original meanings. On the contrary, otherness matters in practices of bricolage; it generates conflicting feelings and requires its domestication, which, as Huggan (2001, 22) says, "manoeuvre difference back again to the same." Thus, heterodox combinations of beliefs and practices are not that playful. The ability to engage with diversity may be in fact relatively small: indeed, an idealized otherness miraculously responds to expectations for universal, authentic, and efficient tools for self-realization. Third, bricolage is much less eclectic than assumed: on the one hand, exotic religious resources are greatly homogeneous due to the neutralization of their particularism and their psychologization; on the other hand, their audience is involved in a very consistent and stable endeavor to actualize one's self for relational and professional purposes in the long term. Fourth, bricolage is not characterized by "self-authority." Indeed, the socialization to norms and values is great, even in privatized and deregulated religious sectors. Besides, bricolage is a class- and gender-based practice, structured by the personal responsibility for realizing one's self in the context of neoliberal politics.

I

The Cultural and Historical Dimensions of Religious Exoticism

THIS FIRST CHAPTER is a preliminary step to the understanding of the dissemination of religious teachings rooted in Hinduism and Judaism in contemporary societies; it aims to provide an overview of the cultural and historical context of this process. Three sections structure this chapter. The first section looks at the emergence and dissemination of Hindu teachings in Euroamerican societies; the second section explores the spread of Kabbalistic teachings, within and without a Jewish environment. These historical sketches also give us an opportunity to present our case studies, the Siddha Yoga, the Sivananda Centres, and the Kabbalah Centre, and to get a sense of the context in which these religious teachings have been disseminated. These two historical overviews are followed by a general discussion, in the third section, regarding the ways in which exotic and mystical religions have been constructed and disseminated.

This chapter underlines that Vedantic and Kabbalistic teachings have been constructed, disseminated, and appropriated in ways which reflect desires and expectations that were, at first, external to traditional Hinduism and Judaism. Nineteenth-century romantic orientalism, Western esoteric movements, and later the youth counterculture of the 1960s all contributed to representations of Vedanta or Kabbalah not only as mystical and mysterious but also as universal and timeless sources of wisdom. Furthermore, these representations are inextricably linked to their polar opposite: the individualistic, materialistic, secular, and decadent West. Accordingly, the exploration and use of these *alternative* religious resources were hoped to revitalize Euroamerican contemporary religious and cultural life. Finally, this historical overview starts to introduce the various ways in which neo-Hindu gurus and Jewish leaders endorsed and contributed to these representations and desires. Overall, this chapter describes the historical and cultural context that makes certain exotic religious resources appropriable, thereby structuring contemporary practices of bricolage. It emphasizes the fact that the elaboration of such appropriable exotic religious resources is not independent from ambivalent cultural relations and encounters. Because they trigger both fascination and repulsion, their appropriation is likely to be selective and to entail their detachment from their cultural environment.

Hinduism for the "West"

The first section of this chapter describes the contemporary popularization of Hindu teachings in the light of the general encounter between India and Europe that took place in the colonial context. Gurus and their teaching of yoga and meditation, as we now know them, have been the inheritors of what has been called a Hindu renaissance or reform. While this renaissance was undoubtedly an attempt to reassert the value of Hinduism, in response to both colonial rule and Christian missions with their civilizing justifications, it inevitably embraced European ideas about what Hinduism is or should be (Halbfass 1988, 1995; Jones 1989; Kopf 1969, 1979). Thus, to a certain extent, the "East" has been shaped in the "West's" own terms, even before being disseminated in Euroamerican societies. In addition, as we shall see, the dissemination of westernized Hindu ideas and practices is itself the result of this particular encounter between India and Europe; it is a form of counter-mission in response to colonial rule and Christian missionary activity in India.

The Emergence of Neo-Hinduism

A Hindu renaissance started in nineteenth-century India, in Calcutta, where European ideas, technology, and social change first spread. An anglicized Bengali elite founded socio-religious reform movements in order to transform society and in particular religious traditions, in order to achieve "progress." This effort involved the application of Western criteria, albeit through a return to a triumphant "golden age" of Hindu civilization (Jones 1989, 212). The emergence of these socio-religious reform movements (and hence of modernized, westernized forms of Hinduism) represents, to a certain extent, a response to Christian missionary work in India, as well as to colonialism's civilizing justification. By the end of the eighteenth century in India, more than 300 Protestant missions had been established; they became involved in moral, religious, social, and political matters. Missionaries unsurprisingly saw Hinduism as an obstacle both for social progress and for the dissemination of Christianity in India. Crusading against idolatry, polytheism, ritualism, and the caste system, missions were providing social services and were the advocates of religious reforms (acceptance of monotheism, rejection of Hindu doctrines and forms of worship, etc.) in order to "save" the Indian population from darkness and bring them enlightenment (Oddie 1979). Far from being tempted by conversion, a section of the Hindu elite instead faced this challenge, making an effort instead to modernize Hinduism. The socio-religious reform movements they founded added a new dimension of social service to Hinduism, which, combined with the defense of monotheism, aimed to combat ritualism and popular religion, and in so doing, to restore the purity of Hinduism (Jones 1989, 208).

In this quest for a restored Hinduism, interactions with European orientalists were crucial. The Bengali elite, with their Brahmin caste status, were perceived by European scholars as the equivalent of the Christian ecclesiastic authority, and they were involved in the European translation and study of India's languages, literature, and religious and philosophical systems. Accordingly, the Bengali elite significantly contributed to the shaping of knowledge and representations of Hinduism (Frykenberg 1997, 89–90). Yet at the same time, they were influenced by the ideas of European scholars, especially by the romantic idealized representations of India (Kopf 1969). European orientalists tended to perceive contemporary India as a civilization in decline, consequently in need of the tutelage of European civilization. Indeed, these Europeans had no interest in popular and contemporary religious life, which was seen as a degradation of Hinduism. Instead, they were looking for its "golden age," an apparently pure Hinduism to be found in the Gita and the Upanishads. A romantic orientalism was looking after untouched mysticism and truths, apparently lost by a soulless modern European society (Inden 1986). Romantic orientalists thus described a primordial, spiritual, and mysterious India, the universal source of all civilizations, which, in the romantic mindset, contrasted with a modern, secular, and decadent West. Accordingly, European scholars were eager to explore Hindu systems of thought in the hope that they would rediscover the ancient sources of their own civilization, thereby sparking a new renaissance in Europe, as had once happened with the rediscovery of ancient Greek and Latin sources. In other words, while nineteenth-century Europe was experiencing rapid and frightening social changes (individualism, industrialization, urbanization, secularization) through which it seemed to lose traditional forms of life, a primordial and religious Indian civilization was expected to provide an alternative source whereby European degeneracy might be overcome (Inden 1986; Schwab 1950). This was the fate of the "mystical East." However, this representation of a Hindu "golden age," capable of generating a European renaissance, was not simply a unilateral discourse imposed on others. It was also orientalism's "most enduring ideological contribution to India's cultural self-image" (Kopf 1969, 284), appealing to the Indian elite, who were trying to reform traditions and shape a national identity through religion. In other words, for the Indian elite, the idea of renaissance meant regenerating India, rather than Europe, even if, paradoxically, this rehabilitation meant the modernization and westernization of Hinduism itself.

The Hindu renaissance relates to nineteenth-century Indian socio-religious reform movements, the most significant of which are the Brahmo Samaj, the Arya Samaj, the Theosophical Society, and the Ramakrishna Mission (I will present the latter in the following section, as its dissemination in European and American societies initiates a new phase of the development of this nascent "neo-Hinduism.") The Brahmo Samaj was founded in 1828 by Ram Mohun Roy (1772–1833), called the "father of modern India" (Halbfass 1988, 198). Ram Mohun Roy was the first Hindu to write extensively on law, religion, education, or politics; his translation of the Upanishads into English greatly facilitated its access to European scholars (Killingley 1993, 2). Born to a Brahmin family, he worked for the East India Company and was therefore familiar with the colonial milieu before dedicating his life to social and religious reform in India. Familiar with the works of European orientalists and intellectuals (Kopf 1969, 198), he explored and interpreted the Vedic literature in search of a pure Hindu tradition; he found it in the Vedas, identifying what he considered to be a monotheistic principle and the universal essence of religion (Sharma 1990). Ram Mohun Roy actually embraced contemporary Western rational theism, defining his religion as "the rational worship of the God of nature." He also used the Enlightenment's terminology and spoke of the "Supreme Being" (Killingley 1993). He thus defended monotheism, rejected Brahmanic ritualism and popular religious practices that he considered idolatrous, polytheistic, immoral, and not in conformity with the true spirit of original Hinduism. In doing so, he was furthering the European distinction between a true Hindu tradition, which he identified with Advaita Vedanta, and a corrupted Hinduism—a representation that other Indian thinkers such as Gandhi and Vivekananda continued to depend on (Killingley 1993, 63–64). Ram Mohun Roy's organization, the Brahmo Samaj, discarded ritual and the use of images, focusing instead on the reading of Upanishads and the singing of theistic hymns (Mukherjee 1978a, 274–275), in ways which reflected the rational theism of the Unitarianism that had influenced Roy. Indeed, interestingly, in 1821 Ram Mohun Roy had founded the "Unitarian Committee" with Unitarians, to promote the worship of one God (it was his followers who suggested establishing a distinct organization, the Brahmo Samaj, in 1828). He was also influenced by Unitarianism's advocacy of social reform when he opened the Brahmo Samaj to all castes. Against the rigidity of the caste system, he defended an egalitarian principle: he insisted on the possibility that anyone could come to know God and find salvation. He advocated access to the Hindu scriptures for all, supporting their translation into vernacular languages. Roy also attempted to apply principles of social ethics and welfare to Hinduism. His most well-known struggle in this respect was against the practice of *sati*, the burning of widows, which was subsequently forbidden in 1829. He also fought against child marriage and polygamy, and he promoted a westernized education system. Ram Mohun Roy was celebrated by European and American orientalists and philosophers as a bridge between East and West. However, he was at the same time criticized by both Christian missionaries and orthodox Hindus, who disliked his westernized interpretation of that tradition. Indeed, Ram Mohun Roy would become the symbol of an affirming Hindu identity, confronting Christianity on its grounds (Halbfass 1988) and claiming the superior universality of Hinduism. Strikingly, his universalism may have been influenced by Western theism. The Brahmo Samaj remained an intellectual movement influenced by European thought, whose audience was limited to an elite (Mukherjee 1978a, 289). While it was pivotal in awakening Indian pride, it declined at the turn of the twentieth century, as nationalism rose and generated new expressions of Indian identity. However, the representation of a monotheistic and universal Hinduism was to become the cornerstone of neo-Hindu teachings, which later spread beyond Indian borders.

The Arya Samaj, founded in 1875 by Dayananda Saraswati (1824–1883), was more conservative and unwilling to incorporate elements of European culture; nevertheless, it also offered a modernization of Hinduism that drew on Western influence. A Brahmin from Gujarat, Saraswati studied Vedanta and yoga and reached the conclusion that the worship of divinities is not contained in the Vedic scriptures (Sharma 1978, 320–321). Contemporary Hinduism was therefore in his views impregnated with superstition and ignorance, and a reform was necessary to return to a certain religious authenticity. Preaching with a solid knowledge of Sanskrit and the scriptures (and of orientalist works on the Vedas; Jordens 1978, 56), Saraswati claimed that in the Vedic literature God is one and infinite and should not be represented as an "idol"; he also rejected some of the taboos linked to caste, ritualism, and popular devotional practices (Jordens 1978, 60–71). His celebration of the authority and the universality of the Vedas underlined a Hindu self-assertion, similar to that of Brahmo Samaj. For Saraswati, the Vedic tradition must become the national religion of India—and the Arya Samaj was to become the seed of emergent Indian nationalism (Jaffrelot 1993, 31). Saraswati frequented the Brahmo Samaj and was influenced by their organizational structure and their liberal approach to education and the social role of women (Jordens 1978). He shared the movement's commitment to monotheism and its critique of popular religious practices. Yet he was opposed to the westernization that, in his view, the Brahmo Samaj represented. More confrontational, he openly criticized Christianity, entered into theological arguments with missionaries (Jaffrelot 1992, 376), and claimed the superiority of the Vedic tradition that, according to him, Christianity had poorly imitated. In its attempt to counter Christian missions, Arya Samaj not only engaged in various educational, philanthropic, and economic programs, combated child marriage, and promoted education for girls, but also aimed to re-convert Christians and Muslims to Hinduism. As Hinduism had not had any ritual of conversion, the Arya Samaj used a ritual of purification for this purpose, thereby imitating Christianity. Like the Brahmo Samaj, the Arya Samaj illustrates the emergence of modern forms of Hinduism in the colonial context, combining Hindu self-assertion with Western criteria (monotheism, rationality, social reform, universality) and representations (a superior Hindu golden age). In other words, reclaiming Hinduism paradoxically meant including Western values and expectations, thereby conforming to the orientalist representation of the "mystical East" while adapting it to modern Western values. Again, this is crucial, as contemporary neo-Hindu movements teaching in Euroamerican societies have drawn from this reformed Hinduism in many ways, as we shall see.

Finally, the Theosophical Society, an esoteric movement founded in 1875 in New York, has usually been understood as part of the Hindu renaissance. Indeed, like Hindu reform movements, the Theosophical Society in India was strongly influenced by orientalism and asserted a Hindu identity in confrontation with what was perceived as European imperialism. Considering that religions practiced today in their exoteric form are shaped by ignorance and superstition, the Theosophical Society aimed to purify them by revealing their authentic and common meaning (Besant, 1993, 13). Its well-known founder, Helena Pretovna Blavatsky (1831–1891), had been impressed by the works of the orientalists, becoming convinced that the Vedas were the source of all religious traditions. The Theosophical Society thus celebrated and looked for India's antique wisdom, although its understanding of Hinduism was undoubtedly closer to Western occultism than to the Vedas themselves (Hanegraaff 1998, 449, 455). This quest for Eastern ancient wisdom was combined with a strong criticism of the colonization of India, the goal of which was to rule rather than learn from its culture. Therefore the founders of the Theosophical Society,

William Q. Judge (1851–1896), Helena Pretovna Blavatsky, and Colonel Henry Steel Olcott (1832–1907), aimed to help Indians rediscover their glorious past, which, in romantic fashion, they opposed to a degenerated Western civilization.[1] It is from this perspective that the Theosophical Society first sought alliance with Dayananda Saraswati, founder of Arya Samaj and vehement critic of British imperialism. This letter, sent by Colonel Olcott to Saraswati, announcing their coming to India, is very revealing:

> A number of Americans and other students who earnestly seek after spiritual knowledge, place themselves at your feet, and pray you to enlighten them. They are of various professions and callings, of several different countries, but all united in the one object of gaining wisdom and becoming better. For this purpose, they, three years ago, organized themselves in to [sic] a body called the Theosophical Society. Finding in Christianity nothing that satisfied their reason of intuition...They stood apart from the world, turned to the East for light, and openly proclaimed themselves the foes of Christianity.... For this reason, we come to your feet as children to a parent, and say "look as us, our teacher; tell us what we ought to do.... We place ourselves under your instruction."
> (cited in Jordens 1978, 209)

This letter illustrates the fact that the fascination for Asian religions is intrinsically intertwined with a romantic and nostalgic critique of Western modernity; I contend that this remains an implicit element of the twentieth century's fascination for Asian religions. Thus, the movement was temporarily renamed as the Theosophical Society of the Arya Samaj of India in 1878 and recognized Saraswati as its leader. At the time, Blavatsky seemed to share with Saraswati the belief in the Veda as the authentic and unique source of truth. But disagreements on doctrines, in particular regarding the theosophists' criticisms of contemporary Hinduism (which is also consubstantial to orientalism and its imperialistic foundation), rapidly led to the separation of the two parties (Kamerkar 1978, 400–402). In India, the Theosophical Society's orientalist discourse attracted as many Indians as Europeans. It condemned the West's imperialism and materialism, its insatiable quest for the technological control of the world, instead celebrating the glorious and ancient past of India, the sacred land that had engendered Western civilization. The Theosophical Society also criticized Christianity for its individualism, while Hinduism was said to replace the individual in the cosmos as a manifestation of the divine, thus fostering a certain sense of service, duty, and solidarity (Bevir, 2000, 164–165). A library in Adyar and schools were opened to promote the study of Sanskrit and ancient texts, with the support and enthusiasm of Hindu religious leaders and the Indian elite, attracted by this study in a flexible and non-religious environment (Oddie 1991, 191–211). Theosophists also contributed to social reform, condemning caste distinctions and promoting education and the participation of women in civil society. The influence of the Theosophical Society in India is far from insignificant—more than 100 branches existed in India in 1884. It responded to Indian resentment regarding European arrogance and fears regarding the possible expansion of Christianity; it also accompanied the emergence of nationalist sentiments and political activities (Risseuw 2000, 184; Oddie 1991, 192). Indeed, the theosophists' discourse on India's golden age and universal wisdom contributed to the shaping of an emerging national identity, providing counterarguments to European contempt and criticisms. British journalist Annie Besant, successor as the head of the Theosophical Society, was to pursue this celebration of ancient India, becoming a prominent political actor who was involved in anti-colonial troubles and who ultimately became president of the Indian National Congress in 1917 (Kamerkar 1978, 406–409; Bevir 2000, 175). Finally, it should be noted that beyond the Indian peninsula, the role of the Theosophical Society for the dissemination of Asian religions was pivotal. The Society renewed Western esotericism to a considerable extent, in drawing on Asian religions. Furthermore, as the first esoteric channel of knowledge of Hindu and Buddhist ideas in Europe and North America, it facilitated the success of the first Hindu personalities who were to teach in Euroamerican societies (French 1974, 92).

Overall, these socio-religious reform movements of colonial India throw light on the fact that certain expressions of Hinduism have been considerably transformed by its encounter with European culture in the colonial context. It gave rise to a "neo-Hinduism"[2] whose leaders, despite their ideological differences, share one common trait:

> Their intellectual formation is primarily or predominantly Western. It is European culture, and in several cases even the Christian religion, which has led them to embrace certain religious, ethical, social, and political values. But afterwards, they connect these values with, and claim them as, part of the Hindu tradition. (Hacker in Halbfass 1995, 231)

Neo-Hinduism is therefore best characterized by a process through which Western values are first embraced and then incorporated into a new vision of Hinduism, in a quest for its primordial purity. In a colonial encounter, the assimilation of those values to which the superiority of the "West" is attributed (rationality, monotheism, universalism, egalitarianism, textualism, and congregational worship) represents a means of more effective resistance (Jaffrelot 1992, 378), even if this meant reshaping "Hinduism" on the model of Christianity (Thapar 1997). Nonetheless, neo-Hinduism, as Hacker stresses, always claims to go back to its primordial and genuine sources. According to Halbfass (1988, 220), what is specific to neo-Hinduism is its particular invocation of tradition as the source of "the power and context for its response to the West."

It is precisely this westernized form of Hinduism that was to spread to Euroamerican societies. Consequently, what has come from the "East" has been profoundly inspired by Western culture, in particular by what the "West" expected the "East" to be: a cultural supplement in the shape of a timeless and universal wisdom, but which leaves behind its rituals, the worship of multiple divinities, and all that the Euroamerican mindset is not ready to value. The reception of religious resources from Asia cannot be understood as a surprisingly natural complementarity between "East" and "West."

Hindu Mission and Westernization

The very idea of a universal and missionary Hinduism results from the encounter with Europe. In fact, the transnational dissemination of neo-Hinduism can be understood as a "counter-mission" (Hummel 1988, 16) that responded to and confronted the colonization of, and Christian proselytism within, India—in such a way that religious revitalization, national identity, and mission abroad could be interwoven. In other words, the popularization of Hindu teaching is partly the result of the colonization of India and the westernization of Hinduism and cannot be understood solely by a tendency of modern Euroamerican societies toward bricolage. Furthermore, disseminating neo-Hinduism in these social environments entailed taking into account expectations of a universal, practical, and inner-worldly Hinduism that emphasizes individual self-realization. Accordingly, the trend of westernization, involving partial detachment of Hindu concepts and practices from their cultural roots, is accelerated as it is widely disseminated. This is already suggested by the Ramakrishna Mission, the first neo-Hindu movement implanted in North America and Europe.

Ramakrishna Mission's leader, Vivekananda (1863–1902), was the first Indian religious figure to successfully introduce Hinduism on the international scene, at the World Parliament of Religions in Chicago (1893). The aim of this event, organized by Unitarians, was to celebrate the unity of people and religions, despite the fact that they expected this convergence would result from the acknowledgment of Christianity's universal value (Bainbridge

1997, 181). Vivekananda was considered to be one of the most outstanding personalities of the Parliament (French 1974, 55). Like the neo-Hindu reformers I have already presented, Vivekananda was deeply influenced by Western culture: in addition to the English education he received at the Scottish Presbyterian College and his familiarity with European philosophy (Halbfass 1988, 229), his initiation into the Masonic lodge of Calcutta in 1884 probably familiarized him with Western esotericism (de Michelis 2004, 93–100). His involvement in the Brahmo Samaj during his youth has also been considered a predominant influence in his approach to the Vedantic literature, much more than the traditional approach of his master, Ramakrishna (1836–1886). Vivekananda's aim in coming to the Parliament of Religions in Chicago was originally to seek material help for his country. However, his unexpected success in the United States encouraged him to begin missionary work instead. It persuaded him that relations between East and West were changing direction, announcing a new era of glorification for India.

Vivekananda's success was the result of the way he expressed the opposition embedded in orientalism between the materialistic, nature-controlling, egoistic, decadent, and secular West, on the one hand, and India's "golden age," where Hindus were the spiritual leaders of the world, on the other (King 1985, 8–11). He therefore embraced the orientalist myth of the East-West difference and complementarity: "You of the West are practical in business, practical in great inventions but we of the East are practical in religion. You make commerce with your business; we make religion our business" (cited in Burke 1986, 160–161). No doubt this opposition between the materialistic West and the religious, spiritual East echoed Western self-criticism and aspiration toward revitalization through Asian religions. Indeed, this was a discourse shaped by the West that was offered to North Americans and Europeans, but which at the same time accorded a primary role to India in the world. In fact, the glorification of Hinduism's spiritual heritage and conversion of Westerners represented a means by which national Indian pride and identity could be revalorized and India's role could be redefined as a spiritual guide for the West. This self-asserting Hindu identity was also clearly evident when, returning to India, Vivekananda spoke to his countrymen:

> Heroic workers are wanted to go abroad and help to disseminate the great truth of Vedanta. The world wants it; without it the world is destroyed.... We must go out; we must conquer the world with our spirituality and philosophy. There is no alternative, we must do it or die.

The only condition of national life, of awakened and vigorous national life, is the conquest of the world by Indian thought. (Vivekananda 1985, 100)

In other words, missionary ambitions in Europe and America were combined with orientalist representations of Indian-ness in a quest for the revitalization of Indian society and the shaping of a national identity. This was made clear by the fact that on his return to India, Vivekananda was acclaimed as a national hero (Mukherjee 1978b, 13; Sharma 1998, 61), despite criticisms from those who thought his teaching was too Westernized. There, he spoke in defense of traditional Hinduism and expressed greater anti-Western sentiments (Beckerlegge 2000, 52–78; Jackson 1994, 30–31).

After participating in the Parliament, Vivekananda spent two years in the United States. He also traveled to France and England, where he made some of his most important disciples (French 1974, 67), and again to the United States between 1899 and 1900, when the neo-Hindu mission spread most successfully. The first "Vedanta Society" was founded in New York in 1895: the Mission would continue to strengthen with Indian disciples whom Vivekananda later sent to maintain local branches. Vivekananda inaugurated the collective teaching of Hinduism to Europeans and Americans. He attracted individuals from the middle and upper middle classes, generally close to the margins of religion in North America—the New Thought, Unitarianism, esoteric circles such as Theosophy and Rosicrucianism. Vedantic societies were adapted to their new environment, for example by giving to satsangs (religious gatherings) the shape of dominical services and using the organizational models of Christian organizations as Vivekananda knew them in India (French 1974, 156; Jackson 1994, *passim*). Vivekananda was actually happy to adapt his teaching to please his new disciples (Killingley 1999); he was aware that Westerners liked only "some" of the ideas of the Hindu scriptures, while some topics like caste, sacred doctrines, or the status of women seemed better avoided (De Michelis 2004, 120). There was a relative absence, on the Western side of the Ramakrishna Mission, of prescriptions regarding practices and behaviors; no particular Hindu god was celebrated, and there was no insistence on a body of doctrine either (French 1974, 156, 158). Vivekananda and his swamis presented Vedanta as "practical" rather than doctrinal, and consequently relevant to modern daily life (Jackson 1994, 64).

The crucial point here is that the transnational diffusion of neo-Hinduism entailed presenting itself in ways that Euroamerican societies would expect and celebrate, in ways which required that its teaching be detached from particular aspects of Indian religious life, social norms, and values (hence a start of de-contextualization). Despite the fact that Vivekananda felt compelled to defend traditional Hinduism in Euroamerican societies against misrepresentations and criticisms by missionaries, this is not the "modern Hinduism with all its ugliness" that he wanted to present (Vivekananda cited in Beckerlegge 2000, 57). Instead, this was a purified, universal, inner-worldly, and practical Vedanta.[3] In tune with Ram Mohun Roy's universalism, Vivekananda claimed that, contrary to Christian transcendence and personal God, only Vedanta could transcend religious creeds.

Furthermore, Vivekananda invited his followers not to consider Vedanta as a doctrine but as a "practical" method of liberation. This definition of the teaching as a "practical spirituality" (Vivekananda 1968), here implicitly opposed to the doctrinal and theoretical character of religion (hence of Christianity), is a recurrent theme among neo-Hindu movements today. It also provides the justification for de-linking these teachings from their religious and cultural roots. For Vivekananda, the "practical" quality of Vedanta mainly meant that it was compatible with engagement in the world—a crucial claim, since the otherworldly character of the Hindu salvation paths was seen, in particular by Christian missionaries, as unsuited for social engagement and activities and hence entailed no moral or social consequences (Halbfass 1988, 241). Thus, while the material world is considered illusory in Vedantic philosophy, Vivekananda innovated in providing an inner-worldly interpretation. This allowed him to see in the Vedanta an invitation to social reform (Beckerlegge 1998, 159–160) and to involve the Ramakrishna Mission in education, social reform, and medical relief in India (Vivekananda was greatly impressed by the social institutions developed by Christian missions; French 1974, 169).

This perspective also contributed to the universalisation of Vedanta: far from only concerning a minority of people who could become ascetics and renounce the world, salvation was instead made compatible with inner-worldly activities (Jackson 1994, 31), and Vedanta therefore became applicable to all, regardless of caste, gender, occupation, creed, walk of life, and so on. This can be understood as a revolution in Hinduism, if one remembers that traditionally Hindus contribute to the cosmic order precisely by rituals and social duties that are specific to gender, age group, and hereditary social group (caste) from which those who are not born in India were in theory excluded (Halbfass 1988, 331).

In the United States, possibly influenced by the New Thought's emphasis on personal responsibility for individual development and healing (de Michelis 2004, 122), Vivekananda's "practical spirituality" also emphasized the presence of the divine in each person and the ability for all to reach self-realization. Indeed, for Advaita Vedanta, Maya generates an illusory sense of personal existence that prevents human beings from knowing Brahman as truth, consciousness, and bliss. Salvation comes from the realization that the self (*atman*) is not an individual "I" but nothing other than Brahman itself. Yet Chapter 5 of this volume will show that in Euroamerican societies, "self-realization" is largely understood as a very individualistic quest for personal fulfillment and growth, rather than the annihilation of individuality. In other words, Vivekananda promoted a profoundly exoteric, inner-worldly, and individualistic path, attracting its first disciples through Vedanta's alleged universalism, its practical dimension, and its distinct methods for encountering the divine (Jackson 1994, 100). Hinduism was thus abstracted away from its collective manifestations (caste customs and duties, rituals, festivals, and pilgrimages) and shifted toward individual salvation (Brekke 1999). It did not have to be consubstantial to the Indian social organization anymore: this combination of universalism and individualization contributed to making Hinduism exportable.

All these aspects—universalism, inner-worldly orientation, religious individualism, and practical character—are still at the core of teachings spread by modern gurus and can be understood as the key to their success outside India. Paradoxically, while we can see with Vivekananda that the drive of this diffusion of Hinduism was a means to assert a particularistic national and religious identity, it entails more adaptation to new expectations. With Vivekananda, the seeds of de-contextualization were already sown, and modern gurus accelerated this process. At a time when the counterculture was to represent a new opportunity for Asian religion, the popularization of neo-Hindu teachings in Euroamerican societies accelerated this universalistic presentation of Hinduism that downplays its particularistic aspects.

The 1960s and Mass Popularization

It is hardly insignificant that it is precisely in the 1960s, when the critique of a utilitarian culture, a bureaucratized social life, and impersonal relations arose (Tipton 1982), that some in the West began to "turn East" in an attempt to reinvent social roles in close-knit communities, reunify the divine and the self, and rediscover emotion and self-expression in religious life. However, the youth counterculture initiated a new approach to Asian religions, as pointed out by Mircea Eliade who, long before them and like orientalists, had taken an intellectual path:

> I made the effort of learning Sanskrit in order to read texts and be able
> to work with the authentic representatives of the Indian tradition. In
> brief, I was approaching Indian spirituality "from inside" as we say, but

without renouncing Western disciplines: philology, critique of texts, ex-
egesis, etc. (in Ceccomori 2001, 113, my translation)

Beyond the rather normative character of this observation, Eliade was right to
underline that the counterculture generation was not motivated by intellectual
or philosophical concerns, but looked for a direct experience detached from
a study of doctrines, as a means to initiate changes in values and lifestyles.
But adapting to this experiential approach entailed a greater detachment from
Hindu cultural roots and norms, as we shall see throughout this study.

Indeed, this new phase of dissemination was also characterized by a far
greater fragmentation and diversification of Asian religions and practices in
Euroamerican societies. By and large, Buddhism, first practiced by the Beatnik
generation, expanded to counterculture students; so did Japanese movements
such as Mahikari and Sokka Gakkai. The counterculture was also a fantastic
period for Indian gurus, and most neo-Hindu movements present today in
North America and Europe spread between 1960 and 1975. Influenced by
Vivekananda's rhetoric, contemporary gurus also represent the continuation
of the mosaic of Hindu sects that had coexisted with Brahmanic orthodoxy
for centuries. Those traditional communities were based on the teaching of a
guru, who relatively freely reinterpreted Hindu doctrines and philosophy for
his own purposes (Renou 1952, 621). Thus, this fragmented and effervescent
religious milieu represented a fertile field for religious innovations, schisms,
and heterodoxies, expanded beyond India's borders.

In North America and Europe, the young generation listened to gurus
giving conferences and lectures on university campuses and even traveled
to India to discover ashrams and practice yoga or meditation. Some of these
gurus are now well-known. Rajneesh, called the "sex guru" for his liberal ideas
on gender relations and sexuality, attracted thousands of Westerners to his
ashram in Poona, where his teaching heavily drew on therapies of the emerging Human Potential movement (Palmer 1994, 46). In the late 1970s, about
30,000 people were visiting his ashram each year (Thompson and Heelas
1986, 19). Transcendental Meditation, introduced by Maharishi Mahesh Yogi
and popularized by the Beatles, claimed to have initiated millions of followers
to meditation worldwide. In reference to a fifteenth-century devotional movement dedicated to Krishna, Swami Prabhupada founded in New York in 1965
the International Society for Krishna Consciousness (ISKCON), a conservative
Vaishnava organization which, at the turn of the 1970s, was already a transnational movement, with thousands of members and more than 75 centers and
communities (Rochford 1991, 10, 277). Through ISKCON, hundreds of young
people were seen adopting this communal life, a strict lifestyle in terms of

gender relations, clothing, diet, and religious practices, dancing and chanting in the name of Krishna, as well as engaging in proselytizing activities in public spaces. While Sathya Sai Baba did not travel to Europe and North America as much as others, he is one of the most famous charismatic Indian gurus today, in particular for his miraculous materialization of ashes, food, and sweets, as well as his alleged healing power. Branches founded by his Indian and Western disciples exist all over the world and have spread Sai Baba's teaching based on the universality of religion, meditation, and healing. Finally, without creating circumscribed religious movements, some Indian masters became highly influential regarding philosophical, spiritual, and psychological issues, such as Krishnamurti and Deepak Chopra, whose books became alternative medicine and personal growth classics.

Hindu practices and concepts also penetrated Euroamerican societies in the 1960s through the emerging quasi-religious therapies of what has been called the "Human Potential" movement. The world of psychology was transfigured in the 1960s: in contrast with classical psychoanalytic schools, emergent and heterodox therapies aimed not to cure mental disease and relieve pain caused by hysteria or depression, for example, but to stimulate personal growth, self-fulfillment, body awareness, or self-realization. These post-psychoanalytic therapies, as Castel (1981b) described them, include "encounter" groups, Gestalt, Transactional Analysis, Humanistic Psychology, Bioenergetics, Primal therapy, and so on. They are generally characterized by a holistic approach uniting body and mind and a quest for self-transcendence, an experience of the divine within. This explains the appeal of Asian religions, which are believed to be holistic, include body practices, and assert the divine nature of human beings—hence the encounter of therapists of the Human Potential with gurus, Buddhist lamas, and yoga teachers in places such as the Esalen institute (Pelletier 1996, 58–59). By and large, Asian religious practices started to be included in increasingly heterodox therapies. Finally, throughout the 1970s, practices such as martial arts and yoga began to develop mass popularity in North America and Europe. This popularization had already taken the shape of a diversification and a fragmentation of teachings, which became "techniques" detached from their original cultural and philosophical context, and used for other purposes than religious salvation.

It is in this context of diversification and popularization of Asian religions that Siddha Yoga and the Sivananda Centres began to spread transnationally. Siddha Yoga is a neo-Hindu movement that emphasizes a strong devotional relationship between the disciple and the guru, who bestows the awakening of divine energy, called *shaktipat*. This experience, as well as meditation and chanting, is supposed to lead to self-realization, that is to say, in Siddha Yoga, the awareness of God within. Muktananda (1908–1982) was the founder of Siddha Yoga. On behalf of his master, Nityananda (?–1961), he claimed to have the mission of creating an ashram, disseminating his teaching and going to the West. A few months after Nityananda's death, in 1961, Muktananda started his own ashram, near Bombay, and welcomed Westerners. The seeds of Siddha Yoga, the "path of the perfect ones," were already planted: the voluntary work of Western and Indian disciples enabled the development of Muktananda's ashram in Ganeshpuri and the first publications of his teaching. Local centers and communities began to be established in Europe and North America in the 1970s by disciples who had come back from India (Brent 1972; Brooks et al. 1997; Yeo 1987, 81–82). It was they who supported his tours in the United States and Europe and introduced him in alternative and spiritual circles. Muktananda made his first world tour in 1970, primarily in the United States but also in Australia and Europe; a second tour in 1974, the Muktananda World Tour, firmly established the movement worldwide, with more than 150 centers and three ashrams since then, administered from the United States by the SYDA Foundation (initials of Siddha Yoga Dham, "abode of Siddha Yoga"). As he was engaging with this second tour, Muktananda declared:

> Today, with my Guru's command and grace, I am going away from India for some time. Owing to our limited vision, we consider various countries as different. For God, all countries are his and all beings are his. In God's house there's no particular region or sect or faith. To him all are the same. I am going abroad to initiate a revolution, a meditation revolution. As a result of this revolution, man will regain his prestige which has been vanished. (Brooks et al. 1997, 82)

It is quite easy to observe the continuity with Vivekananda's missionary Hinduism, combining a claim of universality with the orientalist hope for the regeneration of Western societies by Hindu wisdom. In the United States, some of Muktananda's sympathizers were famous and influential in the counterculture milieu, including Werner Erhard and Ram Dass (Brooks et al. 1997, 75–78). These personalities presented his teaching and introduced him in countercultural milieus as well as on university campuses. In 1982, when Muktananda died, Siddha Yoga represented allegedly 300 centers in 52 countries, which were said to attract 300,000 disciples, a third of whom were American. In France and England together, Siddha Yoga has a thousand disciples, although it may attract many more sympathizers. These disciples and sympathizers are overwhelmingly Westerners: Siddha Yoga does not seem to attract individuals having South Asian origins in the United States or Europe. I do not know the composition of local branches in India, but it seems that they mainly attract Westerners (Healy 2010, 17–18). Currently a woman, Gurumayi (1955–), is the leader of the movement. Like the Kabbalah Centre and many NRMs, starting with the Beatles and Transcendental Meditation, Siddha Yoga attracted celebrities in the 1980s (Graham 2001, 107), and Gurumayi is known to have been the guru of Diana Ross, Isabella Rosselini, Melanie Griffith, and many other "Hollywood dharma-seekers" (Kuczynski 2001), before the Kabbalah craze of the late 1990s. At that time, the media—in particular, Harris (1994) in *The New Yorker*—revealed sexual abuse and secrecy in Siddha Yoga. As a result, many disciples left, and the movement experienced a stark decline in membership and resources. Since then, Gurumayi has considerably reduced contact and communication with her disciples and has closed her ashram to visitors. The new emphasis on the study of scriptures and deeper personal commitment also have contributed to making Siddha Yoga a relatively more exclusive movement than it previously had been.

The name of Sivananda is today associated with one of the most well-known teachings of yoga. Yet Sivananda (1887–1963) never left Asia. Preceding the counterculture's fascination with the "East," he aimed to extend his influence primarily in India (Strauss 1997, 120–121). It is his Indian and Western disciples who disseminated his teaching transnationally. Sivananda established a movement called the Divine Life Society in 1936 in Rishikesh, with the aim of propagating yoga as a means for universal, social, and individual progress. Sivananda's Yoga Vedanta Forest University promoted studies of texts, *sadhana* (religious discipline), and research on Vedanta, yoga paths, and religious studies. The Yoga Vedanta Forest University became renowned for the practice of yoga: at the end of the 1950s, roughly 300 disciples were living in Sivananda's ashram (Miller 1989, 103), with an increasing number of Americans and Europeans at the beginning of the 1960s. After his death, some of his Indian followers were to leave for a less "westernized" ashram (Strauss 1997: 102). The ashram became an extraordinary breeding ground for the diffusion of yoga: called "Swami Propaganda" (Ceccomori 2001, 187), Sivananda urged his disciples to create new branches of the Divine Life Society, to organize conferences and yoga classes, and to translate and publish his numerous books.

One of his students and yoga teachers in his ashram, Vishnu-Devananda (1927–1993), successfully disseminated his teachings outside India. Sivananda was said to have given him this mission: "Vishnu Swami, one day you must go to America. People are waiting there for you to teach them yoga" (Sivananda Centres 1994). What Vishnu-Devananda retrospectively said about his motivation to undertake this mission sheds light on the enduring nature of orientalist representations:

> I knew that although there were many materialistic attitudes in the West, there were also people who could turn towards an inner world. They knew that there was more than the pursuit of material objects; they took to hard discipline. I realized that here was fertile ground to sow the yogic seed. I knew that even Indians wouldn't take his kind of discipline. They wouldn't do what those students did. (cited in Krishna 1995, 40)

This also underlines the enthusiasm of Westerners, learning yoga at Sivananda's ashram and engaging with a new lifestyle. Vishnu-Devananda left India for the first time in 1957, and with the support and help of his first students, he opened an ashram in Quebec in 1959. He had wished to found it in New York, but could not because of US immigration regulations of the time (Sivananda Centres 1998), which explains why the headquarters of the Sivananda Centres are located in Canada. A second ashram was created in the Bahamas in 1967, thanks to the support of an American sympathizer; ashrams were opened in California and New York in the 1970s with the support of disciples. Vishnu-Devananda endlessly traveled, trained yoga teachers, and initiated swamis, enabling them to establish and run centers in their own countries. He never stopped organizing yoga classes, demonstrations, and conferences; hosted in his ashrams, these events drew all sorts of New Age personalities, representatives of different religious traditions, and artists, thereby celebrating the universality of yoga beyond cultural and religious differences. There are today 9 ashrams and 19 Sivananda Centres, located mainly in European and American metropolises. These different ashrams and centers are managed by acharyas, the board of the monastic order founded by Vishnu-Devananda in 1969, called the True World Order. The Sivananda Centres also developed a Teaching Training Course, through which they have trained more than 10,000 yoga teachers. As in Siddha Yoga, Sivananda Centres attract Westerners, and it was exceptional for me to meet individuals having South Asian origins in the French and British local branches. Their ashrams and centers in India certainly welcome Indian followers, yet the ways in which their activities are advertised online show that they do cater to Westerners, for example through the use of English, the provision of "cultural information" and directions for non-locals, and the emphasis on the exotic charm of the locations (Sivananda Centres 2012).

The Kabbalah Craze

The popularization of Asian religions was one of the obvious features of the counterculture. But the 1960s "new religious consciousness" also contributed to one of the most fascinating developments in modern Judaism: a growing popular interest in Kabbalah that has not shown any waning today and spans from Orthodox to secular Jews, and even non-Jews. As Hinduism was supposed to regenerate the West, so Kabbalah is taken for something else: a source of original and ancient universal truths in esoteric and New Age circles, or a vital force for the revitalization of Judaism in a Jewish context. In both cases, it entails an adaptation to the expectations and dispositions of an audience that is only partially or not socialized at all with Judaism. This has led to the diversification of Kabbalistic teachings and their partial or total detachment from Jewish norms and practices, which the Kabbalah Centre illustrates. Again, the processes of idealization, universalization, and de-contextualization make this religious tradition available for appropriation.

A Short Introduction to Kabbalah

Before turning to the dissemination of Kabbalah, it is necessary to present it briefly, to be aware of traditional Kabbalah's esoteric character and marginal place within Judaism. This, indeed, makes its modern popularity a striking and fascinating shift. More important, it is crucial to explain that traditionally, Kabbalah inextricably entails an assertion of religious observance and for this reason seems inseparable from Judaism. It is in light of this that the dissemination of Kabbalah to individuals who, as non-Jews or as secular Jews, do not practice Judaism represents a process of de-contextualization.

Kabbalah is associated with a specific Jewish esoteric trend which, in medieval Spain, France, and Italy, produced a doctrine of the nature of the divine and human beings and their vocations, and which offered keys for understanding and acting upon the world and its divine realms (Mopsik 2003, 11–16; Dan 2007, 8–20). Rather than a simple and coherent system, Kabbalah is an unfinished chain of multiple different and sometimes contradictory religious creations, interlocking more than 6,000 texts, the content of which has been orally interpreted and transmitted over centuries in Western and Eastern Europe, North Africa, and the Middle East (Mopsik 1988, 26; Scholem 1998, 163). It is often argued that Kabbalah emerged with the ideas of *Ein-Sof*, the boundless, inaccessible divine and primal cause of the universe, and the *sefirot*, 10 inter-related "vessels" receiving *Ein-Sof*'s emanation of light that animate all divine realms and beings, thus ensuring passages between the different worlds. This complex activity internal to the divine itself is described in detail in the most influential Kabbalistic book, the Zohar, which was canonized nearly immediately after its appearance. Written in Aramaic, the Zohar is a pseudo-epigraphic work with all the marks of an ancient rabbinical text attributed to Talmudist Bar Yochai, second century C.E.; academics nevertheless describe it as a composite work, written by several Spanish authors of the thirteenth century. This commentary suggests that beyond the Pentateuch's literal meaning, divine secrets can be discovered in the sacred text and each of its letters (Idel and Malka 2000, 63). These secrets would give human beings the necessary knowledge to perfect their souls and positively influence divine worlds through religious observance and righteous actions and intentions. The expulsion and dispersion of Jews from Spain and Portugal in the Mediterranean region fostered the emergence of various poles of Kabbalah studies in symbiosis with new cultures.

Equally important for the history of Kabbalah is the Safedian period that flourished in the sixteenth century with the teachings of Isaac Luria, a charismatic figure whose teaching, influenced by the Spanish tradition, was recorded by his students. Although he died young and taught for only a very brief period, his systematization of Kabbalistic concepts was used to reinterpret the Jewish tradition as a whole, and the great upheavals in Jewish religious thought, such as Hasidism, can be viewed as new interpretations of Luria's doctrine (Dan 2007, 80–81; Mopsik, 2003, 87–102). Luria explained the primordial imperfection of the world in a new way. There is at the start an inherent flaw in the universe: some of the *sefirot* could not contain the emanation of divine light and broke, with the result that sparks of divine light fell and now feed the *kelippot*, the evil powers that govern lower realms, thus causing disharmony and destruction in the divine worlds. The ultimate goal of human beings is to correct the universe, by freeing the captive sparks of light and returning them to the divine realms in order to accomplish their restoration—*tikkun*. This would bring redemption, perfection to *Ein-Sof* itself, and the permanent unification of divine worlds and beings. Kabbalah has therefore a theurgical dimension: it asserts the human ability and necessity to influence or act upon the divine, not for individual purposes but for the restoration of divine harmony and collective redemption.

Kabbalah is also inextricably linked to Jews' observance: *tikkun* is performed by the observance of the divine commandments (*mitzvot*), as well as abstention from transgression and acts of injustice that would delay its achievement and strengthen the power of evil. In other words, "the Jew is responsible for everything, including God," noted Idel (1988, 179), and cannot walk away from this cosmological game (Dan 2007, 58). The fact that

Kabbalah traditionally emphasizes Jews' specific mission and the distinction between Jews and non-Jews means that, like Hinduism's extension to outcaste Westerners, Kabbalah's modern popularization necessarily entailed a process of de-ethnicization.

Indeed, Kabbalah has combined extraordinary doctrinal innovations with strict adherence to *halakha* (Jewish law). As Dan (2007, 59) notes, "The kabbalists thus presented a radical new mythology, which drastically spiritualized Jewish religious culture, but at the same time they enhanced and invigorated the traditional Jewish way of life, giving it powerful new spiritual incentives." For Kabbalists, the revelation of divine law allows heterodox interpretations. Claiming to be the guardians of an immemorial wisdom that contains the secrets of the universe has nonetheless allowed Kabbalists to include notions and beliefs rooted in Christianity, Islam, and Greek philosophy. Since the Middle Ages, a "practical Kabbalah" also involved the use of this teaching for immediate ends: associated with magic, it includes the use of astrology, divine names and formula, talismans, and amulets, to bring health, prosperity, and protection against the evil eye (Mopsik 1988, 122, 140). However, Kabbalah was ultra-Orthodox in the sense that it linked ethical deeds, commandments, prayers, and rituals to processes in the divine worlds; its doctrine incited religious observance and forbade transgression of religious tradition (Dan 2007, 58). Again, this is important to keep in mind when we will explore the modern popularization of Kabbalah and its rejection of religious observance.

The modern diffusion of Kabbalah is also surprising because of its esoteric and marginal status within Judaism until recently. Despite the fact that interpretations and experiences were recorded in writing, texts were often cryptic, and only some of its secrets were transmitted orally by masters to a few chosen disciples. In addition, because of its syncretic tendencies, Kabbalah was often perceived as heterodox or even as a heretical stream in Judaism (Mopsik 2003, 18). It was ignored for a long time by Jewish scholarship and was attacked by Jewish philosophers, who judged its esoteric speculations as an aberration incompatible with reason. Suspicious religious authorities restricted its study to men older than 40, in particular in Western Europe, but Kabbalah remained an important part of religious traditions in North African Judaism and in Eastern European Hasidism (Mopsik 1988, 39). Until the 1960s, Kabbalah was scarcely taught. It could be studied primarily in Jerusalem and only by small numbers of highly observant male students who were completely familiar with the rabbinic literature. The main Orthodox institutions had rarely—and only recently—introduced it in rabbinic seminaries, more as a result of public demand than as a change in Orthodox mentality (Mopsik 2003, 245).

A Christian Kabbalah

To tell the history of the popularization of Kabbalah, we need to go far back in time. Indeed, it has been at the heart of pre-modern and modern Western esotericism as part of Renaissance Neo-Platonism and occultism. As such, it contributed to the contemporary interest in Kabbalah (within or without the Jewish world) and has greatly informed contemporary Kabbalistic teachings, but as "Christian Kabbalah," that is, severed from its Jewish origins.

Christian Kabbalah emerged in fifteenth-century Italy. By and large, the Renaissance was a period of transition in European thought, a period of social change in which a new sense of the past was developing (Blau 1965, 114), so that primordial times and origins could be fantasized and "rediscovered"— hence the incentive for the exploration of arts, sciences, philosophies, and magic that led to the translation and study of a wide range of sources, from Egyptian hieroglyphs to Hermetic treatises. It is in this context that an interest in Kabbalah, then perceived as an ancient wisdom, emerged in Christian circles. The first book of Christian Kabbalah was published in 1485 by Pico Della Mirandola. In a combination of Kabbalah and Hermeticism, Pico presented Kabbalah as the primordial divine revelation that had been lost and found, and which would allow Western thought to grasp Pythagoras, Plato, Moses, and Christianity as a unique tradition (Blau 1965, 113; Goodrick-Clarke 2008, 43; Mopsik 2003, 100). By and large, for Christian Kabbalists, Kabbalah contains ancient and universal truths, including the essence of the Christian message. The leitmotif of the entire Christian Kabbalah was therefore to use Kabbalistic hermeneutics to reveal the mysteries of the Scriptures and to demonstrate the Christian truths they enclosed, the confirmation of tenets such as the trinity or Jesus as the messiah (Idel 1988, 263; Dan 1998, 120; Yates 1979, 17–18). In this venture, Christian Kabbalists were helped by Jews who had converted to Christianity and who could translate texts into Latin. Some did this in such a way that their translation could lead one to think that Kabbalah was actually close to Christianity, which facilitated the "discovery" of Christian principles in Jewish sources (Idel and Malka 2000, 139–140; Dan 2007, 62–63; Yates 1979, 19). This role is not totally different from the one played by the Indian elite for nineteenth-century European orientalists. Here again, the "other" is interesting insofar as they are *useful* to reclaim one's truths. The affirmation of Christianity through Kabbalah is made obvious in the intent to use this discovered evidence in disputations with rabbis and Jewish authorities, and their exploitation in missionary activities. In fact, one of the main aims of Christian Kabbalah was to convert Jews (Idel and Malka 2000, 142; Blau 1965, 77; Yates 1979, *passim*).

Throughout the sixteenth and seventeenth centuries, treatises appear in Italy, France, England, and Germany, and Kabbalah, associated with magic and alchemy, became one of the main components of the emerging Western esotericism (Hanegraaff 1998, 388, 395). More important, this meant that Kabbalah began a new existence outside its Jewish milieu, so that one could study Kabbalah without being Jewish, sometimes with the aim of asserting Christianity's legitimacy and, ironically, without Jews being allowed to practice their religion (Yates 1979, 183). This particular appropriation of Kabbalah implied selections, interpretations, and transformations—a process that we have already observed in the pragmatism with which orientalism considers the "mystical East" as a source of regeneration of the West. Christian Kabbalists were interested in Judaism's conception of language and its various methodologies of textual interpretation. Guematria, the numerical computation of the value of letters, and Temurah, which involved a systematic exchange of letters, allowed new interpretations of texts, but also excited Christian scholars' imagination about great secrets they could then discover. Accordingly, Christian Kabbalists emphasized methodology, rather than the content of the Kabbalistic texts themselves. They were also fascinated by the idea of a divine language as a means to influence reality, in particular the multiplicity of the names of God, and emphasized Kabbalistic elements of magic and astrology. This is the reason that Kabbalah has so often been associated with magic, an existing but secondary aspect of traditional Kabbalah. Similarly, through the works of occultists, Kabbalah began to be associated with alchemy in the sixteenth century, even though this represents a minor aspect of Kabbalah (Dan 2005, 641). Some of Kabbalah's central themes, such as the infinite God and the *sefirot* system, became marginal in Christian Kabbalah, while the trinity and Christological dimensions were included. The importance of observing God's commandments was removed. Stripped from structural religious norms and practices, Kabbalah was transformed into a gnosis for scholars and scientists to fulfill an intellectual and speculative interest, without being incorporated into their daily life as a religious practice (Dan 2007, 64, 66; Idel 1988, 262–263; Idel and Malka 2000, 142–146).

It was again the quest for origins that triggered the dissemination of Kabbalah in the context of nineteenth-century romantic orientalism, the same that aroused the interest in Asian religions. *Fin de siècle* romantic orientalism looked in the religious traditions of the East to satisfy its fascination with mysticism, the occult, myth, and folklore. This was thought to be an alternative to mechanistic and limited views of reality implied by rationalism and modernity, and greatly inspired nineteenth-century philosophers, artists, and esoteric milieus. Judaism could not escape from this orientalist lens: the Jew was the Oriental archetype (Mendes-Flohr 1991; Kalmar and Penslar 2005). Thus, while the Enlightenment was anti-Kabbalah and treated it as a manifestation of superstition, romantic scholars and philosophers such as Schelling were attracted by Kabbalah. In the romantic quest for a new aesthetic, Kabbalah's theory of language became a metaphor for a poetical language (Kilcher 2005, 644). But they were not inspired by any Jewish source of Kabbalah. Their explorations of Kabbalah were overwhelmingly impregnated by Christian Kabbalah. Not only was Kabbalah understood as a speculative system of thought exclusively (Idel 1988, 263), but its Jewish origins were often denied. In fact, nineteenth-century scholars sometimes identified its origins in Christian gnosis, Sufism, or Persian religious traditions (Fenton 1994, 218), but they shared the common assumption of Kabbalah as the universal and primordial knowledge from which other religions emanated (Hanegraaff 2010, 110, 112).

Christian Kabbalah also became very influential in esoteric circles: Swedenborg (Hanegraaff 1998, 425), Eliphas Levi who saw in Kabbalah the source of Christian theology (Fenton 1994), Papus in France, Aleister Crowley and the Order of the Golden Dawn in England (Asprem 2007), the Theosophical Society, Free-mason and Rosicrucian circles (Goodrick-Clarke 2008), which saw in Kabbalah a source of universal occult knowledge (Huss 2007b, 84)—all of these integrated references to Kabbalah that usually drew from Christian Kabbalah exclusively. Accordingly, Kabbalah was perceived as a theoretical knowledge of the structure of the universe; it was also strongly identified with magical practices, with an emphasis on methods of letter combinations or the magical use of divine names (Burmistrov 2010, 86; Pasi 2010, 158; Asprem 2007). We know little about the influence and understanding of Kabbalah in nineteenth- and twentieth-century esotericism, but there is no doubt that speculative Kabbalistic teachings were embraced by people who had little knowledge of Hebrew and Jewish works, if any, and who, in many instances, believed in the idea of a universal Kabbalah without Jewish origins (Hanegraaff 2010, 110). Hence Kabbalah was further detached from Judaism and unavoidably underwent a diversification of interpretations. Crowley thus defines Kabbalah as an "unsectarian and elastic" terminology and "an instrument for interpreting symbols," without referring to Judaism (Asprem 2007, 138). The founder of the Theosophical Society, Madame Blavatsky, drew on esoteric and orientalist publications (in particular, the works of Adolphe Frank and Eliphas Levi) to present Kabbalah as originating in Zoroastrianism (Hanegraaff 1998, 453; Pasi 2010, 160). Trying to establish the primordial character of Asian religion, Blavatsky ignored Jewish sources and claimed that an oriental (Asian) Kabbalah preexisted a Jewish Kabbalah, which she considered to be inferior:

> While the Oriental Cabala remained in its pure primitive shape, the Mosaic or Jewish one was full of drawbacks, and the keys to many of his secrets—forbidden by the Mosaic law—purposely misinterpreted. (cited in Pasi 2010, 159)

What is of note here is the condemnation of Judaism for concealing Kabbalistic secrets: it was indeed possible to combine fascination for Kabbalah and anti-Semitism (Dan 2007, 67; Fenton 1994, 226; Burmistrov 2010, 90). For Mopsik (1988, 114–116), if Kabbalah has been the main source of Christian esotericism, this fact has been silenced and denied by its members, who sometimes used Jewish sources referring to Kabbalah without citing them. This ambivalent relationship to Judaism in Western Europe is also evidenced, he notes, by the anti-Judaism of some Theosophists and Rosicrucian publications of the time. The ways in which Blavatsky situates "Jewish Kabbalah" as neither Western nor part of her Oriental (Asian) occultism (Pasi 2010, 160) also epitomizes this very peculiar relation to Kabbalah. Indeed, while there have been attempts to elaborate a yoga for Christians (Father Deschanet in France), or a Jewish yoga (Rothenberg 2006), its Hindu roots were never denied, as Kabbalah's Jewishness was.

The Rediscovery of Kabbalah in Modern Judaism

Kabbalah's early detachment from Jewish observance and dissemination as a speculative, mysterious, and ancient source of knowledge in esotericism significantly contributed to its popularization in contemporary Euroamerican societies. However, changes that occurred within Judaism in the postwar period have been equally crucial. By and large, there has been a revitalization of the study of Kabbalah out of concerns for Judaism's survival, and it is only in this context that, paradoxically, the universal Kabbalah taught by the Kabbalah Centre can be understood. The historical and cultural context that fostered the revitalization of Kabbalah is not, in some ways, drastically different from neo-Hinduism's first counter-missions in response to imperialism and Christian missions in India. It, too, poses the question of identity and role in the modern world. Here, the concerns regarding Judaism's presence and survival are linked to a national identity claim in the context of the creation of the state of Israel, the Holocaust, and the increasing secularization of Euroamerican Jewry. These three factors have contributed to the revitalization of Kabbalah *within* contemporary Jewry.

Just as neo-Hinduism made use of the romantic and orientalist image of Hinduism for *national* self-assertion, the positive image of the Orient held by *fin de siècle* romanticism represented an opportunity to rediscover Kabbalah's philosophical and literary heritage within Judaism, as part of affirming a Jewish identity. Kalmar and Penslar (2005, xix) called this "internal" or "counter-orientalism," involving the romanticization of the Orient and Jews as "Orientals." Combining the romantic fascination for the "Orient," an interest in esotericism that had embraced Christian Kabbalah, and nascent Zionism, Jewish thinkers and scholars of the end of the nineteenth and the beginning of the twentieth centuries celebrated Hasidism and rehabilitated Kabbalah. Thus, some emphasized the esoteric and metaphysical value of Kabbalah, while others saw in Kabbalah a possible means for the Jewish people to reclaim their historical heritage and shape a new national identity (Huss 2006). True, the dissemination of Kabbalistic works in these Jewish intellectual circles was limited, due to an ambivalent attitude toward Kabbalah. Perceived as irrational, medieval and oriental, Kabbalah was not seen as compatible with modernity (Huss 2006, 212); many European Jews chose instead to identify with the West, its values and aesthetic standards, leading the Reform movement, for example, to purge rituals from its "Orient quality" (Mendes-Flohr 1991, 82). Yet Huss (2006) notes that this intellectual interest in the Oriental sources of Judaism constructed the image of Kabbalah as the vital force of Judaism, an enduring representation, as we shall see further on.

Indeed, the strength of socialist and secular trends of Zionism limited the reference to Kabbalah to build a new national identity; nonetheless, Jerusalem was a vital center of traditional Kabbalah in the early twentieth century and became a central reference for religious Zionism. Abraham Yitzhak Kook (1864–1935), Israel's first Chief Rabbi and one of the most influential thinkers of religious Zionism, integrated Kabbalistic ideas within a national Zionist ideology. Considering Zionism and the birth of Israel as a sign of coming redemption, Kook advocated Kabbalah's dissemination. Kabbalah has kept its significance in shaping national and political identities in Israel, in particular in the cultural and political empowerment of the Sephardic ultra-Orthodox communities (Garb 2007, 2008).

Kabbalah also came to represent Judaism's vital force within some Orthodox communities. The Holocaust, the destruction of communities, and the breakdown of the tradition's continuity have given rise to new echoes of messianism and to the long-standing claim that the study of Kabbalah hastens the process of redemption. Indeed, for some, the Holocaust announced the coming of the Messiah; it was also interpreted by some Orthodox leaders as the result of a lack of Jews' religiosity in general and of the neglect of Kabbalah in particular. These religious ways of making sense of the Holocaust made the study and dissemination of Kabbalah within certain Orthodox Jewish communities an imperative. In addition, the loss of Jewish leaders, in particular from Eastern Europe, left a vacuum and weakened the reproduction of religious traditions, but also paradoxically allowed innovations in Kabbalistic teachings in the Orthodox world. The dissemination of Kabbalah within contemporary Jewish communities was facilitated by the migration of Sephardic Jews to Israel in particular. In North Africa, Kabbalah had been integrated into the religious life, although in a limited and regulated form. The dispersion of Sephardic Jews shattered traditional structures and weakened authority figures who could no longer control the teaching of Kabbalah, hence allowing a diversification of religious practice and beliefs as well (Garb 2007; 2008).

Finally, and more important, the twentieth century revival of Kabbalah is linked to the assimilation and secularization of Jewish communities around the world. This started within American Jewry in the countercultural context and sparked the worldwide popularization of Kabbalah. By and large, the American counterculture was disproportionately composed of youths from Jewish families, both among political activists (Liebman 1979; Rothman and Lichter 1982; Stratton 2008) and in the awakening of the "new religious consciousness."

In *The Future of Religion*, Stark and Bainbridge (1985, 400–401) gathered data from different studies conducted in the 1970s, which shows an extraordinary over-representation of Jews in ISKCON, Scientology, Ananda, Witches, the Unification Church, and the Satchidananda Ashram. In some NRMs, the percentage of Jews was five times greater than their percentage in the general American population (Ariel 1999, 196). In American forms of Buddhism, their representation was even larger; religious surveys have estimated the proportion of Jews in American Buddhist groups between 6 percent and 30 percent. While these estimates are far from precise, they sharply contrast with the proportion of Jews in the total American population, which was about 2.5 percent in 1990 (Roper 2003, 171; Vallely 2008, 20). At the start of the 1980s, 20 percent of residents of Rajneesh's ashram were Jewish (Mann 1993, 29).

Jewish converts to NRMs grew up in homes identified as Jewish, but where parents did not consider themselves to be observant. Their children had attended religious services several times a year, were familiar with Jewish rituals that were observed at home, and had attended supplementary Hebrew or religious school. But they emphasized the lack of stress on transcendence, the lack of "spirituality" in family religious practices, the impersonal and bureaucratized character of their parents' synagogue, and evoked instead a quest for a living religion (Eisenberg 1988, 51; Linzer 1996; Selengut 1988, 97–99). Furthermore, Selengut (1988, 104) explains that young Jews were also attracted by the proclaimed universalism of some NRMs, which responded to a feeling of discomfort with their own religious identity, perceived as marginal, particularistic, and ethnically distinctive. The research findings presented in the next chapter confirm Selengut's analysis: the Kabbalah Centre's opening to non-Jews is attractive to those who have a Jewish background and find there not an exclusive and ethnic, but a universal and cosmopolitan, Judaism.

While most sociologists of religion ignored what could have provided other analyses of the counterculture and its religious manifestations, it did not escape the attention of Jewish authorities (Eisenberg 1988; Jewish Community Relations Council of Greater Philadelphia 1978; Kelly 1990; Rudin 1978). Indeed, Jews drawn to NRMs or gradually leaving Jewish communities were a source of concern for mainstream congregations. Losses through conversion and persecution were actually perceived similarly, a feeling that was probably more acute after the Holocaust, which poses the question of the survival of the Jewish tradition (Feher 1994)—hence the expression a "spiritual shoah" to designate conversion and assimilation, and the development of several Jewish cult awareness organizations. In this context of the destabilization of Judaism, we should not be surprised that it was Kabbalah—which had already been cast in the role of the authentic source of mysteries and truth, and as such, of Judaism's vital force of Judaism—that was drawn upon to revitalize Judaism.

Kabbalah: An Attempt to Revitalize Judaism

I certainly have some deep concerns about the revival of Kabbalah. Young Jews are being caught up in an aspect of Judaism that they often do not understand well, and that is not necessarily making them into better Jews. But I think we must acknowledge that the interest in Kabbalah will be with us for years to come…I also believe that the revival of Kabbalah can be a healthy return to an important and enduring dimension of the Jewish heritage. There is a need for a revitalization of much of Jewish life and practice, and Kabbalah, which has been a source for such vitality in the past, can serve in this role again. (Eisen 1999, 40)

Since the 1960s, Kabbalah has increasingly been at the heart of attempts to revitalize Judaism by competing denominations and organizations. It has been first rediscovered through the renewal of Orthodox movements drawing on Hasidic tradition, on the one hand, and, on the other hand, through the Jewish Renewal, sometimes coined as "New Age Judaism" (Salkin 2000) or "Judaism lite" (Wilkes 2005, 119). The postwar period witnessed a movement of return to Orthodoxy through Hasidism. Hasidism was originally an Orthodox and pietist movement that appeared in the eighteenth century in Southern Russia and spread in Eastern Europe, then in the United States and Israel through the Ashkenazi diaspora. Hasidism emphasizes individual piety and devotion, God's omnipresence, and the importance of communion with God, through fervent praying and singing, rather than the intellectual understanding of religious doctrines. Through popular literature, songs, and sermons using a Kabbalistic vocabulary, Hasidism represents a major factor for the popularization of Kabbalah in the Orthodox Jewish community.

Hasidism has doubled its numbers every decade since the 1950s, and by the end of the Century represented a worldwide movement of about 200,000 Jews (Breslauer 1995, 112). It attracted a large number of young Jews in the 1960s and 1970s, especially those born in American Reform and Orthodox families. In this regard, the Hasidic movement Chabad-Lubavitch has been instrumental. Chabad started in 1940 when the sixth Lubavitcher rebbe (master) fled World War II to America, which he envisioned as the place for the future of Judaism. There, Chabad became the first large-scale Jewish attempt to reach out to secular and disaffiliated young Jews and win them back to the fold of Orthodoxy. In its traditional Hasidic perspective, Chabad viewed Kabbalah as "the 'salt' that flavors the 'meat' of Judaism" (Salkin 2000, 361). Kabbalah could therefore represent a Jewish alternative to NRMs that were taking Jews away from Judaism. Providing a wide range of religious, social, and educational services, Chabad draws on classical Hassidic teachings, referring to Kabbalah that it has slightly adapted to modernity; however, the movement remains Orthodox (Magid 2006; Friedman 1994). Danzger (1989, 81–82) notes that a section of Jewish youth may have found in Hasidic movements such as Chabad similarities with the "new religious consciousness" of the counterculture: strong community bonds, charismatic leaders with spiritual powers, a stress of devotion and emotion, special kosher diet that echoed their interest in macrobiotic and natural diets, and particular clothing. Idealizing this "highly ethnic world of imagination" that saw in Hasidism an authentic Judaism, uncorrupted by the compromises of assimilation in American society, they were also attracted by the mysterious knowledge of Kabbalah. We may note in passing that Orthodox organizations such as Chabad do not seek to attract and convert individuals who are not born into a Jewish family, but to reintegrate secular Jews to Judaism (Ariel 2011, 25; Danzger 1989, 81–83).

Kabbalah also began to be disseminated through heterodox and syncretic expressions of modern Judaism through the Jewish Renewal. The Jewish Renewal is the institutional continuator of the *havurot* movement, intimate fellowship groups created in the 1960s by young Jews dissatisfied with the Conservative and Reform congregations in which they had been raised. Functioning in place of the synagogues and with a countercultural mindset, the *havurot* rejected the enforcement of *halakha* and the exclusive authority of the rabbi. Instead, religious norms were to be accepted as a source of guidance and inspiration only. *Havurot* valued the intimacy of the close-knit community, egalitarian relations between genders, intense forms of prayers, Hasidic chanting, and meditation. They also integrated drama, poems, and pop songs, created new forms of prayers, and developed new interpretations of texts. Finally, in response to the internal divisions of Judaism, *havurot* were post-denominational (Salkin 2000, 354–356; Weissler 1989; Wertheimer 1992).

The Jewish Renewal combined the *havurot* spirit with a heterodox revival of Hasidism. Its main leaders, Zalman Schachter-Shalomi (1924–) and Shlomo Carlebach (1925–1994) were former emissaries of Chabad, from which they inherited an intense religiosity and a strong attachment to outreach activities. But they also had personally explored the beatnik world of the 1950s and early 1960s, met with personalities such as Allen Ginsberg, Leonard Cohen, and Timothy Leary, and Schachter-Shalomi even used psychedelic drugs to develop his religious experience. Familiar with the countercultural ethos, they came to believe that Orthodoxy's rigidity and rejection of modernity would repel the disaffiliated youth of the 1960s (Ariel 2003, 140–143; Danzger 1989, 86; Salkin 2000, 367–368). Instead, the Jewish Renewal movement adopted a counter cultural ethos that had already shaped the *havurot* movement. It insisted on egalitarianism and organized teaching of mixed classes of men and women, celebrated love, and adopted an accepting attitude regarding sexuality and drug use. The Jewish Renewal did not enforce traditional religious rules. Its religious outlook was actually syncretic; it integrated psychotherapy and borrowed from Sufism, Buddhist meditation, or yoga on the basis that all spiritual paths similarly enable individuals to experience the divine and attain self-fulfillment. Yet the aim of embracing other religious practices and teachings was to revitalize Judaism—we should not be surprised that later, Carlebach and his followers would take a more observant approach. At the time, Schachter-Shalomi and Carlebach were aware that young Jews were exploring a wide range of religious alternatives to Judaism and they wanted to show them that spirituality, joy, and intensity could be found in the Jewish tradition, too (Magid 2006, 57; Ariel 2003, 24, 141). Thus they also integrated music (Carlebach, a composer and singer, was known as the "singing Rabbi" during his lifetime), Hasidic folklore, storytelling, and dance in their religious practices. They revalued the act of prayer and engaged in new ways of reading the Torah. In insisting on intention and meaningful justifications for Jewish observance, the Jewish Renewal movement attempted to revitalize Jewish practice beyond its denominational boundaries. Kabbalah was central in this attempt: the mystical and mysterious Kabbalah participated in the re-aestheticization of religion and was presented as a means for a direct and vibrant experience of the divine that is central to Jewish Renewal (Salkin 2000, 366; Weissler 2006, 2011). In short, Kabbalah was "exoticized" within a Jewish context.

By and large, through orthodox and heterodox expressions, Kabbalah became "emblematic of a rebellion against Judaism itself" (Eisen 1999, 32). It was precisely the rejection of the traditional forms of authority, institutions, and imposed religious observance that accompanied the revival of Kabbalah. Attracting secular and disaffiliated Jews, Kabbalah increasingly became a vibrant, mysterious, "spiritual" alternative to mainstream Judaism, despite the fact that this very representation originated in Christian Kabbalah. Thus, secular or disaffiliated Jews may relate exclusively to Judaism through Kabbalah, without belonging to a Jewish community or observing specific practices. In other words, the modern dissemination of Kabbalah within a Jewish environment involves its partial detachment from Judaism as well.

The Popularization of Kabbalah Teaching and Detachment from Jewish Norms

The image of Kabbalah as an attractive spiritual and ancient wisdom is now consolidated. Its popularization is unprecedented; it has shown no sign of decline since the counterculture and is now a transnational phenomenon. In fact, representatives of Jewish institutions and denominations I have interviewed in all four locations said they observed the rapid and growing interest in Kabbalah. Originating in different sources, from Western esotericism to Jewish circles, Kabbalistic teachings are increasingly diversified. It is spread in an Orthodox fashion through Hasidism, and Jewish Renewal–influenced organizations, within proliferating traditional Kabbalistic *yeshivot* (religious schools) in Israel, and is now introduced in Jewish studies in universities and adult education programs in North America, Europe, and Israel. Many mainstream congregations now organize activities and festivals in relation to Kabbalah, such as Rosh Chodesh, a minor holiday celebrating the new moon and now emphasizing femininity, and Kabbalat Shabbat, which involves a prelude to Shabbat services of hymns and songs composed by sixteenth-century Kabbalists. Targeting young adults, some Shabbat services have become more meditative and contemplative. For some denominations, activities referring to Kabbalah also represent a means "to position [themselves] as quite a cool young professionals' synagogue."[4] In fact, Kabbalat Shabbat weekends and classes have become indispensable assets to introduce Judaism to disaffiliated Jews.

Furthermore, in Israel and elsewhere, new communities are emerging, founded by leaders coming from an Orthodox background and attracted by a Jewish Renewal approach or even a New Age trend (Garb 2008; Werczberger 2011). Within the Orthodox world, Israeli Hasidic communities also have experienced a vibrant renaissance that emphasizes ecstatic experiences and entails innovative reinterpretations of classical Kabbalistic literature (Garb 2011). Furthering the influence of Christian Kabbalah, a constellation of syncretic courses have developed in esoteric circles and New Age milieus that blend Kabbalah with other teachings such as yoga or meditation, emphasize personal growth, or identify Kabbalah with magic, alchemy, and astrology. In the last 40 years, hundreds of books have been published, ancient texts have been re-translated and re-edited, and new practices such as rituals, pilgrimages, and the use of amulets have been revitalized or invented (Huss 2007a). The diversification of Kabbalistic teachings is also the outcome of the fact that many teachers of Kabbalah today do not come from a religious background and did not study Kabbalah in traditional institutions (Huss 2007a). Kabbalah has also become a source of inspiration for artists in graphic art cinema and literature, who may or may not have a link to Judaism (Meilicke 2002; Huss 2010). All these references to Kabbalah share a common feature: the "violation" of *halakha*, as Garb (2008, 75) puts it—in other words, a partial detachment from Jewish religious life and its norms. Even in a Jewish environment, it is mostly disaffiliated and secular Jews who are drawn to Kabbalah, in allowing them to feel connected to Jewish traditional culture without observing Jewish law.

The Kabbalah Centre is a perfect illustration of the diversification of Kabbalistic teachings and their partial detachment from Jewish norms. However, the emergence of the Kabbalah Centre at the end of the 1960s was in tune with concerns regarding the secularization of young Jews and may be considered, to a certain extent, as a movement of outreach using Kabbalah, like Chabad and the Jewish Renewal. It shared their enthusiasm and strategies for outreach activities; like the Jewish Renewal, it entails a relaxed attitude regarding religious norms, syncretism, and intense praying and singing to revalue festivals and religious practice that derive from Hasidism. But the

Kabbalah Centre is a fascinating case in that over the course of its development, it changed its rationale, universalized its message, and engaged with
non-Jews.⁵ In other words, the Kabbalah Centre has done what, much earlier, Vivekananda did when he founded Vedantic Societies in America. Like
the "practical Vedanta" taught to Westerners, the Kabbalah Centre's universal
teaching entails a partial detachment from Judaism, and hence a process of
de-ethnicization.

The Kabbalah Centre presents itself as being founded in 1922 in Israel by
Yehuda Ashlag (1885–1954), a Kabbalist who translated the Zohar into Hebrew
and who was also known for his comments on the Zohar and his highly intellectual but modernizing teaching that draws on Lurianic Kabbalah (Garb 2008,
29–32). However, one could argue that the Kabbalah Centre, as such, was created by Feivel Gruberger, (1929–2013), later called Philip Berg, a New Yorker
from an Orthodox family. Berg received a religious education and was ordained
as a rabbi but worked as an insurance salesman while remaining Orthodox. He
began to be interested in Kabbalah in 1962 as he traveled in Israel and met his
first wife's uncle, Yehuda Brandwein, one of Ashlag's students and the head of
the department of religious affairs of the Israeli workers' union (Huss forthcoming a). Berg became Brandwein's book distributor and fundraiser in the
United States, but he also wanted to study Kabbalah and traveled many times to
Israel for this purpose. For Brandwein, Berg established in 1965, in New York,
the National Institute for Research in Kabbalah, to support research and publi-
cation in Kabbalah, "in accordance with the Orthodox Jewish tradition."⁶ When
Brandwein died in 1969, Berg claimed he had made him his successor. This is
contested by Brandwein's students; similarly, Ashlag's descendants deny any
relationship between Berg and themselves (Myers 2007, 39).

Berg moved to Tel Aviv in 1971 with his second wife, Karen, and began
to teach to a community of young Israelis. He, too, considered that "understanding and study of Kabbalah represent a unifying force necessary for the
survival of Judaism" (Berg 1983, 43). Thus, his goal was to reach out to the
young generation of Jews cut from their roots and prove to them that Judaism,
like yoga or Buddhism, also had responses to offer. As in the American Jewish
Renewal, different levels of commitment and observance were accepted. Berg
presented his teaching as non-coercive and inclusive: it proved to be successful among a partially secularized and mixed audience, looking for a spiritualized Judaism. In 1978, it was claimed that 400 students were involved in
the Research Centre of Kabbalah (Myers 2007, 58)—in the light of my interview with old-time students in Israel, I would not be surprised if the group
had been smaller.

The Bergs returned to the United States in 1981. There, the Berg family and some of their Israeli disciples launched activities to spread Kabbalah, first within the Jewish community, going door-to-door to sell the Zohar and offer classes, with limited success. But at the turn of the 1990s, Berg's mission changed its aim to become the "spiritual growth of humankind" as a whole (Kabbalah Centre 2004a). The significance of this shift is reflected in the magnitude of the controversy the movement has generated by celebrating the universality of Kabbalah and teaching it to Jews *and* non-Jews. True, Ashlag and his disciple Brandwein felt the diffusion of Kabbalah was urgently needed in alarming times for Jews, but neither advocated any teaching to women or non-Jews (Myers 2007, 20, 37). Thus, to reach an audience not necessarily familiar with Judaism's beliefs and rituals, courses and literature were simplified and detached from their Jewish background (see Chapter 3). This partial separation of Kabbalah from Judaism was accentuated in the 1990s by a teaching revision toward a greater professionalization and the increasingly pervading use of a secular vocabulary used in popular psychology, teaching, and learning (see Chapter 5). Personal fulfillment and happiness, through the connection to the Light of the Creator, became the central aim of the teaching. Thus, here too the universalisation of the teaching is combined with religious individualism.

The Kabbalah Centre took off with the opening of a center in California, the haven for unconventional religions. The celebrities that it attracted contributed to its fame; they include Barbra Streisand and Sandra Bernhard, who was "seeking something spiritual within the confines of being a Jew" (Tucker 2011), but also Britney Spears, Jerry Hall, Paris Hilton, Roseanne Bar and, of course, Madonna, who joined in 1996 and gave phenomenal publicity to the movement. Visibility, nonetheless, has its downsides: criticism by Jewish authorities, scholars, anti-cult movements, and journalists made the Kabbalah Centre one of the most controversial NRMs of the third millennium. Though it has been accused of debasing and selling Kabbalah in a cult-like organization, some of its detractors credit the Kabbalah Centre with enabling some people to renew their attachment to Judaism through the study of Kabbalah, and to be successful where many synagogues fail.

It is claimed that today no less than 10 million have visited one of the centers in the world, which are primarily located in the United States, or in Israel, Europe, and Latin America—although the number of committed members probably amount to a few thousand only. Seventy percent of these "students" are said to have no Jewish background (Kabbalah Centre 2011a, 6). However, my observation and interviews suggest that the very core of the movement, the "teachers," usually come from a secular Jewish background, a majority of them being Israeli. The population of *chevre*, volunteers who work freely for the Kabbalah Centre in exchange for basic subsistence support, is slightly more diverse, although the majority appear to be born into Jewish families. After Philip Berg's debilitating stroke in 2004, the movement seemed to undergo a new turning point, which could accelerate its de-contextualization of Kabbalah. His two sons, Michael and Yehuda Berg (born in Jerusalem in 1973 and 1972, respectively), and his wife, Karen, are in charge. With a Jewish secular background, Karen Berg is increasingly presented as a spiritual leader in her own right, yet her approach is more tinted by New Age ideas than Kabbalistic notions and Jewish culture.

Synthesis: The Cultural Conditions of Bricolage

This chapter emphasizes that the popularization of exotic religious resources such as yoga, Vedanta philosophy, or Kabbalah cannot be explained exclusively by individual practices of picking and mixing. Nor can one take for granted the "availability" of these resources. Rather, long-term historical processes and cultural encounters have constructed specific exotic religious resources. It is only under certain circumstances and through processes of idealization, universalization, and de-contextualization that these resources are domesticated and become "available" for bricolage in Euroamerican societies.

For a start, the elaboration of otherness precedes bricolage. Neo-Hinduism and Kabbalah, as well as Sufism (Westerlund 2004), Buddhism (Obadia 1999), and shamanism (Kehoe 2000), have been fetishized: they have gradually been constructed as ancient, authentic, mysterious, and vibrant alternatives to religions that are undermined by secularization and, more broadly, to the disenchantment of the modern West. These representations as absolute religious "others" further a romantic and countercultural outlook on modernity, reflecting the nostalgia for the "virtues of a world we have lost" (Wilson 1976, 176). Paradoxically, in its way of understanding cultural differences, this exoticism is self-referential: the representations of exotic religious resources have been shaped by desires and concerns that were at first external to them—hence the categorization of Hinduism or Kabbalah as "mysticism," as opposed to an alleged rational Western civilization. Mysticism was originally a concept used in a Christian context; it has increasingly come to incarnate a very modern distinction between the private and the institutional dimensions of religious life. The application of the term to other religious traditions entails that they have increasingly been perceived as sources of intimate experiences of the divine

(King 1999, 96–97). In addition, as King (pp. 23–24) stresses, assuming that these so-called "mystical" religions are primarily a source of religious experience that are distinct from the collective and institutional aspects of religion facilitates their de-contextualization. Note that it is also the "experience" that raised tremendous interest in shamanism, wrongly and consistently identified with altered states of consciousness (Hamayon 1995). Representations of the Mystical East and the shamanic trance reflect the fact that exotic religious resources are envisioned as desirable alternatives when religious institutions lose their legitimacy in secular societies. In fact, the "insatiable appetite for antipodean plunder" of Euroamerican societies (Clarke 2000: xi) cannot be understood properly without thinking of what they aim to contrast with, and complement. Again, it is not that these religious resources *resolve* tensions and challenges in advanced industrial societies, but that Asian religions, shamanism, or Kabbalah are *desired* to be so; they were pragmatically shaped by this desire, just like the first Christian Kabbalists referred to Kabbalah in order to "prove" the truths of Christianity and to convert Jews. Pragmatism, the expression of a certain entitlement, remains: today, exotic religious resources are cast in the role of healing and self-realization techniques.

This idealization of foreign religious traditions was made on the terms of those entitled to explore these resources, because it results from very specific cultural encounters. Orientalism is hardly separable from imperialism: the feeling of superiority inherent to the colonial context needed to draw a distinction between a primordial and pure Hindu religion, on the one hand, and an obscurantist and despicable contemporary Hinduism, on the other hand. As far as Kabbalah is concerned, scholars and leading figures of esotericism often silenced Kabbalah's Jewish roots, despite it being a pillar of Western esotericism; this appropriation of Kabbalah actually reflects the Christian West's ambivalent relationship with Jews who were simultaneously its insiders and outsiders (Bauman 1993). Another example of the relations between religious exoticism and power relations is shamanism. Lumping together various practices from different regions of the world, "shamanism" is often believed to reach back to the dawn of prehistory, and its alleged primitiveness associates it with a harmonious relation with nature, a romanticized traditional community life, and therapeutic practices. Strikingly, "shamanism," elaborated as one of the West's perfect alterities, has long been attacked by religion and state powers. Siberian shamanism was suspected of political turmoil and resistance in the regions conquered by the Russian Empire. Described as demonic, it became forbidden as Christian Orthodoxy consolidated its hegemony, while Enlightenment philosophers scorned its supposed primitive and superstitious character. Though persecuted, shamans were never eradicated; many

Russians, including officials close to the czar, would ask for their advice and assistance. Nineteenth-century romanticism cultivated a fascination with what was perceived as shamans' magical and healing powers and their ability to travel in others worlds (Hamayon 1995; Jilek 2003; von Stuckrad 2003). Similarly, shamanism triggered colonists' fears and fantasies about "Indian magic" in the context of state formation in South America (Atkinson 1992, 315). In other words, the fascination for, and fear of, other people's supernatural powers are not independent from the attempt to subjugate and control them; in this context they become potentially subversive.[7] Nothing illustrates this ambivalence better than Tantra, which Urban (1999, 123) defines as a nineteenth-century joint creation of Indian texts, orientalist scholars, and Western popular imagination. Tantrism, the sexual practices of which have been exaggerated, aroused moral repugnance and was seen as evidence of Hinduism's depraved state (again, Tantra was suspected of political plots and rebellious activities in colonial India). Yet, reflecting the repressed desires of Victorian society, Tantrism stirred up fascination and excited the imagination. Tantrism, redefined as the art of "sacred sexuality," became popular with the 1960s' sexual liberation and turn to the East in a quest for sensual pleasures (Urban 1999, 2000).

Western controversies and concerns largely contributed to shaping both the Asian religions and Kabbalistic teachings that were subsequently adopted in European and American societies, because in these cultural encounters, the struggle for cultural survival and self-assertion demanded the integration of Western values, expectations, and representations. In other words, the colonial encounter with India and the ambivalence toward Judaism also explain why neo-Hinduism and Kabbalah, presented by those concerned with the continuity and legitimacy of their religion, seemed to fit their audience's expectations. It is not by chance that neo-Hinduism presented itself in Europe and North America as universal, monotheistic, egalitarian, and socially relevant, nor should we be surprised that the revitalization of Judaism entailed the celebration of a mysterious and ancient Kabbalah that had fascinated scholars and esoteric circles for so long. It was also in the context of Western colonialism that a text-based, pragmatic, rational, universal, individualistic, and socially active Buddhism emerged and seduced Westerners in the twentieth century. By contrast, traditional cosmology and ritualism were downplayed, devalued, and considered incompatible with modern times (Baumann 2001). Gombrich and Obeyesekere (1988) even talk about a "Protestant Buddhism" that emerged in nineteenth-century Ceylon.[8] Similarly, Zen in the West results from the transformation of Zen Buddhism that took place during the Meiji era, characterized by the rapid Westernization and modernization of Japanese society. Sharf

(1995; see also Faure 1995) portrays a Japanese elite who, animated by a "defensive strategy" and impregnated by European values, attempted to "purify" Buddhism. Influenced by Protestant anti-ritualism and rationalism, but also by the works of orientalist scholars and the American philosopher William James, the "New Buddhism" (as it was called in Japan) was presented as modern, rational, socially responsible, and having universal creeds. It also made direct experience one of its characteristic features while, ironically, this was not a significant notion in traditional Japanese Buddhism and derived in large part from Occidental sources. Reflecting twentieth-century Japanese intellectuals' concern about the place and future of Japan in the modern world, Zen missionaries in the West presented Zen experience, again, as a universal ground of religious truth, but also as the unique and specific expression of Japanese spirit. Yet, it allowed Zen to be presented as a "spiritual technique" that could be used by anyone, regardless of his or her religion, like Kabbalistic speculations, yoga, and meditation. The experiential and mystical components were also attractive to those denigrating the institutional forms of their own religion (Sharf 1995). Again, there is nothing natural or spontaneous about the "availability" of, and appeal for, "exotic" religious resources. Their popularization has implied that they, to a certain extent, become Western and distance themselves from their original culture; the religious quest of their disciples is therefore less eclectic than we could assume.

Accordingly, these particular modes of dissemination and appropriation unavoidably result in the de-contextualization of exotic religious resources. Indeed, the ambivalence of feelings toward foreign religious traditions is resolved by their universalization. Kabbalah is appropriated more easily if it is not Jewish; contemporary popular Hinduism is contrasted with a universal Vedanta or a yoga practice severed from its Hindu roots. It is often claimed that Sufism, perceived as a mystical (hence "acceptable") form of Islam, is in fact pre-Islamic and realizes the synthesis of all religions (Westerlund 2004, 25–30). Thus, Sufism transcends Islam, as Kabbalah transcends Judaism. Shamanism is equally believed to be universal, primordial like a proto-religion; it is also appropriable as neutral, de-territorialized techniques (Losonczy and Mesturini Cappo 2011). European and American "neo-shamans" substantially refer to Nordic and Celtic traditions while, following the tracks of modern gurus, Buddhist lamas, and Kabbalah Centre's leaders, some Lakota shamans have reformed their tradition themselves. They embraced the "spiritual knowledge of Celts and their druids," emphasized environmental issues, and prioritized therapeutic practices in their teachings (Lindquist 1997; Vazeilles 2008). As an increasing number of Native Americans express concerns about the neo-shamanic appropriation, modification, and commercialization of their tradition, one of the criticized neo-shamans responded: "they must give up tribal mythologies that hurt the planet in order for their leadership and vision to be released to help everyone" (cited in Lindquist 1997, 45). Considering that shamanism should be "accessible for all who look for it," the claim that only individuals from particular tribes can perform certain ceremonies is branded as dogmatic and racist by the neo-shaman. This anecdote is quite telling of a sense of entitlement in appropriating the sacred knowledge of others, but it also sheds light on the fact that universalization is fundamental to the process of appropriation of exotic religious resources. It allows one to sever them from their original sociocultural environment; universalism is what makes them "available."

Thus, exotic religious resources have become ancient and primordial knowledge from which derive all religions and philosophies; a detour through foreign traditions thus offers a return to the origins. Contemporary Islam, Hinduism, or Judaism as lived and practiced are therefore irrelevant. Exotic religious resources are seen as transcending the specific social dimensions of these religions, and this is precisely what facilitates their dissemination outside their boundaries. This is what the two following chapters will demonstrate by exploring, first, the ways in which students of yoga and Kabbalah relate to these teachings, and second, the beliefs and practices being taught in relation to Hinduism and Kabbalah.

2

Religious Exoticism, Belonging, and Identities: The Discomfort of Bricolage

THIS CHAPTER ADDRESSES issues of identity and belonging in relation to, in turn, non-Indian followers of neo-Hindu movements, students of the Kabbalah Centre who are not born Jewish, and finally, those who are born Jewish. In these three cases, exotic religious resources are idealized. "Eastern spiritualities" and Kabbalah represent the mystical and authentic traditions of a world we have lost and which could provide solutions to the problem-ridden, materialistic, modern "West." Yet, this religious exoticism by no means entails a desire to become Hindu or Jewish. On the contrary, when confronted with the religious dimensions and Hindu/Jewish character of the teachings of neo-Hindu movement and the Kabbalah Centre, social actors express clear signs of discomfort and resistance, reflected in selective practices, superficial and short-term involvement, and occasional departures. Jewish students of Kabbalah are equally ambivalent, although for different reasons: they, too, reject Judaism as a religion and a particularism to the extent that their practice of Jewish liturgy in the Kabbalah Centre could be described as a form of neo-marranism.[1] Despite the appeal of Eastern wisdom and Kabbalistic mysteries, the teachings of neo-Hindu movements and the Kabbalah Centre are not adopted because of their Hindu/Jewish character, which in fact has the effect of limiting their popularization. This is evidenced by these movements' limited expansion, low membership retention, and high turnover. Accordingly, these religious resources are more effectively appropriated when perceived as not Hindu/Jewish.

The chapter ends by summarizing the implications of these empirical findings for the understanding of religious exoticism and bricolage. First, religious exoticism is characterized by the fetishization and the aestheticization of religious traditions, in such a way that these traditions, as practiced, actually need to be overlooked. Second, the ambivalence of exoticism is highlighted by the coexistence of appeal to, and discomfort with, religious resources; bricolage thus entails processes of domestication that de-contextualize and familiarize exotic religious resources. These features reveal religious exoticism's ethnocentrism and its roots in uneven macro-cultural encounters. Finally, exoticism underscores rather than disproves the effects of secularization; as many other teachings, neo-Hindu and Kabbalistic, are appropriated in the context of the rejection of religious authorities and claims of individual autonomy. Nevertheless, the assumption of a postmodern "pick-and-mix" through which individuals freely combine resources, indifferent to their particular cultural and religious roots, is inaccurate. Discomfort, aversion, and hence the need to de-contextualize exotic religious resources to appropriate them, clearly demonstrate that *otherness matters*.

Orientalist Nostalgia and Repulsion for Hindu-ness

This section describes the relations of Siddha Yoga's and Sivananda Centres' followers to the Hindu roots of the religious movements they frequent. Undoubtedly, the transnational spread of Siddha Yoga and the Sivananda Centres, as well as a large number of neo-Hindu movements that emerged in the 1960s, has to do with the fascination for Asian religious traditions in Euroamerican societies. However, when the encounter with this fantasized otherness becomes "real" (through language, liturgy, or devotional practices), it proves to be a source of discomfort, if not of culture shock. This repulsion explains the limited numerical success of neo-Hindu movements in Euroamerican societies, of which most followers are lightly involved, often on a short-term basis and alongside other religious incursions. These followers actually render neo-Hindu teaching familiar and appropriable: they understand Hindu beliefs and practices as part of a culturally undifferentiated "Mystical East" and a pool of free resources that can be adopted, rejected, or westernized, according to individual pace and needs. Their pragmatic quest for useful techniques and their belief that truth is beyond all religious particularisms also contribute to rendering the Hindu character of the neo-Hindu teaching they follow irrelevant.

The "Mystical East," the World We Have Lost

Many followers of Muktananda and Vishnu-Devananda traveled to India, sometimes for several months, and those who have not often envisage it. Their travel memories invariably depict India as "another world" or as a "world apart" and what makes India fundamentally "other" is its religiosity. Indeed, interviewees describe how true spiritual attitudes permeate every aspect of Indian daily life and transfigure Indian society, people, and landscape. For instance, Hortense, who lived in Siddha Yoga's ashram in Ganeshpuri for several months, says that the beauty of Indian sunrises and sunsets is unique, because "it's a country where people are completely in relation with the spiritual, which is totally integrated, even among the poor." Guy was involved in Transcendental Meditation 25 years ago and (irregularly) has frequented the Paris Sivananda Centre for 10 years; he had the opportunity to travel to Pakistan, Afghanistan, and India, where he did trekking and visited ashrams:

> In India, religion is something that influences every aspect of life. It's the simplicity of a gesture, the simple welcoming attitude of someone, the simple preparation of a meal, it's always linked to a divinity, it's something sacred. That's the difference, I mean, for me....It permeates every aspect of life. We don't separate, like I'm going to mass so I'm religious, and just after I can do the worse things ever. For me, the philosophy influences all of our daily actions and for me Indians are influenced by religion in all their...Whatever they do, they always think about it.

Hortense and Guy's depiction of India's pervading, spontaneous, and authentic "spirituality" express the romantic nostalgia for a world we have lost, a world not yet de-sacralized, fragmented, and morally corrupted, as the modern West is believed to be. This spiritual and timeless India is not about India per se; rather, it is about Western modernity and its aftermaths. The myth transcends Indian society and culture: in Hortense and Guy's evocation of India, Indians are defined by, and reduced to, their assumed religiosity. By and large, I was struck by the absence, in interviewees' representations and memories, of references to any other aspect of life in India. Indeed, for the orientalist myth to stand in front of the modern decadent West, one must forget that India is also a place where modernization has taken place and where social conflicts, political struggles, and technological progress exist (Kalra and Hutnyk 1998, 346).

The Sivananda Centres in India contribute to this form of "spiritual tourism." The movement offers activities centered on "Spiritual India," offering an initiation to traditional medicine, cultural activities, pilgrimages, fasting, and detoxification programs—"A perfect opportunity to unwind during the year end and to enjoy the silence and peace within. Re-energizing the body and mind with yoga and meditation and starting the New Year with an *experience rich in spiritual culture*" (Sivananda Yoga Vedanta Dhanwantari Ashram n.d.). The numerous existing "sacred tours of India" are, however, less about a discovery of India than about finding oneself. "A spiritual pilgrimage to India is not, primarily about information. It's about initiation," wrote authors of a touristic guide of *Spiritual India*:

> India will bend your mind, assault your body, flood your senses, and shred your nerves....And ultimately, if you're lucky, your old identity will break down....It's this breakdown and the attendant possibilities for transformation—more than a specific teacher or spiritual site— that's the real blessing India has to offer. (Cushman and Jones 1998, 3)

Students of neo-Hindu movements are probably not the only ones to be influenced by orientalist representations about the "Mystical East" in contemporary societies. However, as far as they are concerned, these representations are translated into religious trajectories in which "Eastern" religious resources tend to predominate. A quarter of interviewees, more notably among the French, declare an interest in Buddhism; it would be, they believe, their religion if they had to have another one. To a certain extent, this reflects the wide popularity of Buddhism (Lenoir 1999, 89); nevertheless, followers of the Sivananda Centres and Siddha Yoga are also attracted by less well-known Daoism. Prior to being involved in Siddha Yoga or the Sivananda Centres, many interviewees had also been initiated into meditation techniques by Transcendental Meditation. Several have practiced martial arts, and a quarter of the Siddha Yoga followers I interviewed practice yoga. Half of the interviewees, in both movements, use or practice alternative therapies that are not exclusively but predominantly rooted in Asian traditions—Ayurveda, acupuncture, Chinese medicine, chi gong, shiatsu, reflexology inspired by Chinese medicine, and reiki, a Japanese healing practice popularized since the 1980s. They tend to value the practical and body-oriented techniques—it helps to explain why in fact they have rarely opted for Buddhism. Similarly, many French interviewees started to discover "Eastern" ideas in esoteric circles (Theosophy and Rosicrucianism in particular) but found these approaches too "theoretical." By contrast, there is among some interviewees an assumption that "Eastern" traditions can offer something that is lacking in Euroamerican societies: "For Orientals, whether they are Buddhist or Vedic, it's the importance of the body, which is something we don't see at all in the West," states a yoga student of the Parisian Sivananda Centre. In other words, an undifferentiated "mystical East" transcends cultural and religious particularities.

Interlopers of Hinduism

The first time I was exposed to it, it was in India, I'll never forget it, it was a Sunday night, and I walked into the hall, and we had satsang for about half an hour. . . . And then we all started singing "Hare Krishna," and I thought, "Ooooh no!". . . . And then we had arati [ritual of worship] and the candles, and everybody you know, prostrating, and . . . And food being offered and . . . Yeah, it was very strange, because doing arati for two deities, it was for me, I thought, "this is a kind of worship, I don't understand." (June, Sivananda Centre, London)

While idealizing "Eastern" religious traditions, followers of neo-Hindu movements can feel challenged when confronted with certain Hindu practices and Indian cultural norms. Indeed, it is not the Hindu-ness of the Sivananda Centres[2] or Siddha Yoga that attracted them; half of interviewees expressed indifference toward their particular religious and cultural roots and a quarter found these roots problematic. Léonard, for instance, has practiced yoga and meditation regularly at the Paris Sivananda Centre for five years after a five-month trip to India; he goes to the Centre several times a week to meditate, practice yoga, and teach it as well. He adopted a new lifestyle, became vegetarian, and stopped drinking alcohol. However, Léonard finds the figure of Sivananda culturally remote and does not consider him as his guru. He also explained his issues with the Hindu origin of yoga: "I don't feel Hindu and I think, 'yes it's linked.' So sometimes I feel uncomfortable." Another example is Tina who has been involved in Siddha Yoga for two years in London, after trying various alternative religious and therapeutic practices. When I met her, she had found something new and was moving away from Siddha Yoga because, as she sums up, "I feel that it has helped me a lot to *go into the East*, but I also feel that there are other powerful paths *and it's not my heritage*." In other words, the "East" represents an important landmark in a "spiritual trajectory," but its foreign cultural baggage here justifies the quest for new explorations.

Overall, several interviewees express this paradoxical relationship: adopting a Hindu-based teaching while feeling challenged by its cultural otherness. Lionel, a member of Siddha Yoga, described "disorientating cultural references" when he talked about his first contact in Siddha Yoga; he mentioned a disconcerting "bipolarity" between an inner experience that he considered authentic, deep, and incontestable and "external" references to which he could not relate for cultural reasons. Susan, who practices yoga at the London Sivananda Centre, describes herself as an intruder in someone else's religion:

> I know it is someone else's culture, I mean that that's why Hinduism is potentially problematic because, there is this idea about Hinduism for the Indians you know.... So to me it's still, I still feel like an interloper in Hinduism. So I see yoga as, as a kind of Western artifact.

The image of the "interloper" is particularly interesting: it conveys the idea of trespassing in a territory that belongs to someone else. Thus, Susan expressed a sense of transgression, which explains why she wants to consider yoga as manufactured (hence diverted, de-contextualized) for the Western lifestyle. As we will see below, the need to adopt a domesticated form of Hinduism is of paramount importance: it allows appropriation of exotic cultural resources while preventing or limiting challenging cultural encounters.

Contacts with cultural otherness can be particularly challenging, for example, when these followers of neo-Hindu teachings are confronted with the use of foreign languages. In both movements, satsangs involve prayers and chants in Sanskrit or vernacular languages. In Sivananda Centres, they follow silent meditation; in Siddha Yoga, satsangs primarily consist in singing mantras—a few strophes sung by a group of musicians is repeated by the audience for about an hour in the darkened room, followed by a short silent meditation. Chanting in foreign languages represented Jean's "first obstacle" when he came to Siddha Yoga for the first time, after being involved in Rosicrucianism for 15 years. He now has been deeply committed in Siddha Yoga in Paris for 10 years; however, this first encounter literally repelled him. Devotional practices sung in Sanskrit led him to think that "it was not his thing" and he decided not to come back. It is only six months later, when he participated in an Intensive (Siddha Yoga's initiating event) that Jean started to accept and follow the teaching. Anna, another French Siddha Yoga follower, explains that she does not like singing in Sanskrit either, because in her view the use of a foreign language creates a distance. Interestingly, she also mentioned she would prefer it if songs were in Latin—it was not about understanding the meaning of the song but about cultural familiarity or "intimacy," to use her own words.

The liturgy in neo-Hindu movements is experienced as problematic, too. Rituals are symbolic actions; they activate meanings that relate to doctrines, worldviews, or values that are unavoidably situated in a specific religion and/ or cultural context. As we shall see, contemporary gurus insisted on yoga and meditation as techniques that can be used by anyone to reach self-realization, regardless of their religion, nationality, gender, and so on. To make their teachings universally relevant, they downplayed the importance of rituals and festivals, but without completely eliminating them. For example, despite their strong emphasis on yoga, the Sivananda Centres regularly organize pujas (worship) and festivals to honor Hindu divinities. They are far from being the most popular activities of the movement; while hundreds of students frequent the Parisian or the London Centre to practice yoga every week, the pujas I participated in were not attended by more than a dozen people. I also observed that some of the participants felt awkward during these rituals; uncontrollable laughter once broke out as divinities were covered with milk and honey and were dressed with miniature saris. Laughter and humor in these circumstances are far from being insignificant: they try to ease and de-dramatize the sense of cultural shock. This was obvious in Mick's interview, for example. Mick started to practice yoga three years ago in the New York Sivananda Centre before moving to London for work. I met him a few months after a Shivaratri at the London Centre and we evoked this Shiva festival in which we both took part. He described the ritual practices that took him aback—rice grains sprinkled toward statues of the divinities while repeating Shiva's one hundred and eight names, as well as the worship of the lingam, Shiva's phallic symbolic attribute. Admitting he was playing the "funny black guy" for me, he described forcefully and comically his impressions about this "strange" ritual:

> The milk pouring and, the rice throwing and stuff. That's not my thing. No I can, you know, cook the rice, let's eat the rice, but I'm not gonna count a hundred and eight rice [laughs]!... And they've got this, like, phallic symbol you know, they're pouring milk over it, I'm thinking, "penis! Hello?! What's going on here? Milk on a penis? No way! I'm not going up there pouring milk on this penis thing!" And I'm thinking you know, "we sit here, and people die in India, you know, they could be eating this rice so what's going on!" So I was thinking...[laughs] So I was like, "oh man, what is this?"

Mick's irreverence expresses discomfort with this foreign liturgy and the impossibility, for this reason, to take it seriously. Here, he also referred to the personification of the divine in this Hindu ritual. In fact, the presence of divinities materialized in pictures and statues on the altar is problematic for many followers of the Sivananda Centres. It does not fit with their abstract representation of the divine, which they tend to perceive as immanent and immaterial—the "energy." Thus, they find the personification of divinities naïve and childish and explicitly disapprove of polytheism, if not "paganism." Desiring a direct, unmediated contact with the divine, they also see the presence of these Hindu gods as an obstacle, revealing a strong religious individualism that in this respect may clash with the neo-Hindu environment. Ultimately, this repulsion regarding rituals does not concern the relatively new members only. William has been practicing yoga for seven years in the Sivananda Centre. He undertook the yoga Teaching Training Course in India five years ago, and made several trips to India, Tibet, and Nepal, including a pilgrimage to the Himalayas with one of the Sivananda Centre's acharyas. When I met him he was a full-time resident in London and he would later continue to be so in the Parisian Centre. His status as resident entails that he devotes his time to help running the Centre and fully participates in satsangs, festivals, and pujas. Yet, despite finding a meaning in rituals, William has "kind of a feeling of, this is not quite my world":

> Tonight, you know, there's a homa, a fire ceremony, "cause it's Swami Sivananda's birthday. And, so we get a priest. A priest comes, and delivers us a ceremony in Sanskrit and does this fire ceremony and stuff. And, symbolically, it's a wonderful thing, it creates...It's a cleansing purifying thing with the smoke and I can imagine it is, but it is not my thing, you know, a priest from thousands of miles away, talking a language from thousands of years ago from thousands of miles away.

William could not express more clearly the sense of cultural and geographical distance in relation to Hindu rituals.

Finally, I also found that disciples of both movements were resisting the guru's status and related devotional practices, despite the fact that the figure of the guru is at the very core of neo-Hindu doctrines and has an uncontested authority on these movements' internal organization. Coleman's (2001, 85) study of Buddhism in the United States underscores similar difficulties regarding the obedience and reverence expected toward lamas and teachers. The guru is traditionally presented as having a deep knowledge of the Vedas. Having realized the unity between the individual and the Absolute, Brahman, he acquires a quasi-divine status. He is supposed to transmit the knowledge of scriptures to his disciples and guide them to salvation (Cenkner 2001, 10; Sharma 1993, 2–4; Smith 2003, 170). It may be worth noting in passing that by trying to "rationalize" Hinduism, nineteenth-century Indian socio-religious reform movements opposed the guru tradition and its devotional nature. But by and large, the role of gurus as "godmen" became a core feature of contemporary Hinduism (Clémentin-Ojah and Chambard 1994, 113; Smith 2003, 170). I think that there is another reason for the centrality of the guru in contemporary neo-Hindu movements in the West. Emphasizing the relationship between guru and disciples is to give precedence to the salvation path of bhakti. Bhakti was a traditional response to the elitism of Brahmanism; it is one of the main salvation paths of the Vedas, according to which salvation can be attained through devotion. As such, it does not require renouncement and is accessible to all, including women and low-caste individuals (Esnoul 1952). Accordingly, bhakti may have been perceived as more "exportable" among non-Indian people who are outcaste and have no knowledge of Hindu liturgy and scriptures.

However, it seems that the "exportability" of the guru principle has its limits. The Sivananda Centres reasserted, in principle, the divine nature of the guru and the necessity of his guidance, but in practice Vishnu-Devananda presented himself as a "teacher." One of the current leaders of the movement told me that when he came to the West, Vishnu-Devananda realized he could not teach Sivananda's teaching as such, in particular bhakti, and this is why he started with "very practical things which could hook the Western world"— in other words, yoga postures and meditation. It was only in the later years of his teaching, when he thought that some of his disciples were ready, that Vishnu-Devananda reintegrated bhakti in his teaching. Yet, it repelled some of them, who subsequently moved away. Significantly, Vishnu-Devananda decided not to nominate another guru as his successor. He created a board of disciples, the acharyas, to administer the movement, which led to the routinization of the movement after his death. Sivananda and Vishnu-Devananda are nonetheless considered to be the gurus of the Sivananda Centres. In Siddha Yoga, the guru's role is central and somewhat unavoidable, since the guru rules over the organizational and spiritual dimensions of the movement. Furthermore, by their touch, Siddha gurus are believed to awaken their followers' *shakti* (the energy within) during the Intensive. The importance of devotion is reflected in the weekly recitation of the Guru Gita in local centers, 181 verses in Sanskrit evoking the divine nature of the guru and the guru-disciple relationship, referred to as Siddha Yoga's indispensable text. Lucy, for instance, was introduced to the teaching by this practice:

> I don't think [it] really is the best introduction if you don't understand
> it, because they don't really tell you anything about what Siddha Yoga is.

You go along, you do the Guru Gita and then you go home—so it's like, I don't really understand, it looks like a load of people singing to a picture.[3]... I suppose it's understanding the guru principle because when you look actually into different things you find that everything is inside yourself, and the guru principle is something external from ourselves, and this sort of confused me. I'm not into worshiping external things, deities and stuff like that. Then as you understand more about the guru principle then the more you understand about the guru inside yourself and how this is sort of a reflection.

Lucy emphasizes one more time the difficulties of the first encounters with neo-Hinduism, in particular with its devotional practices. Her interview also illustrates a common resistance against the principle of the guru as authority and the asymmetric relationship it entails. By and large, devotion to the guru, a pillar of neo-Hindu teachings, is seriously questioned or rejected by more than a quarter of followers of Siddha Yoga and Sivananda Centres whom I interviewed. Surprisingly, this resistance includes those who are deeply involved in one of the movements, including some who lived in an ashram. Tina, who now thinks Siddha Yoga "is not her heritage," felt repelled by this emphasis on the guru and only came back a year after her first contact with the movement: "all my conditioning kicked off, surely it means you're really weak if you need a guru, and surely it's really dodgy.... I thought, I don't want a guru, I'm not interested in that." As illustrated by Tina, the guru figure clashes with Euroamerican ideals of individual autonomy—a central issue for these followers who look for tools enabling them to develop their potential by themselves. It conflicts with ideas about egalitarianism as well: "I don't want the gurus because it also says something about inequality" says Mick, "I think it's important that we have teachers but we worship these teachers like gods.... Sivananda and Devananda are like gods. And I don't believe that." By and large, the deification of human beings is unsurprisingly at odds with contemporary religious individualism and rejection of authority—this is why Lucy, above, explains that she now understand the guru as being "inside" herself. This "detour" to find oneself is a common way to accept the guru. Similarly, William calls himself "his own guru." "The higher figure it's here, it's yourself, it's inside of yourself" repeats Christopher. Despite being very enthusiastic about his discovery of yoga at the London Sivananda Centre, he is very uncomfortable with devotional practices and cannot participate in them:

The LAST, that LAST thing, the bow, it's something that strikes a chord in me, I hold back from doing that, I don't do that.... I think the reason

why I'm so interested in Buddhism, is that it's the one religion which
doesn't rely on a on a higher figure.... You follow the Buddha, but only
because you follow what he DID. You don't follow him; you follow his
words, and his teachings.

Like Christopher, several followers of both movements evoked the darshan,
the devotional practice that concludes the satsang, during which followers bow
in front of the gurus' representations. During Siddha Yoga satsangs, I noticed
that some participants systematically left the room before the darshan took
place; interviews highlighted that it was a deliberate avoidance on their part.
Several interviewees dismissed the practice of darshan jokily, referring to
followers who bow in front of the guru's empty armchair in Siddha Yoga as
"kneeling to an armchair." Again, humor is used to minimize cultural discomfort. This discomfort has nonetheless sometimes been expressed in more
forceful terms. Sandrine started to practice yoga in the Parisian Sivananda
Centre three months before the interview; she is therefore a newcomer. She
found the darshan "idolatrous": it is, she says, "something that nearly hurts
me." Sandrine explains she comes to satsangs because to have the benefits of
yoga practice, she believes it must be a "real investment." During satsangs,
she kneels and bows, too, because everyone does it, but it feels like "an inner
rape because this is something that does not come from me," she explains.
Once more, the vocabulary—of being hurt or raped—sheds light on the sense
of transgression and the strength of culture shock involved in this encounter
with Hindu customs that clashes with individuals' socialization.

These feelings clearly show that bricolage is far from being indifferent to
cultural otherness, on the contrary. Not only are cultural elements of Hindu-
ness rejected,[4] but I contend that it is the Hindu-ness of these teachings,
their foreign origins, that limits their appropriation by a large number of
individuals who would become fully committed in a Hindu religion or lifestyle. Indeed, the orientalist fascination for timeless and spiritual India has
so far not led to mass conversion. Quantitatively speaking, neo-Hindu movements attract small numbers of followers; the popularization of "Eastern" religious resources is a cultural trend that cannot be compared, by any means,
with the expansion of, for example, Pentecostal and Charismatic Christianity
throughout the world. I cited several interviewees who described a disorient-
ing first contact with Siddha Yoga or the Sivananda Centres, sometimes followed by a period of rejection. Accordingly, we can imagine that a substantial
number of newcomers do not come back after one or few events, for the same
reasons these followers felt repelled. This would be consistent with the important turnover I observed in these groups over time.

Furthermore, the limits to which individuals engage with Hindu beliefs and practices are highlighted by the structure and mobilization of resources of a great number of neo-Hindu movements. It is only the core members of Siddha Yoga and the Sivananda Centres (and for that matter of Transcendental Meditation, Sahaja Yoga, Osho Movement, and the Art of Living) who fully follow the teaching to such an extent that it is fair to say they have adopted a form of Hindu religious practice and lifestyle. In Siddha Yoga and Sivananda Centres, these quasi-Hindu converts are the swamis: they took monastic vows of celibacy, renounced the worldly and family life, devote their entire life to the teaching, and live communally. They run ashrams and centers, perform ritual activities and initiation, and transmit the guru's teaching. Yet they represent a minuscule proportion of followers: in Sivananda Centres, a few dozens swamis at most have in charge an international network of 9 ashrams, 19 yoga centers, and more than 70 "affiliated centers." It is also an unstable religious elite: Siddha Yoga has a very small number of swamis, partly because a substantial number of them broke their vows and left the movement since their initiation in the beginning of the 1980s by Muktananda (more than half of them by 1985). "Most wanted to return to worldly life or nurtured desires and ambitions that could not be satisfied in their present situation" (Brooks et al. 1997, 127). Thus, Gurumayi decided not to ordain anymore "because people don't keep their promises," a long-term disciple who lived in ashrams in India and the United States told me. Both in Siddha Yoga and the Sivananda Centres, "residents" and "staff" help to support the organization by working for free. They opt for the communal life without renouncing worldly life permanently and in some cases they work outside the movement in order to support themselves. But they, too, represent a minority of followers and commit themselves for a short period of time only (from a few months to a year or two). Thus, the vast majority of Siddha Yoga's and Sivananda Centre's audience are relatively mildly involved. Most Siddha Yoga followers simply participate in festivals, retreats, and satsangs on a more or less regular basis, without necessarily embracing all the norms and rules of the religious teaching. Each Sivananda Centre is run by a dozen swamis and residents only; each week, in London or Paris, they welcome hundreds of participants of yoga classes, satsangs, and workshops, who may not always identify with the movement and its teaching. One of the acharyas I have interviewed in Paris recognized that many of their students in fact use yoga as a technique against stress and are not interested in its "spiritual dimension." Yet, by developing a diversified range of classes, events, training and retreats, the Sivananda Centres deliberately supply a form of spiritual service to a large number of individualistic, sometimes consumerist, individuals who may neither belong nor believe. It is, I believe, what makes it relatively successful, compared, for instance, to the Sri Chinmoy Centre, which requires a deeper commitment of all (including sexual abstinence and celibacy) and do not develop peripheral activities. Comparatively, the Sri Chinmoy Centre only attracted less than 50 students or so in France in the mid-1990s (Altglas 1997).

An Accommodating Eastern "Spirituality"

You don't have to be a Hindu to believe in Siddha yoga, you
don't have to be anybody to believe in Siddha yoga, that's
what I like about it. (Meredith, Siddha Yoga, London)

Followers of neo-Hindu movements clearly express a longing for an Eastern version of a religious golden age in their discourse as well as through their religious trajectory. On the other hand, they are clearly repelled by Hindu traditions that are too foreign and that clash with their values and expectations—sometimes by being, paradoxically, too religious; that is, involving rituals or religious authorities such as the guru. Accordingly, there is a coexistence of fascination and repulsion which, I believe, is resolved by an "understanding" of Hindu-ness that renders it more acceptable. This process of "domestication" is central to religious exoticism: it makes what is foreign more predictable and familiar (Foster 1982, 21). As such, it allows for the assimilation of new cultural resources, yet through their universalisation and de-contextualization. This ambivalence toward exotic religious resources and their domestication, as a result, are intrinsic to practices of bricolage.

To start with, the orientalist representation of the mystical East itself contributes to this domestication of Hinduism. This is particularly well illustrated by the notes that Lisa, who had practiced reiki, meditation, and alternative therapies, spontaneously brought when I met her for an interview, in order to think about her involvement in Siddha Yoga. On the sheet of paper, Lisa associated "Christianity = Western" to the following words: "judgmental, narrow-minded, intolerant, arrogant, rigid, scared, reminded of our inherent weakness/imperfection/sin." By contrast, under "Siddha Yoga = Eastern," she wrote: "accepting, loving, open-minded, gives responsibility + power to the individuals,[5] reminder of our individual/collective greatness." Lisa's contrast between "East" and "West" actually expresses a rejection of the norms and authorities of her religious upbringing (in later chapters we will highlight that social actors like Lisa internalized other social norms that are no less coercive). In addition, these notes reflect the widespread belief, among followers of neo-Hindu movements, that "Eastern spirituality" does not require observance. Lisa's notes echo Alison, a 27-year-old Catholic single woman from Boston who works in London and practices yoga at the Sivananda Centre:

> I've actually always been interested in Eastern philosophy versus Western and I feel more comfortable thinking about it as philosophy as opposed to religion. I think that Eastern religions are probably more...They straddle that line between philosophy and religion better than Western religions, so I've always found it interesting *as a counter point* to Catholicism which is such a Western tradition, so rigid. I do find that interesting but I've always been the sort of person that picks and chooses, you know, whatever sort of framework makes sense for me at the time.... Daoism is probably my favorite, which is Chinese.... But I don't think I could ever embrace it completely because it wouldn't satisfy the Western side of me which wants some more extremes in my life, so I do try to find balance and *that's what you don't get in the Western religions*.... I am very much interested in learning more about Hinduism and the little that I have read, but not in any consistent, methodical way.... I see yoga as a very balancing... It has a very balancing effect on my life and it's very much of that Eastern tradition. It's not all that different from what you would read about in Daoist texts that I've read, so I would say it's definitely related.

First, Lisa and Alison show that the "East" counterbalances a deficient "West" and implicitly conveys a critique of the latter. In this regard, the opposition between "East" and "West" overlaps the opposition between religion and philosophy/"spirituality": the "East" is valued as interesting systems of ideas which, unlike "rigid" Christianity rejected by Lisa and Alison, does not require its followers to adopt certain ideas or lifestyle and can be used freely and selectively. Second, it is therefore possible to explore many of these resources, also because Alison's "Eastern tradition" is culturally undifferentiated. By and large, interviewees tend to envisage Buddhism, Hinduism, and other Asian religious systems as part of a whole, which fundamentally contrasts with the "West." The assumption of such unity allows Alison, Lisa, and other Western neo-Hindus to overlook potential contradictions and to explore a diversity of teachings. Third, here Alison clearly emphasizes the usefulness of the "East": it is about what it does for her, and this usefulness legitimates her religious incursions. Again, it is still about the usefulness of the "East" for the "West." These three features of the representation of Asian religious teachings—an accommodating Eastern "spirituality," pragmatism, denial of cultural differences—are the three core features of the domestication of Hinduism that I intend to discuss below.

Followers of Siddha Yoga and Sivananda Centres tend to perceive Hinduism as a sponge, able to absorb a wide range of beliefs and practices, and hence as fundamentally inclusive and tolerant. David, who has been practicing yoga in Paris for three years, explains that "what [he] like[s] in Hinduism is that

> [i]t's not dogmatic, that it adapts to each one, and that it's something for each individual, that there is a recognition, not of a group, but of the different personality of each one, and that everyone progress at his own pace. *And I like it because I really believe in that;* I think we are really all different.

In other words, the elasticity of Hinduism makes space for contemporary individualism: it allows, as we shall see, each individual to adopt it on its own terms. This is illustrated by the representation of Hinduism of another student of the Parisian Sivananda Centre, Elisa, who traveled to ashrams in India and spent several weeks in the Indian Sivananda Centre:

> I like this idea in Hinduism, which is quite joyful and convivial, and very open: each one chooses what he wants, the perception he wants. I like that, this side of it which offers a lot of things, but which not really impose very defined paths, like in yoga also. There are many ways to approach yoga.... Each one chooses their thing and I really like this.

Similarly, Lydia, a member of staff at the Paris Sivananda Centres, explains that "we are so free in Hinduism" and "it's good because it's not something you have to adhere to." And yet Lydia lived for a year and a half in the Indian Sivananda Centre, which she discovered when working for a volunteer organization in India. These representations transcend knowledge of Hinduism as practiced—that is to say, as involving rules, norms, institutions, and authorities, as a source of contestation between different sects, as a basis for political mobilization in India and among the South Asian Diaspora, as the foundation of Indian nationalism, and as a source of violence against Muslims in India. Instead, the representation of the Hindu tradition as flexible, tolerant, and inclusive, one to which people do not need to convert or conform, reflects the desires of individuals who are secularizing and reject religious authority. On the other hand, it allows followers who are not ready to embrace Hindu norms and practices as a whole to disregard, or to keep a distance from, what is culturally disturbing. "People do not like to introduce the idea that in fact yoga is a religion" explains Charles, who has been practicing yoga for nearly 20 years and even thought of becoming a swami. He then added: "Well basically it is Hinduism, but you can slant it for your own needs whichever religion you are from." Ultimately, since it does not require adherence or conversion, this representation of Hinduism also allows, as we already noted, light, short-term and sometimes plural incursions.

The need to domesticate Hinduism in interviewees' own terms explains why they also praise the westernization of the teaching they follow, despite their nostalgia for India's golden age. Thus, a follower of Siddha Yoga in London praises the fact that "Siddha Yoga is very modern in the way it moves and adapts to today" and "the way [the teaching] is translated or the way that is put across to people, is just so easy to absorb." Similarly, a yoga student of the Paris Sivananda Centre positively described the latter as the "MacDonald of yoga," offering well-organized and successful centers in European and American metropolises. This surprising way of paying tribute to the Sivananda Centre is explained by the recognition of the difficulty for Westerners to embrace Hinduism as such. Daniel, who was introduced previously to Siddha Yoga and is now practicing yoga at the Sivananda Centre, believes that "there are a lot of things to eliminate" in the teaching because "we are not born in India, it's more difficult for us to assimilate all these teachings." Westernization is therefore a positive process. Virginie, for instance, who has practiced yoga for three years after an intensive yoga and meditation retreat in Sweden, suggests that

[y]ou learn fifteen thousand times more stuff once [yoga] is digested by the West, for us yeah...Because, in the sort of Indian chaos, we have to reckon that we're westerners, and if you go there, unless you really settle there, if you just travel there you won't see much.

In short, while neo-Hindu teachings are appealing because they are believed to come from "a world apart" that contrasts with the inadequacies of Euroamerican societies, they are too foreign to be accepted as such and hence need to be adaptable and flexible, so that it can be more of a "Western artifact," as Susan put it. Chapter 3 shows that contemporary gurus' teaching reflect these expectations by claiming that the Indian, Hindu roots of their teaching are irrelevant and that their teaching is a simple, practical technique that does not require conversion and can be adopted by anyone, regardless of their religion, lifestyle, beliefs, and so on. Accordingly, cultural differences that are, on the one hand, dramatized (the mystical East as the "world apart") can be reduced or avoided by this domestication of Hinduism.

Pragmatism and Exoticism

Have you been interested in knowing more things about
Hinduism or about India?
*Not necessarily, no. Now, I'm fine 'cause I know this hasn't got
anything to do with Hindus or India, in a way. You know, it's
a self-discovery journey, so it has to do with your self (Elena,
Siddha Yoga, London).*

A pragmatic approach is core to the exotic relationship with otherness and
allows individuals involved in neo-Hindu teachings to deal with what creates discomfort and resistance in confrontation with otherness. A 30-year-old
artist, David has a passion for India, where he has traveled twice to take photographs of saddhus (renunciates) in Varanasi, one of India's holy cities.
He practices yoga at the Sivananda Centre in Paris and explains that things
coming from "there" interest him, because "they can precisely give me the
possibility to reach something that we don't have here." Thus, the domestication of Hinduism entails the pragmatic attitude of justifying practices by
their usefulness; even chants in vernacular languages, rituals, multiple divinities, or the guru relationship become acceptable. For example, interviewees
often explain that songs and mantras in Sanskrit convey energy. Flavio, for instance, frequents Siddha Yoga in London and believes that "if you're chanting,
you will feel different after chanting, like you have different energies." Eric,
who practices yoga in Paris in the Sivananda Centre, also considers that the
meaning of the chants is not important; the Om mantra for instance, "reduces
the frequency at which the brain works," whether or not one understands
Sanskrit. We can note in passing that this pragmatic logic is extended to the
intelligible dimension of the teaching—and transcends its normative dimension: Eileen reads every day Siddha Yoga's Correspondence Course, but "it's
not just, what you're reading. Again, it's the energy you get from it. It's the
shakti [the energy]. . . . You could read it without understanding and you still get
amazing benefits from it."

The ritual is equally rationalized and tends to become a means, for example, to help slip into a meditative state, be in the here and now, or get
well-being. In other words, Hindu liturgy is not appropriated for the symbolic
world it embodies, it is "diverted" for practical aims. Coney (1999, 83) highlights a similar pragmatic relationship to rituals among Sahaja Yoga members:

Most followers give little real thought to whether they want to express
themselves through the symbols and practices of an alien tradition.

There is no point at which they decide consciously to adopt a Hindu approach to ritual, or even an exotic ritual form. Instead, the decision is made implicitly in their initial recognition and acceptance of the presentation of the ritual as 'a means towards an end.'

Similarly, divinities represented and worshipped during the satsangs of the Sivananda Centres are accepted for what they do: "I always thought Hinduism was about worshiping these deities, but it's not. It's about connecting to the energy, which is quite strange really" says Barbara from the London Sivananda Centre. Both interview abstracts from Barbara and Eric emphasize that they first experienced a phase of rejection before finding a way of—pragmatically—accepting these gods as a means to an end. "Before I was not really interested by Hinduism," says Eric:

> I was seeing deities, I was thinking "yeah right, these are pagan deities." But now I start to be interested because the Centre is saying that Ganesh and all that are archetypes that we find in ourselves. So, Ganesh the warrior, its possibilities, it's our full potential with every possibilities.

Finally, the guru also needs to be "useful" as "someone who can respond to your expectations in terms of self-knowledge and self-realization," to use David's words. And this is how the great majority accept having a guru: as a means to an end. Several students of both movements described the guru as having this ability to answer individual expectations. He or she is described as a "response," a "solution," a "tool," or "the box of matches that can light you up." Claire, one of Gurumayi's French disciples defines the authentic guru as "someone who transmits me her state," since "for me the criteria is the experience she allows me to live," while another follower of Gurumayi defines the true guru by "the degree of transformation they can bring in you." The instrumental quality of the guru can also supplant any other form of legitimacy:

> I question myself about this, is Gurumayi enlightened? And I've come to the conclusion, whether she's an enlightened being or not, if she can help me progress on my path, if she is showing me a way to be a better person and live my life as kinder and more loving to others, then I will progress.... I don't really think it matters whether someone is enlightened or not, if they're guiding you in the right direction, giving you the right information you need to grow, then that's enough. (Lucy, Siddha Yoga, London)

By and large, this pragmatic attitude allows disciples to overcome their initial discomfort and accept the Hindu elements of the teaching, not for their Hinduness but for their practical value. In turn, it allows disciples to disregard what is not felt as being useful—darshan, pujas, for instance. Alternatively, when accepted, it is as a useful means to find and improve oneself. It is also the foundation of these plural and selective incursions in various teachings: "At the end of the day, it doesn't matter where it comes from, whether old or new, if it is effective, then that's for you," says an interviewee. Pervading in practices of bricolage, this pragmatic logic thus legitimizes the combinations of various religious resources. Yet it also "organizes" bricolage around the value of efficiency and usefulness (Champion 2004, 70).

This pragmatism is linked to the light involvement in neo-Hindu movements that we have described. In fact, every interviewee, without exception, claimed that their relation to Siddha Yoga or Sivananda Centres was not related to a quest for belonging to a community, and they do not tend to have relationships with other followers outside the movements' events. The "community" must be useful, too, "allowing you to go forward." Even Jean, who has been committed for many years to running the Siddha Yoga Paris Centre, admits to having an instrumental approach to community life:

> I think that we shouldn't be duped. Self-realization or well-being, we do it ourselves on ourselves. Now, there are a lot of tools to reach this point, the community is one of them. So the community for the community, no; but the community as a tool, yes.

Ultimately, this pragmatism entailed by the domestication of neo-Hindu teachings is enabled by contemporary gurus who, as we shall see further on, emphasize the practical and potent nature of the practices they advocate.

Universalism and Denial of Cultural Differences

Universalism contributes to the domestication of Hinduism by dismissing cultural singularities. Indeed, neo-Hindu converts share the idea that the teaching they follow is universal in essence. Kerry, who practices yoga at the London Sivananda Centre, considers that "all paths lead to the same place. It's the same, their goal is the same but their method is slightly different." For Eileen, Siddha Yoga "makes you realize that all [these] religions are saying exactly the same thing; they're all saying the same thing" so that "essentially, there's no difference." This universalism is encouraged by gurus' universalistic rhetoric (see Chapter 3), but it is also widespread within "spiritual" milieus. Champion

(1993) described what she called the "mystical-esoteric nebulae" (a loosely defined network of personal growth workshops and conference, bookshops, and
groups in continuity with the New Age) and underlined a common belief in
the convergence of all religions in a universal tradition. This widespread belief
was in fact already found in nineteenth-century esoteric thought. Faivre (1996,
30), for instance, underscored the search of concordances between religions
in Western esotericism, leading to the introduction of Egyptian and Asian references. Indeed, Esotericism's Egyptomania and orientalism are linked to the
hope that through other traditions one could discover the one universal and
authentic truth underlying all religions.

Nonetheless, in the case of neo-Hindus, belief in the universality of
the truth de-dramatizes the Hindu-ness of the chosen path, its rituals and
doctrines. This can be illustrated by Mick, who reacted so violently to the
Sivananda Centre's Shivaratri night:

> It's not important that yoga is from India. Because in fact, the reality
> is that there's a connection with all these ancient cultures. If you go to
> Peru, and they talk about chakras, these things are not, Indian, essen-
> tially. Yes the Indian culture, and Peru I remember, there is, they talk
> about these chakras, with the Egyptian culture. So, the point is that, it's,
> yoga again is universal.

In the same vein, Christine, a yoga student and teacher at the Parisian
Sivananda Centre, does not like satsangs, their ritualistic dimension, and the
presence of Hindu divinities; however, she argues, satsangs are about God and
since God is the same everywhere and present in everything, there is actually
no real issue with it.

This way of disregarding cultural and religious particularisms allows some
followers of neo-Hindu movements whom I interviewed to actually rediscover
their initial Christian upbringing through neo-Hinduism. Indeed, many "find"
similarities between the Christian message and neo-Hindu teachings—in other
words, they unsurprisingly understand the teaching in the light of their own
religious upbringing. Mick, for instance, explains about yoga that "it allows [him]
to embrace Christianity." Nigel, a follower of Siddha Yoga for four years, defines
himself as belonging to the Church of England—"I don't go to church to practice, but I believe that there is God, I pray everyday, I read the Bible" he says.
Nigel thinks Gurumayi's teaching gives him a better understanding of the Bible:

> I'm a Christian, and a lot of things which didn't make sense to me
> when I read the Bible, after Gurumayi, after meeting Gurumayi, it

started making sense after that....When I met Gurumayi, I felt that maybe there is more meaning to what I had been reading before in the Bible. So to understand more about myself, I felt then Siddha Yoga is the best place to be.

Other followers of Siddha Yoga described how this teaching represented a sort of "detour" through which they were able to rediscover Christian doctrines and rituals with deeper understanding and serenity. There is absolutely no evidence that in turn they become observant Christians; rather, it helps their finding the familiar in the foreign. In fact, this detour by Hinduism to rediscover Christianity is compelling evidence that what is embraced is not "other" but actually a return to the same with the illusion of difference. It appears clearly, for example, when followers of both movements describe the guru in relation to the Christ. Neo-Hindus sometimes see themselves as having a living guide and identify, explicitly or implicitly, with Jesus' first disciples. Thus Gurumayi is understood as a Christ-figure representing god on earth and delivering his message. She is, for Graham, the savior Christians wait for: he defines her as "Shiva incarnate on earth" and "Shiva is coming back" through her. "She's touchstone, he says, I do believe that It's returning, the Spirit is going to return." This "detour" through Hinduism and back to Christianity is revealing; it is also pervasive—I observed that disciples of Sri Chinmoy and Sahaja Yoga revisit Christianity in similar discourses. It is also a surprising praise of other religions to assert that "I've got more of a feeling for Jesus now that I've started on an Eastern religion than I got before," as one disciple of Siddha Yoga put it.

Non-Jewish Kabbalists: "If People Persist in Saying It's Jewish, I'll Say No"

Non-Jewish followers' ambivalence toward Judaism resonates with neo-Hindus' attitude toward Hindu-ness. They show again that bricolage involves tensions, mixed feelings, and, as a result, a process of interpretation and de-contextualization of exotic religious resources. Like those who discover yoga and meditation but feel repelled by pujas, non-Jews usually discover the Kabbalah Centre's teaching through courses that downplay Jewish references and, when they become more involved, they are confronted with a disorientating, unfamiliar, and unsought liturgy in which their participation is restricted by their not being Jewish or knowledgeable about Judaism. Their ambivalent relationships to the religious and ethnic dimensions of

Judaism entail an exotic process of domestication that is similar to that of neo-Hindus. Partly secularized, these students tend to appropriate Kabbalah as a non-Jewish, non-religious, universal "spirituality"; its raison d' être is to be an efficient tool for personal growth. While some entertain the idea of being "spiritually" Jewish, or having a bit of Jewishness, non-Jewish students of Kabbalah have in fact no intention of being Jewish in an ethnic or religious sense. They never convert to Judaism, display a light and unorthodox level of practice, and have a short-term and peripheral involvement in the Kabbalah Centre, alongside involvements in a wide range of alternative therapies and religious teachings. Overall, the great majority are attracted by Kabbalah despite its Jewish origins and religious dimension; it is detached from Jewish references and liturgy that it has appropriated, much as yoga and meditation are selected from the realms of Hindu doctrines and rituals. Overall, the Kabbalah Centre's Jewish character limits its expansion among the non-Jewish public, even in a deregulated, innovative, and porous religious landscape such as Brazil.

The Kabbalah Centre, an Inclusive Synagogue?

By and large, joining the Kabbalah Centre is clearly not a move toward conversion to Judaism. Through participant observation and interviews, I have not encountered any case of conversion to Judaism among non-Jewish students of the Kabbalah Centre. None of those who said they were interested in converting to Judaism has converted to Judaism when I contacted them, three of four years after their interview. Besides, the Kabbalah Centre does not invite its non-Jewish students to convert.[6] However, I would like to start this section of the chapter by evoking the exception, that is to say, the very few who joined the Kabbalah Centre because of its Jewishness as well as its inclusiveness. Both are women who lived with a Jewish man and embraced a Jewish way of life. Now divorced, they lost their link with Judaism and wish to find it again.

Patricia is a 37-year-old Argentinean working as a fashion designer in London. She received a strong Catholic education before she met a Jewish man at the age of 18 who would become her husband. She discovered the Kabbalah Centre 20 years ago in Argentina, when teachers presented themselves in the couple's shop to offer Kabbalah classes. They both started to study Kabbalah; it provided Patricia with explanations of Jewish rituals and festivals, while her husband was teaching her how to observe them at home—her desire to have a Jewish home was related to her difficulty in being accepted by her husband's family. When she divorced, Patricia "lost the connection," and it was the desire to perform religious rituals that motivated her to go back to the Kabbalah Centre, this time on her own, and in London:

> So I went to Kabbalah Centre and I went to Shabbat because I know [the] Centre was more open and you know the Orthodox I had the experience before [laughs] I don't want to go to the synagogues where they…
> *I have a question, why not go to a synagogue?*
> Because I had the experience. I know, I know, I was coming from a family like that. And I know they were closed. And I know this story. I've been new in the, you know, in Judaism, you know, by work, by boyfriend, by everything, I know very well that world. And then I know I was not going to be accepted and I did not want to risk to have, you know, these things. What I want to do is just to connect myself to the Shabbat thing. So I thought, for sure it's going to be that synagogue [the Kabbalah Centre]. So I went there, I was very welcome.

In other words, the Kabbalah Centre allowed Patricia to join a sort of inclusive Jewish community. Patricia became a regular attendant of the Centre and was thinking about starting a conversion process. I had news from her a year after her interview; she was fasting for Yom Kippur and went to a mainstream synagogue close her home to hear the Torah reading in order to avoid traveling to the West End where the Kabbalah Centre is located. Yet she rejects rigorous observance; she explained that she does not want to "become with the black clothes." Instead, she aspires to a "sincere spiritual study" and to learn "how to run my house in that way." The Kabbalah Centre can familiarize Patricia with Jewish traditions without expecting her to respect them or to convert. Patricia does not fully observe at home but scans the Zohar and recites daily prayers prescribed by the Centre; she practices Shabbat and festivals, usually at the Centre.

In other words, the Kabbalah Centre can attract non-Jews who have a peripheral position in relation to Judaism. Catherine is 53; she is a divorcee with three children and has a small business in clothes repair. She has a French working class background and received a strong Catholic education. Her family did not accept her marriage with a Jew (like Patricia, Catherine is caught in a divided world between Jews and non-Jews), but she felt comfortable in her husband's family, and appreciated its strong family bonds. Catherine straightaway embraced Judaism, which she found beautiful and "close to life." But she did not convert; the fact that she needed to work on Saturdays was in her view an obstacle. This prevented her children from celebrating their Bar mitzvah (children of a non-Jewish mother are not considered to be Jewish by Orthodox Judaism), despite the fact that she raised her children within the Jewish religion. Thus, Catherine described herself as "having adopted the religion without being converted"; she explains that she feels Jewish but does not like "all the constraints." Now a student of the Kabbalah Centre for three years, Catherine feels she has not left Judaism. On the contrary, she perceives her involvement in the Kabbalah Centre as being in continuity with an unchanged bond with Judaism. Simply, the Kabbalah Centre "goes further," as "another way of opening the mind." Here again, the Kabbalah Centre becomes a substitute for conversion and integration into a mainstream Jewish community. Indeed, Catherine does not envisage conversion anymore,

> because I really like the Kabbalah Centre, and I see other openings and I don't want to pretend. I don't want to say, I want to convert, I will do this and this and that, and if I don't do it, I would break my word and this is wrong. So I prefer to remain as I am and practice at the Kabbalah Centre.

Catherine now prefers the Kabbalah Centre, because there she does not have to comply fully with the Jewish law (she mentions working on Saturdays), hence satisfying her need to "be a bit modern" and find understanding in an undemanding Jewish environment. Indeed, she remembers being told off in her husband's congregation once, as she unintentionally transgressed a liturgical rule; Catherine believed that, had it happened at the Kabbalah Centre, members would have reacted differently, "because it's open to everyone, the Kabbalah Centre."

Patricia and Catherine are the only students of the Kabbalah Centre who joined partly because of its Jewishness and have, at some point, embraced a Jewish way of life. They share an ambiguous desire to be part of a Jewish community, but did not convert and are unwilling to become fully observant. Now divorced, they are not part of a Jewish environment anymore. All of this makes it difficult for them to integrate into a mainstream Jewish community. By contrast, the Kabbalah Centre, with its Jewish origins and its universalistic claims, can welcome those who, like them, have a peripheral position in regard with Judaism, without demanding that they convert or fully respect the Jewish Law. It is, however, a profoundly ambivalent position: here, the Kabbalah Centre is joined as a substitute for a Jewish congregation by individuals who are not converted and may be unwilling to do so.

Jewishness: A Limit to the Expansion of the Kabbalah Centre

Setting aside these particular cases, the Kabbalah Centre's Jewishness limits its expansion among a non-Jewish audience, like neo-Hinduism proved to be too Hindu for Westerners. Indeed, the interest in Kabbalah does not equate to an attraction for Judaism. This is particularly well illustrated by the case of Martine, a 52-year-old French woman whose thirst for Kabbalah led her to attend two Kabbalah Centre classes. Martine is a full-time therapist using sophrology and massage. She has a long-lasting quest in esoteric milieus: having a Catholic background, Martine believes her ancestors were Cathars, "the first Christians" as she called them, which explains why many of her relatives are mystics or mediums. Martine defines herself as a medium, too, and she explored Kardecism in her youth. She also dived into Buddhism, Transcendental Meditation, Rajneesh's teaching, chi gong, and shamanism. She was a Rosicrucian for 11 years and discovered Kabbalah in this context; she is now in the process of being initiated into Freemasonry, in the hope of deepening her knowledge of Kabbalah. I met Martine at an introductory lecture organized by Kabbalah Centre teachers in Paris. It was the first time she attended one of the movement's events. In the "spiritual milieu" she said, it is difficult to express an interest in Kabbalah because it is said to be "for Jews." As she explained during an interview, Martine envisaged using Kabbalistic resources in her own therapeutic techniques (on the use of exotic religious resources as cultural capital, see Chapter 7). It is therefore unsurprising that she felt the need to assert that many therapists who use Hebrew letters are not Kabbalists or Jewish and that "really for me [Kabbalah] is universal, it doesn't belong to the Jewish people." She praised the Kabbalah Centre teacher who, in his lecture, also said that Kabbalah was universal. Martine believes that Kabbalah "is the West, it's our tradition"; she refuses to see Kabbalah as having Jewish origins: "Well, if people persist in saying it's Jewish, I'll say no. No, I will not get involved, for sure, no. No. Because that's sectarian and everything that is sectarian, as I say, doesn't suit me." In other words, Martine is ready to explore Kabbalah only as a non-Jewish system of thought. Her association of Judaism as a sect highlights a representation of this religion as being narrow, coercive and exclusive. It also echoes with the neo-shaman calling racist, tribal, and dogmatic those Native Americans who criticize the wide dissemination of their rituals and ceremonies (Chapter 1). Yet, in Martine's case, there is more to it: at one point during the interview, Martine told me the Jewish people have a "bad karma," this is why history repeats itself: referring to a conference she attended, she explains that Nazis are now reincarnated in Israel and this is why Israel is "doing the same thing" to Palestinians.

The Kabbalah Centre presents Kabbalah as not Jewish (Chapter 3), which reassures individuals like Martine; however, its teaching still proved to be too Jewish for her. I met Martine once again at another course given by the Kabbalah Centre. As the teacher was giving an interpretation of the story of Adam and Eve, she interrupted to comment on the snake. "What is the snake? It's the kundalini," she explained, referring to a Hindu notion. Slightly dismissive, the teacher showed no interest in what he called "another philosophy" and pursued his lecture. The Kabbalah Centre does not refer to Hinduism, Buddhism, or any other religious tradition. Martine's knowledge of Asian religions was of no use in this environment, something she found frustrating. "He doesn't know people's level, he thought I was a beginner," she told me repeatedly afterward. Martine also compared the teacher with a well-known figure in esoteric circles, Charles-Rafaël Payeur. Payeur's conferences, she explained, draw on Christian, Kabbalistic, Rosicrucian, Freemasonic, and Eastern symbolisms and are at a very high level of consciousness, while the Kabbalah Centre teacher adapts to his audience. In other words, she asserted her preference for esoteric and speculative approaches that draw correspondences between various religious traditions, a characteristic of Western esotericism, and for Kabbalah detached from its Jewish roots, as it is presented in Western esotericism through Christian Kabbalah. Martine indicated that she did not intend to come back to the Kabbalah Centre. Her case reflects the expectations of a public interested in Kabbalah via esotericism and the New Age, in a form detached from Judaism. In fact, I found that French New Age magazines such as *Nouvelles Clés* (1988–) and *Terre du Ciel* (1991–) address Kabbalah only as esoteric, Christian Kabbalah. Kabbalah, in its Jewish context, seems *too ethnic* to be easily exoticized, although the Kabbalah Centre might have initiated this process.

By and large, most non-Jewish students of the Kabbalah Centre follow its teaching, *despite its Jewishness*. Like Martine, the newcomers usually have their first contact in the Kabbalah Centre's classes. They may deepen their commitment and start to frequent the movement for festivals and Shabbat services. Then, the Kabbalah Centre's Jewish roots are more obvious and confront non-Jewish students with a foreign language and disorientating, "stranger than ever," liturgies. As with neo-Hindu movements, participation in foreign rituals proves to be challenging and stresses the limits of embracing someone else's religious traditions. Indeed, following rituals, songs and prayers in Hebrew is visibly difficult for those who are not familiar with the language and Jewish liturgy, despite the Kabbalah Centre's eagerness to include everyone. A projected PowerPoint presentation in phonetics helps the audience follow the text in Hebrew, and students who are familiar with the liturgy assist those who are not. They, as well as teachers, endlessly reassure the audience that understanding is not necessary since visualizing Hebrew letters allows connecting to the Light of the Creator (in other words, they do exactly the same thing as neo-Hindu disciples who pragmatically insist on the effect of mantras in Sanskrit).

During fieldwork, I observed clear signs of total disorientation, discomfort, and, at times, laughter. For instance, at some point of the Friday night service, while singing in Hebrew, the woman next to me lost track and whispered near my ear, "Help me!" "I can't! But you're doing well," I replied, not knowing Hebrew either, and we were both laughing. Solidarity in disorientation is something I experienced as I was starting the fieldwork and was not more familiar with the Shabbat service than any other newcomer. This is how I met Dahlia, an Australian singer who was trying to develop her career in London. Sometimes sitting together, we were trying to help each other to keep on track with the recitation of the prayers. Dahlia found a trick: she identified the word Adonai (God) in the prayer book, which was helping us to find out at what stage of the recitation we were, once we would hear the word pronounced (I met other students who memorized the shape of one or two Hebrew words to follow the rituals). Dahlia and I would laugh each time we would get to the signposting "Adonai." Here, too, humor proved to be a comforting device to deal with the liturgy's foreignness and feelings of helplessness.

Dahlia's example highlights that participation in Jewish rituals represents a challenge for the long-term involvement of non-Jews in the Kabbalah Centre, like non-Hindus in neo-Hindu movements. Later on, I interviewed Dahlia: after five months in the Centre, the transition from classes that do not refer to Judaism to Jewish services has remained an issue:

Shabbats are obviously...based in, you know, they say it's not Jewish and everything, but there are definitely strong flavors of Jewish tradition in that. So although now I understand it more and I enjoy it, and I'm there and I go with it, it's quite a bit different from the actual courses. So, sometimes I felt like that when I've been at Shabbat cause I don't really know what's going on, and scanning and...but through going there I'm understanding more, and it's becoming less religious, but I had to go through that process, and I was definitely questioning, yes I am being religious here, with no idea, why are we doing that [laugh].

A year after this interview, I asked Dahlia whether she was still involved in the Kabbalah Centre. She told me she still thought its teaching was good, but she was "just not into all these Jewish observances." Again, Dahlia explained that "they had good things to teach," but was put off by the fact that "the further you get into it, the more orthodox Jewish you get. So it starts very spiritual mixed with psychology and then you find yourself taking all the grains out of your cupboard for Pesach!"

Overall, non-Jewish students tend to participate more in courses than services and festivals. For instance, in the London Centre, about 300 students come for psychology-oriented classes each week, while Shabbat usually gathers 80 persons, according to my observation. The attendants of these religious services are not the same; the proportion of Jewish, committed students is more important, while classes attract a more diverse audience.

Being a Kabbalist without Being (Really) Jewish

Non-Jewish students of Kabbalah are clearly challenged by the references to Jewish rules and rituals, which is usually not what they expected or desired by studying Kabbalah. Accordingly, for those who persist in the Kabbalah Centre, Jewishness needs to be dealt with, the same way that neo-Hindus find ways to make Hinduism safe and appropriable—despite the claim by the Kabbalah Centre's teachers that Kabbalah is not Jewish, in order to reach out to a non-Jewish audience. Also congruent with the Kabbalah Centre's discourse, Kabbalah is often seen as a primordial wisdom that preceded and is then distinct from Judaism. Farrah, for example, described Kabbalah as "the seed root of ancient Judaism, which is one of the seed root of the main religions of the world." This belief allows detaching Kabbalah from Judaism: when I asked Bridget about how she feels about the Kabbalah Centre's rituals and festivals that relate to Judaism, she responded: "It actually doesn't. That is what people get wrong. It goes back to BEFORE Judaism. It is just that the Jewish religion remained the closest to the Kabbalah teachings." Just as neo-Hinduism can be seen as a detour to a better understanding of a Christian background, Bridget told me she likes the Kabbalah Centre's teaching because "it was [her] own culture, because as a Christian we were talking about the Bible...in its original form." Therefore Bridget "was finally learning about [her] own cultural background as a Christian."

Furthermore, as a universal wisdom preceding religions, Kabbalah is not perceived as a religion itself and for that reason needs not be adopted as such. Like members of neo-Hindu movements, non-Jewish students of Kabbalah contrast constraining "organized religions" with Kabbalah as "spirituality." Therefore, they believe that, like "Eastern spirituality," Kabbalah does not demand conversion or respect for religious norms—and indeed the Kabbalah

Centre does not encourage students who are not Jewish to become observant Jews. This approach clearly reflects the expectations of an audience, partly secularized and defiant of religious institutions and authorities. Yet it is also a pre-requisite for those students who are ambivalent toward Judaism. Tamara, whose relation to Judaism is particularly conflicted, as we shall see in the next section, states that what amazes her in the Kabbalah Centre teaching is the fact that "you can even keep your religion and still learn this wisdom." Finally, non-Jewish students of Kabbalah share with disciples of neo-Hinduism their pragmatism. Kabbalah is not about embracing Judaism; it is for them a means to understand the laws of the universe and improve their lives by understanding these laws. Tamara for example explains that

> in order for you to be whole and to manifest yourself as your best self, you need to be in-between the worlds. And Kabbalah gives you this formula. And I really need this formula.... I felt it can give me answers but I also felt, it has to give me answers, you know, because if it doesn't give me then I don't really find the meaning.

One of the means of making the Kabbalah Centre's Jewishness appropriable is, however, surprising and distinctive: some of these non-Jewish students "discover" their Jewish identity in past lives through regression, encounters with mediums, and *déjà-vu* experiences in Israel. This form of Jewish identity is in line with the Kabbalah Centre's teaching on reincarnation, admitting the possibility that Jewish souls can be reincarnated in the bodies of non-Jewish students of Kabbalah. Their desire to study Kabbalah is in fact seen as a sign that they might have a Jewish soul. This Jewish quality of the soul is neither ethnic nor religious, but spiritual or metaphysical, and does not require conversion or observance since the individual is already Jewish. Farrah is English; she considers herself a healer and practices different forms of channeling and therapy. She has been coming to the Kabbalah Centre for seven years and is a regular attendant of services and festivals. She stressed the fact that it was easy for her to dive into the teachings of the Kabbalah Centre that she discovered with a girlfriend:

> I really liked the energy of the place and I liked the people and she sort of guided me to it, and there I am coming along. And I kind of did this thing in reverse, because normally with Kabbalah you kind of do the courses, you read the books, and then you gradually may or may not actually go to Shabbat. But with me, I went to Shabbat for a start.... I was also aware of a great affinity for the Jewish faith.

I know I have the Christian background, but it's almost like, I kind of knew when I started to go that I'd been Jewish before.... I'm aware that I have been Jewish in a past life, it's like sometimes when we sing Jewish psalms, it's like I know the words...and sometimes the chevre come up to me and say look, we know you can't read Hebrew, so how come you know exactly where you are? And I say "I don't know, I don't know."

Here, Farrah stresses her awareness of being Christian in a Jewish environment, but she also insists on her familiarity with this environment because of a past life. In great detail she described this previous existence in which she was a little girl who was deported to a death camp during World War II. She believes that it explains why she feels nervous in airports, when seeing soldiers, and dislikes "people talking about cremation or anything like that." It is interesting to note that a stereotypical vision of Jewish identity pervades the discovery of these past lives. Bridget, another student in London whom I have interviewed, was told by a medium she had Russian Jewish ancestors who had their house burned down, which explains why she had been so anxious about losing her house in the past. Note this romantic and reductionist identification to the Jew as persecuted, yet without actually living with the burden of the Holocaust or the fear of anti-Semitic abuse. Farrah evoked particular feelings, vibrations, and visions that she experienced during a trip to Israel to celebrate Rosh Hashanah with the Kabbalah Centre,[7] which reinforced her belief that she was once part of the Hebrew people who left Egypt:

It was like going back home. It was like, I'm getting emotional now. It was like, I've never had the opportunity to go to the Promised Land in that particular lifetime because I believe that I was in one of my lifetimes I was one of the people who escaped from Egypt, but that I never got to the Promised Land. It was a little bit like, well, I'm doing it now.

Through Jewish past lives, Farrah seeks to explain, if not generate, familiarity with Jewish references as well as a sense of belonging. It is highly significant that Farrah is, at the same time, uncomfortable with the Jewishness of the place. Farrah is indeed aware of the religious knowledge she does not possess, compared to some other members of the Kabbalah Centre. For instance, I remember her once discussing the time of the start of the Shabbat service at the Kabbalah Centre (it depends on the sunset and is fixed by rabbinical authorities all around the world). That night, she arrived early because she did not know the starting time had changed. The length of this discussion she was having with another student and myself reflected her frustration with a sense of exclusion and lack of basic knowledge regarding the Centre's activities. The discomfort regarding her not being Jewish was also noticeable. The first time I met her was during Shabbat at the Kabbalah Centre; she sat next to me and noticed I was taking notes. "I don't have a Jewish background but *they* say you can't write on Saturday," she told me, referring to those who have this background and therefore the authority to set the rules. Through our encounters at the Kabbalah Centre, I heard several times Farrah mention she was not Jewish; but she asked me if *I* was Jewish and if I could read Hebrew. She also expressed her discomfort about her not being Jewish during her interview:

> When you go to the London group, there are probably a higher propor-
> tion of people there that are actually Jewish, who have a Jewish back-
> ground and I automatically think I don't want to particularly say about
> my Christian background.

Strikingly, the majority frequenting the Kabbalah Centre in London are not Jewish, but Farrah's perception actually reveals that the core group who do have religious knowledge and authority is overwhelmingly Jewish.

This exotic appropriation of Jewishness reveals a certain ambivalence toward Judaism that is never embraced as a whole. For instance, having a "Jewish soul" can entail rejection of an ethnic or religious Jewish identity—otherwise we could have expected some of these students to convert to Judaism. Mervyn, a former student of the Kabbalah Centre, now studying Kabbalah in Bnei Baruch (a movement created by former students of the Kabbalah Centre; see Chapter 3), explained that being Jewish is in fact a spiritual state, that has nothing to do with being born into a Jewish family or being observant: "A Jew is a person who has their heart open so they begin to ask what is the meaning of my life and want to return to the Creator" and Kabbalah is the means to do so. He mentioned that his great grandmother was Jewish but, he added, "I didn't really go into, too much into that, I didn't want to be weighed down by somebody else's past, to be inhibited by my, my *physical* people." In other words, while a mythical, spiritual, and evanescent Jewishness is valued, the ethnic, cultural, and religious dimensions of Jewishness are rejected. It is an evanescent and short-term Jewishness opted by the individual, invisible to others and therefore inconsequential—it is Jewishness without being perceived as such.

By and large, reminding us of the ambivalence of exoticism toward otherness, I found that several students combine valorization and rejection of Jewishness, sometimes in very contradictory ways. When I met Romy to interview her, one of the first questions she asked was whether I was Jewish; when I replied positively, she said enthusiastically, "Oh give me some! I would like to make Judaism a way of life." Romy is now deeply involved in Bnei Baruch, after having been a student of the Kabbalah Centre in London. During the interview, Romy reiterated her desire to convert, learn Hebrew, and live in a Jewish way in order to "give her structure" in her life and to settle in Israel one day. However, she also adopted a de-ethnicized definition of Jewishness: "The Kabbalah says anybody who studies Kabbalah is already a Jew. Because it means 'straight to God,' you know," she explained. When we evoked the Jewish roots and character of Bnei Baruch, she responded that Kabbalah actually comes from Mesopotamia and is therefore Persian, so

> Judaism doesn't come into it at all.
> *No?*
> No... Jews? [blows out], don't know much about them... like Judaism as such.

In other words, it is possible to desire to acquire "some Jewishness" as a pragmatic means to structure one's life, while ignoring Jews and Judaism.[8] Four years after this interview, Romy is still very enthusiastic about Bnei Baruch's Kabbalistic teaching but explained she was definitely "not in Judaism, which is not to be confused with Kabbalah." Again, the claim that Kabbalah is not Jewish allows individuals to embrace Kabbalah without getting close to Judaism. Romy's dismissive answer about Jews and Judaism suggests that it is an ambivalent relationship to Jews and Judaism that demands Kabbalah's de-judaicization.[9]

This ambivalence is well illustrated by the example of Tamara, a very wealthy woman from former Yugoslavia in her late thirties, living in Paris. From a Catholic background, she started to be interested in "spirituality" and psychology when she encountered difficulties in her marriage and got a divorce. She plainly evoked her lack of empathy for Jews:

> We never had negative, negative attitudes over them, I mean my grandmother had her best friend who was Jewish.... But I can make more connection with an individual than to feel "oh poor Jews, I'm really sorry." No. I cannot say that. Maybe I was sorry for them; maybe I was sorry for everybody who has suffered in their lives.

Tamara contacted the Kabbalah Centre a year before the interview, after she discovered Kabbalah during a trip to Toledo in Spain. She found books about Kabbalah in a library next to a synagogue she visited:

> We came to a little synagogue. And I had an amazing feeling of calm and peace and belonging. I have never had much contact with Judaism and *I could not say I even had much sympathy for Jews, you know?* I had my own rules. But anyway this feeling was definitely a new experience, a new experience for me.

Here, Tamara explains that her lack of attraction for Judaism or the Jewish people was counterbalanced by a subjective "experience" in a synagogue. She stated that she has never been "connected" like this in a church and now could not stand seeing a cross or entering a church anymore. At the time of the interview, she had met an Israeli observant man and she started to practice Shabbat. Tamara started to eat kosher food and put a mezuzah[10] on her door. She told me she ordered a genetic test to know whether she had "Jewish blood" and envisaged a conversion. Paradoxically, as I came back to the idea of conversion, she replied it was in fact "irrelevant": "the label will not sort much but if I need to be connected you know, with some religion, this is the only religion I would be connected to." Four years after our interview, I asked her whether she did convert and was still studying Kabbalah. She replied that she has no contact with any form of Kabbalistic teaching anymore and was currently exploring "energy workings" such as chi gong and "Theta healing," which she finds "more suitable for [her] own growth and enlightenment." It is not surprising that this student did not convert or continue in the Kabbalah Centre. Her ambivalence toward Jews and Judaism made her conversion to Judaism very unlikely.

Peripheral and Short-lived Involvement in the Kabbalah Centre

This ambivalence toward Judaism is reflected in the peripheral and short-lived involvement of non-Jewish students in the Kabbalah Centre. Non-Jews tend to be the peripheral (but predominant) circle of students who frequent the Centre for its courses, rather than for its religious services. They are therefore often involved in one part only of the teaching. Their level of practice is also lighter, not only because the Kabbalah Centre stresses that non-Jewish students do not have to respect the commandments that bind the Jewish people with the Creator or because it does not allow them to perform certain ritual activities (see Chapter 3). More important, non-Jewish students of Kabbalah express their unwillingness to become observant Jews and are unfamiliar with rituals and rules which, in mainstream Judaism, are usually observed in a household rather than by single individuals. It is therefore unsurprising that their practices are relatively unorthodox, despite the fact that they might adopt some of the rules in relation to Shabbat or eat kosher meat for a moment in time. Non-Jewish students of Kabbalah tend to limit their practices to some of the Kabbalah Centre's particular teachings, such as scanning the Zohar or the 72 names of God, and the recitation of a particular prayer, called Ana Bekoach.

Finally, because they do not identify with Judaism, the study of Kabbalah is for them one phase among others in their religious trajectory. All non-Jewish students whom I interviewed have discovered Kabbalah after trying out a diversity of other alternative religions and therapies; they sometimes continue to practice them alongside Kabbalah, and in some cases, they left the Kabbalah Centre for other teachings. Thus, the trajectory of these students of Kabbalah underlines one more time the link between religious exoticism and secularization at the individual level. And, like neo-Hindu followers, their belief in universalism, that "everything is connected," enables them to find correspondences between Kabbalah, Chinese medicine, Daoism, and other paths that they explore, sometimes simultaneously. This is the reason that Farrah has no problem explaining to teachers that the London Centre's entrance hall would be improved by using Feng Shui techniques. Farrah belonged to the esoteric movement White Lodge; she practices reiki, channeling, an "Indian form of Feng Shui" called Vaastu and rebirth. Tamara is now interested in Theta healing; Romy "studied a bit of Buddhism" and has explored a wide range of therapies. Bridget tried past lives regressions, reiki, and has been deeply involved for several years in Mahikari, a Japanese new religious movement. Her discovery of Kabbalah did not lead her to stop practicing in Mahikari. Before discovering Kabbalah, Mervyn explored various religious traditions and created his own spiritual community that drew on Asian sources. Dahlia, in the Australian spiritual hub Byron Bay, tested all sorts of spiritual teachings such as rebirth, Vipassana meditation, reiki, and yoga (she visited ashrams in India), and it is through a Tarot card reader that she discovered Kabbalah. Recently invited to join a Buddhist group, she "would love to go." Ultimately, Kabbalah is one exotic religious resource combined with many others for a short period of time; this is reflected by the Kabbalah Centre's retention rate of 4 percent, according to a student in London.

Kabbalah Chic in Brazil

We complete the study of non-Jewish students of Kabbalah with a discussion of the Kabbalah Centre in Brazil.[11] Indeed, it is significant that the movement has been relatively unsuccessful in a country that is probably less secularized than its North American and Western European counterparts and is characterized by an extraordinary religious diversity.

Brazilian religious diversity and creativity have been described as "the most exuberant and variegated national religious culture in all of Latin America" by Carpenter (2004, 213) who highlighted a New Age or esoteric boom since the 1980s, and to which we could add a sudden interest in alternative medicines and therapies (Magnani 1999), the resurgence of indigenous religions and the emergence of Ayahuasca religions (Dawson 2007), the rapid development of Pentecostal and neo-Pentecostal churches that are sometimes exported abroad (Birman and Lehmann 1999; Corten 1995; Ireland 1991; Oro 2000; Vásquez 1998), and the continued success of Afro-Brazilian religions in Brazil as well as in the rest of South America (Brown 1994; Johnson 2001; Motta 1988, 2002; Pierucci and Prandi 1996; Prandi 2004). The population affected by the New Age is often that of urban professional classes who have been brought up in Catholic households and/or are familiar with Spiritism,[12] Umbanda,[13] and esotericism (Dawson 2007, 7). Dawson links the *Nova Era* in Brazil with an exponential industrialization and urbanization, which started with Kubitschek's presidency in the 1950s, resulting in rising individualism, the erosion of the Catholic Church's authority and privileges, and the diversification of the religious landscape. The diversity of this landscape is also linked to the fact that it is relatively unregulated by the state; there has been no cult controversy in Brazil (Giumbelli 2002). Carvalho (2000), who researched the attraction for mystical fairs and New Age teachings in Brasília, underlines that despite their being new, these healing techniques and forms of manipulation of supernatural forces are in line with the Brazilian religious culture's heavy stress on the world of spirits. In fact, Carvalho claims that the spirit system of thought permeates Brazilian religiosity as a whole. Another important feature of this diverse religious field is a "structural predisposition to porosity." Both Dawson (2007, 160) and Sanchis (2007) emphasize Brazilian religiosity's composite, syncretic, and hybrid trends, as well as its openness to novelty. "Within an overarching spiritist-inspired cosmological framework" (Dawson 2007, 47), a vast arrays of themes and symbols from esotericism, Catholicism, indigenous religions, and so forth circulate among groups that are not possessive of their ethnic markers of identity (Klein 2004). This porosity entails a diversity of affiliations: for example, a survey in the city of São Paulo in 1995 showed that 26 percent of the Brazilian adult population gravitated toward a religion different from the one they were born into. In São Paulo, one in ten who converted had a new religion for a year or less, while three out of ten had it for up to three years (Rocha 2006, 110). Nevertheless, this syncretic and porous characteristic takes place in the context of a Christian conception of the divine (Negrão cited in Guerriero 2003), which will be a significant issue when addressing the diffusion of a religious movement rooted in Judaism such as the Kabbalah Centre.

The Brazilian way of being Jewish is also plural and malleable. Topel's (2003, 2005, 2008) studies of São Paulo's Orthodoxy highlight the absence of central, regulating institutions to organize Judaism's different trends. She also notes, by contrast with North American, Israeli, and Western European Judaisms, the lack of clear-cut boundaries between Reform and Conservative denominations and between Sephardic and Ashkenazi communities, so that rabbis circulate and operate in different communities and institutions without necessarily being affiliated with them. Despite being relatively conservative, the members of the São Paolo Jewish community, for instance, are open to a diversity of religious experiences, frequent various synagogues and feel proud of the different origins of its members, thereby celebrating diversity and tolerances which are held to be distinctive Brazilian values (Klein 2004, 254). Finally, through interviews with Kabbalah Centre's students and rabbis in Rio de Janeiro, I found that Brazilian Judaism's porosity was such that non-Jews also frequent synagogues, reflecting a certain attraction for Judaism. Indeed, Judaism's symbols, values, and practices are reinvented and exoticized (Grin 2005), granting Jewish cultural and religious resources a certain chic.

Brazilian Judaism undergoes a secularization process, as evidenced by a high rate of mixed marriages (Decol 2001). Also congruent with what is observed in Israel and in the diaspora since the 1980s (Danzger 1989; Schnapper et al. 2009; Sharot 2007), an Orthodox trend is developing: new synagogues and educational Jewish institutions have been opened, and there is a renewed interest in Jewish mysticism (Carvalho 2001; Topel 2008). In this context of secularization and revival, Kabbalah has become an unavoidable topic for competing actors in the field of Brazilian Judaism, in particular due to the influence of Rabbi Nilton Bonder. Described to me as the "Paulo Coelho of Judaism," Nilton Bonder is the rabbi of the Confederação Judaica do Brasil, one of Brazil's largest synagogue with 600 families (Schuster 1998). Bonder is also the author of more than 20 books. His trilogy, *The Kabbalah of Food, The Kabbalah of Time*, and *The Kabbalah of Money*, had a tremendous success (half a million were sold in Brazil) and was translated in several languages. This was before the Kabbalah Centre's wide popularization of Kabbalah, which means that Brazil was actually the avant-garde of Kabbalah's mass popularization. These books were followed by many others, combining Jewish mysticism with philosophy and popular psychology. One of these, *Immoral Soul: A Manifesto of Spiritual Disobedience*, was mentioned in the "Best Jewish Writing 2002" of *Tikkun Magazine* (Kepp 2006). The events I have attended with Nilton Bonder highlight the strong influence the Jewish Renewal movement exerted on him, reflected in the full participation of women in the liturgy, uplifting music and singing in Shabbat services, conferences referring to the 1960s American counterculture, and of course discussions of Kabbalah. Bonder, too, uses Kabbalah to give meaning to Jewish rules and rituals in modern life, by referring to science, environmental issues, or consumerism (Bonder 1989, 1991, 1992). His aim is also to revitalize Judaism in a secularizing context, as he explained during an interview:

> At the time, there was this, a big interest for esotericism and let's say, an interest for the East, the Eastern traditions. And since I came back from the United States, I thought that the Jewish tradition has a very interesting outlook, not only for the Jewish community but also as a traditional wisdom and I thought that there was a space for it and I was mainly interested in trying to do it with the youth of the community, who often understand the religious tradition as something of the past, so that they can see here a certain value, since they were looking in yoga, all these things.

Bonder believes that Kabbalah can fill a vacuum in Brazil and, he explains to me, its mystical dimensions fit with ideas of reincarnation, spirits, and invisible forces that are diffuse in Brazilian culture. In sum, Bonder incarnates a form of Brazilian Jewish Renewal that seeks to bring left wing, humanistic, non-Orthodox Jews to observance (Kepp 2006).

An eclectic and porous religious landscape that includes an unregulated Judaism, the absence of cult controversy, and the popularization of Kabbalah by a "cool" rabbi in Rio de Janeiro all represent favorable factors for the development of a movement such as the Kabbalah Centre in Brazil. Indeed, the Kabbalah Centre is uncontroversial there, by contrast with Israel or France, as we shall see in later chapters. I found advertisements for the Kabbalah Centre's courses in the Brazilian Jewish press, and its teacher has been invited several times to give lectures in Jewish institutions. In fact, in Brazil, the Kabbalah Centre started giving courses in São Paulo in the prestigious Jewish cultural center of the city, the *Hebraica*. At the time of writing, despite being in disrepute in many countries, the Kabbalah Centre's teachers still give talks in this institution. Furthermore, the Kabbalah Centre now does not limit itself to use Jewish network and media: Shmuel, Brazil's main teacher until 2011, holds a daily column in *Extra*, one of the most widely sold newspapers in the country. Without any sarcasm or controversy, he was interviewed several times in national television programs, such as the popular *Programa do Jô Soares*, after which, Shmuel told me, the telephone of the Kabbalah Centre in Rio would not stop ringing. Just when the Bergs sent their Kabbalistic astrologer to Brazil to offer astral maps to students from their headquarters in Los Angeles, an article on "the horoscope of Kabbalah" was published in the Brazilian version of *Marie Claire*: it explained Kabbalistic astrology (one element of Berg's innovative teaching), and presented the Berg family and the Kabbalah Centre in a positive way. In the same period, Madonna's tour in Brazil was also an opportunity for the teachers to be interviewed by newspapers and to advertise their activities.

In addition to this favorable social context, the Kabbalah Centre in Brazil had the chance to have a Brazilian teacher, by contrast with most local branches where there is a turnover of (mostly) Israeli teachers, who are often disconnected from the social and cultural environment. Shmuel Lemle, the first Brazilian teacher of the Kabbalah Centre, was born in Rio de Janeiro and is proud of his city and Brazilian culture. His parents are Jewish: his father, a doctor in medicine, is a pillar of the ARI, Rio's Liberal synagogue that his own father, rabbi Henrique Lemle (1909–1978), founded after emigrating from Germany during World War II (Lemle 1998). In other words, the grandfather of the Kabbalah Centre's teacher is the initiator of Rio's Reform Judaism. Shmuel went to a non-Orthodox school as a child; in his youth he rejected Judaism and tried other religious teachings, but decided to find his way back to Judaism when he met a Kabbalah Centre teacher at a service in a Lubavitch synagogue. Both he and Shmuel started to teach in São Paulo in 1995 and in Rio de Janeiro in 2000. At the time of fieldwork, Shmuel was the only teacher in Brazil and was traveling weekly from Rio de Janeiro to São Paulo to teach in both cities. During his courses and Shabbat services, Shmuel makes the teaching relevant by referring to Brazilian popular culture, addressing Brazilian social problems or the place of Brazil in the modern world. This is unusual among Kabbalah Centre teachers, since they very often live full-time in the Kabbalah Centre's premises, do not teach in their own country, in their mother tongue, and do not necessarily stay in the same branch for long. The students I met in Shmuel's classes greatly appreciated him and related to his teaching.

In these conditions, we could easily imagine that the Kabbalah Centre could really take off in Brazil, and indeed Shmuel explained to me that it was extremely easy to teach Kabbalah there, in particular the Kabbalah Centre's main principle—the existence of an invisible and divine higher world, distinct from a limited physical world. Yet, the Kabbalah Centre in Rio de Janeiro is a very small group. In this city of 6 million inhabitants, the Kabbalah Centre's Shabbat gathers 40 participants at most. Its main introductory course, Kabbalah One, which I attended, started with only 50 students; after the eighth class we were only 20. The Kabbalah Centre in Rio does not attract Jewish students in particular; it is challenging for the liturgy, which necessitates the presence of 10 Jewish men. To my knowledge, the Kabbalah Centre in São Paulo is not significantly different from Rio's branch. I do not pretend to be able to explain exhaustively why the Kabbalah Centre is relatively unsuccessful in Brazil. In particular, I am not sure why it does not attract more Jewish students, although we may hypothesize that Bonder's synagogue in Rio attracts individuals who, otherwise, could potentially be students at the Kabbalah Centre—some of the Kabbalah Centre's (Jewish or non-Jewish) students indeed frequent Bonder's synagogue. Nevertheless, the trajectory and discourses of some of the non-Jewish students tend to show that the Kabbalah Centre's Jewishness limits its expansion in the country with the "largest Catholic population in the world" (Arriada Lorea 2009, 81), despite its buoyant religious culture.

Kabbalah Centre's Jewishness is in some ways valorized by non-Jewish students. At one of my first Shabbats at the Kabbalah Centre in Rio de Janeiro, I met Carolina, a 48-year-old woman raised as a Catholic, who has frequented the Kabbalah Centre for seven years. As I explained to her my research project, her response was to stress that Brazil is a fascinating country in terms of religious freedom, and that many people came there to flee persecution. Carolina refers to Brazil's history in relation to Jews: at the end of the fifteenth century, Jews in Spain and later in Portugal were forced to convert or were expelled. Conversion did not prevent those "New Christians" from being accused of heresy and persecuted by the Inquisition; some of them came to Brazil at the turn of the seventeenth century, where no Inquisition tribunals were established and where they found opportunities for social mobility. While we do not know how many they were, they represented a substantial proportion of free men in colonial centers (Chor Maio and Calaças 2001). In other words, for Carolina, the Kabbalah Centre's Jewishness embodies Brazilian values of religious freedom and diversity, as well as Jews' contribution to Brazil's history. It fits with the national representations of Brazil's history of cultural and religious diversity and tolerance.

Moreover, several members of the Kabbalah Centre in Rio de Janeiro I have interviewed, including Carolina herself, identify with the descendants of these

Jews who were converted to Christianity before emigrating to colonial Brazil. When I interviewed Carolina later and asked her how she felt about being in a group rooted in Judaism, she responded that it was actually very easy for her and referred to an argument she had with her mother as she was going to Israel to celebrate Rosh Hashanah with the Kabbalah Centre. Her mother asked her why she changed religion; "I changed nothing, I'm Catholic," Carolina said. Then a relative told her that her family was in fact Jewish: they were descendants of New Christians. Thus, while in Western Europe some non-Jewish students construct a metaphysical or spiritual Jewish identity through past lives, Carolina draws on Brazil's history to identify with Jews forced to convert to Christianity. Both are, in fact, variations of the same exotic phenomena—having "some" Jewishness without being Jewish (similarly, a teacher assured me that in Poland, through their study of Kabbalah, some of his students "discover" that their parents are Jewish but have hidden it since World War II). With Carolina, I found that other interviewees also identified as descendants of New Christians.

This trend has to be understood in the light of the fact that in the last 20 years or so, it has become fashionable for Brazilians to discover their Jewish ascendance. Drawing on academic research on New Christians in Brazil, an increasing number of Brazilians believe that their Jewish origins are revealed by their family names. Indeed, New Christians are supposed to have changed their names to avoid persecution; these names are relatively common, leading to speculations by a large number of people. In very rare cases, and with substantial evidence on their origins, entire families recognized themselves as Jewish; some re-converted and went to live in Israel (Benveniste 1997; Ramagem 1997; Waingort Novinsky 2006, 2010). This fashionable identification as converted Jews is congruent with Brazil's celebration of its cultural and social diversity, as well as the recent official recognition of social groups that, until recently, were marginalized (Dawson 2007, 136). Besides, identification with Judaism is particularly positive as it grants the prestige of being identified with a group that experienced social mobility (Sorj 1997, 82). Lesser (2004, 48) stresses that "for non-elite, non-Jewish Brazilians, discovering a *converso* in the family allows them to both be 'Jews' (the rich and powerful kind) while not being actual 'Jews' (the sneaky and problematic kind)." This description exactly fits with the ambivalent identification with Judaism that I observed in the Kabbalah Centre, in the Brazilian case and beyond. It allows the identification to a restrictive and positive version of the Jew (the successful, the persecuted victim), while religious and ethnic aspects of Jewishness are rejected due to a remaining ambivalent relationship to Judaism and Jews. Besides, it is possible that the Kabbalah Centre drew on this trend of claiming a Jewish identity to appeal to a wider audience in Brazil—a teacher I interviewed in Rio believed there are a lot of "Jewish souls" in Brazil, which represents a potential for spreading Kabbalah.

In the case of non-Jewish students of the Kabbalah Centre, identification as descendants of New Christians also allows them to be Jewish, in such a way as not to prevent them from being Catholic at the same time, which explains Carolina's claim to be Catholic—like Farrah who still defines herself as Christian, despite her Jewish past lives. And one more time, it is a paradoxical way of keeping Judaism at bay. When I asked Carolina whether she felt Jewish, she replied that she did not and explained that she would not convert. Besides, she added,

I was born to be Catholic, so I'm free, I don't need to respect Saturdays, I can respect it if I want, and, I don't need, I can walk with a tight trousers, I can eat what I want, although I'm quasi kosher because I'm vegetarian.

Carolina also explained that Kabbalah is the basis of Judaism but it is also the origin of Catholicism; thus, it reinforced her understanding of the church teaching. Religious exoticism, one more time, is paradoxically a way to go back to the same. Overall, during fieldwork in Brazil, references were often made to Christianity, reasserting that many elements of the Catholic Church originated in Judaism (that Jesus was Jewish, for example) in order to make of Kabbalah a way of reinforcing a Christian identity, rather than of identifying with Judaism. In fact, references to the Jewish roots of Christian symbols and rituals have been underlined slightly more by Brazilian non-Jewish students of Kabbalah than elsewhere. In this regard, it is not insignificant that one of the full-time volunteers I interviewed in the Rio Kabbalah Centre is now living in the United States and has been baptized recently in an independent evangelical Protestant church.

We therefore start to see the limits of the study of Kabbalah for this non-Jewish audience, especially when it is perceived as another religion and contradicts students' Christian beliefs. Sergio's incursion in the Kabbalah Centre illustrates this. Sergio is 71; he is a famous writer of theater plays and scripts for television *novellas*. He has been raised as a Catholic, and when he was young, he was drawn to mysticism through the writings of Teilhard de Chardin and the figure of Teresa of Avila. He started to study Kabbalah a year ago through the Kabbalah Centre's courses, though he felt very uncomfortable when attending Shabbat services. Sergio found ways to deal with the Centre's Jewishness: he, too, thinks he may be a descendant of New Christians because of the name of his grandmother. He also evoked his first contact with Jewish culture when teaching in a Jewish institution in São Paolo, as well as an early fascination for Yiddish literature, which he used to create successful shows. An "oriental" look intimated his belief that he may have "Jewish blood." Sergio also finds Christ's teaching very Kabbalistic and stresses that Jesus was Jewish and consequently celebrated Jewish rituals. Sergio believes Kabbalah helps him get closer to the teachings of Christ. Sergio also believes that Kabbalah is for all humanity and not a religion. Two years after this interview, Sergio left the Kabbalah Centre, yet without completely losing interest in the teaching. But in his correspondence with me, he highlighted the religious and the Jewish nature of the Kabbalah Centre as problematic for him:

> The first thing they insist on is: it's not religion. It is religion. Everything revolves around Jewish History. Every door of energy was about characters and events of the Jewish history. The Jewish members [of the Kabbalah Centre] smile a lot, make a lot of compliments, but it is difficult to enter their circle. Nothing aggressive, but . . . delicately, we are not part of them.

Sergio then explained his views by emphasizing that God is everywhere and among different ethnic groups in the world, thereby responding to the Jewishness of the Kabbalah Centre. The Centre's teachings in terms of self-help are good, he explains, "but they can be also found in the Vedas, in Christianity." Incidentally, during his interview, Sergio had told me that he had been a member of the Japanese Church of World Messianity, which he left after four years, because he found that its philosophy, despite being interesting, was contradicting Christian principles:

> There was a point when I wondered, "come on, are you saying that Meishu Sama is sent by God, is the son of God? Yes." So I said, "ok for me it's only Jesus, not Meishu Sama, so I'm leaving."

Sergio then added: "and this is the same thing, I'm in Kabbalah and if they come to me and say 'listen, your Christ is rubbish,' it's not, for me it's not, but Kabbalah doesn't present this conflict that the Messianic Church did." It seems it finally did.

Disenfranchised Jews in the Kabbalah Centre: New Marranos?

This section explores the relationships that Jewish followers have with the Kabbalah Centre's Jewishness. What must be said at the outset is that these students are also very ambivalent toward the Jewish roots of Kabbalah, which they, too, exoticize. While acknowledging that these roots represent a source of comfort, the Jewish tradition that they seek in the Kabbalah Centre has to be non-religious and universal, thereby refusing Judaism's ethnic markers, particularism and visibility.

Practicing Judaism without Being Religious

As paradoxical as it may seem, Jewish members of the Kabbalah Centre, including the most committed and observant of them, express a rejection of Judaism-as-religion and envisage Kabbalah as an alternative to it. Jewish students of Kabbalah had an upbringing in secularized, mildly practicing families and moved away from the religious socialization they experienced in their youth. As individuals subjected to a process of secularization, they have similar trajectories to non-Indian neo-Hindus and non-Jewish Kabbalists: they reject religious institutions and authorities they perceive as rigid and meaningless. Religion is described as something "being rammed down [their] throat," as one Jewish student put it, and it is contrasted with Kabbalah as "spirituality."

Eyal is characteristic of these followers. He discovered the teaching in the early 1980s. Defining himself as a secular Israeli "involved in tradition" but "not brought up religious," Eyal explains that while being proud to be Jewish, he also holds that "you can't relate yourself to a religious establishment, especially in Israel." He describes his experience of Jewish communities, which he depicts as exclusive and uninviting "bunkers":

> When a non-religious Jew, let's say even traditional, comes to the synagogue, it's very alienating. Nobody helps you, nobody tells you, you have no idea what's going on and it's so disenchanting that it's just like, "why should you come again?" and I remember that as my experience as a kid, as a teenager, of going once in a while to the synagogue and I would sit there with my father and uncle and thinking to myself like, "why is it so boring? Something is wrong with me." But I looked around and everybody else seemed bored. And I said to myself: "there is no way something like that would hold for so many thousands of

years. So we lost something. . . . And when I studied Kabbalah—this is
it, this is what we lost.

One more time, we encounter the idea that an authentic tradition, here
Kabbalah, faded away in the agonies of modernity and needs to be found
again, as well as the polar opposition between disenchanted religious institutions devoid of meaning and a true meaningful wisdom (here Judaism versus
Kabbalah). This is the reason that I contend that these secularized Jews also
have an exotic relationship with Kabbalah; here the distance is a distance in
time and not so much a cultural distance, as with "Timeless India," although
it is Kabbalah's secret and unknown nature that also makes it attractive for
secular Jews.

However, these partly secularized Jewish students have complex relations
with Judaism; it is not for them a religious "other" that, for this reason, needs
to be kept as bay. On the contrary, for those who dive into the deepest level of
the Kabbalah Centre's principles and become full-time members, it is experienced as a *return* to a true Jewish tradition. Eyal, who later became a teacher,
explained that his first courses with Berg "mesmerized" him, because

> First of all, I started to understand what is Kabbalah and how much
> I missed it in my education. Two, it explained to me Judaism in a way
> that I could relate to. Three, I could understand the traditions that I was
> already doing, I could understand it in a way that I can feel comfort-
> able with and *it could make me closer to that tradition*. It gave me a sense
> of belonging to another, because, with understanding. [What else...] It
> made me feel that the establishment has not interfered anymore be-
> cause I don't need it *to connect to my Judaism*.

Eyal illustrates the Kabbalah Centre's early role of a revitalizing Judaism for
a secularizing young generation. Through a renewed understanding of their
religious background, some students like Eyal have become observant Jews,
and have strengthened their bond with Judaism while keeping away from
mainstream religious institutions. To begin with, they link their new observance with having found a new meaning for religious practices. Yitzhak, a
50-year-old Israeli student, remembers going to the synagogue now and then
with his secular father: "we would go to hear the blow of the shofar [horn
used in Jewish liturgy] at the end of Yom Kippur and stuff like that, you know,
but without any explanation. Just, 'it's a tradition.'" Yitzhak explained that,
by contrast, Berg's teaching enabled him to "study and understand what is

behind all those customs," as well as "the deepest meaning of being a Jew and what is the deepest meaning of life." Thus, these students feel that they restore their bond with Judaism while strongly refusing to engage in religious observance when justified by the rule of "tradition." Noa, a full-time volunteer in Tel Aviv, summarizes: "sometimes in religion it's a feeling that you have to do it. But in Kabbalah and spirituality you don't have to do anything. You need to learn why and then you will want to do it." Noa's view clearly echoes discourses on "Eastern spirituality" versus "West = Christianity" observed among students of neo-Hinduism. Partly secularized, Eyal, Yitzhak, and Noa became committed and observant students on the understanding that it was the result of their own personal choice and not the obligation of respecting traditions. Interestingly, I found that some students have been attracted at some point by the Chabad-Lubavitch movement's revivalism and Kabbalistic teachings, but unsurprisingly they found this conservative environment too prescriptive.

The students who have become observant Jews in the Kabbalah Centre constitute the small inner core of the organization—teachers, full-time volunteers, and highly committed students. They often joined the Kabbalah Centre before its universalistic turn, when it played the role of a Jewish revival movement. I observed that these students are often Israeli, and some French students of Sephardic origin share similar trajectories. Indeed, Israelis who identify themselves as "secular" are actually characterized by a higher level of religiosity that one would think, partly because religious symbols and norms permeate Israel's national culture (Ben Rafael and Sharot 1991; Liebman 1990). As for Sephardic Jews, they migrated from North Africa to Israel, France, or Canada in the 1960s and despite being affected by secularization as well, their strong familial and community ties have contributed to their maintaining a certain level of observance (Ben Rafael and Sharot 1991, 99). In other words, the Kabbalah Centre's small inner core is made of *the most traditional of the secular Jews* (this is confirmed by the fact that I did not meet any student who had an Orthodox background). This explains why, despite being disenfranchised from Jewish institutions, these students could become observant and committed on a fairly long-term basis in the Kabbalah Centre. Yet, paradoxically, this minority of followers with the highest level of observance and commitment remain extremely ambivalent toward Judaism. Disappointed by their religious upbringing, they are very dismissive of mainstream congregations and communities. They are attracted by Kabbalah *as a (Jewish) alternative to Judaism as a religion.* This approach of the Kabbalah Centre in Israel can be compared to the research of Haenni and Voix (2006) and Philippon (2014), who found that in Morocco and Pakistan, respectively, an educated, westernized middle class explore Sufism as an alternative to Muslim traditions that they find rigid, ritualistic, and dogmatic. In this case, the Sufism they explore either developed in Euroamerican societies, or is permeated by the values and practices of Euroamerican New Age.

By and large, the Kabbalah Centre's Jewish students all share this rejection of religious institutions and norms for which Kabbalah is an alternative. However, most of them do not reach the level of observance and commitment of the inner circle of the movement. They even sometimes feel challenged by the Kabbalah Centre's relative orthopraxy. Ranit is a designer; she was raised in Israel by parents of Tunisian origins. She has been a member of the Kabbalah Centre for five years. She recalls her first Shabbat with the movement as being "very scary": "you think, "shit, they try to make me religious!" It took her a year to join the Kabbalah Centre for Shabbat. The involvement of these secular students in religious practices proves to be challenging. During my fieldwork, Ranit often told me how uncomfortable she feels about particular devotional songs and practices, up to the point that she would make sure to come late at Shabbat to skip them—just as neo-Hindu followers leave before the devotional darshan. While Ranit refused to join her parents for Passover because they are not religious and "will not do things in the right way," she still found it difficult to keep Shabbat herself, not without expressing guilt and hesitations. She would often ask me questions to know whether *I* was respecting Shabbat's and festivals' rules, in order to compare and evaluate her own level of observance. Ranit's resistances and hesitations are not exceptional among the Kabbalah Centre's Jewish students. Many expressed their reluctance (if not "fear") to engage in the Centre's religious practices at first, thereby shedding light on the conflicting relationships that these secular students have with religion.

Accordingly, for most secular Jews, it seems that the Kabbalah Centre remains "too Jewish" (as too religious), as evidenced by the overall small number of followers of the Kabbalah Centre, as well as its minuscule retention rate. Nathalie is a 40-year-old Londoner; she has been involved in the Kabbalah Centre for four years. She was brought up in a non-Orthodox Jewish family having Shabbat Friday meals, and celebrating some of the festivals. Yet, Nathalie was at first reluctant to attend a course on Kabbalah when she was told about it: "if there was a lecture organized in Golders Green on Kabbalah by a Jewish rabbi I would not be attracted to go, but if Tony Robbins did an NLP seminar[14] I would go to that," she summed up. Drawn into personal growth techniques and spiritual teachings, she nevertheless attended an open class at the Kabbalah Centre. She found the theme interesting and the teacher's discourse not "conflicting"—"not a truth which is too exclusive," like "you must keep Shabbat or you'll be, you know, God will be very unhappy." In other words, she did not hear a religious discourse—the Kabbalah Centre teachers avoid referring to Judaism or religion in general in their lectures in order to reassure both the non-Jewish and the secular Jewish audiences. Nathalie now comes regularly to the Kabbalah Centre for Shabbat and festivals; however, she would gladly avoid them and reckons that "it could be to do with the connotations I have had in the past with going to the synagogue, and I don't really like rules, and although no one tells me I have to go, it is a weekly structure that I resist." In other words, because it relates to her religious background, the religious dimensions of the Kabbalah Centre remain a place of struggle. However, Nathalie finds the teaching useful in relation to personal growth: "I go to Synagogue [the Kabbalah Centre] on Saturday and listen to the Torah on Saturday mornings. It is very hard for me to do that but I do it because I believe and I experience that it brings me some energy." Nathalie does not accept practices and norms as a way of strengthening her bond with Judaism, but as means to an end. It is a pragmatic attitude that we already have identified as part of the process of domestication of exotic religious resources. It is encouraged by the Kabbalah Centre, whose teachers constantly stress that rituals and festivals are not performed because they are traditional, but because they are efficient "tools" to draw the Light of the Creator. For instance, Daren, another student of Jewish origins in London, refused to come to the Kabbalah Centre on Saturday morning for a long time, but he "understood" and "felt" that coming and listening to the Torah at Shabbat was an opportunity to receive more energy: "I keep Shabbat, but purely because I understand that I get a download of energy that will make my week a thousand times better than if I just go and play golf or tennis [instead]." Pragmatism is again core to religious exoticism: Daren considers Kabbalah to be "a very, very powerful system...which is the reason why I'm doing it."

I believe that highly observant students keep Judaism's rituals and commandments, on the basis of the same arguments regarding the connection to the Light of the Creator. However their desire to strengthen their bond with Judaism is not matched by the majority of secular students like Nathalie or Daren. By and large, this large fraction of the Kabbalah Centre's membership reflects the characteristics of secular Jews' relation to religion today—low level of observance, lack of belief in central tenets, highly selective and variable patterns of observance, severely diminished interest in the organizational life of the Jewish community, and expectation of a non-judgmental and less hierarchical Judaism (Cohen and Eisen 2000; Greenberg, 2007; Sharot 1991; Waxman 2003). Secular Jewish students of the Kabbalah Centre share with its non-Jewish audience a quest for a spiritual teaching outside the realms of mainstream religious authorities, where they can select the "tools" that they find useful without being expected to become observant. And this includes religious resources outside the Kabbalah Centre. Nathalie, for instance, continues to use meditation techniques that she learned from Transcendental Meditation and is still interested in personal growth techniques. Overall, the spiritual and therapeutic incursions of secular Jewish students of Kabbalah are sometimes as diverse and plural as those of non-Jewish students.

Inclusive Kabbalah

In sum, apart from the small inner core of the movement, both Jewish and non-Jewish students have exoticized Kabbalah as an authentic and primordial "spirituality" that was lost but whose mysteries can finally be discovered on the basis of individuals' free will. All embrace the Kabbalah Centre's teaching despite its Jewish rituals and norms. However, non-Jewish students are uncomfortable with the Kabbalah Centre's Jewishness, as religious (a coercive and constraining polar opposite of "spirituality") and as other. Indeed, the ways in which Judaism inspires antipathy in some cases shed light on non-Jewish students' discomfort with this religion. Jewish students of Kabbalah clearly express a similar rejection of religious forms of authorities. Their relation to Kabbalah Centre's Jewishness is different, yet also conflicted. It is undoubtedly a source of comfort and familiarity, but at the same time, Jewish particularism is rejected as a tribalism at odds with the modern universalistic ethos, and is implicitly feared as the locus of stigmatization.

Daren is 38, he is a successful professional in the London finance milieu; he has been following the Kabbalah Centre's teaching for more than four years. Beforehand, Daren never had any interest in "spirituality" or religion and was disinterested in his religious upbringing; "I'm born Jewish. I had a bar mitzvah like everyone else, but it had no meaning for me." Yet, when someone mentioned to him they were studying at the Kabbalah Centre, it clicked: "I can't explain in a logical sense, but when I heard the word Kabbalah, I was totally, wow, I have to find out more." I assume Kabbalah evoked esoteric knowledge and hidden mysteries, but the fact that it relates to Judaism was clearly significant:

> I think for myself being Jewish, knowing that *this doesn't compromise my Jewishness* makes a very big difference. I think the fact that I'm Jewish is very convenient. Because in Kabbalah, they teach that whatever your religion, whatever your background, it empowers you to become better in that realm, so if I was Catholic, maybe I would still study Kabbalah,

and maybe I wouldn't care that I was Catholic and I still wouldn't go to church, the same way as I never went to synagogue. And, but that I am Jewish, and that there is *a lot of overlap*, it gives you a *warm fuzzy feeling*; you know I'm familiar with Hebrew for example, and it's just maybe a little *closer to home*.

Daren has never been observant and, as mentioned earlier, first resisted attending Shabbat on Saturday mornings. Yet, the Kabbalah Centre's Jewishness is for him critical: it is about familiarity with the liturgy (in fact, being a Jewish man allows Daren to contribute to the performance of rituals) but also loyalty to his Jewish identity. Similarly, Robin, 52, has been involved in the London Kabbalah Centre for five years. He broke away from a relatively traditional Jewish education as a young adult and is not observant. The Kabbalah Centre's Jewishness is nonetheless important to him, he says, because "the connection with the Torah and the Zohar gives me the connection to my origins. I feel that, because I am Jewish, that my soul, you know, belongs with the Torah." Robin now feels "passionate about the Torah," and the Shabbat services at the Kabbalah Centre allow him to experience this bond: "when I go up to the ark and the ark opens, that is a channel to me, the letters, the whole energy of the Torah is the energy that I draw on."

Jewish students of the Kabbalah Centre do find the movement's Jewishness significant, but it is also a source of difficulties. We noted earlier that Nathalie, for instance, was repelled by the idea of joining a Jewish movement studying Kabbalah. Yet, regarding the movement's Jewish roots, she too admits that "there is a comfort factor, but I would rather that there wasn't. I would like to say that even without the comfort factor it wouldn't make any difference. It is a bit like a *nice bonus*." Thus, while acknowledging the importance of the Kabbalah Centre's Jewishness for her, Nathalie would wish it to be insignificant, for the following reasons:

> It is quite important to me that everyone has the opportunity to study Kabbalah because I think it makes a difference, so *I wouldn't want my Judaism to get in the way of that* and I don't buy into it being *exclusively Jewish* which is why I wouldn't support a . . . I am not interested enough into the pure study of Kabbalah, in the theoretical study of Kabbalah, to go to a lecture like that.

During the interview, Nathalie stresses her Jewish identity, which she also sees as potentially conflicting with the universal and inclusive teaching of

Kabbalah. In fact, not only did she reject Judaism as religious observance and norms, but also as particularism:

> I've never been a big fan of religion particularly, although I am Jewish, and I wouldn't say I am not Jewish. It is kind of an odd thing but, I am not particularly a fan of what it creates. So I was a bit reticent [about coming to the Kabbalah Centre] because I had listened to sermons over the years about, you know from my rabbi about, I don't exactly know what it said but it was things like Jews stick together and all that sort of stuff, which I understand on the one hand but you know it was *against my feeling that there should be world peace and unity*, you know this kind of dream.

Nathalie's interview echoes the childhood memories of other students, who also refuse to consider their Jewish identity as a particular and exclusive marker. For example, Moshe, a Kabbalah Centre teacher, remembers being very upset by a rabbi who told him that non-Jews had no soul. By and large, there is a clear rejection among Jewish interviewees of a sense of difference and separation between Jews and non-Jews.[15] And this rejection of Judaism's particularism is paradoxically shared by those who acknowledge that the Jewish origins of the Kabbalah Centre represent a source of comfort for them. Therefore, in some ways they expect the Kabbalah Centre to be Jewish and not Jewish at the same time. Ben, a young artist I met during a party organized by the London Centre, illustrates this ambivalence. Ben presented himself to me as coming from a Jewish family established in the East End for 300 years. He was educated in a religious school but, he insisted, he always wanted to see everyone love each other, whatever their religion or race. It is the Kabbalah Centre's Jewishness and inclusiveness that made it for him: "when I discovered that these people were doing everything 100 percent, that they connect to my tradition and there was love for everyone, that was it."

Overall, the Kabbalah Centre's Jewishness is a "nice bonus," at the same time as Jewish students praise its inclusiveness. This explains why, by comparison, those who frequented the Chabad-Lubavitch movement could not join it. As mentioned earlier, unsurprisingly, Chabad proved to be too orthodox for the religious individualism of the Kabbalah Centre. But it was not the only reason that was invoked. Robin, for instance, frequented Chabad in London a few times and emphasized that they were not welcoming for those who are not Jewish, which in his case would exclude his wife and children. By contrast, in the Kabbalah Centre he appreciates "it wasn't full of just Jewish people." Arthur, a Londoner whose grandfather was a rabbi, found Chabad's teaching "amazing" and similar to the Kabbalah Centre's, "except it has not been made available for everybody," and he "never really liked being part of anything that was so exclusive that everybody else was blocked out" (incidentally, like Robin, Arthur's wife is not Jewish). Arthur echoes Nathalie's hopes for world peace and harmony: "the thing I like about the Centre is that it crosses all the religions and therefore has the potential to tie all of these religions under a solid umbrella that makes sense of all of the religions. So, the potential for harmony is great, and the potential for peace is great."

During interviews and informal talks, Kabbalah Centre's Jewish students recurrently stress the movement's inner diversity and the universality of its teaching, which has the effect of de-emphasizing, if not refuting, the Kabbalah Centre's Jewishness. Understandably, the movement's universalistic claims make both non-Jewish and Jewish students comfortable, albeit from a different perspective: the former refusing to embrace Judaism, the later refusing to be exclusive Jews. Daren, while having a "warm fuzzy feeling" about the Centre's Jewishness, also praises the fact that "within the Centre, there's a tremendous cross-spectrum of society, there is absolutely everyone and everything" so that the friendships I have are multinational, multi-age, multicultural. It's much richer." Jane is Jewish and has always been celebrating festivals and Shabbat Friday meals with her family. Her sons were raised in the Jewish tradition and were bar mitzvahed. When I met her for the first time at the London Kabbalah Centre, the very first thing she told me was how much she loved the diversity of the Centre. It is something she forcefully reiterated during an interview, alongside her discomfort with apartness: "it's universal. I ... I am not comfortable with anything that is exclusive, I like to think of an all-encompassing God who is not discriminating against anyone." This is why Jane believes that the Kabbalah Centre's Jewish roots were not determinant for her, although she recognizes being familiar with its norms and practices.

Jewish students' appreciation of the Kabbalah Centre as a Jewish but above all inclusive environment reflects larger issues that affect modern Jewry. The apartness of Jewish communities in pre- and early modern times generated "historical familism" (Cohen and Eisen 2000, 103–104), that is to say, a focus on the collective memory of a particular people, hence the sense of "being different" as Jews, "mutual responsibility," and negative perception of non-Jews. However, Jews' progressive integration and successful social mobility in contemporary Euroamerican societies have made Jewish particularism less and less meaningful. Fully integrated Jewries do not need close communal cohesion in order to survive in hostile societies anymore (Greenberg 2007). Rather, historical familism has been increasingly rejected by Jewish communities like other segregating and stigmatizing attitudes that can prevent their acceptance. Indeed, one of the main anti-Semitic arguments referred to Jews'

alleged apartness and unassimilability. As such, they often have been viewed
as unable to participate in the universal progress of society (Fine 2012). By
and large, Jews' integration has often entailed downplaying their Jewishness
in public, even if the rise of ethno-politics and a successful integration now
enable Jewish identity-claims and visibility in particular contexts (Cohen and
Eisen 2000; Gidley and Kahn-Harris 2010; Stratton 2000). Finally, rejection of Jewish familism is also entailed by the contemporary process of secularization. Increasingly involved in mixed marriages, disenfranchised from
religious communities, secular Jews have found less meaning in this particularism, which they find at odds with the values of universalism and cosmopolitanism. Interestingly, Jewish youth who started to join NRMs during the
counterculture highlighted "feelings of alienation from a Judaism which was
seen as familial, particularistic, and ethnically distinctive" (Selengut 1988,
104). In fact, Selengut stresses the appeal of religious teachings presented as
universal among Jewish members of NRMs, looking for a "new religious consciousness" and a new ethos of peace and social justice: "it always bothered
me that Judaism was only for the Jews; redemption should be for all people,"
a Jewish-born member of the Unification church said to him (p. 104), thereby
echoing the universal ethos of the Kabbalah Centre's Jewish students. Cohen
and Kelman (2007, 20) found that Jews who are today disenfranchised from
synagogues and Jewish organizations criticize them for being "claustro-
phobic" and exclusive and see their divisions between social classes, Jewish
denominations, and between Jews and non-Jews as reflecting "prejudice, if
not racism."

Accordingly, as an NRM, the Kabbalah Centre is in a sense "adequate" for
its Jewish students: it "connects" them to their Jewishness *and* is universalistic, inclusive and diverse at the same time. Eyal, who has taught Kabbalah
for many years, is fully aware of the cardinal significance of its universality for
its Jewish audience:

> The message is that the messages of Kabbalah are universal, and you
> have to understand first of all why that's so important, because most
> Jews do not feel comfortable in a small, little place, "us against them."
> It's like maybe the ghetto, the Jews are out but the ghetto is inside the
> Jews. And this has to be over. And most Jews do not want to relate to
> that. That's why they can't find themselves in many, in most Jewish
> communities. Because most Jews around the world are not part of a
> Jewish community anymore. So one goal that I have is that Kabbalah
> can give a solution because it's universal, it goes with science, it fits
> with modern universalism and humanism.

In other words, teaching Kabbalah to everyone regardless of their creed is also a means to claim progressive and humanistic values—openness, egalitarianism, cosmopolitanism, and multiculturalism, to which Nathalie's ideals about "world peace and unity" implicitly referred. Thus, Jewish students seek in the Kabbalah Centre a positive Judaism of which Kabbalistic teaching can make the world a better place; but it is a positive Judaism because of being non-ethnic, depoliticized, universal, and hence welcoming to Jews and non-Jews alike. It is crucial at this point to remember that the anti-Semitic discourse sees Kabbalah as an occult knowledge that Jews keep for themselves, as illustrated by Madame Blavatsky in Chapter 1. Accordingly, one of the greatest paradoxes of the involvement in the Kabbalah Centre is that it leads its Jewish students to refute to a certain extent the Jewishness of the movement, its liturgy and its Kabbalistic system of thought, as well as to keep their personal Jewish identity intimate and invisible so that it does not "get in the way," as Nathalie put it. Thus, the Kabbalah Centre can be seen as a form of neo-marranism, through which Judaism is performed and partly concealed, if not refuted.

For assimilated Jews disenfranchised from Jewish institutions, this particularism may implicitly be perceived as the attribute of tribal, pre-modern, and inassimilable communities, from which they want to maintain distance. Robin, who feels his soul "belongs with the Torah," provided me with an unforgettable answer when I asked him why he stopped going to Chabad: "I would not want to be *Jewished*," he replied, referring to ultra-Orthodox communities' affirmed, hence visible, Jewishness. Strikingly, Robin's refusal to be "Jewished" cannot but echo non-Jewish students' desire to be a bit Jewish but certainly not "really" Jewish. They are, in both cases, a refusal to identify with Judaism, albeit for different reasons. Invisibility has been one of the necessities of Jews' assimilation. The "assimilationist bargain" has meant for Jews in Western Europe and North America the need to find a balance between reducing the scope and visibility of their Jewishness, on the one hand, and to find new modes of expression and identity to exist as Jews, on the other (Cohen 1983: 25; Stratton 2000: 101). In this regard, the Kabbalah Centre can be seen as one expression among others of this assimilationist bargain: its universalism redefines Judaism as positive, modern, and assimilable, at the same time as it allows its members to feel part of a non-Jewish, cosmopolitan, and even glamorous organization. Interestingly, those who do seek to strengthen their bonds with Judaism in the Kabbalah Centre denounce the attitude of concealing the teaching's Jewishness as a form of self-hatred, an internalized anti-Semitism, especially when it is encouraged by the movement's leaders in order to accommodate non-Jewish students. As we shall see in the next chapter, the universalistic strategy that conceals the Kabbalah Centre's Jewish roots is a source of tension and scission in the movement.

Ultimately, it is through this attempt to avoid the stigma of Jewish particularism and be proud of cosmopolitan and progressive values *as Jews* that we can fully understand the significance of celebrities in the Kabbalah Centre. From a pragmatic point of view, these wealthy students are certainly crucial in supporting the movement financially. But by studying Kabbalah, celebrities made a branch of Judaism inclusive, cool, and exciting and gave Judaism a positive public image. In this regard, the significance of Madonna's travels and pilgrimages to Jewish sacred places in Israel, her meeting with President Shimon Peres during which she presented herself as an "ambassador for Judaism" (Weizman 2007), and the use of the Israeli flag and of Jewish religious symbols during her concert should not be underestimated. However, at the same time, Madonna's involvement profiles the Kabbalah Centre as glamorous and positively de-emphasizes the movement's Jewishness.

Synthesis

Despite the appeal of Eastern wisdom and Kabbalistic mysteries, the teachings of neo-Hindu movements and the Kabbalah Centre are adopted in spite of their Hindu/Jewish character, which in fact has the effect of limiting their popularization. Even the Kabbalah Centre's Jewish students express a certain resistance to rituals and commandments and share with Western neo-Hindus and Christian Kabbalists an ambivalence toward the movement's Jewishness, albeit for different reasons. In other words, the popularization of Kabbalistic and Hindu-based teachings is eased by their de-linking from their specific cultural and religious roots—and this is reflected in the official discourse of Siddha Yoga, the Sivananda Centres, and the Kabbalah Centre, as the next chapter will show.

The implications of the ways in which neo-Hindu and Kabbalistic teachings are adopted in practices of bricolage are many. First, religious exoticism involves the fetishization and the aestheticization of religious resources. It is not Hinduism or Judaism as such that is sought, but the mystical East and Kabbalistic secrets that are foreign, mysterious and ancient. Less than an interest in what is different, this fetishization values exotic religious resources as polar opposites of, and complementary to, the materialistic, secular and problem-ridden West. This is the reason that attraction for "authentic others" does not equate to a desire of becoming this other through conversion or drastic change of lifestyle. On the contrary, in its ways of envisaging cultural and religious differences, exoticism is actually very self-referential: it is about finding one's true self, achieving fulfillment, and reclaiming the values of one's religious background through foreign religious traditions.

Second, this is the reason that exoticism necessary rests on the ignorance of the other (Todorov 1993). This was well illustrated by representations of spiritual and timeless India, dismissive of the modern features of Indian society, or trips in Israel through which new Kabbalists immerse themselves in biblical times. Similarly, interest in Native American shamanic practices does not involve any concern or interest in the socioeconomic and political problems encountered by these indigenous peoples (Kehoe 2000, 94). More important, Hinduism and Judaism, as practiced by Hindu and Jewish communities, are ignored; they are supplanted by an "Eastern spirituality" and a non-Jewish Kabbalah. For Todorov, the refusal to see others cannot be seen as a celebration of otherness, and leads us to the third feature of religious exoticism: its ambivalence. Fetishization of and aversion for otherness coexist, as evidenced by neo-Hindus' feeling of being interlopers, dismissive attitudes toward Kabbalah's Jewish roots, resistance to Hindu and Jewish rituals, and peripheral and short-term involvements in Siddha Yoga, the Sivananda Centre, and the Kabbalah Centre. The exploration of westernized forms of Sufism, Buddhism, and shamanism is also, more often than not, short-term and non-exclusive; it is justified by the belief in a primordial and universal tradition (Lindquist 1997; Philippon 2014; Vazeilles 2008).

Fourth, because of this repulsion, religious exoticism entails the "domestication of the foreign and unpredictable" to render them familiar and safe (Foster 1982, 21). The process of domestication therefore entails the de-contextualization of these resources, that is to say their de-linking from their original religious and cultural framework (Appadurai 1986, 28 talks about "commoditization by diversion"). Thus, neo-Hindu teachings are adopted as part of a universal and culturally undifferentiated Eastern "spirituality," which does not require observance, is positively modernized, and is adaptable to individual needs. Similarly, Kabbalah is appropriated as a non-Jewish, non-religious, universal "spirituality." Both neo-Hinduism and Kabbalah are used as pools of efficient techniques for personal growth (see Chapter 5). This process of domestication is observable in the popularization of other exotic religious resources. When embraced and spread by individuals of non-Muslim origins, Sufism, for example, has often been "divorced from its Islamic framework and used as techniques in human transformation" (Taji-Farouki 2007, 405); it is then presented as universal and is sometimes combined with non-Muslim teachings. Taji-Farouki notes that the students of this "universal Sufism," as the author calls it, are generally not born-Muslims and tend not to convert to Islam. The recent popularization of Daoism took a similar route. Originating in Chinese closed agrarian society, "Daoism as a comprehensive cultural package is not yet a real option for the West" notes Clarke (2000, 204). Yet, while its diffusion has not been as significant as Hinduism and Buddhism, Daoism was also de-contextualized and adapted to fulfill demands, ranging from health to interior decorating (Feng Shui).

Fifth, exoticism can be seen as one of the many effects of secularization and certainly does not disprove the existence of such process, even at an individual level. Neo-Hinduism and Kabbalah are desired to be malleable, tolerant, and non-prescriptive "spiritualities" that one can freely choose, by contrast with "organized religions" associated with norms, authority, and constraints. It is on this basis only that most social actors explore these exotic religious resources. Ambivalence toward otherness and religious institutions' loss of authority both result in plural, short-term, and superficial involvement in neo-Hinduism, Kabbalah, Buddhism (Coleman 2001, 16, 121), Sufism (Hermansen 2004; Westerlund 2004), or shamanism (Lindquist 1997, 263).

We now understand bricolage in a new light. Mary (1994) is right to differentiate this "exotic" bricolage from the syncretism of indigenous populations in colonial and missionary contexts. In the latter, bricolage is not "chosen," but results from unequal power relations through which new symbolic resources are associated with the West's domination. This bricolage does generate "free" and unlimited combinations; it is made of dialogues, compromises, and resistances that are constrained and shaped by the original meaning of religious resources. By contrast, the religious exoticism I have described is not the result of relations of domination whereby Euroamericans become subdued by other cultures, imposed or perceived as superior. On the contrary, ethnocentric fetishization, the desire to select and instrumentalize detached elements of other religions and to ignore these religions as practiced, and the distaste provoked by these religions, all point toward the reverse of uneven power relations. However, I disagree with a depiction of the "postmodern collage" through which individuals are believed to elaborate personalized identities, indifferent to the cultural and religious frames of resources that they combine—hence a bricolage free from ambivalence and contradiction. Why would there be feelings of resistance, rejection, and transgression otherwise? These feelings, as well as the limited expansion of not only neo-Hindu movements and the Kabbalah Centre but also Daoism, Sufism, and Buddhism, demonstrate that *otherness matters*. And it is precisely because it matters that religious resources are de-contextualized to fulfill contemporary Euroamerican desires and expectations which, in turn, are not free from "pre-constraints."

3

Universalizing and De-contextualizing Exotic Religious Resources

THE PRECEDING CHAPTERS suggested that while exotic religious resources are idealized, social actors wrestle with feelings of discomfort relating to their foreignness. They overcome these feelings by considering neo-Hindu and Kabbalistic teachings as acultural and universal, and by "slanting them for their own needs," as an interviewee put it. As we shall see, this means appropriating them as techniques for self-realization. In other words, Vedanta is more attractive if partially detached from Hindu institutions, rituals, and culture, just as Kabbalah is often appropriated as a non-Jewish teaching.

This chapter describes the ways in which religious leaders have played an active role in making possible such an appropriation of exotic religious resources. As neo-Hindu movements started to target a primarily non-Indian audience and the Kabbalah Centre began to teach non-Jews, they increasingly presented their teachings as universal and as transcending their respective Hindu and Jewish roots. In order to be able to include everyone, regardless of nationality, religion, and culture, they refused to be identified as Jewish or Hindu. They abandoned their aim to revitalize Hinduism and Judaism, respectively. They reinterpreted central doctrines that make them traditional ethnic religions as well as the significance of rituals. In other words, important processes of interpretation and innovation enable practices of bricolage to be developed. These processes of universalization and de-contextualization are not innocuous; they affect religious tenets, identities, and rationales, and as such, they are potential sources of tensions within religious organizations. Again, such risky and arduous processes of domestication show that in religious exoticism, otherness matters tremendously.

Universal Ambitions and the Denial of
Particular Roots

As they have spread transnationally, some neo-Hindu movements and the Kabbalah Centre have presented themselves as universal while downplaying, if not denying, the Hindu or Jewish origins of the teaching they aim to offer to the world. Hinduism and Judaism certainly proselytized at some points in their history (Sharma 1992; Sharot 2001, 9; Tapper 2002, 28 n.87). Nevertheless, this is a remarkable shift for revivalist movements whose original aims had to do with the affirmation of a particularistic identity. In Hacker's (Halbfass 1995, 233) view, for instance, the chief impulse of the neo-Hindu way of thinking was nationalism; its mission in the West thus reflected the affirmation of an Indian role in the world, in response to Western imperialism and Christian proselytism. Kabbalah hoped to win back secular Jews and rebuild vibrant Jewish communities in the postwar world. In other words, religious movements that were driven by concerns with their particular identities ceased to identify with Hinduism and Judaism, respectively, and de-linked their teaching from the ethnic dimensions of these religious traditions.

When "East" and "West" Merge

Universalism has always been part of neo-Hindu thinking. Neo-Hinduism was, paradoxically, an affirmation of a Hindu identity, a response to the universalistic claims of Western thought itself, which claimed a universalism of its own (Halbfass 1988, 173). This trend is obvious in the neo-Hindu counter-mission in the West: there, Vivekananda avoided referring to his guru, Ramakrishna. His aim was to avoid personalizing and particularizing his message and to develop a universalistic rhetoric. Vivekananda drew on the idea of a universal religion that had already been addressed by Ram Mohun Roy, the Unitarians, and the Theosophists. His concept was nonetheless versatile; it sometimes referred to the diversity of religions, their timeless nature, their unity, or their complementarity (Sharma 1998, 54–65). Interestingly, his "universal religion" also designated a non-particularistic, non-cultural entity, an idea that is recurrent in the rhetoric of contemporary de-ethnicizing religious teachings. This is

> one which will have no location in place or time; which will be infinite like the God it will preach, and...which will not be Brahminic or Buddhistic, Christian or Mohammedan, but the sum total of all these. (Vivekananda 1965, 19)

Thus, there would be a universal religion that transcends differences and particularisms. However, the assertion of a Hindu identity is also characteristic of
neo-Hinduism: Vivekananda presented Vedanta as this universal religion that
stands above history and culture.

> We may remark that this is the unique position in India, our claim is
> that the Vedanta only can be the universal religion, that it is already the
> existing universal religion in the world, because it teaches principles
> and not persons. No religion built upon a person can be taken up as a
> type by all the races of mankind. (cited in Sharma 1998, 63)

Here, Vedanta is implicitly contrasted with Abrahamic religions and their
reverence for prophets. Vedanta is presented as unique in its non-historical
and non-cultural nature, which by the same token detaches it from India and
Hinduism. Yet Vivekananda's universalistic discourse does not dilute but
affirms Hinduism by asserting its inclusiveness and its universalism. In other
words, universalism and affirmation of a particular identity are combined in
Vivekananda's presentation of Vedanta as a meta-religion:

> Ours, as I have said, is the universal religion. It is inclusive enough, it
> is broad enough to include all the ideals. All the ideals of religion that
> already exist in the world can be immediately included, and we can pa-
> tiently wait for all the ideals that are to come in the future to be taken in
> the same fashion, embraced in the infinite arms of the religion of the
> *Vedanta.* (Vivekananda 1964, 251–252)

Vivekananda's presentation of Vedanta in Europe and America is of paramount
importance, because it heavily influenced and impregnated the teaching of
twentieth century gurus who, like him, sought to disseminate their teachings
outside India. For instance, we find in Sivananda's presentation of his organization, the Divine Life Society, a similar discourse. It is "an all-embracing and
all-inclusive institution" whose "objects, ideals and aims are very broad and
universal" and which "includes all the fundamental principles of all religions
and cults" (Sivananda 2000 [1958]). The inclusiveness of Sivananda's teaching
also relies on the idea that only one truth lies beneath the diverse religious
traditions and that "all religions are one." Nonetheless, the only universal,
eternal religion is Vedanta itself (Sivananda 1998 [1947]). Sivananda's writings on Hinduism, Vedanta, and yoga are very often apologetic. They emphasize India's unique and preeminent "spirituality," as opposed to the West's
materialistic culture. This "spirituality" would be the means by which India's

national life is purified and strengthened. In fact, Sivananda's discourses significantly contributed to Indian nationalism (McKean 1996, 164–171).

Neo-Hindu movements that spread in Euroamerican societies in the 1960s onward partially departed from this particularistic and proto-nationalist feature of neo-Hinduism. For instance, in the organization he created on his behalf, Vishnu Devananda did not emphasize Sivananda's apology of India. Vishnu Devananda wrote very little himself; he rather referred to the writings of his guru, today largely available in the Sivananda Centres, yet I found that those of Sivananda's texts discussed during satsangs at the Sivananda Centres or published in their magazine *YOGALife* usually address issues of individual spiritual path rather than the glory of Hinduism. In his initiatives to disseminate Sivananda's teaching, Vishnu Devananda focused on a practical teaching of yoga, which he presented as a means to unite people and reach world peace.

Contemporary gurus who, like Vishnu Devananda, predominantly targeted Euroamerican disciples and lived outside India on a long-term basis or permanently, took distance from the neo-Hindu concern with India's identity and role in the world. Instead, they amplified their universalistic discourse by insisting on unity and denying the significance of national, religious, and cultural differences. In this regard, the motto of the Sivananda Centres, "unity in diversity," by reference to Vivekananda (1968, 175–188) who also used this expression, is far from being irrelevant. Sri Chinmoy (1931–2007), a guru who started his movement in New York in the 1970s by teaching meditation to United Nations staff, provides us with a good example of this universalistic rhetoric:

> There are not as many differences as we think between eastern religion and western religion. We are all children of God. We speak different languages, but when it is about the heart…we are all in tune….And the true spirituality does not know any geographical barrier, neither East, not West, South or North. (Sri Chinmoy n.d., my translation)

Here, the idea of a universal religion, associated with monotheism, seems to undermine the differences between religions. It also de-emphasizes the polar opposition between "East" and "West" that was central to Vivekananda's approach and thereby attenuates the distinctiveness of the "East." Muktananda, for instance, had a very similar discourse:

> Those who have little understanding think that one country is different from another, but all countries are his, all paths are his, all languages

are his, and all men are his relatives. In God's house there is no particular religion, or sect or faith. To Him, all are the same. (Muktananda
1996, 112)

It is important to note that contemporary gurus such as Muktananda and
Sri Chinmoy have been very prolific writers and sometimes made contradictory claims—similar remarks have been made about the teachings of Sahaja
Yoga's guru, Sri Mataji (Coney 1995, 115), and Rajneesh (Carter 1990, 124). So it
is the case that these gurus sometimes *also* continue to attribute to their teachings specific virtues that compensate for Westerners' particular needs: "My
teachings are helpful not only on an individual level, but also on a universal
level," said Muktananda. "For instance, in America only one thing is lacking,
and that is mental peace—a balanced state of mind" (Muktananda 1978, 24).
Nonetheless, the amplification of neo-Hindu universalistic rhetoric (to such
an extent that it refutes Hinduism's uniqueness) represents a significant shift
from Vivekananda's and Sivananda's approach and is typical among contemporary gurus who settled outside India. For example, Muktananda amends the
significance of cultural and religious diversity to the extent that he rejects the
idea of a link between his teaching and India, for fear that such a link would
reduce its universal dimension. In a book of interviews and conversations that
mainly took place in the United States between Muktananda and his disciples,
the guru is asked if it is necessary to believe in Indian religious traditions to
receive *shaktipat* (in Siddha Yoga, the awakening of the *kundalini-shakti*, an
inner energy). Muktananda answers that this is not the case, since all religious
traditions are identical. In addition,

Shaktipat is not exactly a religious phenomenon. If it is a religion, then
it is a religion that transcends religions. It is not the monopoly of the
Indian religious tradition. Shaktipat is something that in earlier times
was also a part of the Christian tradition. (Muktananda 1994, 40)

By claiming that Siddha Yoga is not a religion, Muktananda reassures the
countercultural youth who were critical of their religious education and clearly
responds to the ambivalence of Euroamerican disciples toward Hinduism. It
is therefore not surprising that Muktananda insisted on refuting the Hindu
character of his teachings when he discussed the rituals in Siddha Yoga:

It's only because you don't know the Indian language that you consider these rituals as part of the Hindu religion. If you understood
the meaning of the chants, you would begin to feel that they were

yours.... Only the language belongs to India. But the real meaning, the essence, is not India, nor does it belong to any other country. If someone sang this in English, should I then say that it belongs only to the Christian tradition?...I haven't brought anything new to America; whatever I brought is already here. Kundalini Shakti is already within you.... So what have I brought from India? (Muktananda 1978, 39–40)

It is not so certain that Muktananda actually does not give any significance to Indian language and culture. For example, an old-time disciple told me that once Muktananda became outraged by the suggestion made by a disciple to translate and chant Siddha yoga songs in English. Besides, part of the exoticization of foreign religions is to grant power to their practices and language: thus, it is also stated that "the vibrations emanating from repeating the names of God or chanting sacred Sanskrit texts have a tangible effect on our own inner being" (Siddha Yoga 2003). Note in passing that the Kabbalah Centre embraces the same rhetoric about the sound, energy, and pulse of Hebrew letters. In both cases, it encourages students to see these foreign languages as instruments of power that do not require understanding.

In the same vein, Muktananda's successor, Gurumayi, later claimed that "Siddha Yoga is not a religion but a way of life" (Brooks et al. 1997: 27, 592). Siddha Yoga is not an exception in this regard. Maharishi Mahesh Yoga, founder of Transcendental Meditation, claimed that India has a superior science of the soul in his early writing, before making his teaching transnational. Yet, in the 1970s, he distanced himself from Hinduism and presented his teaching as "the science of creative intelligence," "without the resistance invited by labeling his message 'Hindu,' or 'religious'" (Humes 2005, 65). Humes (2005, 66) quotes this fascinating abstract from the 1975 bestseller *The TM Book* written by TM teachers:

The TM program is not a religion? I've heard it was some Westernized form of Hinduism. No, no—it's absurd to assume that just because the TM technique comes from India it must be some Hindu practice.... The TM technique is a scientific discovery which happens to come from India.... The TM program does not involve any religious belief or practice—Hindu or otherwise.... Does TM conflict with any form of religion? No. People of any religion practice the TM technique.

TM declined in the 1980s (Bainbridge and Jackson 1981). Incidentally, and while it may not be the only cause, it is in this period that Maharishi Mahesh

Yogi started to refer more heavily to the Vedas and to ask his disciples to pay more respect to Hindu values and principles (Hume 2005).

To summarize, contemporary gurus who focused on a non-Indian audience have tended to present their teachings as meta-religions transcending religious traditions, including Hinduism itself. This can lead them, strikingly, to refute the Hindu origins and character of their teaching. Accordingly, the diffusion of neo-Hinduism outside Indian borders has entailed a de-contextualization process. By contrast, as we shall see later in this chapter, some contemporary gurus who live in India and have a significant proportion of disciples there developed a very particularistic and exclusivist discourse.

From the Revival to the Disavowal of Judaism

The Kabbalah Centre followed a similar trajectory to neo-Hindu movements such as Siddha Yoga and Sivananda Centres, by taking distance from its original revivalist goals and by presenting Kabbalah as a universal wisdom. Kabbalah was therefore "never meant to be just Jewish" (Y. Berg in *USAToday. com* 2004). In the previous chapter, we contextualized the Kabbalah Centre with other movements of Jewish revitalization which, in the second half of the twentieth century, tried to respond to the destruction of traditional Jewish communities and the undermining effects of secularization. Then, the Kabbalah Centre aimed to revitalize the observance of Judaism:

> Our Kabbalah classes help people define the world around them from a Judaic point of view and answer some of the esoteric questions *that conventional Judaism often overlooks.* Topics like the purpose of creation, the "Big Bang" theory, the effects of repentance, prayer and meditation, death and resurrection, cosmic-consciousness and Judaism, astrology, reincarnation, kabbalistic terminology and concepts, man's purpose and the messianic era are all intensely explored within the context of Jewish philosophy. (Brochure for introductory lessons, 1983, New York, my emphasis)

The Kabbalah Centre's position in relation to Judaism is clearly stated here: its primary aim is to show the relevance of Judaism for its members. Berg (2000, 57) wished that "all of Israel would return to religion": his teaching and writings thus endeavored to demonstrate the significance of Judaism's practices and to stimulate observance in "introduc[ing] the fiber of spirituality that is interwoven into each of the mitzvot" (cited in Lifschutz 1975, 17). Berg envisioned the Kabbalah Centre as offering what he believed was lacking in "conventional Judaism" and which could bring back younger generations into the fold of religion. Hence the reference to Kabbalah and other topics that, it was hoped, would attract a secularized audience. The Kabbalah Centre's adaptability and eclecticism would later develop greatly, but at the time, in order to demonstrate the significance of Judaism to young Jews attracted by Asian religions, Berg was eager to emphasize the differences between them by claiming Judaism's precedence and doctrinal superiority. For instance, the yin and yang's presentation of good and evil as part of the same reality proved to him that "[t]he Eastern mystic strives to transcend the realm of intellectual concepts" (P. Berg 1983, 98).

It was in the 1990s that the Kabbalah Centre started to dissociate itself from Judaism and adopt a universalistic rhetoric. This reflected a change in its diffusion goal: it ceased to be an Israeli movement focusing on secular Jews' return to observance and became a worldwide organization teaching individuals, regardless of their religious background. In a sense, the Kabbalah Centre could have remained a revitalization movement by converting its new students to Judaism, but precisely it did not. It started to present itself as not Jewish, but universal. The Kabbalah Centre is now introduced as

> the largest, leading educational organization on the wisdom of Kabbalah worldwide. Our purpose is to make accessible the ancient wisdom and tools of Kabbalah in order to illuminate the minds and hearts of individuals, groups, and organizations—regardless of faith, political belief, or race. Motivated by no other desire than the spiritual growth of humankind, the Kabbalah Centre...transforms people's lives by helping them understand and connect to the spiritual nature of the universe. (Kabbalah Centre 2004a)

The Kabbalah Centre's goals and identity no longer refer to Judaism, but insist on their inclusive and universal nature. Just as the orientalist idea of a universal and timeless Vedanta allowed Vivekananda to present it as a meta-religion, the Kabbalah Centre draws on long-held representations of Kabbalah that emerged with Christian Kabbalah, making this branch of Judaism a primordial and universal source of wisdom. Kabbalah is therefore "the world's oldest body of spiritual wisdom [which] contains the long-hidden keys to the secrets of the universe as well as the keys to the mysteries of the human heart and soul" (Living Kabbalah System 2006a). It becomes a timeless meta-religion, predating Judaism itself; it transcends race, religion, and politics, which are seen as being illusory and ephemeral distinctions (P. Berg 1987b, 152–158). Accordingly, like contemporary gurus, the Kabbalah Centre leaders refuse to "reduce" their teaching and associate it with the idea of religion itself. The Kabbalah Centre was certainly avant-garde in this rhetorical universalism but did strike a chord that many would later play: the reader of this book will have no difficulties finding teachings that call themselves "Universal Kabbalah" as opposed to "Jewish Kabbalah."[1]

This universal rhetoric is directly linked to potential students who do not identify with Judaism and paradoxically look for a non-Jewish Kabbalah. Thus, while it is acknowledged that "historically it is true that many of the kabbalists have been Jewish," Kabbalah is said to have practical applications for people of any faith, even those who do not have any religious affiliation. Echoing Siddha Yoga's gurus, Kabbalah becomes "a way of life that can enhance any religious practice" (Kabbalah Centre n.d.a.) and as such is not incompatible with any religion—as yoga and meditation are presented in neo-Hindu movements. In other words, part of this universalistic rhetoric is to make Kabbalah an "all-denominational" and "inter-spiritual wisdom" (Y. Berg in *USAToday. com* 2004; M. Berg 2005) that does not demand conversion. "Kabbalah is not about leaving your religion," states Yehuda Berg. "We have plenty of Protestants and Muslims, people of all religions who learn our teachings and [go] back to their religions. It's about becoming a better Jew, a better Christian or a better Muslim. It's about becoming a better you" (cited in *USAToday.com* 2004). Once more, we note that the emphasis on individual self-realization contributes to the universalization of the teaching.

The Kabbalah Centre's decision to teach Kabbalah as a universal wisdom is a remarkable shift for a movement of religious revitalization, yet it seems that the experience of teaching secular Jews prepared the Kabbalah Centre to direct its efforts toward students with no Jewish background. Indeed, a former teacher who joined the group in the 1970s in Tel Aviv explained that in Israel they were careful not to present the teaching as religious, so that it would not ward off their secular students. Accordingly, teaching in the United States was not dissimilar in the sense that "again, you have to kind of hide the religious stuff," so that "it's very good in a way that you are not too Jewish." In other words, the Kabbalah Centre smoothly shifted from avoiding being "too religious" to being "too Jewish":

The courses at the beginning were very Jewish, religious,[2] all Israeli. Then, when you give it in America, you put less sources from the Bible, less sources from the Talmud, less sources from the Zohar, and more ideas that are more, that people are...acquainted with? So it was too much quotes, whatever, it gets people very tired. For Israelis, like everybody knows the quote, so it's just like, you just have to mention the book, everybody knows what you're talking about, you move on. For Americans it's like, it's foreign. And then also to take the subjects, so Kabbalah what we used to be taught in Kabbalah One was spread on the new Kabbalah One and Two. It became more and more like a lot of topics that were passed, like "What is a Jew?" . . . That class was taken out.

The example above of an excluded class shows that the transformations of the teaching were not only about adapting to a public that did not have sufficient knowledge of Judaism, but also to those who would not be interested in such a topic because they do not identify with Judaism. Similarly, kosher food and circumcision were originally part of the standard classes and have also been removed, notes the same interviewee.

The detachment of the Kabbalah Centre's teaching from Judaism is noticeable in the movement's literature as well. Berg's first books constantly drew on Jewish biblical figures and history, citing scriptures, rabbis, and Kabbalists. They were subsequently re-edited with fewer references to Jewish sources and Hebrew terms. "Torah," for example, is often replaced by the "Old Testament" or the "Bible" in more recent editions. God's commandments to the Jewish people, the *mitzvot*, are now called "connections" (with the Light), "deeds," or "precepts." The words "Judaism" and "Jew" appear less frequently. Since it would be impossible to remove all references to "Jews" and the "Jewish people" in the literature, they are often replaced either by "man," "mankind," or "people" in order to universalize the arguments being made, or by "the Hebrew" and the "Israelites." Thus, by referring to biblical Jews only, Jews become a historical, abstract, and mythical reference, distinct from the "living" teachers and students of the movement who are ethnically Jewish and who literally embody Jewishness. By contrast, recent books written by Philip Berg's sons and wife contain increasingly eclectic references to mainstream popular culture, ranging from the movie *GI Jane* to figures such as Shakespeare and the Dalai Lama. The religious concepts they use are also diverse and refer, more than they used to, to the age of the Aquarius, astral projections and auras, cosmic consciousness, chakras, and equate *tikkun* with karmic law. References to Christianity may well have increased in recent years: Jesus is recognized as a Kabbalist, while the Zohar, written at "the time of Jesus" (Kabbalah Centre 2006b), was presented as being the Holy Grail to an interviewee. Recent written material and conferences insist on the fact that Kabbalah reveals the mysteries of Christianity such as the trinity, the messiah, or the resurrection; as such, Kabbalah allows one to become a better Christian (Kabbalah Centre

2011b). This rhetoric clearly resonates with Christian Kabbalah, thereby under-lining the ambivalence of such an approach—that is, using Kabbalah as a way of asserting Christian truths.

It is difficult to be certain of the reasons that this universalistic shift hap-pened, but the circumstances in which it did are hardly insignificant. Unlike the Jewish Renewal in the United States, the Kabbalah Centre's mixed classes of secular men and women and its eclectic teaching topics were quite un-precedented in 1970s Israel. This triggered criticisms and campaigns from Orthodox Judaism (Huss forthcoming a); Berg's credentials and legitimacy to teach Kabbalah were questioned and his personal life was criticized (he had divorced and left his eight children before marrying his second wife, Karen). In addition, the authority and social role of Orthodox institutions in Israel were becoming stronger; it was "the return of the repressed" in post-Zionist Israel (Loss 2010, 86), a context that would unavoidably challenge the development of the Kabbalah Centre. The Berg family came back to the United States in 1981, probably because as a very pluralistic religious environment it seemed to be more favorable for its development (Myers 2007, 56–61). It is after the Bergs re-turn to North America that the teaching and the dissemination strategies were transformed; part of this transformation was its detachment from Judaism.

Thus, the Kabbalah Centre today refutes being a Jewish movement or teaching anything relating to Judaism, but also disavows Judaism by contrast-ing it with Kabbalah (and itself):

> Is Kabbalah Jewish? It is quite understandable that Kabbalah could be confused with Judaism. Throughout history, many scholars of Kabbalah have been Jewish. But there have also been many non-Jewish scholars of this wisdom, such as Christian Knorr von Rosenroth, Pico Della [Mirandola] and Sir Isaac Newton, just to name a few. The star-tling truth is that Kabbalah was never meant for a specific sect. Rather, it was intended to be used by all humanity to unify the world. (Kabbalah Centre 2007b)

Again, by addressing this question, the Kabbalah Centre tries to reassure its audience about the non-Jewishness of the teaching. As primordial and uni-versal wisdom, Kabbalah is contrasted with Judaism, which had become a "sect," a posterior and particularistic organization embracing but also con-cealing Kabbalah. There is here an implicit criticism of Judaism for being exclusive and limiting access to Kabbalah—"You can't say God wants his best stuff saved for the Jews" explained Michael Berg (in Rifkin 2007). Berg's writ-ings and other teachers' discourses often blame "conventional Judaism" and its representatives for maintaining their power by keeping Kabbalah secret and for their dogmatism devoid of spirituality. By contrast, the Bergs are presented as the champions of the popularization of Kabbalah: despite criticisms and abuse, they defy the religious establishment and dare to teach its secrets to the masses. Accordingly, we could read the Kabbalah Centre's mission to popularize Kabbalah as a direct challenge to Orthodox Judaism's role and legitimacy, and its universalistic claims as a contribution to the conflicted dialogue within a divided Judaism.

However, it is quite striking that, in the citation above (as well as in the literature and introductory lectures I have attended), the Kabbalah Centre makes references to Christian Kabbalah as evidence of Kabbalah's non-Jewishness. It is not surprising in the sense that what Christian Kabbalah did for centuries is what the Kabbalah Centre is now doing—detaching Kabbalah from Judaism. But by refusing to consider Kabbalah as Jewish, presenting Kabbalah as a way of becoming a better Christian, and criticizing Judaism's attempt to limit access to Kabbalah, it reiterates a discourse found among students of Christian Kabbalah such as Madame Blavatsky and which, to say the least, expressed a clear ambivalence toward Judaism. In other words, the expression of its conflicted relationship with Judaism has led the Kabbalah Centre to embrace arguments used by others that had an anti-Semitic flavor; the criticisms of Jews' exclusiveness is certainly one of them.

The Kabbalah Centre's conflicted and ambivalent relationship with Judaism can be disturbing for some Jewish students—not the least because these criticisms of Orthodox Judaism are embraced and repeated by non-Jewish students, who may find there a legitimated expression of their personal ambivalent feelings toward Judaism. Tamara, for instance, believes that "more Jewish people are opposed to Kabbalah than those who are non-Jewish." Francis, who thinks his grandmother may be Jewish "so [he] can say this," considers Jews "agreed to do a job and they haven't done it, they have kept the bits and pieces to themselves, for themselves in their own family and forgot the rest of their family, which is now 7 billion people." Also, "it is the Jews that thought they were chosen, we know that they agreed to take on the mantel and the covenant which is different from being chosen. How can the creator...choose one child over another?" And here we touch upon a crucial difference between the Sivananda Centres and Siddha Yoga, on the one hand, and the Kabbalah Centre on the other. Leaders and students of the former are overwhelmingly non-Indian; they neither developed a significant membership in India nor attracted a section of the South Asian diaspora in the United States, Canada, and Britain. By contrast, today, a minority of the Kabbalah Centre's membership are ethnically Jewish and identify in a way or another with Judaism. We can therefore presume that the movement's universalistic rhetoric and condemnation of Judaism is a potential source of tensions and divisions. The second section of this chapter explores this issue in detail.

De-ethnicizing Interpretations: Dharma and Torah for All

A crucial aspect of the universalization of these movements' teachings relates to the ways in which neo-Hinduism and the Kabbalah Centre have reinterpreted some of the fundamentals of Hinduism and Judaism, so that they can apply to everyone. Indeed, the de-contextualization of these popular Vedantic or Kabbalistic teachings is precisely entailed by reinterpretations of the tenets that make traditional Hinduism and Judaism ethnic religions. This is why, here, this de-contextualization is also a de-ethnicization. Both Hinduism and Judaism traditionally entail the reference to a particular geographical territory (India or Israel) and a specific people (those belonging to the caste system or the chosen people of Israel). These tenets need to be re-thought so that they can become universally inclusive. Second, and more important, the de-ethnicization process results from the *practical* consequences of these reinterpretations of who can be a member, participate in practices, or become a leader. Interpretations are, of course, countless; therefore their exploration could not be exhaustive and making such an inventory is not our objective. Accordingly, I focus on central concepts such as dharma, the law of karma, and Judaism's notion of the chosen people, in order to illustrate the de-ethnicization process involved by the universalistic ambitions of Siddha Yoga, the Sivananda Centres, and the Kabbalah Centre.

Traditional Hinduism has been characterized by a certain exclusiveness that has limited the recognition of foreigners. Dharma is a key concept of Hinduism, which has several meanings and understandings; it is the cosmic order that, by analogy, manifests itself through social order. It also designates duty and norm: Hindus are meant to participate in this cosmic order through rituals and social obligations in relation to their caste, gender, and stage in life. Thus, traditional Hinduism's notion of dharma orders society and draws hereditary distinctions between different castes, as well as between "Aryans" and "non-Aryans" (outsiders). The latter cannot honor or violate dharma: born outcaste, "they stand outside the sphere of dharmically relevant action" (Halbfass 1988, 331, 333). In addition, since dharma is inseparable from Indian social order, it is only in India that it is effective. Here, it is not so much India as a nation, but Bharat Mata (Mother India), a sacred space that transcends political borders. Accordingly, transforming Hinduism into a universal religion that could include foreigners meant reinterpreting the notion of dharma, and this is one of the core features of neo-Hindu thinking (Halbfass 1988, 337).

Therefore, neo-Hinduism broke with Hindu orthodox systems, especially through a reinterpretation of dharma that grants it a universal dimension. This did not start with contemporary gurus in the 1960s or even with Vivekananda, but with the nineteenth-century encounter with Europeans in colonial India. Dharma was first translated as "religion" by missionaries who aimed to evangelize Indian populations. Thus, a "Hindu dharma" started to coexist side by side with a Christian and a Muslim dharma—Christianity being presented as the "true dharma." Yet this allowed unprecedented comparisons and responses from Hindu reformers. For Ram Mohun Roy or Dayananda Saraswati, it became a tool for a Hindu self-assertion as they contrasted different dharmas with *sanatana dharma*, a timeless and universal dharma—Hinduism. This clearly responded to Christianity's claims of universality, but also to the European notion of ethics: neo-Hindu intellectuals reinterpreted dharma as an ethical code applicable to the whole of humanity. In Europe and North America, Vivekananda presented dharma as an individual duty of self-realization detached from Indian social organization and hence applicable to everyone (Brekke 1999; Halbfass 1988, 338–347).

Accordingly, this universalization of dharma entailed the extension of the law of karma to the whole world. In principle, actions (karma) influence future lives in accordance with their moral quality. They allow the attainment of better reincarnations and, ultimately, liberation (*moksha*) from the cycle of reincarnations (O'Flaherty 1980). This is a central issue shared by the different Hindu philosophical systems: while Brahmanism insists on ritual duties to act upon one's karma, yoga advocates ascetic practices that abolish individuality, Advaita Vedanta emphasizes the realization of Brahman, and the Bhagavad Gita insists on devotion and selfless action. Yet the law of karma is traditionally socio-centric: only in India can one control and influence karma, while the rest of the world is subjected to the manifestations of the consequences of actions (Halbfass 1988, 323). Within orthodox Hinduism, the law of karma is inseparable from the caste system: to influence positively their next lives and attain ultimate liberation, Hindus need to respect specific duties (rites, professional occupations, etc.) in relation to their social status (Weber 1996, 117–123). However, contemporary gurus provided the law of karma with a universal dimension by claiming that everyone is subjected to it and can influence it, and by insisting on its moral character:

Jesus taught "do unto others as you would have them [do] unto you." These are all expressions of the law of karma, of cause and effect. It works something like a boomerang. Whatever thought or deed comes from a person will be returned to him. It may not come in the same form, but sooner of later each will confront the results of his own actions. A joyous and giving person immediately draws a response of warmth and love. If a person is hateful, he will be disliked—until he removes this negative quality. This is the law. (Vishnu-Devananda 1978, 6)

It is striking that Vishnu-Devananda refers to Christianity to explain the law of karma to Europeans and Americans (Sivananda 1999 [1946], and other contemporary gurus do, too). His emphasis on personal responsibility also outlines the detachment of the law of karma from Indian social organization, in particular the caste system. Consequently, these breaks from Hindu orthodoxy and the will to include non-Indians have contributed to the de-emphasis of ritual duties, which unavoidably refer to Indian social organization. Movements such as Siddha Yoga or the Sivananda Centres do celebrate certain Hindu festivals and anniversaries in relation to their gurus, nevertheless their emphasis is primarily on other practices such as meditation and yoga. Ritual duties may also have been downplayed by neo-Hinduism's emphasis on the more exportable path of bhakti. Because devotion is part of all religions, Swami Durgananda (2010, 15), one of the current leaders of the Sivananda Centres, asserts that "Bhakti is not tied to any religion."

Let us now turn to the Kabbalah Centre's interpretation of Judaism's core tenets. Like Hindu orthodoxy, traditional Judaism draws a line between Jews and non-Jews. This is linked to the central role of the covenant, the contractual relationship between God and the tribes of Israel. At the same time, Judaism reclaims universalism: it insists on the fact that God is the God of *all* creatures (Danzger 1989, 296) and that through the respect of God's commandments, the people of Israel will redeem the whole world (Ben Rafael 2005, 368). There are therefore tensions between universalistic and particularistic orientations within Judaism, which has limited efforts to reach out to adherents (Eisenstadt 1992, 27; Danzger 1989, 4–5). Of course, these issues regarding Jewish identity and relation to non-Jews have become complex as Judaism fragmented into different denominations, which hold varying doctrinal interpretations. Reform Judaism, for example, tends to de-emphasize this distinction between Jews and non-Jews. However, the idea of the chosen people as having a specific role of repairing the world for humanity is very important in Kabbalistic texts themselves (Idel and Malka 2000, 81); Kabbalah's emphasis on *tikkun* makes of "every Jew a soldier in the battle between good and evil" (Dan 2007, 78). Furthermore, the Zohar describes souls of non-Jews as different, "impaired," and originating from the "darker side" (Myers 2011, 183). Thus, the Kabbalah Centre, referring to these texts, had to offer new interpretations, although Myers's (2007) and my observations are that most of the time, during the usual activities and events organized by the Centre, teachers deliberately avoid addressing the challenging theme of distinctions between Jews and non-Jews.

The Kabbalah Centre is fascinating in the sense that, in its universalistic ambitions, it could totally refute the distinction between Jews and non-Jews. It does not. Berg maintains the distinction between Jews and non-Jews, but tries to erase the ethnic nature of this distinction: being Jewish is not about being born into a Jewish family but having a different sort of soul—although many Jewish interviewees clearly understand that those who are born Jewish have, de facto, a bigger soul than those who are not born Jewish. Thus, those who are in the Kabbalah Centre and work for their spiritual development may be Jewish souls. Here, Berg drew on Luria, who evoked reincarnations and the possibility for Jews to be born in non-Jewish bodies—and vice versa (Myers 2011, 184). Therefore, in the Kabbalah Centre, being Jewish means having a bigger soul, which therefore has a greater desire to receive and can be filled by more light from the Creator. Accordingly, a Jewish soul can and has the responsibility to undertake spiritual transformation in order to remove the chaos from the world. It is then agreed that Jews have more responsibility and have to respect the commandments, while non-Jews do not need to. Thus, Philip Berg does not deny Jews' pivotal role in human history in accordance with Jewish messianism and Kabbalah, which grant Jews the mission to accomplish the *tikkun* for all of humanity. We will see later to whom exactly, in practice, these responsibilities are attached.

The Kabbalah Centre also had to reinterpret the covenantal foundation of Judaism, according to which God chose the people of Israel as he revealed his commandments in the form of the Torah to them and thereby drew a distinction between them and other nations. The Kabbalah Centre now claims that the Torah has been given to everyone: while Berg (1983: 33) wrote in the early edition of *The Kabbalah Connection* that "the Jewish people must first realize why the Torah was given to us," it is stated in the new edition that "we must first realize why the Bible was given to us" (2009, 21). Rather than presenting the Torah as God's commandment to the people of Israel, the Kabbalah Centre emphasizes the traditional Kabbalistic understanding of the Torah, a code that needs to be deciphered to understand the universe. There is nonetheless ambivalence in the sense that the Kabbalah Centre still considers the reception of the Torah on Mount Sinai as a dramatic moment for all: "mankind will return to this level of consciousness achieved by the people of the Exodus, when they stood at Mount Sinai" (P. Berg 1993, 127). In other words, rather than removing the significance of Judaism's particularism, the Kabbalah Centre seems to affirm its relevance for humanity as a whole. This way of *judaicizing* the world is reflected in countless details in the Kabbalah Centre and in fact parallels neo-Hinduism's inclusivism. For example, Jesus and Muhammad are described as Kabbalists (Y. Berg 2008a, 78), which echoes neo-Hindu interpretations of Jesus as an avatar (Mayer 1989, 29) or a yogi of a superior order (Sivananda 2001 [1938]). Hebrew is claimed to be the universal language (P. Berg 1993, 158). Israel, as symbolizing a higher level of spirituality to which everyone aspires, includes humanity in the symbolic frame of the Exile: "Each of us has the same mission and destiny as Abram. All of us are commanded to migrate to Israel" (Y. Berg 2003a, 93).

This inclusion of humanity within Judaism is nowhere more striking than in the Kabbalah Centre's approach to festivals. Judaism's rituals, festivals, and practices recurrently refer to the history, and specificity of, the Jewish people: Passover celebrates the liberation from Egypt, Sukkoth commemorates the march toward the Promised Land, Shavuot recalls the acceptance of the Torah at Mount Sinai, and Purim and Chanukah express a yearning for the land of Israel (Mittleman 2010, 360). Yet, not only are Jewish festivals and Shabbat practiced in the Centre, but they are given tremendous importance. For example, "Rosh Hashanah is our opportunity to confront the negative energy aroused through the wrongful acts we've committed during the preceding year" (Kabbalah Centre 2004e), while Passover has the power to "interrupt the dominion of ego and chaos over the world" (London Kabbalah Centre 2008a). It is agreed that everyone, regardless of their religion, can receive fulfillment and happiness from these festivals. Similarly, "[n]othing in Kabbalah is more fundamental than the concept of Shabbat and its observance," wrote Michael Berg (2001, 178). While the Kabbalah Centre celebrates Jewish festivals and holds gatherings for the Shabbat service, teachers endlessly repeat that "it's not about tradition, it's not religion." They present these practices as "tools" to connect with the Light; each Shabbat and holiday, respectively, has a specific significance "for connecting to particular forms of spiritual energy" (M. Berg 2001, 186). New practices were also invented or introduced to reach a wider audience unfamiliar with Judaism, such as scanning the Zohar or the 72 names of God, and the recitation of a particular prayer, called Ana Bekoach.

Finally, it may have been easier for the Kabbalah Centre to simply eliminate or de-emphasize the observance of *mitzvot*, which implies the distinctiveness of the "chosen people" of Israel, for they have the specific duty to respect ethical and legal precepts given by God (Eisenstadt 1992, 24). While Christianity insists on faith, Judaism emphasizes acts, thus the performance of *mitzvot* is literally at the heart of Judaism (Danzger 1989, 4–5), and of Kabbalah in particular, since it emphasizes their cosmic effects for the repair of the world (Dan 2007, 53–59). By and large, the Kabbalah Centre does not depart from Kabbalah's attachment to observance. Berg took great pain in his writings to insist on the fact that commandments were not prescriptions and orders, but opportunities to draw more light, hereby reiterating their significance. However, on the basis of their particular metaphysical nature and mission, only Jews have to respect the 613 Jewish commandments given by God, whereas non-Jews simply need to comply with the seven noahide laws.[3] And here, again, lies an ambiguity: as we shall see further on, *in practice* these commandments do not apply to metaphysically "bigger souls" but to "ethnic" Jews within the Centre.

Tensions and Contradictions of the De-contextualization Process

We now turn to the modalities and challenges of the de-contextualization of exotic religious resources. Indeed, responding to the expectations of individuals who fetishize otherness while at the same time being repelled by it necessarily generates some tensions and contradictions. On the one hand, there is a temptation to exoticize religious teachings to make them appealing. On the other hand, devices are used to downplay particularisms: organizational strategies, transformations of leadership and membership, and, as far as the teaching is concerned, interpretations, innovations, and concealments. As it will be shown below, this intense, conflicted re-writing of religious identity and purpose clearly represents a potential for conflict and division. In this regard, playfulness and fluidity are hardly the best words to qualify what bricolage involves.

Exoticizing Religious Teachings

For a start, it is obvious that the process of de-contextualization cannot but be ambivalent, simply because, from a sociological point of view, no religious teaching can fully transcend cultures and religious traditions. Every social fact—here, religious concepts, norms, and practices—is by definition historically and socially situated. In addition, precisely because they are new and peripheral religious organizations, NRMs are prone to refer to traditional institutions and respected figures as sources of legitimacy. For instance, contemporary gurus often refer to their own guru and a lineage of gurus, which could be traced back to Shiva himself in the case of Siddha Yoga. Gurus often present themselves as ordained monks in respected Hindu monastic orders—they may wear the orange robe of renunciates and be called by their initiation name as swamis. Some of them, such as Vishnu-Devananda and Muktananda, had their close disciples initiated in these traditional orders; known as being conservative and in support of the caste system (Cenkner 2001, 192; Hulin 2001, 224), the reason that these orders would accept the initiation of Westerners and women remains unclear. But the gurus' motive for such initiations is more obvious, as explained by members of Siddha Yoga:

> In contrast to some other contemporary Indian teachers who created orders of sannyasis [renunciates] that had legitimacy only within their own movements, Muktananda consciously did everything he could to make sure that his monks could be recognized by the wider community of traditional dasanami[4] swamis. (Brooks et al. 1997, 104–105)

Similarly, the Kabbalah Centre also refers to respected figures and mainstream Jewish institutions to establish its legitimacy. It evokes an unbroken lineage of Kabbalists linking Philip Berg to Ashlag, but also to Luria and Shimon bar Yochai, who is said to have revealed the Zohar more than 2,000 years ago. Philip Berg mentions having been ordained as an Orthodox rabbi and defines himself as an Orthodox Jew; he is called "the Rav" by his students, an honorific term for rabbi, and his wife "rabbanit Karen." Similarly, their sons are presented as ordained rabbi; the yeshivot where they studied is indicated in the Kabbalah Centre's official discourse (Kabbalah Centre 2004c, 2004d). The first pages of the movement's prayer books display the approbations received in 1995 by the Jerusalem Ashkenazy Rabbinical Court, Kabbalist Yitzchak Kaduri, and other authorities (Meir 2011, 164; Huss forthcoming a).[5] Those who study NRMs will recognize a standard practice of recent religious minority groups whose authenticity and legitimacy are questioned, if not contested. Here we want to point out the fact that neo-Hindu movements and the Kabbalah Centre paradoxically find their legitimacy in their respective particularisms, which is obviously in tension with the ambition to transcend these particularisms.

Furthermore, the process of de-contextualization is inherently ambivalent because of the fascination for otherness that makes these NRMs successful. Despite the controversies that some of them may raise, exotic representations of Vedanta, yoga, or Kabbalah precisely make neo-Hindu and Kabbalistic teachings appealing. Accordingly, the movements studied here do not intend to provide a teaching devoid of religious and cultural references; they present Vedanta or Kabbalah as unique, universal, and timeless sources of wisdom. Furthermore, exoticism, the desire for differences, implies the construction and the fetishization of otherness. It is therefore not surprising that NRMs that popularize exotic religious resources are prone to "stage their marginality" and "dramatise their 'subordinate' status for the imagined benefit of a majority audience" (Huggan 2001, xii). A good example is Muktananda's particular reference to Kashmir Shaivism. Kashmir was a place of reformation of Shaivism; this is not considered to be a unified religious system but includes a diversity of sects and tantric practices that were particularly influential between the ninth and eleventh centuries (Thursby 1986; Dyczkowski 1987). The significance of Kashmir Shaivism for Muktananda is hardly philosophical. In the early years of his teaching, he emphasized Vedanta—of which some principles are antithetical to Kashmir Shaivism. He introduced Kashmir Shaivism only in the late 1970s (Caldwell 2001, 21) and referred to other Hindu philosophical schools and sages as well. In a book in which Muktananda comments on Shaivite scriptures, a preface written by one of his disciples is quite telling of Muktananda's relationship to Kashmir Shaivism:

> It is not quite correct to say that Baba [Father] is a follower of Kashmir Shaivism. The Shaivite scriptures that Baba uses here deal with a vast amount of intellectual and technical material that doesn't interest Baba at all. His merciful and practical eye catches only those ideas that are directly helpful to minute-to-minute, real life sadhana [religious discipline]. (cited in Muktananda 1977, 10)

Thus, references to Kashmir Shaivism are not about adopting its doctrines, but about its evocative power, an ancient and specific tradition enshrined in a remote and attractive region of Asia.

We find in the Kabbalah Centre another example through which religious and cultural otherness is staged and fetishized. The Kabbalah Centre often refers to Moroccan Judaism, hereby reflecting a modern revival of a romantic representation of a pure Sephardic Kabbalistic tradition (Meir 2011, 165). As a result of the Spanish emigration and periodic visits from emissaries of the yeshivot of Safed since the sixteenth century, Kabbalah permeated North African religious life. In Morocco, the Zohar nearly reached the same sacred status of the Torah and Talmud. The Zohar not only was studied by brotherhoods of Zohar readers and rabbis, but also was popularized through liturgy, songs, tales, and popular customs (Ben

Rafael 1982, 33; Zafrani 1996, 173). During my fieldwork, I heard several times teachers and leaders referring to the great Kabbalists of Morocco and some of them, with their students, undertook pilgrimages to their graves. These pilgrimages, called *hillulla*, are a tradition originated from Moroccan Judaism that has been revived in Israel in recent years (Ben-Ari and Bilu 1997; Bilu 1991). In Tel Aviv, I participated in a *mimouna*, a traditional North African celebration that occurred at the end of Passover and which has become popular in Israel. In London, a Moroccan party was organized to celebrate the anniversary of the death of Avraham Azulai (ca. 1570–1643), a renowned Kabbalist from Fez. For this occasion, the Centre was redecorated with oriental rugs, cushions to sit on the floor, and low tables; typical North African food was served. This emphasis on Sephardic culture may be attractive for students of North African descent in France, for instance, or in Israel. Indeed, Sephardic Jews have been often labeled as "oriental"; associated with traditionalism, they are contrasted with a European, modern, and intellectual Ashkenazi heritage. In Israel, they are concentrated in the lower strata of the population and experience relative deprivation and social rejection (Ben Rafael and Sharot 1991, 99). Accordingly, this emphasis on the North African Kabbalistic tradition may serve as a tool for self-assertion for students of Sephardic origin. However, the Kabbalah Centre's emphasis on Moroccan Judaism serves other purposes in the North American context where the movement developed. There, and in local centers like London, in the absence of Sephardic Jews, it provides an "exoticized" and attractive Judaism that the London Moroccan party, described above, illustrates. This echoes Fader's (2008) ethnography of a synagogue in Manhattan, B'nai Jeshurun, that became increasingly popular among an economically secure upper middle-class congregation, due to its "spiritual" turn. Influenced by the Jewish Renewal, it emphasized self-discovery and healing; it also became hip by embracing Sephardic ritual, music, and material culture, through which "a Jewish Other was created and then consumed by the predominantly Ashkenazic congregation" (Fader 2008, 41).

In other words, through references to Kashmir Shaivism and the Moroccan Kabbalistic tradition, Muktananda and the leaders of the Kabbalah Centre, respectively, dramatize the particularism of their teaching. They exoticize it, while claiming that it transcends religious, geographical, and national boundaries: this paradox reflects the ambivalence of religious exoticism, combining a fetishization of, and repulsion for, otherness. Indeed, bricolage demands resources that are "special" and mysterious while at the same time acultural and universal.

Israel, Axis Mundi?

I now explore the ways in which these ambiguities of religious exoticism are translated in neo-Hindu movements and the Kabbalah Centre, as well as the tensions and contradictions they may generate. The Kabbalah Centre illustrates this issue particularly well. It was originally an Israeli movement of religious revitalization. As a transnational religious organization claiming to be beyond national, cultural, and religious boundaries, it needs to manage its attachment to Israel. This is relatively challenging due to, first, the symbolic and geographic significance of Israel in the Kabbalah Centre's teaching; second, the importance of Israeli students' religious knowledge in the movement; and third, the unavoidable political issues entailed by this attachment in the context of the Israeli-Palestinian conflict.

To begin with, Israel is of paramount significance for symbolic reasons. According to traditional Judaism, Israel is the past and the future of the Jewish people, who live in exile in all the other places in the world (Ben Rafael 1998, 33). The Kabbalah Centre maintains the Land of Israel's centrality to Judaism, while trying to give this a symbolic and universal meaning detached from its actual geographical and political existence. Israel thus expresses a higher level of "spirituality" and a deeper connection with the Light of the Creator; hence migrating there means attaining a certain level of spirituality. This is why Philip Berg asked for photographs of Jerusalem and the holy temple, and also of the graves of Kabbalists (such as Luria's in Safed), to be displayed in every local branch of the movement, so that the land of Israel could be brought closer to students in their "spiritual exile" (P. Berg 2000, 68). This aspiration to elevate oneself is what students are supposed to understand when teachers, during Shabbat and festivals, ask them to "tune their consciousness" to, and connect with, Israel.

Berg also recognized the uniqueness of Israel as a physical place: he indeed presented Jerusalem and the holy temple as channels of energy (P. Berg 1983, 32, 67–68). Thus, Israel is described as the "metaphysical epicentre" and "source of the creation of the world" (Brochure for Rosh Hashanah 2007, London). An Israeli interviewee who studied the Kabbalah Centre's teaching for 13 years, explains:

> One of the things that are unique to Israel, to the geographical place of Israel, is that it is near the Holy of Holies, which is the geographical place where the Light of God enters planet Earth and the entire Universe. It's the nearest geographical place to the spiritual source. And the nearer you are to the source of light, the more intense the

Light is. Okay? So the Light here is intense. That's why the news here are always more intense than in Dubai or in London or in New York.

This comment shows that Berg's reinterpretation of Israel as a symbol of a higher level of "spirituality" does not prevent, in practice, the understanding of Israel as an exceptional geographical location. By and large, several teachers and students, whether they are Israeli or not, or Jewish or not, described Israel to me as a unique place. "As a centre of energy of the world, you probably feel it is different from any other place," said a teacher to newcomers at an introductory lecture in English in Tel Aviv. Furthermore, religious practices reinforce the significance of Israel as a physical place. Students periodically travel to Israel for "Energy Tours" and participate in pilgrimages to the graves of saints and Kabbalists, such as Luria's in Safed and Shimon bar Yochaï's in Meron. During religious festivals, Kabbalah Centre students go to Jerusalem at night in order to make "visual connections": from Mount Scopus, they "visualize" the place where the holy temple is supposed to have been and make a wish about what they want to change in their lives. These activities primarily involve Israeli students, but also those who, precisely because of the importance of Israel, come from overseas to participate in pilgrimages and festivals with members of the Tel Aviv Centre. Finally, the use of communication technologies sometimes allows students all over the world to share these specific events in Israel. When I was in Tel Aviv for Passover, the Bergs asked the Tel Aviv Centre to find a way to broadcast live one of these "visual connections" on Mount Scopus to the United States. Thus, Israel's geographical significance is reiterated by practices—pilgrimages, festivals, and rituals.

In other words, as a student of the Tel Aviv Centre told me, "Israel is where the real thing is happening." Yet, the Kabbalah Centre now has its headquarters in Los Angeles. This is where the leaders live, manage their transnational organization, train teachers and volunteers, and reshape teachings and practices. In addition, festivals such as Pessah and Rosh Hashanah, which allow students to gather around the Bergs, usually take place in the United States. Organized in large hotel resorts, these events are prominently advertised in local branches and can gather thousands of students. This recent centralization of the Kabbalah Centre in the United States generates misunderstandings and resentment, in particular from Israeli students. Ninette, for instance, is an Israeli student of the Tel Aviv Centre. Born in Morocco, she studied in Paris before migrating to Israel, where she married and brought up her children. During informal discussions and an interview, she expressed several times her love for Israel, the importance of living there as a Jew, and the sacrifices it had entailed at first. She has been a regular and enthusiastic student of the

Kabbalah Centre for several years, yet she made clear to me that she had "her own views on things." When I asked her what she meant by this, she referred to the Kabbalah Centre's incentives to come to the United States for festivals:

> Me, I found this so STUPID, I was telling myself "we are lucky enough to be in Eretz Israel [the Land of Israel], to live here, I'm going to go in exile for the festivals, but I'd be stupid to do this!... We had the luck to come and live in Israel, I am not going to leave Jerusalem, Israel, to put myself in a *bled* of Los Angeles.

Bled is an Arabic word for place, or village, used in French in a derogatory way to designate an isolated place.[6] It is quite telling that Ninette associates Los Angeles with a *bled* and contrasts it with Jerusalem, *the* place, outside of which she feels in exile.

But Israel is central for more than symbolic reasons: not only did the Kabbalah Centre start in Israel and kept local groups there, but its core members are predominantly Israeli. Senior teachers are old-time students who started with the Rav himself in the 1970s in Tel Aviv; they have the knowledge of the original teaching. Whether in London or Los Angeles (Myers 2007), these are very often Israeli teachers and full-time volunteers who, under the Bergs' leadership, run the Kabbalah Centre. For cultural reasons, the Israeli staff, whether senior of junior, possess forms of knowledge that are central to the Kabbalah Centre. They speak and read Hebrew fluently. They are also very familiar with Jewish customs that new teachers, coming from an American or European secular Jewish or non-Jewish family, would not know. Consequently, Israel is to a certain extent the depository of the ways and works of the Kabbalah Centre, at least in the view of the Tel Aviv students, who do not hesitate to criticize teaching modes imported from Los Angeles and contrast them with an Israeli way of doing things. Even the son of Philip Berg himself can be disapproved: during a Shabbat in Tel Aviv, a local student found he recited prayers too fast. "Us, we don't do it like that," she told me, hereby affirming that in Tel Aviv they have their own customs. At another Shabbat, one of my informants asked me with contempt, "Who is that guy?" about a new teacher saying prayers; "for sure he's coming from Los Angeles," she added, "they're all hyper there." This informant criticized the sending to Israel of young American teachers who are trained to express their enthusiasm in their body language and singing. On another occasion, she regretted the fact that changes in ritual songs were imposed from the American headquarters: "We are not used to this!" she explained, emphasizing again the importance of their local traditions. In other words, despite the Kabbalah Centre's claim to transcend illusory cultural boundaries, it is nevertheless confronted with the fact that its teaching unavoidably draws on local knowledge and customs. The cultural changes involved by the recent transnationalization of the movement are therefore a potential source of tensions with those who consider them-selves the bearers of the original knowledge. Indeed, while elsewhere students sometimes expressed criticisms about certain aspects of the teaching, they did not question the legitimacy and centrality of the leaders' religious knowledge.

Finally, the divisive nature of the Israeli-Palestinian conflict is another source of tension for the Kabbalah Centre's universalism. Given its attach-ment to Israel as a sacred place and the importance of Israeli members in its organization, it is an issue it cannot totally ignore. Myers (2007, 178) argues that the Kabbalah Centre prioritizes its universalism in relation to Israeli na-tionalism. Yet, despite its support of children in Malawi and its distributions of Zohar to fight darkness in various regions of the world, there is on the part of the Kabbalah Centre members a particular involvement in Israel-Palestine. One of its main educational projects is "Kids Creating Peace," a separate nonprofit organization registered in Israel as a charity for children. Drawing on the volunteer work of Israeli students, this program started in the early 2000s. It is intended for Jewish and Arab children and is taught in schools and youth centers by members of Jewish, Arabic, and Christian communities. These educators and facilitators, I was told, are not always Kabbalah Centre students; some in the Arabic community are hired and trained by "Kids Creating Peace." Taught in Arabic or Hebrew in separate settings in various parts of the country, common events are also organized to introduce the chil-dren to each other. A universalistic perspective shapes this educational proj-ect: when I was in Tel Aviv, the staff from Kids Creating Peace were starting to work with a Sufi master to teach Jewish and Arab teenagers in Jaffa, "to show to the kids that yes, actually there is a universal principle," says one of the Kids Creating Peace's directors. Recently, the Kabbalah Centre organized in London a "Kabbalah Power of Peace Conference: Unrest in the Middle East" and support for a two-state solution was addressed by the speakers, Karen Berg and the widow of former Egyptian president Anwar Sadat (*The Jewish Chronicle* 2011). *The Jerusalem Post* reported that the Bergs gave a Zohar book to Palestine President Abbas (Cashman 2012). Accordingly, the Kabbalah Centre tries to combine with subtlety its universalism with a particular attention to the Middle East. This can also be illustrated by the ways in which the Kabbalah Centre justified a campaign of Zohar distribution in the region:

> Rav Berg has said on many occasions, "As goes Israel so goes the World." The Zohar states that "Israel is the heart and the rest of the

world corresponds to the organs of the body." In the same way the heart furnishes blood to the body, Israel furnishes Light to the rest of the world. When there is a lack of blood flow in the human body heart attacks can occur. Similarly, when there is a lack of Light in the body of the world, hatred, terrorist attacks and war occur. As the Middle East peace process begins anew between Israel and Palestine, it is imperative that we inject Light into the region. (Kabbalah Centre n.d.b.)

Consequently, the "Zohar Projects" are particularly focused on the Middle East. In 2006, during the conflict between Israel and Hezbollah in Lebanon, the Zohar was distributed to Israeli soldiers and those under attack in Lebanon and Syria (Myers 2007, 178–179). At the start of the second Intifada, it was handed to the Israeli Defense Force and Palestinians (Hazan 2003). However, while the universalistic and peace-oriented initiatives are officially celebrated in the movement, an interviewee suggested that the distribution of Zohar books in occupied territories after the second Intifada had not been understood by all Israeli students. Some may have wanted the Kabbalah Centre to be more openly supportive of Israel. This reflects the divisions in Israeli society on political issues, but it also has consequences for the Kabbalah Centre's attempt to transcend cultural and national boundaries.

Indeed, there is potential for tensions between the movement's universalistic discourse and the Israeli nationalism shared by some students. Despite its relation to Israel, the Kabbalah Centre claimed that "Kabbalists are not pro-Israel, pro-Zionist, pro-Arab. Kabbalists are pro-humanity, pro-human soul, pro-God's children" (Y. Berg cited in Myers 2007, 178). On various occasions, I heard teachers and leaders blaming both sides for the Israeli-Palestinian conflict: both Israelis and Palestinians want to receive without giving, or are unable to cry over the death of one another's children. The Orthodox Jews are also to blame: one old-time French student heard Berg explaining that, by throwing stones at secular Jews, the ultra-Orthodox generated darkness and caused the second Intifada. These views on Middle Eastern politics could be in stark contrast with those held by students in Israel, as suggested by observations made during fieldwork. For instance, one old-time Israeli student talked about the special collective meditations he participated in to nullify the negativity of Hamas and Iran. This is not at all, as far as I know, a typical practice of the Tel Aviv Centre. However, in this particular local branch, the list of names circulating for Shabbat's prayer for healing included all Israeli soldiers wounded in Gaza at the start of 2009, as well as Ariel Sharon. A student told me this was relatively common in Israeli synagogues. But for the Kabbalah Centre, it may well be unique: in branches elsewhere in the world, I only saw the names of students' relatives and friends on the list of people in need of healing.

Of course, every transnational organization has a certain degree of local variation. But in the case of the Kabbalah Centre, these are rather contradictions, revealed to students as they come into contact with its universalistic and particularistic trends. Avi is a former student who had joined the Kabbalah Centre in Israel. As he became a volunteer he lived and worked in other branches in the United States. While he is still fond of Berg's teaching and still attracted to the study of Kabbalah, Avi was disturbed by what he associated with anti-Semitism:

> In every Shabbat, every synagogue in Israel, everywhere in the world basically, there is a prayer to the soldiers, to the soldiers of the IDF. May they be successful and bla bla bla. While I was in New York and in Los Angeles, they didn't have this prayer. And I felt.... I felt really bad about it. Somebody, maybe my supervisor, who was very Zionist was telling me, "listen guys it's not good," and they've changed it. But they really, even when they can come to Israel, they come to Israel because it is a Holy place, they are not coming to connect to what is happening here.

Here, this student regrets that the Kabbalah Centre tends to make of Israel a symbolic place, detached from its political and national dimension. This is, in a way, the opposite of Zionism, which made of Judaism a national identity, a source of common values and symbols, and which associates Jewishness with peoplehood. For Avi and for other students in Israel, it is therefore difficult, if not meaningless, to separate them, for "Israeli Jews are not ready to reduce Judaism to either religion or to bluntly secular nationalism completely detached from Jewish legacies" (Ben Rafael 2005, 390). Avi recalled being deeply hurt when he spoke to a teacher in New York about the importance of Israel and Zionism for him. The teacher, an Israeli national who had lived in New York for more than 20 years, replied that for him "Israel is only the *tzadikim*'s [the righteous one's] graves." By labeling this anti-Semitism during the interview, Avi may suggest that, in his view, a lack of support for Israel equates with disavowal of Judaism. But he also implicitly refers to the notion of self-hatred. The idea of "self-hating Jews"—the notion that some Jews have internalized anti-Semitism and are uncomfortable with their own Jewishness—is often controversially used to label those who criticize or oppose the state of Israel (Lerman 2008). So the interviewee could be suggesting that by their lack of support for Israel, Kabbalah Centre's leaders are hiding, or renouncing, their Jewishness in order to please their new international audience. Avi also evoked a gathering in the Tel Aviv Centre for Rosh Hashanah, at which students from all over the world participated:

> There was a lecture given by an IDF hero, a war hero. And many people there said "come on, what's going on here? He's talking about war on Rosh Hashanah; he's talking about Zionism? We didn't come to Israel to hear that. We came to hear spiritual stuff" and... even Michael [Berg] was almost... he was apologizing to his whole congregation about that, he was saying "listen, it was out of place, it was not our idea," lalala and... but all the while, they are trying to make different things, like they made a new garden, like a retreat garden and an officers' club of the IDF, contributed by the Kabbalah Centre. And they hand out free Zohar to soldiers, so it's like a mix, but it's...

This "mix" refers to the difficulty for the Kabbalah Centre to find a balance between contradictory rationales—the importance of Israel, which is hardly merely symbolic and metaphysical, and its universalism, believed to suit students outside Israel.[7] Again, it underscores the challenges of de-contextualization for a recent movement whose current members may have either adhered to a revivalist Israeli movement or, more recently, to a "trans-denominational" wisdom. Important, painful issues lie behind the processes that make exotic religious resources available for bricolage and, as we shall see below, the survival of a movement such as the Kabbalah Centre can be at stake.

Nationalism and Contemporary Neo-Hinduism in India

The Kabbalah Centre is not unique in its contradictions: overall, transnational movements that developed a universalistic rhetoric need to address in one way or another their particularistic origins. The universalization of neo-Hinduism is similarly challenged by reference to India as a sacred land and a nation. I have underlined that neo-Hinduism's assertion of Hinduism's uniqueness aimed to respond to Western imperialism and Christian proselytism, as well as to affirm the spiritual role of India in the world. There is, therefore, a strong link between neo-Hinduism and Indian nationalism. Sivananda himself (1999 [1947]) defended the idea that "[t]his name Hindu is not only of geographical, but also of national and racial importance" and his writings have been used to support nationalism (McKean 1996, 166). Indian nationalism indeed draws on belief in India's religious achievements, asserts unity in Hinduism, and claims that India has a message to proclaim to the world. Contemporary Indian nationalism has been directly inspired by figures such as Dayananda Saraswati (founder of Arya Samaj), Vivekananda, and Aurobindo,[8] who all emphasized the significance of Hinduism for the Indian nation and the world as a whole. In the 1920s, reflection on Hindu identity was significantly renewed by *Hindutva*, written by Vinayak Damodar Savarkar (1883–1966). This founding text of Indian nationalism granted Hinduism a central role, but also introduced the idea of the Aryan race and defined "Hindu-ness" by combining nation, race, and religion. *Hindutva* deeply influenced Keshav Baliram Hedgewar (1889–1940), initiator of the main Indian nationalist organization, the Rashtriya Swayamsevak Sangh—RSS, the "National Volunteers' Corps" (Bhatt and Mukta 2000, 411–413). As the RSS sees Hinduism as the core of India's national identity, it founded the Vishwa Hindu Parishad (VHP), the "World Hindu Council," in 1964. The VHP is one of RSS's most important branches; its aim is to unify and thereby protect Hinduism from Western and Christian influences. In line with this objective, the VHP functions like an ecclesial structure that gathers religious leaders and gurus who support the idea of a universal Hinduism, despite the fact that many of them perpetuate the internal diversity of Hindu salvation paths (Jaffrelot 1993, 1994). The RSS also founded a political wing in 1951, the Jana Sangh, precursor of the Bharatiya Janata Party that was in power in India from 1998 to 2004.

The links between neo-Hinduism and nationalism are not only ideological. One of the founders of the VHP and a major ideologue for the nationalist movement is a disciple of Sivananda, Swami Chinmayananda (1916–1993). Yet, as McKean (1996, 165) explains, "in order to protect its international reputation as a proponent of universal religion, the Divine Life Society does not publicize its links with Hindu nationalist leaders and organizations." The successor of Sivananda in the Divine Life Society, Swami Chidananda (1916–2008), was also a member of the VHP's Central Advisory Council. By and large, McKean (1996) suggests that many priests, gurus, and ascetics have had key roles in the growing support for Hindu nationalism: they legitimate the VHP, popularize nationalist ideas, and provide nationalism with ideological content. In turn, thanks to the VHP, they have become influential political players.

In the light of the Kabbalah Centre's struggle with its attachment to Israel, we could imagine that the particularism of neo-Hindu movements supporting Indian nationalism would unavoidably hinder the de-contextualization of their teaching and limit its appeal for Westerners. The study of some of them, such as the Art of Living and Sai Baba's organization, helps us to understand the ways they may be able to spread in the West while supporting Hindu nationalism in India. Sri Sri Ravi Shankar (b. 1956) founded the Art of Living in the 1980s. It is one of the rare neo-Hindu movements that became remarkably transnational after the counterculture. Since the mid-1990s the movement has experienced rapid expansion in India and abroad, claiming to be implanted in more than 140 countries (Sri Sri Ravi Shankar n.d.). Since 1996, the Art of Living is a nongovernmental organization with a consultative status at the Economic and Social Council of the United Nations. Like Sri Chinmoy and Vishnu-Devananda, Sri Sri Ravi Shankar presents himself as a peace ambassador. A humanitarian leader, he is said to actively combat violence and to support interfaith education and multiculturalism. The core practice of his teaching, Sudarshan Kryia, is a breathing technique said to increase vitality, and to overcome stress and violent behaviors. Presented as a therapeutic tool, Sudarshan Kryia is meant to be used by everyone, whatever their nationality, religion, or culture. The Art of Living's main center is in Bangalore. In India, Sri Sri Ravi Shankar became a celebrity and his statements are covered by the media. He calls for the reconciliation between castes and the unification of the Hindu community, as conditions for India to face the modern world and achieve progress. In fact, Sri Sri Ravi Shankar's discourse has clearly political and nationalistic tones. In 2003, for example, he criticized the state of Karnataka for allegedly granting more funds to mosques and churches than to Hindu temples. In May 2004, he spoke against the designation of Sonia Gandhi as India's prime minister. Recalling that "India as a nation has been chosen by destiny to stand and live for the values which its ancient rishis [authors of the Vedic hymns] and sages have expounded from time to time through its existence for thousands of years," he considered it "disturbing and even humiliating" to install an Italian-born person as prime minister. This, in his view, should be stopped at all costs for it would undermine India's spiritual and civilizational direction (*India Link International* 2004). It is therefore not surprising that the VHP recruited Sri Sri Ravi Shankar to reach the moderate masses in India and among the diaspora, hoping that a discourse on religious, national, and environmental issues would strengthen the Bharatiya Janata Party (Nanda 2009; Narain 2008). Sri Sri Ravi Shankar's political positions are received favorably by his Indian disciples, a successful business and political elite concerned with India's position in the global world. However, Adveeff (2010, 184–185) observes that his nationalistic discourse is not really perceptible among his Western audience, except in his reiteration of the orientalistic opposition between a spiritual India and a materialistic West. Indeed, his Western disciples are mainly interested in what the "East" can bring them: a therapeutic and personal growth tool. They are often ignorant of the Indian social context; few have visited India and when they had the opportunity to do so, it was often a trip organized in one of the Art of Living Foundation's ashrams. The paradox between Sri Sri Ravi Shankar's universalistic teaching and his political militancy in India results, Avdeeff (2010, 185) concludes, in a cleavage between Indian and Western disciples.

Sathya Sai Baba (1926–2011) represents a similar case to Sri Sri Ravi Shankar. Claiming to have millions of disciples around the globe (Srinivas 2010, 12), he was one of the most famous gurus in India, in particular for his magical materialization of objects. Sathya Sai Baba claimed to have an ecumenical mission; he referred to Jesus, Aurobindo, and Ramakrishna and incorporated elements from different religious traditions. This universalism is embodied by the symbol of his organization, superposing the symbols of various world religions, and reinforced by values of love, peace, and nonviolence. Yet Sathya Sai Baba also affirmed India's spiritual role and superiority. He was an outspoken opponent of westernization and modernization and considered the modern capitalist West, its violence and its greed, to be destructive for India (Urban 2003, 87). Instead of accepting Western influences, India should follow its own path and reclaim its glorious religious heritage. In fact, Sathya Sai Baba's teachings had a "persistent note of cultural nationalism" (Babb 1986, 172). His discourse reflected his middle-class followers' concerns and ambivalence toward the erosion of traditional values and social change in a growing capitalist society (Urban 2003, 75)—more broadly, this is what has favored the growth of Hindu nationalism in India in recent years (Morris 2005, 141). When Sathya Sai Baba died, the leaders of the RSS paid tribute to the guru:

> Revered Baba had a special affection for the cause of Hindu unity and reform and always showered his choicest blessings on the activists of the RSS and VHP engaged in that mission. In an intuitive gesture revered Baba sent word to the RSS leaders to visit him on March 18, 2011. About 60 senior functionaries of the Sangh visited Puttaparti and received Baba's blessings, which will remain as cherished memory for ever....On behalf of the RSS we pay our most respectful homage to the cherished memory of the great soul. (Mohan Bhagwat and Suresh Bhayyaji Joshi in *Vishwa Samvad Kendra*)

Sai Baba's devotees abroad who are not part of the Indian diaspora might not be enthusiastic about this aspect of their guru's message. For instance, a study of the movement in the United States underlined the concerns of American devotees, expressed during the preparation of the Seventh World Conference of the International Sai Organization in 2000. Among other issues, American devotees wished to make American centers "more culturally relevant" by downplaying the ritual dimension of their religious practices and singing their songs in English rather than in Sanskrit—in other words, to make the teaching less Hindu. To promote "unity in diversity," they also insisted on the celebration of the unity of all religions and "separating spirituality from religion, culture and nationality" (Palmer 2005, 116). This, to say the least, contrasts with Sai Baba's discourse to Indian disciples. Accordingly, there may be a cleavage between Indian and overseas devotees that allowed Sathya Sai Baba to hold two different discourses, a universalistic one and a particularistic one. In this regard, it is quite telling that the Sai Organization divides devotees into two groups, "Indian" and "Global" (Srinivas 2010, 243).

During fieldwork among neo-Hindu movements in Paris at the end of the 1990s, I noticed that five groups of Sathya Sai Baba's devotees existed, along ethnic lines. Three of them were composed of "white" Parisians; two gathered members of the South Asian diaspora, in different locations and for different practices. In my visit to French-born devotees, the emphasis was on the guru's universalistic discourse and healing power. Prayers and songs were different in the group of South Asian devotees, as well as the language used for the gathering. It was in fact my presence that forced the leader of the group to translate the discussion into French. I do not know whether this organization is generalized within the transnational organization of Sai Baba devotees. However, a thorough study of Sathya Sai Baba's devotees in Bradford in the 1980s shows that most members were Gujarati (Bowen 1988). While not ethnically exclusive or caste-bounded, Bowen (1988, 44) describes the Bradford branch as an "ethnic enclave," despite the guru's universalistic claims. Some research show that "there was a gradual defusing of the explicit Hindu content of the movement's presentation to suit circumstances in Britain" and a stress on universalism (Taylor 1987, 89). Furthermore, the Sai Organization's affirmation of Indian heritage can generate tensions along ethnic lines. For example, Bowen (1988, 121–122) mentions conflicts and rivalries among British leaders (Indian Gujarati, Sri Lankan Tamil, and "English white"), in relation to liturgical orientations that affirm a Gujarati identity and Indian heritage. More broadly, the disciples' motivations are different: as migrants, South Asian disciples in Britain see in Sai Baba's teaching a means to protect themselves against Western materialism and secularism, to reconstitute a social network, and to affirm their ethnic and religious identity (Taylor 1987, 87). Klass (1991) notes that in Trinidad the movement predominantly attracts disciples of Indian Hindu descent. Wealthy and educated, they found it difficult to relate to Trinidad's rural Hinduism, but are attracted by Sai Baba's universalistic rhetoric that both suits their cosmopolitan outlook and allows them to reassert their Hindu identity. The organization's attempts to attract disciples not of Indian descent have been limited. On their part, Afro-Trinidadians are not willing to join a movement they understand as a form of Hinduism. Overall, Klass (1991, 171) states that, reflecting Trinidad's ethnic divisions, the Sai Baba movement "provides the devotees with what they perceive as an intellectually valid and respectable basis for maintaining Indian culture and ethnic separation." Kent (2000) explored Chinese participation in the Sai Organization in Malaysia and outlines similar issues. Chinese members are desired insofar as they evidence the fact that the movement transcends an Indian ethnic particularism, but Indian members still perceive themselves as "the rightful protectors of spirituality" and limit Chinese devotees' access to leadership roles. Kent claims that Malaysian devotees are split into two groups: some operate under the control of the Sai Organization and coexist with a loose unofficial network of branches and devotees. This is where Chinese members, who are wary of exclusive Indian leadership, Hindu-Indian self-assertion, and the Hindu flavor of religious practices, are predominantly found.

These two examples, the Art of Living Foundation and the Sai Organization, provide us with some reflection about the ways in which "nationally oriented" neo-Hindu movements manage two contradictory rationales. To begin with, these two gurus have been predominantly based in India—Sai Baba left India only once (Srinivas 2010, 94). Their Indian audience is numerically significant, reflecting Sri Sri Ravi Shankar's and Sai Baba's focus on political and social issues that are relevant for Indian society and the Indian diaspora. This facet of their discourse is not openly shown to Westerners, whose ignorance is reinforced by a limited knowledge of the Indian sociopolitical context and its complexities, their lack of exposure to Indian media, and their lack of knowledge of Indian languages that gurus may use for specific purposes. As they expand globally, these movements reiterate the neo-Hindu universalistic rhetoric and emphasize peace, the universality of religions, healing, and self-fulfillment. A discourse opposing the materialistic West to spiritual India echoes Westerners' orientalistic representation of the "mystical East" and their hope to find something that their own culture seems to lack. Finally, it would be interesting to assess the extent to which, in countries where these movements have disciples from the Indian diaspora, distinct branches are created to reflect specific cultural, linguistic, and religious affinities.

By contrast, "universalistic" movements such as Siddha Yoga, Sivananda Centres, and many others had a different trajectory. Their gurus often lived and remained in Europe or North America; they have not become figures of the politico-religious scene in India. Focusing on teaching Euroamericans and not on promoting Hinduism among Hindus in India or abroad, their teachings were geared toward Western expectations, in terms of healing and self-fulfillment—although this proves to be also attractive for the Indian urban middle classes (Warrier 2003). As described in the first section of this chapter, neo-Hindu movements in Euroamerican societies today are likely to de-emphasize the polarization between East and West, and to dismiss cultural differences and even the Hindu origin of their teaching. Universalism becomes a means to reassure an audience who is not believed to be ready to convert to Hinduism. This Western-oriented discourse may explain why many of these neo-Hindu movements (Siddha Yoga, Sivananda Centres, and Sri Chinmoy, for example) did not attract the Indian diaspora. An extreme case would be Rajneesh, whose teaching was heavily influenced by Gurdjieff and the Human Potential movement. Actually, even when Rajneesh started his ashram in Poona, his criticisms of Hindu religious leaders and the "free love" and violent behavior of his controversial therapies undermined the appeal of his teaching for Indians. Most of his ashram's residents and visitors were foreign; his poor reputation in India partly explained his move to the United States in the 1980s (Carter 1990, 63, 113; Mann 1993, 22; Sharma 1985, 117). We can expect that the more "universalistic" neo-Hindu movements end up having mostly Western-born members and are estranged from the Indian social context, the more meaningless it would be for their teaching to be in tune with Hindu nationalism.

In addition, neo-Hindu movements founded and disseminated mainly outside India tend to have an increasingly Euroamerican leadership. As such, they may well contribute to de-emphasizing the particularistic component of neo-Hindu thinking, hence to the teaching's detachment from Indian culture. For example, most swamis of Siddha Yoga are not originally from India (Thursby 1984). The Sivananda Centres have a totally non-Indian leadership: in 1988, Vishnu-Devananda left the responsibility of managing the mission to students he met and trained in Europe and North America. It is striking that even the swami in charge of the Indian Ashrams and Centres, Swami Mahadevananda (b. 1939), was born in Italy (Sivananda Centres n.d.a.). No acharya of the True World Order, the monastic order that Vishnu-Devananda created to manage his organization, was born in India or has Indian origins. In continuity with Vishnu-Devananda's approach, this leadership reflects the expectation of its Western audience, more than Sivananda's concern with reclaiming India's national vitality. The fact that these neo-Hindu movements developed a non-Indian leadership and membership has tremendous importance. It means that the ethnic component has become irrelevant since non-Hindus can follow the teaching, practice rituals, become initiated to a Hindu order, lead the movement, and teach to new students.

Overall, the homogeneity or the separation of members constitutes a crucial factor in the popularization of Hindu-based teachings in Euroamerican societies.[9] This is also suggested by the tensions currently affecting the Vedanta Societies created by Vivekananda more than a century ago. While their initial objective was to teach Vedanta to Americans and Europeans, there has been an increasing number of members from the Hindu diaspora and a decrease of white American disciples. Indeed, the Hindu diaspora found in the Vedanta Societies an organization they knew, at a time when, in the 1960s and 1970s, there were no Hindu temples to welcome them. Now prevailing in the American centers, there is a new emphasis on rituals that is particularly contentious with non-Hindu members, who give precedence to meditative, individualistic practices over the social and family dimension of pujas. Overall, the culture of American Vedanta Societies are increasingly perceived by their members as overwhelmingly Indian, making non-Hindu members uncomfortable, in particular regarding hierarchical and devotional relations to swamis, the use of Bengali to communicate, or even new ways of preparing food. This Indian culture is also maintained by the tendency of the Indian headquarters of the Vedanta Societies to appoint swamis born and trained in India (Cimino 2008; Giles n.d). This confirms the ambivalence of Westerners adopting exotic resources: Hindu practices and beliefs are adopted insofar as they are, to a certain extent, extracted from their original cultural context.[10]

The Ethnic Dimension in the Kabbalah Centre

A universalistic rhetoric tends to take precedence over an assertion of India's spiritual role in those neo-Hindu movements that focused on a Western audience. By contrast, the Kabbalah Centre and "nationally oriented" neo-Hindu movements somewhat maintain a relation between religion and nationhood, which potentially challenges the universalization of their teaching. Consequently, the transnational diffusion of Sri Sri Ravi Shankar's and Sai Baba's teachings could have involved a cleavage between two different types of disciples, either attracted by the universalistic or by the nationalistic rhetoric, as separated geographically and/or linguistically.[11] In this regard, the Kabbalah Centre is more vulnerable to internal tensions, because of the paramount importance of Israeli students and teachers in nearly all of its branches. Moreover, the Kabbalah Centre also faces contradictions by not having a similar cleavage of membership between ethnically Jewish and non-Jewish students. The following section sheds light on the ways in which the Kabbalah Centre's teaching *as practiced* paradoxically performs and even maintains differences between Jews and non-Jews within the movement. This inevitably generates contradictions with the claims that Kabbalah is not Jewish and transcends cultural, ethnic, and religious boundaries.

The demarcation between different members is reflected in their differentiated participation in activities at the Kabbalah Centre. Since the 1990s, the Kabbalah Centre has developed a broad range of courses and classes to attract a wide audience. Participants in these courses indeed represent an eclectic attendance. Some only attend classes and are not strongly committed to the Kabbalah Centre; they may know very little of its doctrines and practices. By contrast, Jewish festivals and Shabbat are attended by fewer but more committed members, of which a higher proportion are ethnically Jewish. These different forms of involvement in the Kabbalah Centre are maintained by the fact that Shabbat and festivals are usually not advertised to course participants and are not featured on available brochures in local branches. These are meant to advertise Kabbalah as a universal wisdom and to reassure students who could be repelled and confused by the obvious practice of Judaism within the Kabbalah Centre. Through informal discussions and interviews with relatively recent students in Rio, Paris, and London, I found that some were not aware that festivals and Shabbat were actually taking place.

Furthermore, while the movement claims it has nothing to do with Judaism, its valorization of Jewish concepts and practices unavoidably leads students to associate it with Judaism, even though they are told that this is neither Judaism nor religion. In short, for a minority, it is obvious they have joined a Jewish movement, despite the official universalistic discourse and other students' assumption that the Kabbalah Centre is not Jewish. I would like to illustrate this point by a fieldwork example of a Shabbat evening in Paris. The Torah scrolls were circulated among the participants; people approached the scrolls, and touched and kissed them, which is a practice I often observed in the Kabbalah Centre. At this moment, a woman said to another one with surprise: "We were not doing this at the synagogue," explicitly referring to her former socialization to Judaism to understand and contrast the Kabbalah Centre customs. As her interlocutor answered right away, "But we are not in a synagogue," the first replied: "Yes, but I'm getting confused!" In other words, she knows she is not in a synagogue (although I heard students and teachers sometimes call the Centre "the synagogue"), but she still perceives continuity in religious code and practice. Thus, she refers to her early socialization and norms for an understanding of the teaching. Minutes later, as the Torah came nearer again, both joked about whether they would dare or not to touch the scrolls and one stated, "in the synagogue we were doing it." Some even dismissed the Kabbalah Centre's universalistic claims: Robin, a Londoner of Jewish origin who has been involved in the Kabbalah Centre for a few years, was cynical about it. He remarks, "[the teacher] says that Muslim or Catholics won't be in contradiction with their faith but that's bullshit, what the Kabbalah Centre offers is pooh-pooh religion."

Unsurprisingly, the Jewish identity of the Kabbalah Centre is unquestioned in its Israeli context. This became clear to me when I asked Israeli interviewees whether, according to them, the Kabbalah Centre was Jewish: the answer was so obvious to them that they could barely understand why I was posing such a question. Elsewhere I had received nuanced answers for what was considered to be quite a subtle issue. Throughout my fieldwork in the Tel Aviv Centre, I found that despite teachers' warnings not to behave in a religious way, there was a relatively high level of conformity among students, which revealed that, there, the Kabbalah Centre tends to reinforce the observance of Judaism. During a Shabbat on a Saturday morning, one of my informants told me that the student who was reading the Torah in front of us owned several restaurants in Tel Aviv and had opened new premises near the Kabbalah Centre. I told my informant that I had passed the new restaurant that morning and it was not open. She replied immediately, to state the obvious: "you don't even think someone who studies Kabbalah, his restaurant would not be kosher, right?" In Judaism, it is one of God's commandments not to work during Shabbat. I should have known, in other words, that he is observant *because* he was a student of the Kabbalah Centre. Overall, my fieldwork in Israel contrasted with the other fieldwork phases in the sense that the fundamentals of Judaism were taken for granted, not only by a small core of teachers and volunteers, as in London or Rio, for example, but by the majority of students and teachers. The fact that these fundamentals were given a new spiritual significance, contrasted with a religious "robotic" approach, meant that Jewish norms and practices were actually enhanced and reasserted (Chapter 6). Furthermore, the Kabbalah Centre's practices and norms are congruent with Israeli social values. Judaism's majority status in Israel means that its symbols, values, and practices are recognized and experienced as part of national culture. As a result, it would be difficult for Israeli students not to consider the Kabbalah Centre as being Jewish. Finally, in Israel the ethnic identity of the Kabbalah Centre's members is taken for granted since nearly if not all students are born Jewish. As everyone is therefore perceived as part of the "chosen people," the potential exclusiveness of the Kabbalah Centre's teaching is unproblematic. Actually, despite the fact that the students in Tel Aviv are well aware of the Kabbalah Centre's outreach to non-Jews and publicly express a positive outlook on this, they may still implicitly consider it as a movement for Jews. While conducting fieldwork in Tel Aviv, some of my informants knew my husband was coming to Israel to visit me for a few days. During this period, I was often asked why was he not coming with me to the Centre. Once, a participant responded before I could answer: "Ah yeah that's right, he's not Jewish!" Here, Jewishness is clearly understood as an ethnic category. Ranit, a female interviewee in her early forties, explained to me that she was told off for having non-Jewish boyfriends by the teachers, in reference to disparaging sayings, in the Zohar, about Jewish women who are attracted to non-Jews.

The status of the Kabbalah Centre in Israel is very specific. Nevertheless, I found that elsewhere the movement's teaching also maintains a demarcation between Jewish and non-Jewish students. It first does so by granting Jews a higher level of "spirituality" and the responsibility to repair the world for the whole of humanity. Berg described this not as an ethnic but as a metaphysical distinction so that, by their presence and desire to grow, all students of the Kabbalah Centre potentially demonstrate having a Jewish soul. However, the ethnic dimension of this distinction is in fact reified through practices. It is on the basis of Jews' metaphysical characteristics and particular mission to repair the world that the Kabbalah Centre explains why only they have to respect the 613 commandments given by God. Transgressions are believed to generate "short-circuits," which undermine the student's connection to the Light. By contrast, those who are not Jewish only need to comply with the seven noahide laws. The performance of Jewish rituals, by definition, requires *those who are born Jewish or who converted to Judaism* only to perform certain actions, giving them de facto particular roles that differentiate them. For example, the Kabbalah Centre respects the traditional rule that requires a minyan, a quorum of at least 10 male Jews, to perform rituals and ceremonies. As in Orthodox synagogues, a Cohen then a Levi are first called to read the Torah in front of the audience on Saturday morning Shabbat. Yet these rules are unspoken; it is by asking questions as part of the fieldwork that I discovered them. They are ambiguous as well: every man can be asked to hold the Torah scrolls, but only Jews can read the Torah. To prevent a sense of alienation from students who are never called to do so and cannot follow prayers in Hebrew, the teachers invite the assembly to connect with the power of unity and re-mind them that "we're all equal, everybody gets the energy." It actually does not prevent this sense of alienation. I found that non-Jewish students are very conscious of being excluded from core knowledge and activities. They are also very conscious of the presence of Jewish students who can read Hebrew, read the Torah, and perform certain ritual acts. Like Farrah (Chapter 2), they may overestimate the proportion of Jewish students in their local branch. I also found that in Rio, for instance, several students felt excluded from the branch's inner (Jewish) circle, for not being Jewish. Interestingly, I observed that while there may have been a close group of members around the Brazilian teacher and his wife, the "Jewish divide" was not relevant, for similar criticisms were made by students of Jewish origin. Yet these perceptions are important in that they reveal a sense of exclusion on the basis of Jewishness.

Finally, there is an amazing consequence of this demarcation in the ritual participation and observance of the commandments. The coexistence of Jewish with non-Jewish students who are not required to follow the same rules helps the former to perform their *mitzvot*, through a complementarity of roles. Doing so, it cannot but dramatize the demarcation between observant Jewish students and the others. Again, it seems better left unspoken, and this only appeared through fieldwork, by being myself caught up in this organized complementarity between students. In London, I often used to come to the Kabbalah Centre before the start of Shabbat and help the *chevre* (full-time volunteers) in the kitchen to prepare the dinner. It was, especially at the start of fieldwork, a good way to participate in the Kabbalah Centre's casual activities and speak with students. One Friday evening, as I reached the kitchen, I bumped into volunteers who asked me to turn on the light of the storage room for them. At first, I did not understand why I had to since they were themselves standing in front of the door; I probably looked puzzled and they impatiently repeated their request. It was only afterward that I realized what happened: they could not turn on the light on Shabbat. Assuming I was not Jewish (this is indicative of Israeli volunteers' perception of the peripheral students at the London Centre), it would not therefore do any harm if *I* turned the light on. I was then asked by another *chevre* to do other things because she "couldn't do it." In other words, I played the role of the "Shabbat goy"—traditionally, the Gentile who assists Jews by performing actions forbidden by religious rules. The fact that some *chevre* are not Jewish seems to reinforce this organizational complementarity, as suggested by an Israeli student:

> Another thing I like about them is that it's a very even and balanced place between the Jews and the not-Jews who are chevre, and they really accept each other, it's amazing because at Shabbat, the Jews would never do anything that is forbidden and the non-Jews would do everything for them, they would, I don't know, press the buttons for the elevator, someone would make the video screen work.

Therefore, in some ways, the presence of non-Jewish students facilitates the observance of Jewish students. This is not only a religious divide between observant and non-observant students: I expect that those who are known as Jewish but not observant would not be asked to perform these tasks. It is thus an ethnic demarcation that is maintained and reiterated by this organizational arrangement.

Apart from very committed members such as teachers and *chevre*, non-Jewish students seem relatively unaware of rules and norms that underlie the teaching in practice and which demarcate them from ethnically Jewish students. I agree with Myers (2007, x, 124) who writes that the "Kabbalah Centre's method of outreach...tends to conceal the core component of its teachings" and that "[f]ew people are aware of the leadership's and the inner core's loyalty to traditional conceptions of Jew and non-Jew." Except for references to biblical stories, students rarely hear about "Jews" in the Kabbalah Centre, no one in the movement is explicitly identified as Jewish or not Jewish, and the central role that "ethnic" Jews hold for ritual practices is not explained to attendants. It is unclear, even for very involved members, whether non-Jews can be *chevre* or teachers. As a result, the demarcation between Jews and non-Jews implied by the Kabbalah Centre practices is not obvious to those who have a limited knowledge of what Jewish observance and rituals imply. These concealments remind us that religious exoticism and, by extension, bricolage can only operate by ignoring certain aspects of what is appropriated.

The Kabbalah Centre: De-judaicization and Crises

It has only been a little more than a decade that the Kabbalah Centre started to present Kabbalah as a "universal wisdom" de-linked from Judaism. Yet, for its first students, its teaching continues to revitalize Jewish values and practices. Doing so, it unavoidably reiterates the ethnic demarcation between Jews and non-Jews within the movement. While we can expect that some students are drawn to the teaching partly *because* it is believed not to be Jewish, others strengthen their bond with Judaism in the Kabbalah Centre. The coexistence of contradictory rationales is relatively concealed by the constant work of universalistic reinterpretations, the silence on what could reveal the particularistic dimension of the teaching, and the unawareness of Judaism's rules by a large number of students. Yet, for critical students in Israel, the cultural changes resulting from the Kabbalah Centre's transnational diffusion are more obvious. Looking positively at the teaching to non-Jews, the Kabbalah Centre remains for them a means to reinforce religious and national values, which is in some ways at the antipodes of the Kabbalah Centre's recent detachment from Judaism. In this last section of the chapter, I explore crises and scissions that the Kabbalah Centre has experienced as the result of its ambivalent relationship with Judaism.

The Kabbalah Centre struggled with its position in relation to Judaism from the start. Indeed, its early attempts to revitalize the Jewish tradition through an unconventional teaching of Kabbalah led to an internal crisis that nearly put an end to the Kabbalah Centre after just a few years of existence. A first scission occurred in the 1980s in Israel when a student left to create a more orthodox movement for the study of Kabbalah. Today, this movement, Bnei Baruch, is competing with the Kabbalah Centre for the worldwide dissemination of Kabbalah. Michael Laitman (1946–) came from Belorussia to Israel in 1974. He was one of Berg's students in Tel Aviv but in 1979 he also started to study Kabbalah with Baruch Ashlag (1907–1991), son of the Kabbalist Yehuda Ashlag. Baruch Ashlag lived in a religious community in Bnei Brak; he had been taught Kabbalah by his father and possessed most of his unpublished works. As Laitman embraced the more orthodox and strict approach of Baruch Ashlag, he started to criticize the Kabbalah Centre's libertarian and unconventional approach. When he left in 1984 to create his own movement, all the senior members of the Tel Aviv Centre but one left and joined him. The Kabbalah Centre was wrecked (Myers 2007, 60; 2011, 205). This episode shows that Israeli students in the 1980s were clearly expecting a revitalization of their practice of Judaism through Kabbalah: "It was a crisis because people had more inclination towards being more religious," recalls a former student.[12] According to the same interviewee, the Kabbalah Centre in Tel Aviv gradually found a new wave a students, by spreading a "message that is universal, that is open"—that is, not orthodox. Indeed, making Kabbalah a teaching for all is another matter.

This is what the second scission within the movement tends to show. Interviews of individuals who were directly involved or witnessed this crisis led me to understand this scission as resulting from the contradictions and tensions generated by the Kabbalah Centre's new universalistic rhetoric. In 2008, one of the oldest teachers of the Kabbalah Centre left. Shaul Youdkevitch had been a full-time member for 28 years, having taught at the Tel Aviv Centre since the split that affected it in 1984. Based in Los Angeles for a few years, he came back to Israel to run a new organization that he founded: "Universal Kabbalah Communities." The idea of a "universal Kabbalah" is definitely enduring. Yet, interestingly, Youdkevitch initially aimed to develop a curriculum and program that could be adopted by synagogues and Jewish communities (Tugend 2008). What struck me in the descriptions I was given of this crisis was the emphasis on changes to the teaching that amounted to hiding the Kabbalah Centre's Jewishness. This was blamed on the new leadership. Since Philip Berg's stroke in 2004, his wife and sons have directed the movement in a more authoritarian and commercial fashion, I was told. Eyal, a former teacher, believes that "when the drive is selling, then you have a natural selection," which involved removing "whatever disturbs selling and having people around enough." The Kabbalah Centre's commercial trend already existed under Philip Berg's leadership, but what is crucial here is that the alleged commercial aims seem to have involved concealing the Jewishness of the movement. Eyal described what, in his views, happened in the Kabbalah Centre in recent years:

> Everything is about what will sell. How to say it in a way that will sell to as many people as possible, okay? So now you have this idea that to be too Jewish is not to do good business. Very simple, so you hide it. Anyway, the ideas of Judaism are universal so that's not a big problem. You know, you're not, you're not lying too much. Right? But then, they start to get mixed up about, "are we Jewish or are we not Jewish?," you know, eating Kosher. And starting you know, okay, you know what, we can eat in a non-Kosher restaurant because we don't want the students to see that we are too Kosher. We will just play with it. We will just eat salads. This is okay.

This interview confirms that popularizing Kabbalah in the widest possible way entails its partial detachment from Judaism. But Eyal also points out the painful implication—to be popular, it is better not to display Jewishness. This culture of concealment to reassure and make comfortable non-Jewish students is implicitly related, once more, to the "self-hating Jew" by Eyal:

> You start to be having a lifestyle of hiding stuff all the time. And it becomes part of your nature and that's not good. Because you're always like, you always have to hide it. This is, you know, don't be ashamed of who you are, say it, or don't be it.

By and large, the removal of references to Judaism in courses that increasingly draw on popular psychology brought resistance among the old generation of teachers. For instance, interviewees mentioned the growing influence of Jamie Greene in the Kabbalah Centre. Jamie Greene was born in England and has a Jewish secular background, I was told. A musician in the 1980s, he became a psychotherapist and coach in Los Angeles, addressing issues such as "overcoming fears, phobias and anxiety," "hidden addictions" and the "art of negotiation" (Greene 2010). He closed his practice in 2004 and became a full-time teacher in the Los Angeles Kabbalah Centre until 2009. During this period he and Yehuda Berg developed a new teaching method, "Living Kabbalah

System (LKS)," which strongly blends Kabbalah with popular psychology. LKS is presented as a set of three packages of courses and exercises on CDs. They allow individuals to study by themselves but are complemented with cycles of classes in the Kabbalah Centre. Again, the emphasis on self-fulfillment did not start then, but the increasing psychologization of the teaching is linked to its detachment from Judaism, for example by Avi, who was a full-time volunteer in Los Angeles at the time:

> With Jamie Greene we had a leader who was not Israeli, who was not, who doesn't know Hebrew, so he was becoming a powerful person there. So he came, like pushing into that direction and they're like, others younger, younger generation from LA who became teachers, were also pulling it to that direction because, they didn't know Hebrew, they didn't know all the texts.... They were second generation Kabbalah Centre students who were not familiar with Judaism in other ways.

In other words, the psychological dimension of the teaching, more accessible and rooted in American culture, has become more important as the Kabbalah Centre recruited students and teachers who are not Israelis and, as non-Jews or secular Jews, do not have the linguistic, cultural, and textual knowledge involved in the study of Kabbalistic texts. Shaul Youdkevitch, who before he left was working on the "Kabbalah University" project, which aimed to gather courses and texts for the study of Kabbalah, was visibly not pulling in the same direction. The knowledge of the leaders themselves is also an important factor. Philip Berg's stroke led Karen Berg and her sons to have increasing authority in the movement. Presented as a spiritual leader, Karen Berg, however, makes very little reference to Kabbalah or Judaism. Her writing and speeches are oriented toward women and often deal with family issues and relationships. They also are, like Yehuda's, permeated by popular psychology and New Age ideas. This psychologization (see Chapter 5), combined with a universalistic rhetoric, accelerates the de-contextualization of the Kabbalah Centre and greatly increases its potential for dissemination. But it unavoidably creates tensions with students and teachers who thought they entered a revivalist Jewish movement. They may be a minority, but they are core to the Kabbalah Centre's organization and teaching transmission. Bricolage seems fluid, easy, playful, and unaffected by differences and particularisms; its backstage actually reveals difficult interpretations and dangerous transformations.

Synthesis

This chapter corroborates the argument that the wide popularization of exotic religious resources entails their domestication, hence their de-contextualization. Among neo-Hindu movements and the Kabbalah Centre, this process takes the shape of a universalistic rhetoric. This rhetoric presents Vedanta and Kabbalah as unique meta-religions, in other words, as universal wisdoms transcending religious, cultural, and national differences and boundaries. As such, it also refutes the idea that Vedanta and Kabbalah are, respectively, Hindu and Jewish. The objective of this universalistic rhetoric is to reassure an audience drawn by "Eastern spiritualities" or Kabbalah's secrets who do not identify with these religions, do not wish to convert, may be reticent toward "organized religions" in general, and are not familiar with these specific religious customs, scriptures, and practices. Accordingly, the Kabbalah Centre cannot be associated with "Judaizing movements" (Parfitt and Trevisan Semi 2002) involving conversions or "ethnic identifications with the people of Israel" (p. xi). Similarly, some Sufi groups have developed a universalistic approach in Europe and North America. Predominantly attracting individuals who neither consider themselves to be Muslims nor desire to convert, they promote the spiritual advancement of humanity as a whole, they may even cease to refer to the Koran, the Islamic law, or the tradition of the Prophet Muhammad (Philippon 2014; Westerlund 2004). Shamanic practices and vocation are also considered to be universal and not religious in the "neo-shamanism" that emerged in Euroamerican societies (Lindquist 1997, 24–27). In these groups, ceremonies, workshops, and indigenous shamanic rituals are de-contextualized, by being used to revive romanticized Celtic and Pagan traditions. By contrast, few Japanese religious movements attracted individuals who are not Japanese. Cornille (2000) underscores the nationalistic and ethnocentric tendencies of movements that promote Japanese ethnicity and the restoration of traditional rituals and values. Those that became popular worldwide among non-Japanese (e.g., Mahikari and Soka Gakkai) are those that developed a universalistic orientation as described in this chapter.

By and large, making exotic religious resources "available" for practices of bricolage potentially may entail: staging particularisms while deleting references to certain religious concepts and customs, re-interpreting core tenets that bind religiosity with a particular land and people (hence a de-ethnicization), downplaying or re-interpreting the meaning of rituals, introducing new practices, renewing leadership and membership over time, separating different constituencies, adopting a double language, and concealing contradictions. In other words, the processes by which exotic religious resources become ready to use are multifarious, contradictory, and perilous for religious organizations. Assuming that bricolage is playful and that particularisms are unproblematic means being mystified by the domestication of exotic religious resources. There is a "backstage" to bricolage, where, again, otherness is the crux of the matter.

4

Universalistic Ambitions, Local Realities: Bricolage in (National) Context

ULTIMATELY, UNIVERSALISTIC AMBITIONS are also affected by local realities. Indeed, despite their ambitions to transcend their particularism and become a meta-religion, transnational religious organizations necessarily interact with their local social environment. Influenced by local social environments, their adaptive strategies have led them, in some places, and in particular phases of their development, to identify with Hinduism or Judaism, or to insist on the religious character of their teaching. And conversely: developing universalistic ambitions may affect the dissemination of these teachings locally and entail growth, decline, or changes in the teaching. Accordingly, the de-ethnicization and development of these religious teachings depend in part on national constraints and opportunities, in particular specific responses to religious diversity and the local religious landscape. In other words, exotic religious resources are not "available" and free-floating; their availability and content depend on social, political, and religious conditions. The possibility of practices of bricolage therefore needs to be placed in their national context.

This chapter explores the interactions of neo-Hindu movements and the Kabbalah Centre with their respective social environments through a multidimensional comparison. To begin, this comparison sheds light on the ways in which local branches of the same transnational movement respond to different local social environments—for example, why do some neo-Hindu movements claim to be universal in some places, but Hindu in others? It also aims to explain why in the same country, some neo-Hindu movements present themselves as religious and/or Hindu when other similar groups do not. Second, it explores the ways in which internal changes in a religious movement affect its local branches in different ways—for example, why some branches declined while others expanded when the Kabbalah Centre started to present itself as a "universal wisdom" de-linked from Judaism. This multidimensional and empirical comparison focuses on the British and French contexts in particular, so that the interactions of neo-Hindu movements and the Kabbalah Centre may be evaluated in the same countries.

Neo-Hindu Movements in France and Britain
ISKCON: The Re-ethnicization of a Neo-Hindu Movement

The first section of this chapter deals with neo-Hindu movements in Britain and focuses on the International Society for Krishna Consciousness (ISKCON). Indeed, no other case study could better serve as a cornerstone for an exploration of the opportunities and constraints that the British context represents for neo-Hindu movements, and the effects that these constraints and opportunities can have on their universalistic ambitions. ISKCON is one of the counterculture's iconic movements. The devotees' saffron robes and shaved heads, their dance and chants in the streets, and their bookselling in public spaces all made the popularization of Hindu-based teachings highly visible. ISKCON was founded in 1966 in New York by Swami Prabhupada (1896–1977). An Indian man from Calcutta, Swami Prabhupada had been a successful businessman before following an ascetic path of devotion to Krishna and embarking for the United States in 1965 on a preaching mission. In the 1970s, ISKCON represented 45,000 members and more than 75 centers and communities in the world (Carey 1987, 82; Rochford 1991, 177; 1995, 215). It now claims to be a network of 400 centers, including 60 farm communities, 50 schools, and 60 restaurants (Cole 2007, 46). ISKCON is distinct from most neo-Hindu movements in the sense that it traces its origins to Gaudiya or Chaitanya Vaishnavism, a movement of devotion to the God Krishna that appeared in Bengal in the nineteenth century. Gaudiya Vaishnavism developed independently from the socio-religious reform movements that were influential around Calcutta at the same time (see Chapter 1) and fostered the development of a transnational neo-Hindu mission, in particular with Vivekananda. Thus, unlike many contemporary neo-Hindu teachings, ISKCON's doctrine departs from Vivekananda's neo-Vedantic, westernized, and inner-worldly approach and rejects its universalism (Carey 1987, 99). In fact, Wallis (1984) saw in ISKCON a typical world-rejecting religious movement, thereby contrasting with many neo-Hindu movements in Euroamerican societies (this is, however,

changing; Nye 2001, 20). Originally, ISKCON devotees were all full-time volunteers. They lived in ashrams and turned to intense devotional practices
and service in order to detach themselves from an illusory and threatening
material world. ISKCON's teaching, only recognizing the Bhagavad Gita and
Prabhupada's writings, is often described as exclusive. It promotes a relatively
rigid orthodoxy that is reflected in very strict lifestyles and conservative views
(on sexuality, for instance, see Palmer 1994).

In its early days, ISKCON was mainly composed of Westerners and, unsurprisingly, the founder presented ISKCON as being non-Hindu. Swami
Prabhupada wrote that ISKCON "has nothing to do with the Hindu religion
or any system of religion" and therefore "is not preaching the so-called Hindu
religion" (cited in Brzezinski 1998). Fearing that ISKCON would be identified with Hinduism and would become unattractive for Westerners, Swami
Prabhupada intentionally ignored Indian migrants in America (Rochford
2007, 182). Thus, ISKCON's early days tend to confirm the claim made in
the previous chapters of this book, that the popularization of such teachings
is likely to entail a partial detachment from Hindu roots. Nye (2001, 30), for
instance, notes that most Western devotees do not consider ISKCON to be
Hindu. However, since the end of the 1980s, scholars started to describe dramatic transformations of ISKCON in terms of "indianization" (Carey 1987) or
"hinduization" (Nye 2001, 27). By these terms, they point out the fact that
over the last three decades, in Britain and the United States, the number of
Western disciples has consistently declined, while the number of South Asian
members has increased. For instance, Rochford (2007, 181) notes that in 2005
a majority of the 25,000 American members were of Indian descent; some
of them reached leadership roles (Rochford 1995, 220). These new members
have had a significant influence on ISKCON's religious culture, encouraging
Western members to change "their religious behaviors and identities to fall
more in line with an Indian ideal" (Vande Berg and Kniss 2008, 88). Also,
ISKCON officially redefined itself as being Hindu in North America, as well
as in Britain, where it became a key representative of the British "Hindu community."[1] In other words, ISKCON shifted its universalism geared toward
Western disciples to undergo a process of re-ethnicization, centered on its
relationships with Hinduism and "ethnic" Hindus. This identification with
migrant populations meant losing the attractive power of exoticism as well,
and it is therefore not surprising that ISKCON's Western members have not
grown since then.

This transformation is atypical among neo-Hindu movements. Certainly,
ISKCON's rigid orthodoxy was less flexibly adapted to the Western lifestyle
than other neo-Hindu movements—accordingly, this "hinduization" may not

be as dramatic as it would be for groups such as Siddha Yoga, the Sivananda Centres, Transcendental Meditation, or the Rajneesh movement. Furthermore, a vital quest for legitimacy and resources contributed to ISKCON's motivation for reaching out to Indian Hindus. Indeed, in the late 1970s and the 1980s, anti-cult campaigners criticized ISKCON's recruitment and fundraising methods, accusing the movement of brainwashing and family breakup; serious allegations of physical and psychological abuse of children surfaced (Rochford 2007, 74; Knott 2000, 156). These sexual scandals, the death of Swami Prabhupada in 1977, and the challenges of responding to the needs of its first-generation devotees, now having families to support, all led to the defection of many devotees. These defections in turn resulted in a dramatic fall in financial resources (Rochford 2007, 185), a crucial issue for members who were fully involved in community life and had no source of income but bookselling and donations. In order to survive, ISKCON chose to shift their image from a cult to a Hindu denomination, as an American ISKCON leader explained to Rochford (1991, 271):

> it is a tactical strategy to have the Hindu community come forward and say what they really think about ISKCON. We are Hindus. We are part of the Hindu culture and therefore the same kind of First Amendment rights as any religion....I admit that this is a strategy. But this is also their feeling as well. I mean, when ISKCON is persecuted, they feel that they are persecuted too.

ISKCON's survival took the shape of a re-ethnicization; nevertheless, this can only be understood in the light of the national contexts in which the movement is implanted. Indeed, studies in Brazil (Guerriero 2000), in Hungary (Kamarás 2000) or my own observations in France do not show any signs of "hinduization" of these ISKCON local branches. This adaptive strategy is, however, noticeable in North America and Britain. There, an increasing number of devotes are of Asian descent (Knott 1986, 56) and the British branch became a key representative of the "Hindu community" in the public sphere, despite having emerged in the countercultural milieu. ISKCON contributed to the founding of the most important umbrella organizations that represent Hinduism in Britain. It is a founding body of the National Council of Hindu Temples (NCHT). Set up in 1978, the NHCT aims to unify Hinduism in Britain, to represent Hindus' interests when negotiating with the government and other institutions, and to contribute to interfaith dialogue as Hindus (National Council of Hindu Temples 2005). In 1994, ISKCON was also involved in the launch of the Hindu Council of the United Kingdom, a network of Hindu organizations also aiming to be the voice of British Hindus. Thus, despite the fact that Swami Prabhupada refused to identify his teaching with Hinduism and offered a relatively exclusive teaching in relation to the diversity of Hindu doctrines and philosophies, ISKCON's involvement in these organizations inevitably identifies it with Hinduism. But there is more: it grants ISKCON a decisive role and influence on the representation of Hindus in Britain. This observation led Nye (1996b) to talk about an "iskonisation" of British Hinduisms.

ISKCON and the British "Hindu Faith Community"

ISKCON's re-ethnicization results from two main factors, which have the potential to affect the universalistic trend of neo-Hindu movements. The first of these factors has to do with the characteristics of the local religious field and, in this case, the presence of a Hindu population in Britain and North America. The postwar period marked the emergence of a Hindu diaspora in Britain and North America (Coward 2000; Kurien 2001; Peach and Gale 2003; Vertovec 1997, 2000). ISKCON temples slightly preceded these South Asian migration trends; consequently, they were able to offer services that were essential to the Hindu diaspora in their new host societies. The lack of financial and human resources, and the fact that many Hindus from India were used to having domestic shrines, meant that the Hindu diaspora had been slow in organizing its own religious activities (Peach and Gale 2003, 478; Vande Berg and Kniss 2008, 86). Existing organizations in Britain, such as the Ramakrishna Mission, were not particularly proselyte and often attracted populations from particular linguistic-regional backgrounds. Therefore ISKCON temples were, in the 1970s, among the very few places available to a diverse Hindu diaspora—for instance, the opening of the first ISKCON temple in London coincided with the migration of East African Hindus who, by contrast, were used to frequenting temples regularly and had a Vaishnava background (Carey 1987, 86). ISKCON's rigorous ritual observance, the high standard of its worship, its training facilities for priests, and its very organized temples with full-time committed members all greatly impressed the Hindu diaspora, who started to use ISKCON's premises like any other Hindu temple in Britain (Nye 1996b, 9), the United States (Rochford 2007, 183), and Canada (Banerjee and Coward 2009, 45–46). In addition, ISKCON's provision of educational facilities and activities for youth gave it a definite advantage over other Hindu organizations (Nye 1996b, 12) and resonated with migrants' desire to transmit a Hindu heritage to their children. Since ISKCON had started by teaching Westerners, that is to say, individuals who had no previous knowledge of Indian culture and languages, it probably had acquired a useful experience to reach out to the Hindu second-generation through Sunday schools and youth clubs (Banerjee and Coward 2009, 45–46; Nye 1996b, 11; Carey 1987, 90). ISKCON leaders believe that their youth group, with 5,000 regular participants, is the largest Indian youth group in Europe today (Cole 2007, 48). Finally, "ethnic" Hindus saw ISKCON's mission as asserting the significance of Hindu values and beliefs in Euroamerican societies. This responded to their concern with the preservation of their cultural heritage in a foreign society that they associated with materialism and corrupted values (Rochford 2007, 183; Vande Berg and Kniss 2008, 93).

ISKCON deliberately and actively chose to serve the Hindu diaspora (Cole 2007, 43). As early as the mid-1970s, ISKCON created a Life Membership Program in the United States to connect with their South Asian sympathizers, providing them with access to facilities and social networking in ISKCON branches in exchange for their financial support (Rochford 2007, 184–185). In 1979, ISKCON set up an Indian Community Affairs Program, whose aim was to respond to the needs of the Hindu diaspora in Britain as well—hence ISKCON's provision of festivals, pujas, and ritual services and its impressive development of educational services. ISKCON encourages the visit to their temples by the public, and its representatives regularly visit schools to introduce Hinduism and provide resources and training for teachers (Knott 2000, 160). Their publishing branch, the Bhaktivedanta Book Trust, maintains relations with educational institutions and encourages schools to buy their books (Scheifinger 1999). Thus, its representatives claim that ISKCON headquarters receive an average of 150 school visits per year and that around 1,000 schools possess their educational resource pack on Hinduism (Cole 2007, 48). ISKCON is now the "faith partner" of the Krishna-Avanti school, the first state-funded Hindu school in Britain, which opened in 2008.

The support of the Hindu diaspora has been vital for ISKCON, not only financially but also for changing the movement's public role and image.[2] Adapting to the needs and expectations of the Hindu diaspora is nevertheless not without difficulties. "Ethnic" Hindus tend to have a pragmatic and non-exclusive relationship with ISKCON and only a minority become fully committed to the community of devotees. To them it serves as an Indian-Hindu community center where they can socialize. They may appreciate Swami Prabhupada's conversion of Westerners without agreeing with his teaching or sharing his belief in Krishna as the supreme deity. They are not always comfortable with the ways in which Westerners chant and dance, which they find disrespectful and loud. New elements of Hindu rituals, in particular a stronger emphasis on deity worship (and even the worship of other divinities), are introduced, while Swami Prabhupada's specific teaching is downplayed. Undoubtedly, "in coming to ISKCON to worship and strengthen their ethnic identities, Indian Hindus reshaped ISKCON's religious culture and overall mission as a new religious movement" (Rochford 2007, 131). Indeed, "ethnic" Hindus frequenting ISKCON often do not feel committed to ISKCON's preaching mission and question the necessity of maintaining its support to full-time volunteers—in Philadelphia, Indian board members who fund the temple distinguish between Indian members and temple residents (Zaidman 1997, 341). Vande Berg and Kniss (2008, 90) also state that, by and large, Indians attend ISKCON in Chicago "*despite* Western involvement and leadership." Zaidman (2000, 215) notes that in Philadelphia, non-Indian ISKCON priests are not accepted as proper temple priests by Indian participants, who sometimes choose to go to another Hindu temple for certain rituals. On the Western devotees' side, some express their regret at ISKCON becoming a Hindu temple. The fact that Indian Hindus come mainly to socialize with other members of the Hindu diaspora makes them feel like outsiders (Rochford 2007, 190–191, 181). Interestingly, we can note in passing that the previous chapter evoked similar tensions in the American Vedanta Societies founded by Vivekananda as a result of the increasing number of "ethnic" Hindu members. Finally, there is, in some American branches at least, an ethnic divide between Asian and Western members. This divide is reflected by limited interactions between ISKCON's two constituencies, the rejection of Western devotees by Indian members as appropriate mates for marriage, or the fact that some temples organize separate activities for these two constituencies (Rochford 2007, 190–191; Zaidman 1996, 2000).

Britain's Religious Politics and Hinduism

ISKCON's adaptive strategy takes place in the context of the new British religious politics, and this is the second factor of ISKCON's re-ethnicization. Until the incorporation of the European Convention of Human Rights into British law in 2000, the Race Relation Acts had protected minorities recognized as ethnic or racial since 1965. Accordingly, most planning issues relating to the religious practices of Hindus, Muslims, and Sikhs were discussed in terms of ethnicity or race, and there was a tendency to racialize these minorities (Beckford et al. 2006, 56; Wolffe 1994, 100). These categorizations were significantly arbitrary: Jews and Sikhs were legally recognized as ethnic groups, by contrast with Muslims, for example, due to the diversity of ethnic origins of Muslims in Britain (Asad 1990; Modood 1994; Monaghan 2001; Robilliard 1984). Finally, by taking for granted the existence of homogenous ethnic categories, Britain's race relations entailed a reification of cultural identities, a process necessary for the state to be able to interact with its "minorities." Indeed, British multiculturalism aims at social cohesion through dialogue and cooperation between local authorities and these ethnic minorities—through local "community relations councils," for instance. To be included in this consultation, defend one's interests, and have a role in the public sphere, social actors have to present themselves as a united, clearly bounded, and legible entity, and develop a capacity to mobilize its presupposed constituency despite internal divisions in terms of culture, language, or religion (Lapeyronnie et al. 1990, 185–187). While a shift "from race to religion" (Allen 2005) undeniably took place in British politics over the last 15 years, this construction of homogenous "communities" in response to political pressure has been maintained in the state's relations with religions.

Several factors led to the increasing significance of religion in the British public sphere at the turn of the new millennium: the incorporation of the European Convention of Human Rights into British law, minorities' demands and identity claims, and more important, a growing decentralization of power. As local authorities are increasingly expected to provide public services, the third sector has been envisaged as potential partners in this service provision (Beckford et al. 2006, 11, 77). Religions therefore gained the opportunity to interact and cooperate with public institutions. There had been, since 1992, an Inner Cities Religious Council (ICRC), which was set up to allow religions to have their say on regeneration policies. In 2003, under Tony Blair, the Cohesion and Faith Community Unit was set up within the Home Office to pursue similar aims: to ensure that policies and services engage with the entire population, but also to make efficient use of the "social capital"[3] that religious organizations possess—local knowledge, skills, social networks, paid workers, organizational structures, premises, funds from other organizations, and so on. Seen as a pool of resources, "faith communities," as they have been called since then, are envisaged as providing voluntary activities, suggesting and implementing policies in order to promote interfaith activities, social cohesion, and urban regeneration (Department of the Environment, Transport and the Regions 1997; Home Office 2004; Local Government Association 2002). It is therefore a pragmatic approach toward religion that allows them to have a public role, as illustrated by this interview with one of the civil servants of the ICRC:

> What you probably gather from this conversation, is that we engage with faith communities not just for the sheer fun of it, because it's

intrinsically good in itself, but there are two various broad concerns: re-generation, community cohesion. And so there are practical aims in mind, for why we do this.

It is arguable that the idea of "Big Society" launched by Conservative Prime Minister David Cameron is a continuity of this neoliberal pragmatism, which promotes religions' public role and aims to limit state interventions (British Prime Minister Office 2010).

British religious politics impact on religious organizations, in particular the identification with Hinduism of neo-Hindu movements such as ISKCON. The public arena is open to organizations that are believed to be orthodox, respectable, and representative and can present themselves as single, clearly bounded entities, with a potential for community cohesion and regener-ation—as opposed to "the unofficial, the deviant, the private, and the con-tested" (Gilliat-Ray 2004, 459), or the divided with few resources. And while Hinduism in Britain is socially recognized as a major religious tradition, the numerical importance of the Hindu population contrasts with the extreme diversity and fragmentation of British Hinduism[4]—hence the constitution of an "ecumenical Hinduism" (Williams 1992, 238), which attempts to tran-scend Hinduism's heterogeneity. This is the raison d'être of umbrella organi-zations to which ISKCON contributed, such as the National Council of Hindu Temples and the Hindu Council of the United Kingdom, both gathering a wide range of organizations, community centers, and temples from all over the country "for a United Hindu Voice" (Hindu Council of the UK 2012). It includes distinctive groups such as Arya Samaj and the Chinmaya Mission, groups linked to Aurobindo's and Vivekananda's teachings, and Sathya Sai Baba groups, in the attempt to transcend their divisions in order to assert com-mon identity-claims and interests. Neo-Hindu movements predominantly composed of Western disciples, such as Siddha Yoga or Sivananda Centres, do not belong to these organizations.

Another effect of British religious politics on Hinduism is increasing com-petition among various organizations to represent Hindu-ness. For instance, emerging in 2004, the online Hindu Forum of Britain claimed to have become the largest Hindu umbrella organization, with 200 bodies, and launched con-troversial public campaigns to raise its profile as the voice of British Hindus (Zavos 2008, 335).[5] Similarly, outside India the Vishwa Hindu Parishad aims to support and represent a unified Hinduism—an objective consistent with its nationalist ideology. While being involved in violent campaigns against reli-gious minorities in India, in Britain the VHP is part of the main Hindu um-brella organizations: it obtained state funding for its welfare activities, engages in interfaith dialogue, and has been very influential regarding the ways in which Hinduism is presented in state schools (Mukta 2000). Other particular religious organizations strive to become Hinduism's public representative, despite their particular regional roots or sectarian nature. This is the case, for instance, of the Swaminarayan Mission, a Vaishnava organization that emerged at the start of the nineteenth century in Gujarat and which spread to Britain, the United States, and East Africa (Knott 2009; Williams 1984, 2001).

It is precisely in this political and social context—a mosaic of Hindu organizations competing to engage with the state as "the" representative of the "Hindu faith community"—that we can understand ISKCON's adaptive strategies, its involvement in umbrella organizations, its accommodating effort toward the Hindu diaspora, and its educational projects. Its teaching is certainly not representative of Hinduism as a whole; nevertheless, the fact that it is not attached to any particular regional-linguistic group or caste-based organization is a definite advantage over other movements, and ISKCON has become a key player in the public representation of Hinduism in Britain within the competitive arena of other "faith communities." Its quest for legitimacy therefore finds its way through British religious politics and the construction of a "Hindu faith community," unavoidably leading the movement to a process of re-ethnicization, and this despite the universalistic ambitions of its early days. In this context, ISKCON ceased to be "exotic" by becoming overtly political and identifying with specific ethnic minorities, thereby limiting the appropriation of its teaching for bricolage, from those who are not born Hindu and who represent a minority within the movement nowadays. ISKCON in Britain illustrates the fact that bricolage is affected by the political and religious landscape in which it takes place.

France versus "Oriental Cults"

Neo-Hindu movements do not find in France an "ethnic" Hindu presence comparable to that in Britain. In France, the population originating from South Asia is relatively small; Indians represent a minority of the South Asian migrants, and they usually have not organized religious activities. Most Hindus in France are actually Tamils from Sri Lanka, estimated between 50,000 (Lakshmi Dassaradanayadou 2007, 69) and 70,000 (Goreau-Ponceaud 2009). They represent a relatively recent migration trend that started in the 1980s in the context of the Sri Lankan ethnic conflict. By and large, religious practices have been affected by migration; because of the lack of facilities and the rupture of family networks, religious observance has often become private. However, their two temples are frequented for important festivals. One

of these Parisian temples, the Sri Manicka Vinayakar Alayam, has gained visibility in Parisian city life by organizing a Ganesh festival every year. During
this festival, a chariot carrying the statue of the divinity is pulled through the
18th district's streets that have been covered with smashed coconuts and little
altars along the procession route. Around 25,000 people attend the event (*Le
Parisien* 2011), reaching well beyond the Tamil population: I observed curious
residents of the neighborhood as well as middle-class Parisians, charmed by
the exoticism of the festival. Despite this moment of celebrated religious diversity in Paris, Hindu Tamils in France represent a small and vulnerable population, mainly composed of unskilled workers who are funneled into niches such
as catering, where speaking French is not required (Goel 2008; Percot et al.
1995). My interview with the person in charge of the Sri Manicka Vinayakar
Alayam temple outlined their lack of resources. He explained the difficulties
they faced to have suitable premises for their temple, or to have permanent
priests, due to migration laws and the absence of training resources in France.

On the one hand, this particular religious field—a small, recent, and relatively isolated Hindu community—explains that, despite the fact that some
Tamil families have sometimes participated in ISKCON's satsangs and festivals in France, there is no particular attempt by the latter to accommodate,
adapt, or represent them, as explained to me by ISKCON French representatives. On the other hand, as a vulnerable minority in France, Hindu Tamils
may not see relations with neo-Hindu movements as desirable. Indeed,
I asked the representative of the Parisian Tamil temple about contacts with
ISKCON or Sahaja Yoga whose disciples, I observed, had joined the previous
Ganesh festival. He confirmed he had been contacted by these groups but, he
added, they are not "the same" and he explained he did not feel comfortable
about them coming to the festival. Indeed, as I will show further on, in France
many neo-Hindu movements are suspected to be dangerous "cults" and therefore are themselves marginalized minorities, with some having a disastrous
public image.

The situation of neo-Hindu movements is therefore radically different
in France and explains why a re-ethnicization, such as ISKCON's in Britain,
has not occurred. To begin with, it has to do with France's particular relationship with religions. One of the most important principles of the separation of church and state in France is that the Republic neither recognizes nor
supports any religion. This means that, in principle, the French state gives
precedence to a constitutional equality of all citizens, without any distinction
in terms of ethnicity or religion. It favors the dissolution of particularism and
makes cultural and religious differences a private issue. In response to religious and cultural diversity, Britain emphasized community cohesion, while

France aims to "assimilate" minorities into its republican norms and values. The French state therefore refuses to work with the notions of minority or community and, in contrast with Britain, the idea that religions could influence social policies is highly contentious. For all these reasons, and because France has a strongly centralized state, the public role of religion in France is very limited.

Moreover, the cult controversy in France (Altglas 2008, 2010) significantly shapes neo-Hindu movements' adaptive strategies. Again, this contrasts with the British context, where there has been limited controversy over NRMs and a relative absence of political commitment (Beckford 1983). Britain gave precedence to freedom of choice and individual responsibility, while French parliamentarians engaged in combat against so-called cults claimed that "the state cannot let grow what seems, in many respects, a real plague" and that "to remain passive would be...dangerous for the democratic principles on which our Republic is founded" (Gest and Guyard 1996, 125, my translation). In French anti-cult discourse, NRMs represent an attack against reason, free-thinking, and citizens' loyalty to the Republic (Beckford 2004, 35). In the infamous list of cults elaborated in the 1990s (Gest and Guyard 1996) were included many neo-Hindu movements such as the Osho Information Centre (Rajneesh), the Sri Chinmoy Centre, the Sathya Sai Baba movement, the Brahma Kumaris, Sahaja Yoga, Transcendental Meditation, and ISKCON. Siddha Yoga escaped from being listed in the report; it seems this was because the latter had been prepared in haste and UNADFI could not provide any evidence of complaints in due time.[6] But the exclusion from the list of movements such as Vivekananda's Ramakrishna Mission, the Aurobindo Centre, or the Sivananda Centres may be seen as due to another rationale and actually resulting from a normative distinction between "orientalist cults" and an authentic "Eastern wisdom." The teaching of these gurus has been presented and studied by a small public of intellectuals, artists, and scholars in France, outside—and sometimes before—the counterculture craze for Asian religions. By contrast, the popularization of a diversity of neo-Hindu teachings to a wider audience in the 1970s is perceived as superficial and inauthentic, as illustrated by Eliade's citation in the first chapter of this book. Ironically, the Sivananda Centre in Paris, like most other European branches, was established in the 1970s by swamis and disciples sent by Vishnu-Devananda.

Indeed, the anti-cult discourse presents the popularization of Asian religions as degrading and corrupting their teaching; it becomes a "perverted East" manipulated by cynical charlatans (Bruckner 1982; Gest and Guyard 1996:16; UNADFI 1990a, 2002). There is the idea that movements referring to Hinduism are actually a superficial, debased copy, a "thick caricature of spiritual and mystical trends" made by "usurpers who uses [sic] Eastern colors in disguise to seduce idealistic minds" (UNADFI 1990b, my translation). At the same time, the difficulty in differentiating an authentic mystical East from its perverted forms is precisely what is perceived as dangerous. The danger also comes from practices: the public is warned against fasting and vegetarianism, but also against the prohibition of coffee, alcohol, and tobacco, which, it is claimed, can weaken individuals and threaten their physical integrity. The intensive practices of chanting and trance are associated with hallucination and collective hysteria and are said to be used to destabilize disciples. Meditation allows the guru to relieve his followers from their autonomy and critical thinking (UNADFI 2002, 1990b; GEMPPI 2003, 9), and even more: "When practiced intensely, especially in front of a candle and the picture of the guru, it provokes mental and visual hallucinations and rapidly becomes a dangerous drug" (CCMM 2005, my translation). As illustrated by this naïve and ethnocentric warning, it is not only the lack of authenticity of "cultic practices" that is seen as problematic. The unknown efficiency of—implicitly foreign—practices is seen as a threat. Like meditation, despite being part of respectable world religions, the use of mantra is also claimed to be dangerous:

> Be careful! Each mantra is supposed to link the follower to a particular energy which should deeply awaken them....The mantra is not neutral. (UNADFI 1990b, my translation)

"Oriental cults" are felt to be dangerous because they also embody Western fantasies about Eastern religions and provoke excitement. In other words, the cult controversy reflects the threatening side of exoticism: otherness is exciting at the same time that it is also felt as being dangerous, precisely because what is other is unfamiliar. Finally, the guru is central to the anti-cult discourse on neo-Hindu movements. The term itself has become extremely pejorative in French and now designates every "cult" leader, and beyond this, every manipulative and deceptive personality. We find again this thin normative line: the guru is supposed to contrast with the real sage who "draws on a tradition in which he was trained or of which he knows the scriptures, even if he renews them" (UNADFI 1990a, my translation). The "guru" is perceived as a megalomaniac individual having a "dreadful authority" over his followers, thus UNADFI denounces the personality worship in Transcendental Meditation, Sathya Sai Baba, Rajneesh, Divine Light Mission, and Siddha Yoga (UNADFI 1990a), while another anti-cult group accuses the Siddha Yoga guru of "spiritual dictatorship" (GEMPPI 2003).

Loyalty to the French Republic

In the light of this context, it is probably fair to say that in France neo-Hindu movements find themselves in a precarious if not marginalized position in many cases. As previously explained, the opportunity to identify with a "Hindu community" in the French context is very limited—in addition to the fact that this is not the favored option of universalistic neo-Hindu movements targeting Westerners. Both Siddha Yoga and the Sivananda Centres respond to the French context through the legal frames for associations that organize religious activities. This is actually not surprising: these legal frames, namely the 1901 and 1905 laws, are the two main pillars of France's separation between the state and religions. It is through these laws that the French Republic historically shaped its relations with religious organizations. They instigate the state's independence and neutrality toward religions, define its role as protector of the freedom of religion, and address religions' practical and organizational issues. Three different types of legal status are open to religious groups in France. First, not-for-profit groups with any sort of goals (religious or not) have the right to register as an association under the 1901 law ("association loi 1901"). This frame supports France's third sector and social networks. Second, religious groups can use the status of "religious association" defined by the 1905 Law of Separation of Church and State. This kind of association can only be created for assisting with the costs, upkeep, and public exercise of worship. There is a third status that is defined by the 1901 law and that is also specific to religious groups. It offers the same legal privileges as the "religious association" but is concerned with "religious congregations," that is to say, groups with an organized communal life—the statuses of "religious association" and the "religious congregation" actually reflect the distinction between secular and regular clergies within the Catholic Church. These two statuses for religious organizations are controlled by state agencies: organizations are free to register as "religious associations," but civil servants decide whether to grant the legal privileges entailed by this status (for instance, the ability to receive donations and legacies, and the exemption of donations from tax); as for the status of "religious congregation," it is granted by decree from the Council of State—France's supreme administrative tribunal. Thus, these legal frames can be used as a discretionary power by the state to regulate and control religious organizations, by giving privileges only to those deemed respectable and refusing them when there is a risk of trouble to the public order (Boyer 2001; Messner 1997).

Siddha Yoga and Sivananda Centres opted for different strategies, which partly derives from the fact that the former is seen as belonging to the "perverted East" by the anti-cult movements, while the latter is generally associated with the authentic "Oriental wisdom." The Sivananda Centre could therefore hope to benefit from the legal privileges granted to "respectable" religions, whereas Siddha Yoga is simply an association under the 1901 Law. Indeed, Siddha Yoga would probably find it difficult to obtain the privileges of "religious association" status and does not have, in France, the legitimacy and the communal life that would allow it to be registered as a "religious congregation." This is particularly relevant to us because, as we shall see, it affects the universalistic ambitions and the functioning of these movements.

Siddha Yoga started in France in the 1970s, following Muktananda's visit. However, the movement remained informal and followers simply gathered at the home of one of them. It was only in 1982—the year Muktananda died—that the Parisian branch became formally an association, Siddha Yoga Dham France, and started to publish a magazine, *Nouvelles du Siddha Yoga*. Throughout the 1980s, two swamis organized conferences to present Muktananda's teaching in the main cities (Siddha Yoga Dham France 1983, 30). There had been two ashrams, in Evry and Lyon, for a short period of time, between 1984 and 1988. The visit of Gurumayi in 1987 seemed to have successfully mobilized followers, the number of which increased until the 1990s. There are now eight Siddha Yoga meditation centers in France (Siddha Yoga France 2011), Paris being the most important in terms of members. There are also small informal groups of members who meet to chant and meditate together at their domicile (Siddha Yoga Dham France 1983). Reflecting Siddha Yoga's evolution on the transnational level, the number of followers in France has decreased in recent years.

The 1901 Law association is a status open to everyone; it is not constraining and can accommodate any group and its organizational ethos. Nevertheless, Siddha Yoga rigorously respects the republican spirit of the 1901 law, which the French tend to associate with freedom of association, hence democracy and civic participation. Thus, Siddha Yoga organizes annual general assemblies, distinct from the usual meetings for satsangs and other "spiritual" activities. During these general assemblies, only formal members of the association are allowed to attend and vote; in other words, it is not necessarily those who are recognized as most advanced spiritually but those who pay their annual membership dues who can make decisions. During these assemblies, these members elect an administrative committee of officers, the treasurer presents the annual accounts, and the elected president submits his annual report and makes proposals that are, again, put to the vote of members.

Accordingly, Siddha Yoga has adopted a very secular organizational structure, despite the fact that it fundamentally contrasts with the ways in which religious organizations exert power in general, and Siddha Yoga in particular. As in most neo-Hindu movements, the guru is the absolute authority in Siddha Yoga; having achieved a state of self-realization, he or she is considered to have reached a nearly divine state (Clémentin-Ojha and Chambard 1994). Moreover, the unconditional surrender and devotion to the guru is central to followers' progress on the path—this is the principle of bhakti yoga itself. The swamis initiated by the guru represent a group of advanced followers and accordingly have a certain authority over the organization of communal life or the transmission of teaching. Based on this religious order, Gurumayi with her swamis oversees, through her headquarters in the United States, the functioning of the local branches. While it is probably fair to say that local associative structures always involves a certain amount of adaptation from transnational organizations, the secular and republican spirit of the French "association loi 1901" disrupts the functioning of Siddha Yoga's religious authority, the guru's authority, and her total control of local branches. In fact, the representatives of the French branch expressed the difficulty for them to be fully included in Siddha Yoga as a global movement.[7] One might wonder also to what extent the republican frame affects the "exotic" feel of the movement.

Yet scrupulously respecting the secular principles of the "association loi 1901" is a way for Siddha Yoga to avoid "giving the opportunity to be caught," as one of the interviewees explained. In other words, as a group suspected to be a "cult," Siddha Yoga cannot afford to present itself as having principles and rules that could be seen as conflicting with French values. "In the intention of our path," a representative of the Parisian branch said, "it is impossible to do anything else but to adapt to customs and rules of the country in which Siddha Yoga settles in." By and large, responding to the assumption that cults represent a threat to the French republic and its values, Siddha Yoga demonstrates its desire to observe these principles through the 1901 law, a cornerstone for the Republic foundational values. It also responds implicitly to the criticisms of the anti-cult discourse regarding the guru's authority. In other words, for organizations labeled as "cults," showing their loyalty to the Republic may be more vital than for anyone else.

The Sivananda Centre, First Hindu Congregation in France

The Sivananda Centre also aims to avoid being labeled as a "cult" but, by contrast with Siddha Yoga, they have not been considered as such, and this explains their different response to the French context. The Sivananda Centres engaged in a 10-year administrative process, at the end of which it obtained the status of a "religious congregation." Recognized as such in 1997, it is the first Hindu congregation among the 500 French congregations that are predominantly Catholic. This registration as a "religious congregation" is therefore a remarkable achievement for the Sivananda Centres, and even more so if we think that the movement is overwhelmingly composed of Western followers. When I asked the swami in charge of the Parisian Centre why they engaged in this process, she explained that Vishnu-Devananda himself had explicitly expressed the wish to see the Centre having legitimacy:

> Firstly, it was about material organization, to situate ourselves in relation to the government, because there is always the government. Also the government always had a bit of suspicion towards associations, so in relation to this, we wanted to make a distinction . . . and also in relation to other yoga centers. In France the teaching of yoga is generally very focused on yoga's physical side, that is to say on postures; in addition the problems of cults came on top of that, so it was very important for us that our status is clear in relation to the government.

Therefore, the Sivananda Centre's registration as a "religious congregation" resulted from a quest of legitimacy in two respects. As suggested by the Parisian swami, with this status the Sivananda Centres first aimed to be officially and publicly differentiated from the so-called cults, hence her insistence on the "government." Now the Parisian Centre presents itself as a "monastic congregation recognized by decree of the French government" and added this sentence to its logo (Centre de Yoga Sivananda n.d.).[8]

Second, presenting itself as a "monastic congregation recognized by decree of the French government" positions the Sivananda Centre among other yoga schools and centers. The wide popularization of yoga since the 1970s has entailed the growth of a whole new sector. In order to obtain an official recognition of their activities in the fields of sport and public health, federations of yoga schools were set up—like the British Wheel of Yoga, "recognised by the Central Council for Physical Recreation (CCPR) and Sport England as the national Governing Body for Yoga" (British Wheel of Yoga n.d.). However, in France there have been several competing federations through scissions and reunifications. Interestingly, these federations sought to establish a monopoly of "French" yoga techniques, against a Hindu yoga represented in France by Vishnu-Devananda and other Indian teachers (Ceccomori 2001, 322). However, due to the image of Sivananda himself, the Parisian Sivananda

Centre is an important site for the teaching of yoga in France. In the 2000s, 400 to 600 students were visiting the Centre each week, mainly for yoga classes.[9] Vishnu-Devananda (1985, 14) himself commented on these federations and their teaching:

> The attitude of [yoga] federations can only be understood in terms of commercial interests since they are not founded on the wisdom of a lineage of masters and disciples, the ancient tradition of yoga, the spiritual wealth that is inherited from one's master. I think that these federations are only tools which aim to create a "controlled market" for a limited number of teachers who have the agreement of the organization, generally without qualification, and not a tool susceptible to teach a yogic, spiritual and traditional way of life.

Here Vishnu-Devananda positions his teaching very clearly on the side of "tradition," which he links to a lineage of gurus and disciples, to demarcate it from French yoga federations. By contrast, their teaching of yoga is seen as profit-driven, superficial, and inauthentic; it is not spiritual since, as mentioned by the current representative of the Parisian Centre, it focuses on physical postures. The status of "religious congregation" is a way for the Sivananda Centres to embody this distinction from other forms of yoga teaching. This explains why the French Sivananda Centre has refused to engage with other yoga schools or federations. But by the same token, it implicitly leads the Centre to insist upon the religious character of their teaching. It presents itself as a "tradition" and insists on the guru-disciples lineage. More important, as core practice of the "religion congregation," yoga is implicitly part of a wider system of religious values and practices and not simply a set of postures that improves bodily flexibility.

To be registered as a "religious congregation," the Sivananda Centre had to insist on the religious nature of its teaching and organization. But there is more to this: the French legal frame was originally created to organize the state's relations with Catholic congregations. In fact, non-Catholic congregations have only been officially accepted since 1988—alongside the Sivananda Centre, three Protestant, six Orthodox, and nine Buddhist congregations (Bureau des Cultes 2003). Accordingly, the law assumes a very specific type of organizational structure, which may not shape communal life in other religions. This is the reason that the status of "religious congregation" is rather difficult to obtain for non-Catholic groups, which have to present themselves with a structure that reflects the organization of the Catholic clergy. Ironically, in terms of structure and internal regulation, Hinduism could not be more different from the Catholic Church. Therefore the Sivananda Centre had to redefine statuses, roles, and structure in order to be recognized as a "religious congregation":

> It had to look like something they know in the organization and the spirit, that is to say, to a Christian congregation. So Swami Vishnu is like the Pope, Swami Durgananda [one of the acharyas] is like the archbishop... We tried to create similarities to show them that, despite that the spirit is a bit different, because Hinduism is not hierarchic like this, despite this, there is still a master who transmit a teaching to his disciples, and this, in the structure, can be similar to the Christian tradition we know better here in the West. (A swami in charge of the Parisian branch)

In other words, while Vishnu-Devananda never presented his teaching as religious, the Sivananda Centres redefined themselves as a religious monastic order, and in addition, one that is similar to a Catholic congregation. At the same time, it also had to give evidence of its "Hindu-ness." To obtain its registration as a "religious congregation," it had to be able to provide a guarantee of its seriousness, that is to say, to establish its ancient and traditional origins—this excludes most NRMs from obtaining this status. In the case of the Sivananda Centres, they had to present themselves as part of Hinduism—it is, after all, registered as a Hindu congregation. This was not taken lightly: because of its foreign origins, the Minister of Foreign Affairs was asked to collect information on the Hindu branch to which the Sivananda Centres are attached in India.[10] Therefore the Sivananda Centres had to highlight their affiliation with Hinduism, whereas, again, Vishnu-Devananda never insisted on the "Hindu-ness" of his teaching but reached out to Westerners. To what extent it affects the ways in which the movement is perceived is uncertain, in particular because people can attend yoga classes without engaging with the more religious activities that take place on the premises. But this example shows that the management of religious diversity and the religious landscape of each country affect, at some level, the universalization and de-contextualization of exotic religious resources. For instance, one of the acharyas of the Sivananda Centres told me they have a big temple in Canada, "which Swami Vishnu [Devananda] did primarily for the Indian community that is there, in Montreal; it's not only for us, because there is a big Indian community in Montreal so he did it also for them." Accordingly, it is possible that the more a "Hindu community" is politically valued in multicultural politics (as in Britain and North America), the more those neo-Hindu move-ments could be torn between two contradictory forces: the institutional pressure to accentuate the reference to Hinduism, and their universalistic ideology, which aims to transcend particularism to target a Western audience.

The Kabbalah Centre in France and Britain

National responses to diversity and the local religious landscape shape the pool of religious resources available for bricolage: this is also illustrated by the comparison of the flourishing London Kabbalah Centre, and the Parisian branch that declined in the late 1990s before closing its doors in 2005.[11]

After a first attempt at door-to-door contacts and courses in the East End of London, which had been relatively unsuccessful 10 years earlier, the London Kabbalah Centre has significantly grown. Opened in 1998, it is today consid-ered to be the main European Centre, coordinating activities and projects for the entire region, because of its important human and material resources. The presence of Madonna, who regularly visits the Centre, attracted newcomers. In addition, her financial support could have helped the development of the London branch—the media often claimed that she bought two buildings in London for the Kabbalah Centre. Now located in the heart of London, near Oxford Street, the London branch hosts up to 200 persons for Shabbat and festivals that attract followers from other European countries; it welcomes the Bergs, who regularly visit the London branch. Around 300 students every week attend a wide range of classes, organized by around 15 full-time volun-teers—this numerical evaluation highlights that this "success" is relative, since the Kabbalah Centre remains a small movement, even in its most lively local centers like London. This luxurious place tends to attract the privileged, with some of the most involved students working in the entertainment and music sectors, as well as in communications and life-coaching. The London Centre is also outstanding for its cosmopolitan diversity: it is our observation that half of these well-off students are probably not British. According to one of the teachers, at least half of the London students, if not more, do not have a Jewish background.

By contrast, while the Kabbalah Centre in London was slow to kick off, Paris had a tremendous start in the late 1980s. At the turn of the 1990s, the city was hosting the first and most promising European branch, and it was teachers from Paris who were crossing the Channel every week with boxes of books and material to teach in London. "Zohar were flying," said a teacher who remembers selling up to eight Zohar a day in Parisian and suburban

Jewish communities. The Kabbalah Centre was attracting up to 100 people for beginners' classes, and people were coming from all over Europe for Shabbat and festivals. Up to 15 teachers and volunteers were present full-time to offer several courses per week, to up to 200 participants. However, at the end of the 1990s, the Parisian branch began to decline. It was selling fewer and fewer Zohar, and was losing students without attracting new ones. The Centre closed down and its teachers left in 2005. Today, two teachers meet their students at home and organize a small number of courses and festivals in rented conference rooms. As they had kept contact with students at distance through "student support" by telephone, they have been able to gather 30 motivated people and now hope to re-open a permanent site. Some of the students involved in the early days have also come back, but I also met several students who, despite feeling faithful to Berg's teaching, keep their distance from this new venture.

The Kabbalah Centre, a Jewish Controversy?

Surprisingly, the difficulties of the French branch of the Kabbalah Centre cannot be explained primarily by France's cult controversy. For a start, the media coverage of the Kabbalah Centre has not been more negative in France than in Britain. Across the whole world, as celebrities began to frequent the Kabbalah Centre in Los Angeles at the end of the 1990s, the movement became the subject of tremendous interest. This media coverage provided the "hip 'Jewish' sect" (Rothschild 2007) fantastic publicity, yet it became more critical in the early 2000s. In France, in Britain, and elsewhere, the movement has rapidly and consistently been associated with Scientology for its instrumentalization of celebrities and has been referred to as a "cult." National daily newspapers, such as *Libération*, *Le Figaro*, and *Le Monde* in France, and *The Guardian*, *The Evening Standard*, and *The Daily Mail* in Britain, have exploited this appealing topic and have conducted investigations, often involving the visit of an undercover journalist to the Kabbalah Centre in order to reveal what are presented as scandalous secrets. The "Kabbalah business" (Lecadre 2003) has systematically been denounced: merchandising, prices of classes and events, and high-pressure sales techniques. Selling the Zohar to people who cannot read it has been seen as a fraud, as has the commercialization of "Kabbalah water" bottles, said to cure various diseases. On both sides of the Channel, devastating television programs have covertly investigated the Kabbalah Centre and interviewed ex-members and relatives in order to warn the public against the movement. The BBC2 report, *Sweeney Investigates*, in 2005 featured a potential student (in fact a person sent by the TV crew) who visited the London Centre for the first time and was advised by a teacher to buy bottles of Kabbalah water to cure his cancer. It also showed a teacher giving a course during which he explained that Jews who studied Kabbalah, such as in Morocco, were protected from dying in the Holocaust.[12] This program, which drew two million viewers in January 2005, had devastating effects on the group's image in Britain, and as a result the London teacher was relocated to Los Angeles. Similar investigation programs were broadcast in France in the early 2000s. Retracing the emergence of the movement and its influence on Madonna and other celebrities, these programs were filmed inside the Parisian Centre. They included interviews with two poorly regarded French celebrities[13] whose positive appreciation of the Kabbalah Centre's teaching may not have been entirely helpful, and a member who claimed that the Kabbalah water had cured cancer. Students' relatives testified with their face covered and explained the damages inflicted by this "cult" on their family. Both programs then presented the opinions of various experts, all being negative: a renowned scholar in Jewish studies, the chief rabbi himself, a parliamentarian involved in anti-cult combat, and the president of UNADFI. In both countries, the Kabbalah Centre has since been presented as more "New Age nonsense" (Magnet 2004) and as "pop psychology dressed up in the impenetrable prose of scholarly mysticism" (Shelden 2003).

It is also important to note that the controversy surrounding the Kabbalah Centre has also been deeply religious. Indeed, the American, British, and French media have systematically discussed whether the Kabbalah Centre was legitimate *as a Jewish movement*; this, because they have constantly referred to, and interviewed, religious leaders in order to evaluate and establish the Kabbalah Centre's credentials. The majority of interviewed religious leaders expressed a very critical opinion regarding the Kabbalah Centre; therefore the impression was given that there was a "general consensus of those who are knowledgeable about the 'legitimate' study of Kabbalah" (Horn 2005). More important, asking representatives of Jewish institutions and congregations to evaluate the Kabbalah Centre's legitimacy unavoidably presents the movement as a Jewish issue, even if, paradoxically, they have been eager to reject it as outside the Jewish tradition and to label it as a cult. Indeed, rabbis and other religious authorities have continuously been quoted to establish the lack of authenticity of the Kabbalah Centre *with regard to* Judaism.[14] Journalists have accordingly often insisted on the Kabbalah Centre's illegitimacy on the basis of conservative religious norms. They have, for instance, reiterated the argument that study and strict observance are necessary to learn Kabbalah and sometimes have accepted indiscriminately the conservative principle that Kabbalah must not be shared with women and non-Jews. This view is not accepted by all trends of Judaism, yet many journalists (see, for example, Gilmore 2004) and, below, the French anti-cult movement UNADFI (2005) referred to it:

> According to the Jewish tradition, to be allowed to study Kabbalah one must fulfill a certain number of criteria: be Jewish, male, be at least forty, married, be a father of at least two children and having acquired a deep knowledge of the "sacred scriptures" (Torah and Talmud)....As far as he is concerned, Philip Berg neglects these rules and offers his teaching to all, including non-Jews. (my translation)

By and large, the controversy around the Kabbalah Centre has been religious. The Kabbalah Centre has been evaluated as a Jewish movement and has been contrasted with "respectable" Judaism, presented in its more conservative aspects. Indeed, by asking the normative expertise of the religious leaders who are eager to provide it, the media have in fact found themselves in a complex, divided, and competitive religious field. In this field, various actors, in particular within Orthodox Judaism, aim to embody the true Jewish tradition and exclude those who depart from a strict observance. My analysis of media discourse and interviews sheds light on the fact that the Orthodox have most keenly expressed hostility toward the Kabbalah Centre, as they sometimes do toward Reform Judaism and other secular Jewish movements (Huss, forthcoming a, makes the same observation). Representatives of Reform or Liberal Judaism, suspected themselves by the Orthodox not to be proper Judaism, usually have refrained from making similar comments on the Kabbalah Centre and have not taken any action against it in any way. Ultimately, this unquestioning use of religious leaders' discourse by the media helps establish the illegitimacy of the Kabbalah Centre as much as it strengthens the legitimacy of other collective or individual actors as the repository of tradition. Thus, the media have inherited unquestioningly these conflicts internal to Judaism and have ignored that some of the religious authorities they refer to may directly compete against the Kabbalah Centre in the religious field. For instance, Lappin's (2004) article on the Kabbalah Centre in *The Guardian* draws on criticisms made by Michael Laitman (under the recognizable pseudonym of Jordan Lightman). The article presents him as one of Berg's former students and as an "orthodox and serious Kabbalah scholar," but does not state that his movement, Bnei Baruch, directly battles against the Kabbalah Centre to teach Kabbalah to the masses. His writings and public talks often contrast his own teaching (as genuine, non-commercial, and free from superstition) with Berg's. Some of the most hostile religious leaders toward the Kabbalah

Centre are Lubavitch rabbis[15] whose teaching also draws on Kabbalah to bring secular Jews into the fold of tradition.

Accordingly, the media coverage of the Kabbalah Centre has reflected—but also concealed—a debate internal to Judaism. This is obvious in the fact that the topic was particularly addressed in Jewish media and aroused the interest of journalists working for these media and/or identifying themselves explicitly as Jews. They sometimes have discussed the Kabbalah Centre from a personal Jewish point of view and whether it represents a meaningful way to modernize Jewish life (Eshman 2007). However, their accounts have been overwhelmingly disapproving because of the image it gives of Judaism: as Cohen (2003) put it in *Jewsweek*, "it's the sect we Jews love to hate." In Britain, it is Elena Lappin (2004), former editor of the *Jewish Quarterly* in the 1990s, who conducted the most thorough critical investigation on the Kabbalah Centre for *The Guardian*. Several pieces denouncing the movement have been written in *The Evening Standard* and *The Times* by David Rowan (2002, 2004a, 2004b), who is currently editor of *The Jewish Chronicle*—the magazine recently denounced the introduction of Spirituality for Kids (SFK, the Kabbalah Centre's educational program) in state schools. I interviewed a journalist who works for Jewish media, such as the magazines *Arche* and *Actualité Juive*, and who wrote the first articles on the Kabbalah Centre in France. Her interest in this movement emerged when her rabbi asked her to help an Israeli anti-missionary and anti-cult organization, Yad Laahim, in finding funds in France. Her articles draw on anti-cult discourses as well as the condemnation of the Kabbalah Centre by the Israeli and French religious orthodoxy. As she recounts a course given by a teacher on Rosh Hashanah in Paris, she argues against the Kabbalah Centre on religious grounds in one of her articles:

> As it should be, in such a venture, not all what he says is untrue (it would be too good to be true). For instance, when he's speaking about the necessary kanavoth (intentions) to play the shofar, the necessity, that day, to confuse Satan, or when he's using guematria...to explain a concept, theoretically there is nothing to criticize about it. The problem has to be found elsewhere; in the audience, to begin with. Since when is Kabbalah taught to everybody, men, women, Jews and non-Jews, observant or not, all together? And since when do we make young girls wearing trousers or tight skirts spread the Zohar?[16]

It is worth noting that she personally incited France's chief rabbi to write an official statement against the Kabbalah Centre. At the time, she said, the Consistoire (the body officially representing the French Jewish community

188 FROM YOGA TO KABBALAH

and chaired by the chief rabbi) has not done anything about this. Some rabbis have even authorized people to frequent the Kabbalah Centre (which would confirm similar claims made by teachers of the Kabbalah Centre, as we shall see further on). She also warned the UNADFI, which until then, she said, had no knowledge of the Kabbalah Centre. Again, the responsiveness of the Jewish media world reflects an internal debate about Judaism and its norms, and tends to reinforce the idea of the Kabbalah Centre as a Jewish issue.

The Kabbalah Centre and the
French Cult Controversy

Despite this intense and highly negative media coverage, the Kabbalah Centre has never become a focus for organizations fighting "cults" in Britain or France. In both countries, anti-cult movements have very rarely been contacted by ex-members or relatives, although some have contacted Jewish authorities instead. The Kabbalah Centre is not a "big cult," I was told by a volunteer of the French anti-cult group CCMM, by contrast with what they named "real issues," such as the Jehovah Witnesses, Scientology, or "cultic aberrations" of psychological therapies; "it's not our object," they explained. At UNADFI I was told that it was more a "swindle" than a "cult." A representative from the British Cult Information Centre (CIC) explained that the CIC does not have evidence that techniques of psychological coercion were used in the Kabbalah Centre. This representative explained that, if asked about the Kabbalah Centre, they would be cautious because it is not because a movement is new, or is criticized by the community it represents, that it is a "cult." Strikingly, at the time the Kabbalah Centre was flourishing in Paris, it was not mentioned in the list of "cults" of the parliamentary report *Les Sectes en France* (Gest and Guyard 1996), nor did it feature in the French cult controversy at the end of the 1990s. In fact, the person in charge of the Kabbalah Centre at UNADFI believes this movement only appeared in France in 2003. This is when the organization was contacted by two families with involved relatives, but also when the Kabbalah Centre ceased to reach out to Jews only. UNADFI then alerted the Inter-ministerial Mission of Vigilance and Combat against Sectarian Deviations (MIVILUDES); this explains why the Kabbalah Centre is mentioned in the Inter-ministerial Mission's annual reports in 2004, 2005, and 2007, although in a very brief and anecdotal form.[17]

I believe that anti-cult movements have been cautious if not indifferent toward the Kabbalah Centre *because* it was perceived as relating to Judaism. Interestingly, the first initiatives of both main French anti-cult organizations, UNADFI and CCMM, had been to contact Jewish authorities, either to ask whether they would confirm the cultic nature of the Kabbalah Centre or to call on them to take action. This underlines the fact that the Kabbalah Centre has been perceived as a problem internal to the Jewish community that could be addressed by Jewish authorities themselves (by contrast, Jewish anti-cult organizations in Israel and the United States have been particularly hostile; Huss forthcoming a). Anti-cult movements may have felt the need to be cautious when dealing with such a group: by attacking a somewhat Jewish organization, they could be accused of anti-Semitism. For instance, the CCMM representative confirmed engaging with Jewish authorities in case of problems, "but there were never anything serious," she added. Similarly, the volunteer I met at UNADFI in order to talk about the Kabbalah Centre and access their documents told me she was in charge, among other topics, of cults in Judaism although, she suggested, there are very few "cults" in Judaism. At this point, she mentioned the Lubavitch, but this is more about fundamentalism, she added, because they separate themselves from the world. "Still, it's a bit cultic," she stated, but she immediately made clear that she would say they are not a cult if she were asked about them. In fact, anti-cult organizations have often been accused by their detractors as threatening religious freedom, and charges of anti-Semitism have been indirectly brought up at least on one occasion.[18] We could therefore understand why anti-cult organizations would have wanted to be cautious in dealing with the Kabbalah Centre.

Finally, the combat against "cults" is not the predominant factor determining challenges encountered by the Kabbalah Centre in France, because by the time that anti-cult movements showed slight interest in it, the Centre already had lost most of its members and was about to close. The Kabbalah Centre had been declining since the end of the 1990s and only a handful of disciples had remained when it shut its doors in 2005. This is why students and teachers do not perceive media coverage or France's lack of openness to "spirituality," as they would put it, as the main reasons for their difficulties. I was, in fact, surprised to discover that teachers had no knowledge of UNADFI's or MIVILUDES's purpose or name; they simply knew that the Kabbalah Centre was not on France's "list of dangerous cults." To them, explanations were to be found elsewhere.

The Kabbalah Centre and Orthodox Judaism

Rather than the anti-cult discourse in the media or a French combat against NRMs, the Kabbalah Centre's relationships with Jewish communities and authorities seem decisive in understanding its developments at a transnational but also at a local level. To start, the characteristics of the institutions representing Judaism in France and Britain are particularly significant. Everywhere in the world, Orthodox Judaism has proved to be very reactive and prompt in rejecting the Kabbalah Centre as debasing their tradition. The opposition of Orthodox Judaism to the Kabbalah Centre started in Israel and, as we explained in the previous chapter, this is probably what led the Kabbalah Centre to present itself as a universal wisdom detached from the Jewish tradition. As we shall see, the reactions of bodies representing Orthodox Judaism have been relatively similar in France and Britain. Nevertheless, the impact of these oppositions has been much stronger in France, due to the centralization and legitimacy of Orthodox Judaism.

Chief Rabbi Jonathan Sacks, whose United Synagogue is the main Orthodox synagogue grouping in the United Kingdom, does not want to directly engage with this controversial issue. However, some members of his cabinet are the Kabbalah Centre's most virulent detractors in Britain, regularly denouncing the movement in the press for being a cult unconnected to Judaism. Following an interview request, I was told that "this is something that the United Synagogue does not wish to be involved in." I was advised to contact another member of the chief rabbi's cabinet who actively participated in the dissolution of the Centre in another country some years ago. His opinion was that "they operate in the same way as many of the cults": the Kabbalah Centre breaks family ties, lets its overworked members live in poverty, and has abnormal practices and norms in relation to Judaism. Their "proximity" is also a moot point in his views:

> We need to warn our own community that this is a group that has nothing to do with the Jewish community.... We also feel a responsibility towards the general public that they shouldn't think that this is just another alternative form of Judaism, because it isn't.

As illustrated here, the priority of Orthodox Judaism is to distinguish the Kabbalah Centre from Judaism and hence to draw normative religious boundaries. In fact, the chief rabbi himself made a public statement published by the media in that direction to warn the Jewish community itself, while another declaration from his office and the London *Beth Din* (rabbinic court) "wish it to be known that the Kabbalah Centre does not operate under its auspices or the auspices of any recognized *halachic* authority."[19] In other words, they want to insist on the fact that this movement is not part of Judaism.

These conflicting relationships are not different in France. It is again significant that direct communication I attempted to make with the French chief rabbi, Joseph Sitruk, was not possible. Rabbis of the Consistoire avoided sharing any information about their interaction with the movement or giving me their opinion—although they made it clear that they considered the Kabbalah Centre to be a cult problem.

Several publications, declarations, and events give evidence that it has actually been a concern. One of the chief rabbi's closest advisors clearly referred to the Kabbalah Centre at a conference organized by MIVILUDES: he vehemently rejected "a movement which, for [him], is obviously cultic, claims to be a form of Judaism." Telling the audience that the Kabbalah Centre wished to engage with rabbis on a television program, he said he ensured that "no rabbi went there—as I have some influence on them":

> I managed that no rabbi went there simply because the image of a rabbi discussing with this movement would mean that in the end either we discuss inside religion, or from religious person to religious person.[20]

Here again, drawing boundaries around genuine Judaism (from which the Kabbalah Centre is excluded) motivates the response of Jewish authorities. The French chief rabbi condemned the movement in a public statement as early as 1992 (Fajnkuchen 1997, 2–3). His courses on Kabbalah (1997–1998) in the synagogue of La Victoire, the heart of the Consistoire, were primarily a warning against the Kabbalah Centre, even it he did not name it explicitly. Yet, he mentioned the terrifying dangers faced by those who imprudently manipulate the names of God (the Kabbalah Centre has particular practices around the 72 names of God), outlined that astrology was forbidden by the Torah (the Kabbalah Centre uses a "Kabbalistic astrology"), and mentioned the selling of improper Zohar books (Kabbalah Centre's main fundraising activities in the 1990s was door-to-door selling of Zohar). More broadly, the chief rabbi spoke against the study of Kabbalah without a true master and without the fear of God. Kabbalah, he explained, should be studied exclusively in the respect of *halakha*, that is to say, in the strict observance of Jewish law. Those who claim to be Kabbalists but do not respect these conditions should not be approached (Sitruk 2006).

Books, indeed, have been buried: in 1997, a respected rabbi of Sarcelles (an important Jewish community in the Paris suburbs) and member of the rabbinic council of the Paris Orthodox Jewish community took an openly militant position. Referring to statements made by Israeli rabbis and Kabbalists on the dissemination of the Kabbalah Centre's Zohar (Meir 2011, 173; Huss forthcoming a), he demanded that people bring back the Zohar they had bought from the movement without delay, in order to have them destroyed. The Zohar printed and sold by the Kabbalah Centre was declared not kosher. This event is attested by several interviewees, Kabbalah Centre members, and an independent scholar, who remembers "surrealistic discussions" with rabbis about the conformity of this Zohar: despite being an obvious copy of the original text, they feared it was maliciously modified or printed, for example, on a Shabbat. The magazine *Actualité Juive*, which recounted the affair, described tons of books being returned to the Sarcelles synagogue, to the point that its rabbi had to intervene to stop this wave of panic (Fajnkuchen 1997; interview with a journalist of *Actualité Juive*).

Several interviewees recounted orders given by Jewish authorities, notices posted in synagogues warning against the "cult," forbidding the Kabbalah Centre to give courses in synagogues and excluding their members from coming to services or to the *mikveh* (ritual bath). "People hated us," recalls a teacher, mentioning rumors and threatening phone calls. Another one evoked accusations relating to religious transgression, such as Karen Berg sharing the *mikveh* with men or the Bergs not eating kosher food. According to one of the teachers, rabbis were not always personally opposed to the Kabbalah Centre but they had asked their congregations not to attend its activities anymore and, Kabbalah Centre teachers claim, this is how their students increasingly abandoned the movement. Students left the group, one of them said, because they found it increasingly difficult to attend synagogues and participate in the activities and events of the Jewish community while being involved in the Kabbalah Centre.

Indeed, students' accounts consistently convey a strong feeling of exclusion and conflict that characterizes members' perception of their relationship with Jewish authorities. An irrefutable link between the Kabbalah Centre and Orthodox Judaism is emphasized, whether both parties want it or not. The discomfort of French and British Orthodox Judaism in relation to this research may be understood as an attempt to avoid appearing publicly intolerant and confrontational, but also to clearly exclude the Kabbalah Centre from what they believe to be authentic Judaism. Representatives of Orthodox Judaism have felt compelled to take the Kabbalah Centre into account in order to secure religious boundaries. But their repeated efforts to publicly deny the Kabbalah Centre's Jewish character and its initiatives in France to cast out their members are, in themselves, an avowal of this Jewish character itself. In turn, despite the fact that the Kabbalah Centre denies being Jewish, interviews with teachers and students highlight the importance that they attach to their relationship with Orthodox Judaism. One teacher in Paris explained that Jewish authorities were afraid that the Kabbalah Centre would be successful and spread like the Lubavitch movement, thus attributing to the Kabbalah Centre the role of challenger to Orthodox Judaism. As this teacher went on to say,

> We do everything that another Jew does, but take a religious person, you ask him all the questions of why we are doing this and why we are

doing that, you won't have any responses, you go to the Centre, you'll have responses. This is what makes the difference between us and the others. But again, this is why we don't want to be assimilated to religion, or to Judaism.

In other words, as much as Orthodox Judaism needs to respond to the Kabbalah Centre while denying its Jewishness, it seems that the Kabbalah Centre, despite its alleged universality, still positions itself in relation to Orthodox Judaism.

In France, the Kabbalah Centre's teachers and students easily name and blame the Consistoire for their difficulties, whereas London teachers express indifference toward Orthodox Judaism and insist on their independence. The latter claim to see a real benefit in the fact that they do not need the approval of any Jewish institutions. This clearly reflects the different organizational structure of Judaism at a local level. British Judaism is a "house divided" (Alderman 1992, 321): the chief rabbi's United Synagogue is the largest congregation and represents 62 local communities (United Synagogue 2010). However Reform and Liberal Judaism represent, respectively, 42 and 34 communities (Reform Judaism 2010; interview with a representative of Liberal Judaism). Besides, nearly 37 percent of British Jews do not belong to a synagogue.[21] In sum, the United Synagogue never has had a monopoly on British Jews. The diversity of British Judaism and the importance of progressive Judaism limit the authority of the British chief rabbi, while his French counterpart is at the head of a unique and unitary institution.

French Judaism is indeed very centralized: it is represented by one body, the Consistoire, which was founded in 1808 under Napoleon to organize and officially represent Judaism in France. The Consistoire enforces the predominance of Orthodox Judaism: it was only after the 1905 law on the separation of state and religion that privileges were no longer granted to any organization and that a liberal synagogue could be created in 1907—the Union Libérale Israélite de France. Most liberal communities are very recent, such as the Mouvement Juif Libéral de France founded in 1977, and the Communauté Juive Libérale, founded in 1995 by the first woman rabbi in France. The Consistoire is nevertheless still perceived as officially representing France's Jewish community, with 250 local communities and 135,000 individuals (Schnapper et al. 2009, 94), while liberal synagogues, which are not included in this body, remain a minority and strive to exist. The centralization of French Judaism gives authority and legitimacy to a body only representing, legitimating, and reproducing Orthodox Judaism; it has therefore not favored the development of non-Orthodox congregations. This regulatory and authoritative role of the Consistoire could have made its initiatives against the Kabbalah Centre efficient and pervasive, especially because a high proportion of the Kabbalah Centre's students in France were Jewish.

This intra-European comparison could be extended to others branches of the Kabbalah Centre to highlight the impact of its interactions with Jewish authorities and communities that have different characteristics. It is worth remembering that the Kabbalah Centre grew in the United States, characterized by general religious pluralism and diversity. With possibly the largest population of Jews in the world (US Census Bureau 2009, Table 74), American Judaism is fragmented into a mosaic of congregations and institutions with no chief rabbi or regulatory body (Herberg 1960). For this reason, and because Liberal Judaism is predominant, Orthodox Judaism does not have the authority it has in France or Israel, and there is more space for religious diversity, as epitomized by the Jewish Renewal. By contrast, in Israel, a powerful Orthodox Judaism challenged the Kabbalah Centre's development. It is there that the first public denunciation of the Kabbalah Centre occurred: in 1981, the chief Sephardic rabbi of Israel, Ovadia Yosef, publicly condemned Berg for teaching to a mixed audience of men and women and advised people to keep away from him. A group of Hasidic Jews also attacked Kabbalah Centre students in 1983 during a pilgrimage to the grave of Bar Yochai. Religious authorities have officially denounced the Kabbalah Centre many times and have retracted the approbations they had given to the movements' prayer books. In 1998, the chief Rabbinate of Israel, Ashkenazy and Sephardic chief rabbis, and other religious figures signed a decree against Philip Berg and his movement, which was also denounced by Israeli anti-cult groups (Huss forthcoming a). Such hostility from religious leaders against the Kabbalah Centre is probably not unrelated to the Bergs' return to the United States at the start of the 1980s.

In the only Jewish state, the Kabbalah Centre has probably not gathered more than 200 or 300 members. Indeed, here the authority of the Orthodox is stronger than anywhere else. For a start, Israel does not separate religion and state.[22] It is defined as a Jewish state and its nationalistic ideological basis, Zionism, draws on religious symbols. In addition, since the 1980s the Orthodox have wielded greater political and social influence in the public sphere. Governments have often compromised with ultra-Orthodox and nationalist-religious Jews to gain their support, in particular after the wars of 1967 and 1973. In this period of crisis of Zionism, religion was seen as enhancing national unity and sense of purpose (Beit-Hallahmi 1992, 62; Sharot 2007, 672–676). Moreover, Orthodox Judaism has considerable influence on many aspects of individuals' lives, because the Orthodox rabbinate is sponsored by the state and remains the main provider of religious services. Accordingly, this predominance makes the situation of minority religions quite uncertain (Ferziger 2008; Sharot 2007). Reform, Conservative, and Reconstructionist Judaism have been unsuccessful in Israel and were denounced as foreign and non-Zionist by the Orthodox (Tabory 1991). There is equally very low tolerance toward NRMs: again, reflecting their influence in Israeli society as well as their desire to regulate Judaism, Orthodox and ultra-Orthodox organizations are particularly influential in the combat against "cults" (Zaidman-Dvir and Sharot 1992).[23] Despite the low numbers of individuals involved (Sharot 1996: 121), an official inter-departmental government commission was set up in 1982 as a result of pressures from parents' organizations, Orthodox anti-cult movements, and the media. Its recommendations were never implemented, but the general opinion regarding NRMs is relatively negative, as is the secular media coverage (Beit-Hallahmi 1991; Sharot 1990).

The Kabbalah Centre and its Public

In Britain, the impact of Orthodox Judaism is also limited by the fact that the Kabbalah Centre was at first unsuccessful in attracting Jewish students exclusively in London. The movement started and grew after its "universalistic turn," among people who are not predominantly Jewish, which means an audience that is not familiar with, or affected by, local issues and controversies involving Jewish organizations; it is an international and upper-class audience attracted by the psychologized orientation of the Kabbalah Centre's new teaching. In addition, the presence of Madonna, as well as other members of the entertainment industry, "de-judaicize" the image of the Kabbalah Centre while granting it glitter and making it attractive to a wider audience.

By contrast, in France, the Kabbalah Centre was successful before its "universalistic turn," when it predominantly attracted students with a Jewish background. For Ruth, a student who became involved in the "glorious" 1990s, it was *evidently* a Jewish group: "All those I met around me, who were regularly attending classes, were of Jewish origin. And I didn't even think about it, if there were others who were from another religion," she said. According to my observations, today the core of remaining students in Paris has clearly been socialized in a Jewish environment and are familiar with the Jewish liturgy.[24] In addition, the religious characteristics of these students are important to understanding their relationship with the Kabbalah Centre. While French Jews had previously been mostly of Ashkenazi origin, between 1955 and 1965 the Jewish population doubled with migration predominantly from Algeria, Morocco, and Tunisia, bringing with them North African Jewish community life and profoundly transforming French Judaism. Today, 70 percent of French Jews identify themselves as Sephardim, while 24 percent declare to be Ashkenazi (Cohen 2000). Strikingly, Sephardic Jews are said to be relatively traditional, but they also are more familiar with Kabbalah: in North Africa the reading of the Zohar is included in the liturgy and there was nothing extraordinary in having a Zohar at home—hence the ease with which the Kabbalah Centre sold the Zohar door-to-door in France. "Actually it was their culture," explained one of the teachers,

> They are people who have been brought up with the Zohar, who grew up with the Zohar, so...The Zohar, it was sold very easily and people were very quickly hung up on this teaching which is Kabbalah, a lot wanted to study.

These students have probably responded positively to the Kabbalah Centre's references to Sephardic Judaism. As explained in the previous chapter, this emphasis on the North African Kabbalistic tradition may be exciting and exotic for the American or British students, but could assert the religious and ethnic identity of French students of Sephardic origin. Students were therefore interested in the Kabbalah Centre, not because Kabbalah was attractively exotic, mysterious, and secret, but because it was traditional. "They were religious people, they knew about the Zohar, it was an 'automatic response' only from their own religious upbringing," recalled another teacher. But then teachers pointed out the ways in which these students' expectations are at odds with the Kabbalah Centre's teaching, in their view:

> Here from time to time I meet people who, as soon as they sit, they wear their *kippa*. I don't say anything, by respect, but...[laugh] Because immediately they associate [Kabbalah Centre's teaching] to religion. And that's it, in people's minds, especially the French, especially in France. They don't do it elsewhere. Or very rarely. (a teacher in Paris)

In other words, these students were attracted to Kabbalah as a result of their religious upbringing and values. A teacher analyzed the Paris Centre at the time as being "religious," attracting a religious public that was joining for Shabbat and festivals but was not interested in participating in classes or the goal of self-realization, aspects that would become dominant in the Kabbalah Centre's teaching from the end of the 1990s. By contrast, students of Jewish origin interviewed in Britain expressed a rejection of Judaism as religion and made clear they would never have joined a mainstream congregation.

In France, I interviewed several former students who recalled "exceptional" moments at the start of the 1990s. They described a sense of strong community bonds between members as well as a shared enthusiasm, and they illustrated these nostalgic memories by referring to the Shabbat nights and festivals they organized and celebrated altogether. They are those who left the Kabbalah Centre, dissatisfied with the evolution of the teaching and the way it was then transmitted. The case of two students, David and Thérèse, illustrate this: born in Tunisia, they abandoned traditional religious life when they migrated to France during their childhood, but they gradually became observant as they began to follow the Kabbalah Centre's teaching 25 years ago. Despite remaining faithful to Philip Berg, whom they knew personally, they said that, like other students they know, they maintained a distance from the Paris Centre. As for a reason, they vaguely talked about the development of "American influences," "something modern," and gave the example of courses that were not free anymore: "and this" David believes, "seems more like an American method. Because we didn't really pay for the teaching *elsewhere.*" This word, "elsewhere," is critical. Here, David implicitly compares the Kabbalah Centre with Jewish cultural centers and synagogues he is familiar with (which shows that he was engaging with other aspects of Jewish life, at the time or prior to the Kabbalah Centre), where religious knowledge is transmitted differently. In response to the opinion that funding was needed, David responded that, instead of paying for courses, forms of *tzedakah* (charity) could provide resources, then referring to traditional religious practices. David also explained that *tzedakah* is not about *paying* for a course, but *giving* in order to get closer to the teaching. Again, the Kabbalah Centre is clearly compared with Jewish norms and not with other personal growth teachings.

In sum, this North African Jewish constituency familiar with Kabbalah almost certainly represented an opportunity for the Kabbalah Centre. But it limited its development in the long term: we can assume that the Consistoire's response against the Kabbalah Centre has been more efficient because students belonging to this rather traditional Judaism might have been more obedient and left the movement if they were instructed to do so. In a close-knit community, being excluded from the synagogue and community life would be a high price to pay. More important, the teaching's recent and partial detachment from Jewish references, identity, and modes of teaching have repelled some of these Jewish students and have limited the Kabbalah Centre's expansion among them. French Jews are more traditional than in Anglo-Saxon countries, where progressive Judaism is influential, and they proved to be more motivated by community life than by a psychologized quest for self-realization. For example, there is no equivalent of the Jewish Renewal in France and, contrary to the United States or Britain, demands for Kabbalah courses in synagogues remain scarce, as representatives of Liberal Judaism have noted. They also observed that due to the predominance of Sephardic Jews from North Africa, overall the French Jewish population is relatively traditionalist, even in liberal communities. Unsurprisingly, Orthodox structures have been relatively successful in fulfilling the needs of this traditional Jewish milieu, which is currently undergoing a strong revitalization of community life focused on the importance of Jewish identity and religious observance. The expansion in France of private Jewish schools, religious courses, and Hebrew classes since the 1990s underscores a re-appropriation and legitimation of religion as a mode of identification among the observant section of the Jewish population (Schnapper et al. 2009; Benayoun 1990), a trend that does not concur with the increasingly cosmopolitan and universalistic Kabbalah Centre.

While the Kabbalah Centre lost its initial public in France, it was not able to draw enough students attracted by its universalized Kabbalistic teaching, like in London. The decline of the Parisian branch was accelerated when it moved to one of the most expensive districts of the city (the 16th) in order to attract an exclusive type of membership, in the hope that the success the Kabbalah Centre encountered among celebrities in Los Angeles or London could be replicated. "[Parisian students] thought that if they had a beautiful center then persons of quality would come," recalled a teacher. This very costly place never took off and remained empty: it did not answer the needs of its initial members and did not attract "persons of quality" either. There is an intellectual interest in Kabbalah in France, with which the Kabbalah Centre cannot really compete, and which is fulfilled by a substantial literature, conferences from scholars of Jewish studies, and intellectual circles. This philosophical interest in Kabbalah is very specific to the French Jewish intellectual environment of the twentieth century.[25]

Furthermore, in the French context, the movement's detachment from Judaism makes it vulnerable to anti-cult sentiment. At the turn of the 2000s, the media started to investigate Madonna's new craze and journalists visited (covertly or overtly) the new Parisian Centre. Anti-cult organizations started to campaign against the Kabbalah Centre. Following critical television programs, the two or three celebrities who had publicly endorsed the Kabbalah Centre denied having any link to the movement and refused all interviews on the subject matter. These minor celebrities may have feared adverse consequences for a career that was not to be compared with Madonna's and that, in turn, could not give the Parisian Centre the same level of glamour. Presented as a cult, the Centre found it difficult to find new students while, as shown in Chapter 2, it may still remain "too Jewish" for students familiar with esotericism and attracted by Kabbalah. Unable to support itself financially, the Centre closed in 2005.

Overall, the contrast between the Parisian and London branches of the Kabbalah Centre is not quantitatively important: while the first closed, the latter only attracts 300 students every week at most for classes, and less than 100 participants for Shabbat services. But their different trajectories are particularly significant. The Kabbalah Centre in Britain attracted a population outside the sphere of influence of Orthodox Judaism and was not affected by the hostile reaction of the latter. In contrast, its temporary success among the French Jewish population protected the Kabbalah Centre against anti-cult attacks, but made it vulnerable to Jewish authorities' opposition. The detachment of the Kabbalah Centre from Judaism has had a very different impact on the British and French branches. It certainly made the London branch more appealing to an upper middle-class public interested in personal growth and coaching methods (including Jewish secular students who are repelled by mainstream congregations), but in France it disappointed students who saw the Kabbalah Centre as a place to strengthen their ethnic and religious identity and build up a Jewish community. Its subsequent attempts to outreach for a new audience outside traditional Jewish communities were unsuccessful: depicted by the media as a New Age celebrity fad with cultic tendencies, the Kabbalah Centre did not find its audience in the French environment and did not benefit from the presence of a star such as Madonna.

Synthesis

The analysis of neo-Hindu movements in Britain and France underlined the significance of local contexts for the "availability" of exotic religious resources and their assimilation in practices of bricolage. In some cases, these movements respond to their social environment in such ways that they sometimes downplay, if not abandon, their universalistic discourses. Accordingly, despite being prone to de-ethnicization, depending on local constraints and opportunities, they may present themselves as a religious tradition and/or to identify with a Hindu minority. Two contextual factors appeared to be crucial in shaping these adaptive strategies: national responses to religious diversity (such as policies encouraging religions' engagement in the public sphere or the intensity of a cult controversy) and the local religious landscape (in other words, the numerical importance but also the local structure of Hinduism). For instance, the fragmented and extremely diverse physiognomy of British Hinduism allowed ISKCON to develop its particular strategy, namely competing with other organizations to be the voice of British Hindus. By doing so, it ceases to be exotic and thus becomes less attractive for those who are not born Hindu and are looking for a universalistic, fetishized expression of the Mystical East. ISKCON's association with the identity politics of ethnic and religious minorities made it rather unsuitable for bricolage—ISKCON has been able to attract new members from the South Asian diaspora but not Westerners, and tensions seem to exist between these two different constituencies.

The Kabbalah Centre has grown by redefining its teaching as not Jewish, thereby making Kabbalah available for practices of bricolage. This facilitated the development of the London branch among a cosmopolitan middle-class audience, but in France the de-contextualization of Kabbalah was detrimental. It did not attract new followers, possibly repelled by the accusations of cultic tendencies, and disappointed its first generation of students who through Kabbalah sought to renew their understanding of, and revitalize their bond with, Judaism. Reflecting the fact that Judaism in France is relatively traditional, these students appear to be have been discouraged by the hostile reactions to their involvement in the Kabbalah Centre in their synagogues and social networks. In fact, broadly speaking, the predominance of Orthodox Judaism in France has not favored the development of liberal and eclectic expressions of Judaism.

Accordingly, this chapter highlighted that, while being decisive for bricolage, the process of de-contextualization of exotic religious resources is not invariable. It entails a complex and conflicted negotiation of identity in response to local social environments, the consequences of which may be hazardous for religious movements. Thus, not only are national responses to religious diversity and the local religious landscape determining factors, but characteristics of the audience also are essential to determine what religious resources are available and desirable for practices of bricolage. Bricolage, in other words, is not independent from national contexts.

5

The Psychologization of Exotic Religious Resources

AS I ASKED Dahlia why she came to an introductory lecture at the Kabbalah Centre for the first time, she replied: "I suppose I was definitely feeling unfulfilled, and I think maybe I liked the fact that [the teacher] was sort of mentioning the manifesting things, and making a change, really making a change." At this point of her life, Dahlia was unhappily single and found it difficult to develop her career as a musician in London. After trying yoga, Tarot, and many other "spiritual" means, she started classes at the Kabbalah Centre because she believed "something in her" or something she was "doing" was "blocking" her and preventing her from fulfilling her desires. Kabbalah, she believed, was effectively helping her to change daily, in contrast with other esoteric and spiritual teachings she had explored previously. Dahlia has now left the Kabbalah Centre and is attracted by Buddhism. Like Dahlia, most disciples of neo-Hindu movements and students of Kabbalah started to explore alternative religious resources and therapies in order to improve their lives through the transformation of the self and its attitudes. In fact, it is precisely because neo-Hindu and Kabbalistic teachings (along with many other therapeutic and religious traditions) are believed to offer efficient means for undertaking such processes that they are appropriated. Interviewees report no intention to practice Judaism and Hinduism as such; nonetheless, they have idealized Kabbalah and "Eastern spiritualities" as timeless and authentic sources of wisdom that hold promises of regeneration. This chapter thus addresses the popularization of neo-Hindu religions or the Kabbalah Centre in the context of burgeoning "therapies of normality" that offer methods for assessing, improving, and realizing the self.

Religious Exoticism and Psychologization of Social Life

The use of exotic religious resources for personal growth needs to be understood in the context of the "psychologisation of social life" (Rose 1989, n.d.) in advanced industrial societies, also described as an increasingly pervasive "psychologism" (Castel 1981a), a "therapy culture" (Furedi 2004), and a new "therapeutic emotional style" (Illouz 2008). These notions address the growing tendency to interpret life's everyday problems, as well as their solutions, in psychological terms. Evident in a growing range of domains such as education, poverty, crime, family life, intimacy, efficiency in the workplace, and so forth, social issues are increasingly believed to find their resolution in the transformation of the self. The "psychologization of social life" also sheds light on the proliferation of a wide range of techniques and practices that aim to help individuals change their attitude, develop their potential, realize their self, and reach self-fulfillment. In other words, selfhood and its transformation have gained an unprecedented importance in contemporary societies. Understanding the main features of this "therapy culture" is crucial, since its representations of selfhood and social relations are at the heart of social actors' involvement in yoga and Kabbalah.

Therapy Culture

Therapy culture, it has been argued, finds its roots in American Puritanism and its emphasis on self-examination. By recording feelings and daily events, Puritans were seeking to monitor their spiritual progress and find signs of divine approval to gain greater reassurance of their salvation. This form of self-discipline aimed to respond to the risk of fragmentation deriving from Protestant subjectivism (Ehrenberg 2008, 300). Accordingly, "self-examination serves a dual purpose: to inspire religious allegiance and reinforce social order" rather than encouraging individual autonomy and self-interest (Imbarrato 1998, xvii). While a more liberal form of Protestantism developed in the nineteenth-century United States, the traditional ethics of "self-control" persisted among the urban Victorian bourgeoisie, who were particularly sensitive to an emerging ideal of self-realization and social mobility. Thus, a growing importance was given to introspection and emotional life, as shown by "confessional autobiographies, self-portraits, diaries, letters, and sentimental and self-referential literature" (Illouz 2008, 48).

Similar religious narratives of progress were popularized by evangelicals in Victorian and Edwardian Britain, underscoring the significance of therapy culture's Protestant roots. But perhaps equally important are the affinities between the Protestant emphasis on faith, personal conversion, and voluntarism with capitalism. They converge in the significance of progress, self-reliance, and individual responsibility and as such resonated with those "on the move spatially and socially" (Brown 2001, 38). Thus, in nineteenth-century Britain, novels and magazines told the life stories of "exemplars," their moral battles and their journey (and its obstacles) toward spiritual fulfillment. Structured around the narratives of "error, crisis and conversion," these life dramas conveyed salvation metaphors whereby learning, progress, success, and spiritual fulfillment were earned by self-examination, virtue, and piety. Thus, life became "a road with a moral destination," and these widely disseminated narratives constituted a "guide of behaviour" for such journeys (Brown 2001, *passim*).

In the continuity of American Puritan exemplary biographies, a popular self-help literature started to account for biographies of men who, thanks to their virtue and will power, became socially successful. These new emotional needs around social success and self-betterment were addressed by liberal pastors, but also by new religious movements such as the New Thought and Christian Science, which became enormously popular in the nineteenth century. The so-called "mind cure movement" insisted on the healing power of faith and "positive thinking," thereby reiterating the importance of self-discipline and self-examination in American culture. The combination of the Protestant voluntaristic attitude, self-help techniques, and the mind cure movement made "spirituality and self-help a central aspect of American culture." This might also explain the particular receptivity toward psychoanalysis in the early twentieth century, although American culture did not share "the profoundly pessimistic and deterministic framework of the Freudian outlook" (Illouz 2008, 157). Accordingly, psychoanalysis infused popular culture through advice literature, advertising, and movies, yet within the frame of an American representation of selfhood, involving an ethos of self-improvement and autonomy, the quest for happiness, an optimistic outlook on the perfectibility of the self, and references to faith and moral virtues (Illouz 2008). These characteristics of American representations of selfhood and self-improvement have largely contributed to today's therapy culture.

This process of popularization of psychoanalysis in an American cultural frame solidified during twentieth-century counterculture. The 1960s witnessed the emergence of therapeutic techniques, which epitomized and popularized new perspectives on selfhood and the role of therapy. What has been called the "Human Potential Movement" comprised, for example, transactional analysis, gestalt, rebirth, Erhard seminar trainings (EST), bioenergetics, massage, and other body techniques. Since then, supported by an increasingly widespread quest for personal growth and well-being, new psychotherapies have emerged relentlessly and have become more widely popular. While 50 new therapeutic techniques emerged in the first half of the 1970s, there were 400 in the 1980s and since then have continued to proliferate (Otero 2003, 18).

Their apparent diversity is nonetheless misleading in the light of their relatively standardized paradigms and methods (Garnoussi 2008, 278; 2011, 264). Their first common point is their emancipation from the orthodoxy of psychoanalysis, which is the reason that Castel (1981b, 164) defines them as "post-psychoanalytic." Indeed, these therapies inherited the counterculture's rejection of reason's hegemony and its distrust of intellectual speculations (Furedi 2004, 159; Otero 2003, 22; Tipton 1982, 24). Post-psychoanalytic therapies also intend to differentiate themselves from what they perceived to be the elitism of psychoanalysis. In contrast with the long, costly, uncertain, and intellectual psychoanalytic process they aim to offer simplified responses to very general demands in terms of well-being. They present themselves as efficient methods of short-term investment, focus on the patients' here-and-now trouble rather than the historical dimensions of their lives, and give precedence to direct experience. In addition, post-psychoanalytic therapies tend to value flexible and "practical" techniques that may involve bodywork. Assuming the existence of a biopsychic energy that binds the body and the mind, psychological problems are believed to express themselves in the body as emotional blockages; thus techniques such as yoga, meditation, or massage may be used to release these blockages and to allow the development of the self's true potential (Castel 1981b, 164).

Post-psychoanalytic therapies shifted the focus from treating pathology to the realization of the self and were influenced by the countercultural anti-psychiatry movement and the emergent humanistic psychology approaches of Abraham Maslow and Carl Rogers. The anti-psychiatry movement criticized the repressive dominance of this medical field manifest in its construction of mental illness and its so-called remedies (including medicalization and enforced hospitalization), whereas humanistic psychology simplified the Freudian theoretical frame and made self-realization the fundamental need and drive of human beings (Illouz 2008, 159–160). Thus, post-psychoanalytic therapies tend to promote a human model possessing a capital or a potential, which can be endlessly developed as long as the individual wants and tries. The aim of post-psychoanalytic therapies has become helping people to find their true self and grow, which considerably extends psychotherapies' sphere of remit. They have thus become therapies of normality (Castel 1981b, 155) and hence address dissatisfaction in a wide range of domains—family, love, relationships, sexuality, work, and so on.

Post-psychoanalytic therapies are relatively pragmatic. In the name of individual well-being, any technique that works here and now for a particular individual is legitimate—although, as Otero (2003, 49) emphasizes, patients' needs are fundamentally shaped by specific social expectations. Their legitimacy relies more on their proclaimed effectiveness than on particular intellectual or theoretical heritages, thereby reducing the therapeutic process as the application of a "technique" (p. 15). Therapeutic methods are therefore used in an interchangeable and complementary manner, and therapists may bring them into play successively or simultaneously in order to respond to the needs of their patients. Strikingly, this epistemological devaluation and this propensity for eclectic experimentation facilitated the introduction of religious notions and practices (Briffault and Champion 2008, 136; Castel 1981b, 166–170; 1982, 138).

Indeed, the therapy culture has, in some respects, contributed to the blurring of boundaries between the religious and the therapeutic. As mentioned above, the American culture of self-betterment had religious foundations, from Puritanism to the mind cure movement,[1] well before the new religious consciousness of the 1960s. To this we must add the considerable influence of Jungian psychoanalytic teachings over the countercultural and spiritual milieu of the second half of the twentieth century. Jung envisioned psychotherapy as a religious movement of revitalization for modern society. Fascinated by antique mystery cults, Jung encouraged the exploration of esoteric and exotic religious resources while rejecting Christianity as an institution. Through the reach of a primordial unconscious mind, his psychoanalysis promised the experience of the god within, leading to self-realization and rebirth (Noll 1997).

Maslow's work has also been instrumental in connecting religion and therapy. Maslow celebrated religious experience as a source of self-realization—therapy then becomes a means to attain spiritual fulfillment. But he also asserted the existence of an exclusively personal and private religion that one can discover beyond the rituals, myths, ceremonials, and dogmas of so-called organized religions (Carrette and King 2005, 76). This claim can be read as an incentive for the pragmatic appropriation of a diversity of religious practices in order to achieve a form of self-actualization. Inspired by Maslow's quest for peak experiences, by Jung and his passion for the East, and more broadly by the 1960s countercultural attraction for Asian religions, many post-psychoanalytic therapies integrated yoga, tai chi, shamanism, meditation, and traditional medicines such as acupuncture, shiatsu, chi gong, or Ayurveda in support of a holistic and transcendental vision of the human being (Stone

1976; Tipton 1982). It is once more the belief that exotic resources possess what the West lacks that motivated their appropriation—mysticism fostering direct experiences of the divine, authentic wisdom and healing traditions, a divine and holistic definition of the self, and techniques to realize the self.

The more recent success of "Mindfulness" shows us that the therapeutic use of exotic religious resources has not disappeared with the counterculture. Mindfulness (or Vipassana) is a meditation technique, which retains minimal elements of the Buddha's teachings; it is presented as a portable, flexible, and efficient self-help method for personal growth. Mindfulness is increasingly recognized, in particular by cognitive behavioral therapists, for its effects on mental health difficulties such as anxiety and depression. Its techniques are now popularized through various therapies, but also through books, websites and institutions (Garnoussi 2011). By and large, in recent years and in some countries, the "spiritual" has made inroads into the mental health sector, often through the acknowledgment of the importance of patients' "spiritual needs" in the therapeutic process. This is shown by Champion's (2013) study of the "Spirituality and Psychiatry Special Interest Group" of the Royal College of Psychiatrists in Britain. This relatively contested group has nonetheless gained legitimacy and has grown since its creation in 1999.

Post-psychoanalytic therapies converge on a central theme: individuals' adaptation to their environment as the *sine qua non* condition for their self-realization (Otero 2003, 4). Post-psychoanalytic therapies consider that solutions to life's problems lie in the change of individuals' attitudes, thereby making them responsible for their destiny. They are faithful to Maslow's belief (and maybe to Protestant voluntarism) that "it is the person's responsibility as a free agent to realize as many of his or her potentialities as possible" (Illouz 2008, 160). However, they have departed from the countercultural and anti-psychiatric denunciation of social institutions and the ways in which they exerted authority, which was believed to generate guilt, negative self-image, and the repression of emotions (Garnoussi 2008, 276; 2011, 264). While in the 1960s "liberation psychotherapy" (Rice 1998, 29) such as Maslow's asserted that individuals must be set free from cultural and social repression (the source of psychological problems), therapies increasingly encourage individuals' adaptation to their social environment through the development of communication, relational, and emotional skills, as well as of the capacity to manage external constraints. EST, for instance, invites individuals to become "winners" rather than "victims," by accepting the world as it is and learning adaptive skills, instead of trying to reform their social environment (Castel 1982, 138; Castel et al. 1979, 298, 325). By and large, the objective of new therapies is to provide patients with the necessary tools to build self-esteem, evaluate situations, negotiate conflicts, control emotions, or develop particular skills allowing them to adjust to particular situations. First guided by the therapist, individuals will learn to autonomously adopt the techniques discovered during the therapeutic process (Otero 2003, 56)—it is not surprising, therefore, that the main concern of psychotherapy users was about developing self-reliance through self-discipline (Briffault and Champion 2008, 135).

As Zilbergeld (1983, 17) notes, this encouragement to endless personal growth somehow implies that people are not as healthy and fulfilled as they should be. Consequently, it could be argued that the therapy culture's focus on people's "potential" and methods to realize this potential convey a sense of deficit, lack of fulfillment, and vulnerability, which are the conditions one needs to overcome to reach self-realization (Furedi 2004). Thus, it is the presumption of this lack or deficit of the self that "motivates" the therapeutic process and prompts the search for techniques enabling one to ward off a sense of powerlessness. It has been argued that, by its emphasis on self-realization, the therapy culture of advanced industrial societies paradoxically cultivates a general sense of vulnerability. Furedi (2004) emphasizes an increasingly pervasive language of suffering and victimhood, as illustrated by Rice's (1998) study of "co-dependency." By and large, "trauma," "stress," and "low self-esteem" feature more and more in the public discourse to describe selfhood and a life course scattered by plentiful risks of being emotionally scarred. Emotional ills such as depression, addiction, post-traumatic stress disorder, and panic attacks have been ascribed to an increasing number of individuals and have become growing social concerns.

This language of emotionalism reflects the fact that an increasing number of social issues are now understood and codified in psychological terms. They are also believed to find their solution in the management of attitudes and emotions, which justifies the use of psychological techniques. And this is the reason that these social transformations can be called a "culture" rather than simply a diversification and popularization of psychotherapies. This "psychologization" of social life entails the increasing intervention of new experts in ever more spheres of social life, as well as the modification of the practices of existing forms of authorities. Managers, social workers, teachers (on the "therapeutic school," see Rice 2002), judges, and nurses use new norms and techniques that are infused by a psychological understanding of social relations (Rose 1998, 17). By and large, authors such as Rose, Otero, and Castel advance that therapy culture contributes to maintaining and reproducing a particular mode of political management of social relations, through which the mode of intervention is on the self. In other words, the transformation of the self has become the solution to everything; social conflicts and tensions are codified through a psychological language. Therapeutic techniques are thus used "for teaching the arts of existence as social skills"—communication, weight control, addiction, crime, stress management and so forth (Rose 1998, 97)—in other words, to regulate behaviors. Therapeutic interventions indeed reveal the various social, cultural, and political injunctions placed upon individuals, in particular being responsible, self-reliant, and adapted to their environment (Otero 2003, 2). This new mode of regulation of behaviors is reflected in the fact that an increasing number of individuals receive a form of therapy or counseling. Furedi (2004, 9–10) found that, while 14 percent of Americans had experienced a form of therapeutic intervention in the 1960s, by 1995 it was nearly half of the population. By now, it is estimated that 80 percent of Americans have used the services of therapists. In France, 4 million people have used psychotherapy, a third of whom have followed more than one therapy (Briffault and Lamboy 2008, 101, 105). It goes without saying that new experts and professionals proliferated to answer these new social needs: for instance, in Britain, half a million individuals work as part-time or full-time counselors (Furedi 2004, 10). Finally, the pervasiveness of therapy culture can easily be measured up by the fantastic success of self-help and personal growth literature, which in 1998 represented a $581 million profit in the United States. There, the self-improvement sector as a whole (literature, seminars, coaching, audio and video material) has become a $2.48 billion-a-year industry (Illouz 2008, 162).

Yoga and Kabbalah, "A Bit of Life Coaching"

> In New Orleans, during Gurumayi Chidvilasananda's first American tour, someone asked me, "how did you become interested in Eastern philosophy?" The answer that came out of my mouth surprised even me. I said: "I don't give a damn about Eastern philosophy. All I ever wanted was to be happy. I'd try a philosophy that comes from the moon if it could give me that." (Hayes 1988, 11)

Therapy culture largely contributes to shape the meaning that students of the Kabbalah Centre, Siddha Yoga, and the Sivananda Centres give to their religious trajectory. To begin, exotic religious resources are appropriated as means to support and develop the self. The belief in the efficiency of authentic and immemorial wisdoms for the realization of the self is the key of their popularization. Lyn is a 50-year-old teacher. She had started to practice yoga 10 years before I met her in the London Sivananda Centre, in order to find a "practical philosophy" that could enable her to understand her life better. Suffering from depression, Lyn says that yoga helps her to deal with this issue:

> It just gave me a technique for controlling depression and the ups and downs of the mind. Things like if you have low self esteem and so on, because the whole philosophy of yoga whereby you have this notion of that's not really who you are, and that you are something beyond this, whether you think you are great or whether you think you're terrible, it's not really important. It's this idea of detaching, and just trying to practice calming yoga, trying to be an instrument of the divine, just makes you feel that your life has a purpose. So mentally you feel much happier, and that gives a meaning to the life, physically, mentally, because it gives you a framework for that spiritual dimension in your life. You just feel you are going in a direction and growing and you just feel that it's a positive thing.

Lyn also describes yoga as a "technology of spirituality" to control the mind and to address low self-esteem and anxiety. The notion of detachment aims to ward off Lyn's sense of vulnerability and purposelessness. By and large, many interviewees define yoga or meditation as a form of psychotherapy, a "therapeutic technique" that can "unblock many things," or "an opening of the mind, also an opening of the body which can help people to grow." "What is Kabbalah about, but transformation!" asserts Farrah, who thinks Kabbalah is "a bit like life coaching, it does teach you more how to deal with situations." Lisa, 29, works in the artistic field after studying marketing. She believes it is Siddha Yoga that has given her the courage to be a musician for her living, hence proving that the teaching "works":

> Things changed in me and I think Siddha Yoga has been part of that. It is like it helped to transform myself and to realize that nothing is permanent. You know, this idea of, you can't change the way you are looking, you can't change your personality, that you are who you are. Like "a leopard doesn't change its spots." ...I know it is quite radical but I totally agree that we can be what we want to be, *it is a matter of choice and change and healing* because I really see it in myself since I have been to Siddha Yoga, I have totally changed, it seems like, incredible, like a miracle. I mean, it often seems like a miracle because I have never thought before I could change these things.

Lisa's narrative underlines a crucial point: religious resources are seen as a means that helps the individual to make the necessary inner change, which in turn can "unblock" situations. Therefore, life's achievements are implicitly obtained through the voluntary transformation of the self—with the support of religious resources. Thus, most interviews conducted with students of the Kabbalah Centre, Siddha Yoga, and the Sivananda Centres are narratives of life transformation and achievement, as a result of a process of personal betterment. Buying a country house, feeling confident in a stressful work environment, changing occupation, improving interpersonal relations, healing, dealing with divorce or bereavement are presented as challenges successfully overcome with the help of these teachings. For interviewees, self-fulfillment is generated by personal choice and initiative, encouraging the development of new personal skills such as detachment, strength, optimism, confidence, ability to cope, control anger and fear, or being open to love.

The ability to change oneself is therefore central in the personal trajectories of individuals such as Lisa or Noa, a full-time volunteer in Tel Aviv who describes the effects of the Kabbalah Centre's teaching on her life:

> It's basically being less reactive to different things you know? It's a bit like having a victim consciousness. I used to be really into, even you know, being aware of it or not I felt you know like a victim. I felt like life is dragging me wherever, I'm not really in control of things and it's not that I really had something traumatic or something bad had happened to me, but I felt like something here is missing you know? So it was basically being less reactive to life. Starting to really be *on top of it*. Starting to really, *knowing that I have the power to change.*

Noa exemplifies particularly well an overwhelmingly pervasive quest among research participants: becoming a strong and autonomous individual, in control, unaffected by the outside and able to overcome challenges and difficulties. Patrick's depiction of the benefits of his yoga practice is equally illustrative. It is about having:

> ...more distance with daily life problems. At the end of the day, I realize now that nothing serious can happen to you. A divorce, your mother's death, things like that; ultimately, if you can take some distance and tell yourself that it's not personal, it's ok....Everything that is going to happen to me has already happened to everybody else. It will happen to you...Actually nothing is serious. See, you can be happy, no matter what happens, whatever circumstances maybe...Strength is inside.

In short, the adoption of exotic resources is associated with, and motivated by, life changes through personal growth, understood as an ability to change oneself, and in particular to developing resilience and self-sufficiency. As in the therapeutic field, self-help methods that do not undermine but promote individual autonomy are sought in the religious field by partially secularized individuals. This desire for empowerment through self-sufficiency is very clear in Kim's description of Siddha Yoga's benefits for her:

> Before I didn't think I could help myself, like I have to go somewhere to get that help, you have to look outside to find it. Whereas now I'm thinking: "yes I actually have the tools to do this," I can sit down and work through my crap, even though it might be painful and horrible. It's almost like when you go into a rescue mode for yourself. . . . That's really the first thing, that's "wow I've got the power to transform emotions, I have the power to transform myself if I choose to." I think that's very much the best thing you can be given, because if it's very much you're healing me then you become reliant on this outside thing. So it's good when that teacher can give something back to you and say "have the tools as well" so if I'm not here you can still continue to heal.

Here, Kim describes the guru as providing methods for self-empowerment. Yet personal growth is linked to individual effort, learning, and personal merit by social actors. "If I meditate, or if I practice yoga, I don't expect anything from the outside," explains Virginie, when comparing yoga and psychoanalysis; her progress is therefore the result of her own discipline and nothing else.

Furthermore, these narratives about resilience and self-reliance I have cited so far paradoxically contribute to a discourse about vulnerability and uncertainty. Lyn and Stephen mentioned a state of depression; Noa talked about having had a "victim consciousness" while Dahlia spoke of her "blockages." This narrative of deficit and vulnerability takes many shapes: when asked about what yoga has done for him, Mick explained that it has helped him to be less angry and fearful. These are feelings that he described as being "destructive" to him as "slow[ing] down [his] progression." Similarly, yoga helps Alison "not to worry as much because I can be more productive about dealing with problems, instead of just worrying and worrying and worrying and not knowing what to do and how to handle it or putting off, being a procrastinator." In various ways, interviewees evoke a sense of powerlessness that religious and therapeutic resources are believed to address. As noted in the therapy culture, the narrative of deficit and vulnerability is generated, in part, by the endless nature of the ideal of self-realization, the assumption that one has never finished realizing his or her potential. "There's something more to this," believes Lucy, a student of Siddha Yoga in London, "there's something I have to achieve or there's more to me."

Another important characteristic of these narratives about personal growth and involvement in exotic religions relates to the nature of this resilience. Indeed, interviewees tend to describe resilience as an ability to accept and adapt to circumstances, to become "flexible" in life. Underlying this attitude is the general view that misfortune actually does not exist. Instead, it brings about challenges that one needs to learn from in order to improve and ultimately reach happiness. Individuals' responsibility for their life is therefore implicitly a central tenet taken for granted. This is often described as an important principle that interviewees claim to have learned from Kabbalah, yoga, or meditation. "Even big problems," says Sylvia, who attends yoga classes at the London Sivananda Centre, "I realize that they happen for a reason. I'm able to see the good sides of it, and why it's happening, trying to understand a lot more in step with that situation." The idea that "everything happens for a reason" is particularly strong among students of the Kabbalah Centre, as illustrated by Jane:

> The thing that I think is a big challenge for most of us is when things don't go our way and we are going through a challenge [is] to see it as a gift. And that is one of the things I learnt at the Centre now is when a challenge comes along I try and see beyond the box and the bow, and try to look to see what the gift has given me. *Because when things go well I am not learning....* So it's to look at the challenges to find where the gift is and when to use it. And usually that means changing.

Statements such as "your problems are actually sometimes your greatest gifts," "maybe it's part of life's bigger plan," "things are meant to happen to us" were often made by interviewees to explain the meaning of their "spiritual" path. In these popular self-help principles, they found the means to develop this "positive" attitude toward life (in other words, to accept difficulties as opportunities to grow), which, in turn, fosters life improvements. Life is thus seen as an ascending trajectory of personal progress, and conversely, "learning," "growing," or improving oneself, as illustrated above, is what constitutes the meaning of life. "We have come here to learn a lesson and to make a change," explains Nathalie from the Kabbalah Centre. Lucy from Siddha Yoga considers that "life is to learn through the people that we're with, the experiences we have, to grow stronger in ourselves, to test our faith, and to trust it will help us to connect."

In this lifelong and voluntaristic learning process, depicted as a "spiritual path" or "journey," exotic religious resources are pragmatically conceived as a means to an end. Kabbalah, yoga, and meditation are described as "tools," but also as "ladders" and "stairs," both underscoring aspirations of elevation and progress. "Going higher and forward" in the evolution the soul has to make is what Martine, a medium and a therapist, seeks in Asian religions, Kabbalah, and esotericism. "So no matter the tools, we can take several" because, she adds, "every path leads to the mountain and we can change tools along the way. It is not a problem, it is not important. What counts is to reach up high." Similarly, when asked about the Hindu origins of yoga, Patrick answered this was not a relevant issue. He explained having simply chosen any possible "means" to reach happiness and fulfill his "quest of himself." Thus, "any ladder is good for me, as long as it goes up" and yoga, Patrick believes, is a good ladder, "its steps are good, they're clear." It is on these premises of efficacy that these religious teachings are pragmatically adopted. Nathalie, for instance, reluctantly participates in the Kabbalah Centre's rituals. It is for her "like taking a medicine" but she explains, "I do it because I know it works"; "it is a tool, a technology—I am very cold about it—that makes a difference in my life," she adds.

This pragmatic approach explains why the exploration of exotic religious resources is not motivated by a quest for a new religious identity, why it is characterized by short-term and non-committal involvements, and why it entails the successive or simultaneous combination of diverse religious and therapeutic resources. Above all, individuals seek practical methods for personal growth in a "lifelong religious learning," beyond religious particularities. "That's the thing about Siddha Yoga, there's nothing to believe, it's what you experience and this is those sort of experiences that tell you that you're on an incredible journey," says Eileen. Thus, despite an apparent eclecticism, religious incursions in yoga, meditation, or Kabbalah often contribute to a quest which, for social actors, is relatively coherent and stable, in which any teaching that promotes self-fulfillment is considered. In other words, rather than making successive different choices, they reiterate, in fact, a consistent religious orientation motivated by personal growth. Besides, we could even say that the imperative of self-improvement constitutes an incentive for not stagnating and endlessly trying new techniques that could hasten this improvement.[2]

This pragmatic attitude is better understood if we consider that these individuals increasingly use religious resources for therapeutic purposes, often along with various post-psychoanalytic therapies and traditional healing techniques (see Chapter 2). Infused by the ethos of self-realization of the therapy culture, the spiritual path is often perceived to be similar to therapy in its objective and effects and is authenticated through an evaluation of cost, length, and effectiveness. June, for example, compares her past psychoanalysis with the benefits of yoga:

> It took up a lot of time and it was a very slow process, and it cost a lot of money. And I think what's being better for me, I've felt happier over a shorter period of time, a more balanced way, for less money [laugh] and a far more natural way ... Just over the last four months that I have with yoga. I think it's a valid form of psychology, of psychotherapy, in a way.

June interestingly describes yoga as more "natural," hence bringing about the representation of a traditional and authentic practice, as opposed to the modern and intellectually driven Freudian method. A quest for "a practical philosophy" also predominates: rather than intellectual knowledge, they look for self-help methods they can apply by themselves, as "how-tos" for daily life. Darren explains that "Kabbalah teaches you how to get the very best out of life. It's a very practical system, it gives you very specific, down to earth and physical tool that when you apply, improves your life completely." Applicability is also raised by Lucy to explain why she follows the teaching of Siddha Yoga:

> I went through a long period where I looked at so many different things, shamanism, all these New Age things, I've done some channeling. Channeling was certainly an experience, but they're not *a teaching which will take you on your sadhana in your everyday life where you can actually apply something.*

Applicability is linked to efficacy: when asked about what drove her to Kabbalah, Nathalie answered: "the fact that it makes a difference to my life, that the study of something is applicable to my behavior and my life." Thus, yoga and Kabbalah are often described as a way of life, a "method to live well," or a "guide to life." This practical approach makes doctrines secondary, if not unnecessary: "I don't need to know the physics and the engineering and all that, just tell me what to do: meditate, chant, I don't want to know why, just how," explains Lewis, who finds Siddha Yoga helpful to overcome his drug addiction. Patrick also defines yoga as a strictly practical means in this enlightening metaphor: "One can know to do anything, know everything on water, what water is made of, the Pacific, Atlantic, Antarctica, what matters is that you know how to swim. That's it."

In short, individuals look into Kabbalah and neo-Hindu teachings for practical and efficient techniques that develop self-empowerment and self-reliance. But they also find in these exotic religious resources an ethos of personal growth that includes references to transcendence. As such, they decisively contrast with classical psychological therapies for social actors. Christophe, a member of Siddha Yoga in Paris, explains that he had to stop the course of his psychoanalysis because he found it was conflicting with his convictions. For instance, he felt that his psychoanalyst was considering his belief in karma and reincarnation as part of his neurosis, a perspective Christophe strongly rejects. In his view, it is the psychoanalytic rationalism that is actually invalid. Christophe decided to put an end to his psychoanalysis because he "didn't want to be judged on what [he] think[s] is completely wrong." Since then, he practices "energetic" and "holistic therapies," which he finds more aligned with his worldview. Martine, a therapist interested in Kabbalah, considers that one cannot undertake this profession without being spiritual. Underlining the inaccuracies and limits of "non-spiritual" therapies, she refers with horror to the medicalized treatment of autism, which in her view overlooks the fact that this condition is the manifestation of something occurring "at the soul level," that is in fact linked to a person's karma. "Certainly scientific psychology like behaviorism, that's awfully terrible," says Colin, a British disciple of Siddha Yoga. He thus emphasizes transcendence and direct experience: "There are people writing and researching in fields of psychology whose perspective is really very narrow, they've had no experience themselves of anything transcendent. So they just treat the mind as a machine. . . . If they had half a second of the experience that I had when I first met Baba [Muktananda], all of that would just go out the window."

Personal Growth as Salvation Good

Meditate on your Self. Worship your Self. Kneel to your Self. Understand your Self. God dwells within you as you.
(Muktananda 1993, para. 31)

The process of psychologization of religion implies that the ethos of therapy culture is infused in the religious life of students of neo-Hinduism and Kabbalah, as expressed in rather standardized biographical discourses. The desire (and urge) to realize one's self, a perception of life as a process of self-improvement, the emphasis on autonomy and resilience in response to vulnerability and dissatisfaction, a sense of individual responsibility and voluntarism in the process of self-improvement, an accepting attitude—all of these are fundamental elements of interviewees' narratives about their religious or "spiritual" life. It is this ethos that grants a particular meaning to exotic religious resources: they are understood as the self-help tools helping to acquire detachment, strength, optimism, and acceptance, which as such pave the way to self-realization and self-fulfillment. An efficient self-help method with references to the divine (as energy, as a higher self, or as power of a charismatic religious leader) is sought in Hindu-based and Kabbalistic teachings, as well as in other religious teachings and alternative therapies.

This psychologized understanding of religion is made possible by the fact that the teachings of movements such as Siddha Yoga, the Sivananda Centres, and the Kabbalah Centre have been gradually shaped by the mold of the therapy culture. They present an inner-worldly and individualized version of the Hindu and Jewish salvation path, making the law of karma and *tikkun* a learning process toward the realization of the self. Their teaching is accordingly introduced as simple (yet powerful) techniques that one can acquire, use, and apply autonomously to reach this goal. Finally, these movements have drawn on the field of therapy, coaching and self-help methods to structure the transmission of the teachings to individuals who are not socialized to the Hindu or Jewish religion.

From "self-realization" to Self-realization

Modern gurus have clearly endeavored to answer their audience's expectations in terms of personal growth. Not only have they presented their teaching as a path toward self-realization, but they have also directly addressed, if not confronted, psychology. This was, at first, a response to Western science and hence a form of Hindu identity-building rhetoric. Sivananda (1998 [1940]), for instance, claimed that the yogi's knowledge of the mind was superior to the one of "Western psychologists" who "know only a fragment of mind":

> The doctors are still groping in utter darkness. Their minds need drastic flushing for the entry of Hindu philosophical ideas. It is only the yogins and those who practice meditation and introspection that know the existence of the mind, its nature, ways and subtle workings. They know also the various methods of subduing the mind.

"Modern psychology of the mind is nothing compared to the ancients' understanding of it," similarly wrote Vishnu-Devananda (1988 [1960], 18) because "[n]o one, of course, can really understand mind and souls as long as he experiments on the outside, not turning inward and stilling all his thoughts to watch his own mind and soul."

This confrontation of neo-Hinduism with psychology was also linked to their new audience's quest for self-examination and self-realization techniques, and of course by their orientalism—the assumption that the "mystical East" possesses authentic and timeless *savoir-faire* enabling one to fully experience the self. Muktananda is among those gurus who met the longing and hope for self-realization with relative success. Indeed, he found a receptive audience in the Human Potential milieu. He was introduced in the Erhard Seminar Trainings, which inspired the format of Siddha Yoga's initiating event, the Intensive. Muktananda gave talks on university campuses to students and teachers of psychology; he participated in Transpersonal Psychology conferences in Boston in 1979 and in Bombay in 1982, where he made the opening speech on the topic "modern science and eastern wisdom" (Siddha Yoga Dham France 1982, 10). The title of his contribution underlines the significance of Western orientalism: the East is the guardian of what the West lacks and craves for. While he observes that dissatisfaction seems to be a pervasive problem in the West, Muktananda (1978, 92) asserts that "since ancient times," psychologists in India have explored the human mind and, as a result, Indians "have many rituals and methods of worship that are meant for the purification of the mind, and they are becoming popular even here in the West." Yoga and meditation are indeed "true psychology" (Muktananda 1981, 40). Muktananda's desire to match his new audience's expectation by providing superior means of reaching self-fulfillment is also to be found in his claim that Siddha Yoga was a therapy rather than a religion (Anon., *The Larger Perspective*). As suggested by the writings of one of these transpersonal psychologists (Mann 1984, viii), it is also the "appreciation of the divinity of each human being—the inner self" that made Siddha Yoga so attractive to them. Indeed, Transpersonal Psychology aims to explore the transcendent and spiritual dimensions of experience in order to foster the development of human beings' ultimate potential, hence its interest in meditation and yoga, as well as all forms of exotic healing and mystical traditions (Stone 1976, 95).

Today's leaders of the Sivananda Centres present yoga as a way to control the mind and develop skills such as willpower. They recognize the need for them to consider their students' psychological needs. "We have to take care of people on that side too," explains the acharya in charge of Parisian Centre, who spends a lot of time speaking with her students about their psychological problems and past experiences. By and large, the countercultural and post-psychoanalytic mindset represented a receptive context for gurus in the 1960s. This could not be better illustrated than by Rajneesh, whose teaching fully embraced therapy culture's ideas and practices. Influenced by the writings of Wilhelm Reich, Rajneesh advocated "active meditations" to free the repressed modern mind by letting out emotions and breaking taboos. He also integrated a wide range of post-psychoanalytic therapies as a central part of a spiritual discipline that many participants described as "personal growth." At the end of the 1970s, 60 different forms of therapies were practiced in Rajneesh's ashram in Poona, alongside tai chi, yoga, Vipassana meditation, and Sufi dancing (Palmer 1992).

Contemporary gurus' adaptation to the ethos of personal growth is striking in their presentation of what salvation is about. Indeed, they have undertaken an inner-worldly interpretation of "Self-realization." The notion "God" or "Self-realization" derives from the Upanishads and represents a core Vedantic principle. It deals with the relationships between *Brahman* (the Absolute) and its individuated manifestation, *atman*, often translated as "Self." For Advaita Vedanta, human beings need to recognize that what animates them (the Self) *is* Brahman in order to free themselves from the cycle of reincarnations. Indeed, *atman*/Self is not the individual soul itself: by giving an illusory sense of personal and finite existence, the individual soul (*jiva*) and the "I" thought (*ahamkara*) generate ignorance, pain, and prevent one from knowing *Brahman* (Hulin 2001, 122). Accordingly, the sense of individuality is classically an obstacle that must be overcome through the study of scriptures, the guidance of a guru, the renunciation of worldly activities, and an ascetic discipline (yoga). Vivekananda initiated "Self-realization" as one of Neo-Hinduism's cardinal issues and presented it as a goal for all human beings. He thus made of Advaita Vedanta an inner-worldly and practical philosophy, which does not require renouncing the world and evoked instead an "inner renunciation" (cited in Burke 1986, 456). The inner-worldly interpretation of Vedanta of twentieth-century gurus went further by allowing, if not encouraging, an affirmation and a divinization of the self. In line with therapy culture, they have fostered an understanding of "Self-realization" as "self-realization" by presenting personal fulfillment and empowerment as the goal of religious practice. Also, the notion of "realization" in Vivekananda's time designated a form of "consummation of religious experience" and not a process of personal growth (Bharati 1970, 130). Today's disciples of Siddha Yoga and the Sivananda Centres approach "S/self-realization" as a process of "becoming oneself," "finding one's true self," "and achieving one's potential." In other words, the notion that Vedanta's ultimate goals (the knowledge of *Brahman*) entail the denial of individuality has been lost in contemporary neo-Hindu movements, while personal growth has become the ultimate objective.

Unsurprisingly, some interviewees express their perplexity about the "loss of individuality" that is sometimes evoked in gurus' writings.

In fact, the *atman/Brahman* relations have often been presented (and therefore understood) as a divinization of the self. While Sivananda (1949) advocates the "destruction of the ego" through the practice of yoga, he also teaches to his disciples: "you are the Lord of lords, the God of all gods, the Emperor of emperors. You are in possession of the inexhaustible spiritual wealth" (Sivananda 1998 [1947]). Similarly, Muktananda (1993, *passim*) teaches that it is a mistake for someone to think that something beside his own Self exists but also that meditation allows one to realize that we *are* God. This ambivalence is translated in the movement's core practice: Siddha Yoga's main meditation mantra is *Om namah shivayah, mantra* ("I bow to Shiva"), which is translated as "I bow to the God within" or "I am God" in the movement's gatherings. Therefore, in a somewhat Jungian perspective, it is commonly understood that yoga, mantra recitation, and meditation allow one to "find our divine nature" or to realize that "we all are God."

"Shiva is me," explains Eileen, a disciple from London, "so I'm bowing to myself." For Meredith, the mantra was what attracted her the most, reflecting the fact that Siddha Yoga "teaches to love and believe in yourself." "When I met Gurumayi, I became aware that God is within, explains Nigel, I also became aware that I *am* God." This divinization of the self resonates with a quest of self-empowerment, as suggested by Lisa, also a disciple of Siddha Yoga:

> A big difference that was really exciting for me is that with Christianity or Western religions is that God is outside of you or above you and separate from you and God is perfect and you are not, you are weak and you are a sinner and feeling totally disempowered by it, it is like you totally need this person to save you whereas Siddha Yoga and the kind of things I've read that are more Eastern, it is all about empowering you and you are great and we are all great beings.... It is so exciting, it is so lovely to be, to have that, to be told that you are perfect, you are powerful, you are courage, happiness, you are love, compassion, you have all these things, it is so self-affirming, the God within.

Lisa's statement is particularly interesting. It also underscores, one more time, the extent to which exotic religious resources are shaped by the orientalistic gaze of their new audience. Here, the notion of self-transcendence is valued as a self-affirming principle, which concurs more with therapy culture's ethos than with traditional Hindu doctrine.

Another example that sheds light on the psychologization of Hinduism relates to reincarnation. Classic Hinduism's discussions of reincarnation are diverse and highly complex, but the main principle is that the cycle of reincarnations constitutes an "unending, blind, and meaningless" process that entails upcoming suffering (Hacker in Halbfass 1995, 250). Accordingly, life's ultimate goal is to be free from the cycle of rebirth, and reincarnation is therefore the opposite of *moksha* (liberation). Reincarnation and the law of karma are not central in the teaching of contemporary gurus, who prefer to insist on methods to realize the s/Self instead. Yet, when reincarnation is evoked, it is presented optimistically as an evolutionary process and an opportunity for self-improvement: "progress advances from the existence to the next... until the final and stainless state of perfection is reached and the individual soul merges itself in the Supreme Soul" (Sivananda 1999 [1946]). Accordingly, Sivananda's purposeful and "evolutionary karma" is the exact opposite of the classical notion of the cycle of reincarnation. It is nevertheless not unique. Minor (1986, 15–16) pointed out a similar interpretation of reincarnation as a form of progress in the writings of Aurobindo and philosopher Radhakrishnan, which he analyzed as a neo-Hindu response to Western criticisms about the unscientific and fatalistic nature of the law of karma.

This optimistic idea of successive lives resonates with the inner-worldly orientation of contemporary society. It probably explains why reincarnation is one of the few religious beliefs that progressed in postwar Europe among young generations, contrasting with the declining belief in the afterlife. This popular belief in reincarnation is in addition uncorrelated with belonging to any particular religious groups (Bréchon 2000, 2001; Lambert 2001; Waterhouse and Walter 1999). In fact, the neo-Hindu optimistic approach of reincarnation has strong affinities with the modern injunction of personal growth and the representation of life as a learning process. Vishnu-Devananda (1988 [1960], xiv), for instance, embraces this vision of endless life as a "school for the development of character, compassion, and the realization of the Divine All-pervading Self." Echoing the guru, an interviewee explains that reincarnation is indeed the possibility "to work on what you have not understood" and hence to develop one's potential. Hélène, who practices yoga at the Parisian Sivananda Centre, finds the Catholic idea of paradise not "motivating" because "there is nothing at stake"; she contrasts this with reincarnation, which she describes as "stimulating":

> If you tell me "you have the opportunity, through your actions, to have a slightly different life," to improve a bit, because that's what the cycle

of lives is, if you endlessly come back on earth, it's because you have a path to walk on. That's the idea. I like believing in this. If you reach another behavior, if you make some efforts, then you will be born differently and with what you have achieved you will go a bit further and then reach superior levels.

Hélène sheds light on the crucial importance of individual learning and progress, as what grants meaning to life. Life needs to have a direction, a purpose along an evolutionary process of personal growth. "The more you practice, the more you will develop and grow, explains Lyn about yoga. And if you think in terms of reincarnation, if you are practicing in this life then in the next life you will start off a bit further on." This vision of reincarnation is also predominant in New Age (Hanegraaff 1998, 62) and among Westerners practicing Buddhism. Like Hinduism, Buddhism is about putting an end to a painful cycle of rebirths; however, a majority of new Buddhists look for a process of individual progress rather than reaching Nirvana (Lenoir 1999, 337). In her studies of the mystical-esoteric nebula, Champion (1990, 42–43) noted that the karma law is understood as a form of cosmic justice that eliminates what seems arbitrary in life. Life difficulties as the result of actions in past lives are explained—the understanding of the law of karma is made congruent with the psychoanalytical framework, which understands individuals' present difficulties as the result of early traumatic experiences and their unconscious repression (Stone 1978, 130). Learning and acceptation will be rewarded: "what you do now doesn't change the karma you have to work out, which is all the result of your action in the past. A true *yogi* accepts his present condition, whatever it is" (Vishnu Devananda 1995). Kim, another member of Siddha Yoga, sees reincarnation as "positive" because it means

> being able to transform at any time, or transform anything and without fear.... Because you must be transforming all the time.... So I'm obviously here to learn more lessons and you're here to learn more lessons whatever they may be, who knows you might be enlightened at the end of it all, who knows! It really does amaze me.

Kim's definition of enlightenment, the outcome of a *learning* process, illustrates one more time the strong link between reincarnation and personal growth. In fact, the ultimate realization of the Self leading to salvation is not described by interviewees as their primary goal in life; personal growth is the aim.

Tikkun and Personal Growth

We came to this world to grow and raise our consciousness by connecting to a hidden reality called the tree of life. In spiritual coaching you will learn how to tap in to this reality and so grow to your next level. What is your next level? When your soul is learning and growing...when it is not, the real you stagnates, so gain the wisdom and support your need to grow in your true potential which is more than you can imagine. (London Kabbalah Centre 2008b, 8)

Contemporary Kabbalah movements are equally affected by psychologized reinterpretations of religious doctrines (Huss forthcoming b). The Kabbalah Centre teachers in particular present personal growth as the core of religious practice and describe life as a learning process, which in turn leads to self-fulfillment and happiness. In fact, the very same ethos structures neo-Hindu and Kabbalistic teachings, which underscore that the psychologization of religion acts as a process of standardization of religion.

The popularization of the Kabbalah Centre was accompanied by a move towards greater professionalization and the development of a more therapy-oriented teaching. Today, the Kabbalah Centre aims to carve a niche for itself in the field of personal growth, as shown by the themes of some of its courses, ranging from "spiritual coaching" in London to "creating yourself" in New York. The advertisement for the latter on the social networking website Meetup (Manhattan Kabbalah Centre 2010) is particularly revealing. Here the Centre presents itself by using the following keywords: Judaism, self-improvement, self-empowerment and exploration, spiritualism, lifestyle coaching, metaphysics, spirituality, personal growth, meditation, law of attraction, Kabbalah, consciousness, and life transformation. The recent literature, in particular written by Yehuda and Karen Berg, presents their relationships with their students as one of "counseling." Reflecting the standards of self-help literature, these two authors illustrate their argument by analyzing the real life difficulties of some of their students (K. Berg 2005, 194; Y. Berg 2008b, 20). In recent years, post-psychoanalytic and coaching methods have increasingly shaped the Kabbalah Centre's doctrines, norms, and practices. Full-time volunteers and teachers are now trained in coaching, selling, communication, mediation, and personal growth techniques; it has become part of the curriculum. In that matter, the Kabbalah Centre is helped by students who work in these domains and who voluntary train full-time members in acquiring these new skills.

In the same manner in which gurus presented yoga and meditation as the "true" psychological path, Kabbalah is said by its teachers to function "like psychotherapy but much faster" (Pereira 2003). Most important, Kabbalah surpasses psychology. One of my Israeli informants, Ranit, experienced traumatic events during her childhood, which affects her physical and psychological health. She sometimes wondered whether psychoanalysis would help her, but was discouraged by her teachers: "they don't like psychoanalysis at the Centre," she said, "they say that going to the psychologist and talking for years about your problems does not resolve anything." This is because psychology is believed to be limited by discarding the self's connection with the Light of the Creator, the only real source of health and fulfillment.

While not referring to Vedanta, the Kabbalah Centre's teaching emphasis on self-realization is strikingly similar to neo-Hinduism:

> The purpose of our lives is to transform ourselves so that we can receive complete and ultimate fulfillment. We are here in this world to reach our potential and literally become like God, with giving and sharing as the foundation of our being. (Kabbalah Centre 2007c)

Thus, explained a teacher during a course in Paris, one of people's biggest "diseases" is to think their life is fine as it is. The inability to see limitations, lacks, and problems prevents any spiritual progress. By contrast, "the work of Kabbalah" is the "work of spiritual transformation" (Y. Berg 2008b, 45). The Kabbalah Centre offers an empowering promise through "mystical tools" (Kabbalah Centre 2006b), similar to yoga and meditation in order to, as the course materials explain: "go to the next level." Scanning the Zohar and participating in Shabbat services, festivals, and prayers are presented as efficient means to "connect" with the Light. The key points of its introductory lecture, designed for potential students who come for the first time to the Centre, are highly revealing: Kabbalah promotes constant changes; it uses mystical tools that go beyond self-help to create these changes; the Kabbalistic lineage has been here since the creation of the world, and Kabbalists believe that we can create global change when we, as individuals, transform. In other words, the value of Kabbalah is to be found primarily in its ability to initiate self-transformation.

The hoped for and promised changes are fundamentally worldly in kind. The "top 10 list" of Kabbalah's benefits, drawn by Yehuda Berg (2003b, 29), actually emphasize the enhancement and empowerment of the self: personal fulfillment, peace of mind, relief from fear and anxiety, contentment, love, freedom, control, wisdom, happiness, health, financial security. Indeed, material benefits are not excluded. In some instances, the movement's leaders remind their students that the ultimate objective of Kabbalah is the removal of chaos from the world, which in turn will recreate harmony with the upper divine worlds. "At the Kabbalah Centre, we present Kabbalah as a deeply but practical system for improving your life in all areas—with the added understanding that your personal transformation will hasten the unity of all mankind with God," underscores Michael Berg (2001, 33). Yet, Kabbalah Centre students predominantly look for personal transformation for mundane benefits in the here and now. For Robin, who himself works in the field of coaching, the Kabbalah Centre's teaching is "about helping people to really realize their potential and to understand what life is really all about." Tamara explained her interest in Kabbalah by a need to grow: "I also came to the stage of realizing that religion was not my solution because with religion I am sticking in the place where I am. I needed to *move forward.*"

As in neo-Hinduism, the presentation of Kabbalah as a path of personal growth has entailed reinterpretations of religious doctrines. Philip Berg primarily drew on the teaching of Yehuda Ashlag, who developed a modernized and psychologized interpretation of Lurianic Kabbalah for a wider—but Jewish only—audience. Through a capacity of developing kindness and altruism, Ashlag envisaged Kabbalah as a remedy for the 'bitterness' of the modern existential quest" (Garb 2008, 30). He described the world and human beings as manifesting two fundamental impulses: the desire to give (which characterizes God) and the desire to receive. Drawing on Luria's depiction of the universe (10 interrelated "vessels" receiving the boundless divine's emanation of Light, which in turn animate all realms and beings), Ashlag explains that God created vessels in order to give. But some of these vessels were ashamed to receive without being able to give in return: one of them then stopped receiving Light in order to give, and the vessels broke. Ashlag believes that in order to restore cosmic harmony, human beings have to improve themselves and be like God by learning to receive the Light in order to share, instead of receiving for the self alone. They therefore need to control their desire to simply receive for the self alone because this generates cruelty and injustice in human society. Accordingly, Ashlag emphasizes human beings' responsibility for "repairing the world" (*tikkun olam*) by becoming more generous and compassionate. However, *tikkun* has for Ashlag a collective dimension because in his views social justice and equality can reshape society and foster altruistic individuals. Ashlag was, in fact, influenced by Marxist materialism and thought that communism was the most compatible political system with Kabbalah. He hoped that both could be integrated in the future Israeli society (Huss 2005, 616; Myers 2007, 18–20).

The Kabbalah Centre's approach of *tikkun* is drastically more individual-istic, secular, and psychological. While it retained Ashlag's principles around the need to connect to the Light and share, the concern with transforming society through a socialist or even political outlook disappeared from the teaching. It is the transformation of the individuals that is emphasized and, while it may contribute to *tikkun olam*, the fulfillment of individuals is clearly the focus. Indeed, the Kabbalah Centre asserts that by giving in order to share, students will receive more Light, strikingly echoing Jung, when in a letter to Freud the former suggested a motto for psychoanalysis inspired by Mithraic liturgy, "give what thou hast, then you shalt receive" (Noll 1997, 126). More largely, the Kabbalah Centre's emphasis on self-improvement drastically de-emphasizes Judaism's concern with the world's redemption. Indeed, in classical Kabbalah, the purpose of the Jewish people is *tikkun*, understood as a synonym of redemption (Scholem 1998, 239). The repair of the world is thus supposed to be achieved by commitment to the Torah, its ethics and divine commandments: when every Jew will refrain from religious transgression, the messiah will come and redemption will occur (Dan 2007, 77–79). This entails a sense of shared responsibility for the redemption of the whole world, yet the Kabbalah Centre tends to individualize and psychologize the notion of redemption, understood as personal growth. Philip Berg's (2000, 20) inter-pretation of the messiah is interesting in this regard: in his views, the messiah is "already present as a spiritual potential in each of our hearts."

Thus, in the Kabbalah Centre, *tikkun* has become what individuals need to change in their attitude. K. Berg (2005, 153) presents *tikkun* as:

> a term referring to the part of ourselves that we need to work on in this lifetime. Your particular *tikune* is everything you do when you follow the path of least resistance, as this path is usually made up of self-centered bad habits. You can have a *tikune* with money, health, ca-reer, or any other area in your life.

Echoing aspirations of acquiring the ability to change oneself, *tikkun* "means that we *can* repair and correct any aspect of ourselves (Y. Berg 2008b, 204). Sometimes used as a synonym of "having a karma," students describe dis-satisfactions, addictions, difficult relationships as "it is my tikkun." *Tikkun* is therefore understood as difficulties, which result from past lives and reveal the lessons that one must learn in order to grow. In other words, as teachers explained in courses I attended, it is because of individuals' need to progress and polish their soul that they reincarnate. Personal growth is reincarnation's raison d'être. As a teacher said during one of his classes, one of the rules in reincarnation is that an individual cannot "go backward." Lurianic Kabbalah certainly addressed reincarnation (Dan 2007, 82); nonetheless, the idea of reincarnation shared by students of the Kabbalah Centre is no different from that of neo-Hindus. It reflects an ideal of endless opportunities for the self to learn and progress through a succession of lives. From this perspective, "what seems to be a problem is actually a gift: a chance to remove an internal obstacle that stands between ourselves and the unlimited happiness that is our real destiny" (Kabbalah Centre 2007c), so "love the pain," explained a teacher during one of his classes. For Arthur, this is actually the best part of the Kabbalah Centre's teaching, because then "even the bad times are good."

Finally, the Kabbalah Centre strongly insists on individual responsibility. Not only are people responsible for what occurs to them (it is *their tikkun* provoked by *their* past behaviors) but it is only by accepting life as it is and learning from it that individuals may achieve fulfillment. By contrast, resistance and opposition are discouraged. This principle is absent in Ashlagian Kabbalah but is fundamental in the Kabbalah Centre: one of the main "tools" that students are provided with in the introductory cycle of the Kabbalah One course is a "formula" by which they are invited to refrain from being a "reactive" and to become "proactive" instead:

1. An obstacle occurs.
2. Realize your reaction is the real enemy.
3. Shut down your Reactive System and invite the Light in.
4. Express your Proactive Nature by sharing.

Thus, the "obstacle" is not the problem, but individuals' emotion and attitudes, their tendency to blame others and circumstances, to lament to themselves, to express anger and jealousy. Instead, the self can find some comfort in trusting the Light for having sent an intended opportunity to correct and perfect itself. Ultimately, this approach to life's problems is similar to neo-Hindus' perception of reincarnation: it addresses the uncertainties and arbitrariness in life by giving them an optimistic meaning as part of a process of self-improvement for which individuals are nonetheless fully accountable.

Religion as Self-help Methods

So far, I have shown that the popularization of exotic religious resources entailed a reinterpretation of salvation shaped by an ethos of self-realization. Accordingly, religious doctrines reiterate core narratives of the therapy culture: the existence of the self's unexplored potential, the possibility (and the need) to develop this potential, the individual responsibility for inner change and life transformation—this voluntarism being associated with accepting life's challenges as an opportunity to learn lessons. However, the ethos of therapy culture is much more pervasive than granting a psychologizing meaning to religious doctrines. It actually shapes the ways in which the teaching is delivered. On the model of coaching and group therapies, Siddha Yoga, Sivananda Centres, and the Kabbalah Centre, as well as many other religious movements, present their teaching as self-help techniques that they mainly deliver through courses, workshops, and seminars. This presentation of religious teachings as therapeutic methods contributes to the relative standardization of religious teachings. It also domesticates the foreignness of exotic religious resources by rendering their aims and practices familiar, expected, and desirable as self-help methods.

Simple and Accessible

The presentation of exotic religious teaching as self-help methods first entails a pervading insistence on accessibility and simplicity. This is particularly striking and meaningful when we remember that the Sivananda Centres, Siddha Yoga, and the Kabbalah Centre are structured around a small core of virtuosos who respect a demanding lifestyle and follow complex religious rules. Muktananda, for example, called Siddha Yoga "easy yoga" in several instances. Sivananda insisted on the fact that his teaching, the "yoga of synthesis," was fundamentally accessible and suitable for everyone. This exoteric orientation is reflected in the latter's effort to provide a didactic method. He repeated similar principles and ideas in numerous publications, but also summed up the spiritual discipline's principles under a short list of instructions, the "science of seven cultures." This manual to life intends to "give the essence of the Eternal Religion (Sanatana Dharma) in its purest form" in a few key points that are adapted to the daily life of "modern busy householders with fixed hours of work" (Divine Life Society 2011). Still used in the Sivananda Centres, this *vade mecum* includes the "culture" of health (diet, physical exercises), energy (silence and celibacy), ethics (moral values and attitude), will (control of want and bad habits), and heart (devotion). The "psychic" and "spiritual" cultures concern the study of scriptures and various aspects of religious observance. This simplification and codification of religious discipline was intentionally amplified by Vishnu-Devananda when he spread his master's teaching worldwide. Again, the emphasis is on adapting the teaching to the students' needs and abilities: "By closely observing the life-style and needs of the modern men and women, I have synthesized the ancient wisdom of yoga into five basics principles, which can be easily incorporated into everyone's own pattern of life" (Vishnu-Devananda 1988 [1960], xi). These five principles constitute the structure through which the Sivananda Centres teach yoga, for the reasons explained by the acharya for European centers:

> You really have to take people at the starting level.... You have to teach your five principles, which are really down to earth, but at the same time really very deep if you put them into practice, which can take you far, but [Vishnu-Devananda] had to take us at our level. He saw the level of spiritual education we have here. So it's not that easy.

Thus, the wide range of yoga's philosophical approaches and ascetic practices are synthesized as "proper exercise" (yoga postures), "proper breathing," "proper relaxation," "proper diet," and, strikingly, "positive thinking (Vedanta) and meditation" (Sivananda Centres, *Teachings*). Note that Vedantic philosophy is equated with "positive thinking," therapy culture's central value of acceptance and individual flexibility. Doctrine and philosophy are therefore supplanted by a particular attitude to life, and more broadly by practices—yoga, meditation, breathing, relaxation, and diet.

In relation to simplicity, gurus' teaching of meditation is particularly interesting, since this new practice may have been perceived as difficult by Westerners at first (Lowe 2011, 56). Lowe notes that the Transcendental Meditation's success was linked to its founder's revolutionary claim that "meditation should be effortless, simple and natural." Similarly, both Vishnu-Devananda and Muktananda have compared meditation to sleep and concentration to underscore its natural and innate character. Therefore, "it cannot be taught, just as sleep cannot be taught" (Vishnu-Devananda 1978, 9). But the emphasis on meditation's naturalness also detaches it from its cultural and religious particularism, as illustrated by Muktananda (1980, 19):

> Meditation is universal. It is not the property of any particular sect. Or cult. It does not belong to Hinduism, Buddhism, or Sufism. Meditation is everyone's property, just as sleep is everyone's property: it belongs to humanity. Meditation is not something difficult or strange. All of us, in our daily lives, are already familiar with it. Without meditation, a doctor could not diagnose a disease, nor could a lawyer prepare a brief, nor a student pass an examination.

Kabbalah is equally said by the Kabbalah Centre's members not to require the intellectual knowledge and understanding of scriptures and is repeatedly presented as accessible to everyone. This is a significant shift for Kabbalah, which has been an esoteric teaching for a long period of its history. Moroccan Judaism and Hassidism have integrated Kabbalistic references in popular religious culture; nevertheless, Kabbalah has often involved the study of complex and cryptic texts by a very few individuals with the guidance of a master (Idel and Malka 2000, 191–120; Myers 2007, 7–8). The Kabbalah Centre's trademark is precisely to claim to make a break with the esoteric tradition of Kabbalah and to make it accessible. "We teach a hipper, user-friendly form of Kabbalah," explained Karen Berg (in Tugen 2005), echoing her son's claim: "In the past, we worked at encouraging 3 percent of the world to follow 97 percent of the Kabbalah. Now our realistic goal is to get 97 percent to follow 3 percent of the Kabbalah" (M. Berg in Myers 2007, 72). There is therefore a deliberate intention to simplify and condense Kabbalah, so that this "workable system" can be spread as widely as possible (Living Kabbalah System 2006a). Thus, through courses and the literature, students are introduced to a very simple, systematized presentation of Kabbalah, as expounded by Ashlag, called the "rules of the game of life." These "rules" evoke the existence of the Light and the upper worlds, the need to connect to the Light to reach permanent fulfillment, the possibility to do so by changing ourselves, being confident, proactive, and resisting reactive impulses when facing challenges. Finally, they insist on the importance of receiving the Light in order to share it. These rules actually strongly resonate more with the 10 steps to happiness of Indian-born Deepak Chopra, one of the most famous New Age personalities in the United States (who in other instances synthesized Vedantic notions in "seven spiritual laws of success").[3] Students insistently praise the Kabbalah Centre's efforts to transmit Kabbalah in this manner. Indeed, many explained how, before joining the movement, they had bought books about Kabbalah but felt unable to understand its principles.

The Source of Direct Experience

Ultimately, the insistence on simplicity is associated with the prevalence of direct experience rather than intellectual understanding. In this respect, these religious movements share therapy culture's anti-intellectualism and the countercultural quest for intuitive experience and a focus on the self. The insistence on intuitive experience is also found in New Age and spiritual milieus (Champion 1990, 31), but it has affected the popularization of Asian religious traditions in particular. Indeed, as noted earlier, Western orientalism constructed the powerful representation of a "mystical East" as the ultimate source of religious experience that modern societies have lost in such a way that the association between "mystical experience" and the "East" has been central in the popularization of Asian religions (King 1999). In addition, neo-Hindu thinkers and religious leaders have confirmed this representation by presenting Hinduism as the religion of experience, which they contrast with Christianity, associated with rigid institutions and dogmas—this, despite the fact that the father of Advaita Vedanta, Shankara, did not consider subjective experience as the road to liberation and insisted on the study of scriptures (Halbfass 1988, 390). For example, the Sivananda Vedanta Centres (n.d.c.) consider that "the beauty of Vedanta is that it transcends dry philosophy and mere intellectual concept. Vedanta is an actual life experience, a philosophy in practice." To be united with Shiva or the knowledge of Self, claims Muktananda (1994, 38), it is not necessary to refer to Hindu scriptures and mythology, but to have an experience, the awakening of the *shakti* through the guru's touch. By and large, his disciples consider that "Muktananda's basic grounding was always in the experience rather than in the texts," and his references to literature were rather a means to authenticate his personal experience, the true source of apprehension of philosophy (Brooks et al. 1997, 519). In short, as one Siddha Yoga member put it, "I don't need to think it. I experience it."

Anti-intellectualism is reflected in a general distrusting attitude toward the mind. A source of fear, anxieties, and negative thoughts, the mind needs to be controlled and tamed by focusing on uplifting objects, otherwise it is prevented from reaching self-realization (Muktananda 1981, 36; Vishnu-Devananda 1978, 2). Hence meditation and yoga are overwhelmingly presented and understood as means to control undesirable thoughts and emotions—stress, anger, disillusion, which are defined as "negative thoughts" generated by the mind. Classical texts of yoga certainly insist on detachment and the control of mental activity through the intensive practice of yoga, but it does not exclude the study of scriptures or the performance of rituals, and besides it has a strong ethical dimension (Michaël 1995). Rather, the supremacy of personal experience as a source of knowledge and salvation finds its roots in the countercultural mindset. Indeed, it is easy to find a similar emphasis of experience in a diversity of NRMs, including the Kabbalah Centre. Philip Berg (2000, 11–12) wrote himself that we can learn a lot about Kabbalah by reading the works of Gershom Scholem, "but we can come to know more about Kabbalah simply by connecting to one Shabbat with our whole hearts." As explained by a teacher:

> I think if any the biggest misunderstanding is that the wisdom is intellectual. I think that it is a common thread among people, either those who haven't studied before and think it is an intellectual spiritual teaching or those who have been around for a long time and love to learn.... The real Kabbalah is about living it and experiencing it and

tasting it and changing and trying and failing sometimes and learning and pushing through from that place, and really living Kabbalah.

Kabbalah thus should be experienced. The Kabbalah Centre, however, values study, through life guidance books, learning packages and classes, but its approach to study contrasts with that of traditional Judaism, in which the text is at the center of religious life. To uphold the Jewish tradition, Judaism made of scriptures a "homeland in the mind," in which meticulous discussion of religious texts can serve as guidance (Danzger 1989, 4). As in any synagogue, in the Kabbalah Centre the Torah is recited during every Shabbat and festivals and the Zohar is highly valued. However, it is because these scriptures channel the Light of the Creator; accordingly, concentrating on, and visualizing, their letters allow one to connect with the Light. Aware that many in the audience cannot read Hebrew, they invite participants to "connect with the power of unity, of love" by visualizing particular letters. The Zohar's power, it is said, "does not depend on understanding or belief" (Kabbalah Centre 2012a). The "scanning" of the Zohar has become a central practice that one should observe daily.[4] The relationship to the text, here, becomes a means to experience the divine and receive its benefits.

Practical and Efficient Methods

The "five points" of yoga taught by the Sivananda Centres underline an essential feature of the psychologization of exotic religious resources in the fact that they are transmitted as "practical" teachings. They are said to be practical in two respects. First, they can be *applied* by individuals, who thus hope to be able to carry out their personal development by themselves. Vivekananda (1968, 291) already used the notion of "practical Vedanta" or "practical spirituality" in this way: "The Vedanta...as a religion must be intensely practical. We must be able to carry it out in every part of our lives." Second, as already suggested, neo-Hindu movements increasingly emphasized "practices" over "theory" and "doctrines" to render their teaching exoteric. Accordingly, they gave precedence to yoga, meditation, and chants as "practices" and gave them precedence over rituals and study of texts. Siddha Yoga's core teaching entails meditation and chanting, which "concretize spirituality in daily life," as a disciple put it. Vishnu-Devananda (1988 [1960], 5) focused on yoga as a "science of self-discipline" that "gives a practical and scientifically prepared method of finding truth in religion."

As practices, religious teachings become a means to an end. "Kabbalah is meant to be used, not merely learned," claim the founders of the Kabbalah

Centre (Living Kabbalah System 2006b). The Kabbalah Centre downplays the importance of Judaism's traditional study and discussion of the scriptures and aims to insist on "practices." Accordingly, rituals, Shabbat services, holidays, and commandments are presented as practical means that enable people to connect with the Light of the Creator and bring change in their lives. They are called "spiritual," "practical," "actionable," or "operational tools" (P. Berg 1995, 137; Y. Berg 2008, 196) and Kabbalah in general is very often talked about as a "technology" or a "workable system," and even "a goal-means system" (P. Berg 1987a, 120). Hence it is about *what it does*. During Shabbat services and festivals, the audience is repeatedly invited to "get the energy and make something out of it." Portions of the Torah are systematically commented in response to the questions "What's in it for us?," "What's the energy of the story?" In this way, teachers present an interpretation of the text that aims to show students "what opportunity is available" for their personal growth during each particular Shabbat or festival. The practical and pragmatic orientation of the Kabbalah Centre is extensive: everything from life's problems to relationships, tolerance, effort, and honesty are defined as tools for spiritual growth and transformation. It responds to students' quest for applicable, self-help religious techniques, "something I could use in my life," as one put it, reflecting an ideal of self-reliance. In this regard, I was struck by a remark from a student of the Kabbalah Centre from Rio de Janeiro, who previously had been involved in Afro-Brazilian religions. Priests of Candomble and Umbanda have "a power in their hand that they do not share" she said, while all is "revealed" in Kabbalah. Indeed, the Kabbalah Centre claims to empower its students by providing "tools" they can use by themselves (in practice these tools are learned and discussed through classes as well as through one-on-one meetings between students and their teacher). Exotericism and practical means are combined to provide a religious self-help method.

Ultimately, this instrumental approach toward religion entails that their mode of legitimacy is about efficiency: what matters, as with any therapeutic or self-help method, is that it "works." For instance, Muktananda (1978, 110) explains that "through chanting or japa, repetition of a mantra, one can accomplish anything. Chanting has tremendous power. This is why we do a lot of chanting in all our programs." Vishnu-Devananda (1978, 53–54) describes the same practice by underscoring that as the mantra contains the name of God, "the power of sound is tremendous," therefore it is "one of the most direct ways of self-realization, or universal consciousness." Dramatic effects and the tools' potency are also systematically stressed in the Kabbalah Centre. For example, "a tremendously powerful technology is encoded and concealed inside the celebration of Pesach" (London Kabbalah Centre 2007b). Currently, the main cycles of courses that introduce Kabbalah are called "*Power* of Kabbalah" One, Two and Three—they are interestingly described as "an instruction manual to life" (London Kabbalah Centre 2007a, 7). Legitimating exotic religious resources as efficient and practical methods reflects, by and large, the undermining of religion's symbolic power in secular societies, which can today be evaluated along rational criteria deriving from science and technology. Willingly or not, it encourages the audience of these religious movements to have a pragmatic relationship with religious practices and norms.

"Teaching Not Preaching"

Finally, these religious self-help techniques are delivered under the format of self-help seminars, coaching, or therapies. It is about "Teaching Not Preaching":⁵ again, in the mold of these secular domains, a consumerist and pragmatic relationship with exotic religious resources is encouraged. Through these intense spiritual trainings, individuals who may neither belong to these movements nor be familiar with their religious beliefs and norms pay to learn methods for personal growth that they can apply on their own. The psychologization of these neo-Hindu and Kabbalistic teachings entails a pragmatic relationship with the teachings, which are, to a certain extent, commoditized.

All around the world, the Sivananda Centres' daily routines are structured around impressive timetables of "classes." Yoga courses follow each other and are diversified to cater to the needs of their audience, with sessions for beginners, intermediate, and advanced learners, pregnant women, children, pensioners, or English-speaking students in Paris. They are completed by cycles of "workshops" and "intensives" on "positive thinking," relaxation, "concentration, memory and will power," meditation, vegetarian cooking, and yogic diets. Ashrams organize summer yoga camps and the "Teacher's Training Course." The TTC "graduates" would have respected the "work study program" in terms of requirements of class and lecture attendance in order to receive an "internationally recognized certification" (Sivananda Ashram Yoga Camp n.d.). Siddha Yoga also provides a calendar of "teaching and learning events," which include retreats structured around "study sessions," as well as local courses on the guru's message. The description of the objectives of one of these courses by the French branch of Siddha Yoga (2005) is unambiguous:

It invites each participant to take responsibility for his life joyfully. Its gives tangible tools for acquiring determination, strength, clarity of the mind, which enable him to make choices in his daily life reflecting the greatness and the beauty that are within him. (my translation)

The fact that Siddha Yoga's initiating event, the Intensive, borrowed its structure from the Erhard Seminar Training underscores the extent to which contemporary gurus intentionally embrace the therapeutic framework. Rajneesh, who integrated post-psychoanalytic therapies in the life of his ashram, is an example in point.

The Kabbalah Centre's expansion is similarly linked with the presentation of Kabbalah as a self-help method. North American followers who were professionals in the fields of advertising, marketing, design, and communication were eager to "brand Kabbalah," as a former teacher, Eyal, described it. They contributed to the redesign of the course, opened a "media department," and created a marketing strategy. "The thing was to create an institution of teaching," says Eyal, who contributed to the systematization of this through written and audio media, as well as through a curriculum that could be taught anywhere. Reflecting the ethos of these middle-class professionals, the core mode of teaching increasingly uses methods and practices of personal growth seminars, coaching, and adult training. The Kabbalah Centre presents itself as "the world's leader in Kabbalah Education" in some brochures and posters and a "spiritual and educational organization" (Kabbalah Centre 2006a). The movement accordingly gathers "teachers" and "students"—yet Berg continued to use his title of rabbi. "Courses," "classes," "seminars" and "workshops" are now the entry point to the Kabbalah Centre. The brochures of the London branch present their course's learning outcomes and requirements in no different way than any educational institution would. In practice, these courses involve small group sharing, note taking, question and answer sessions, and "homework."

The embedding of Kabbalah in the self-help and coaching environment is also illustrated by the development of the "Living Kabbalah System," a CD-delivered self-improvement program with Yehuda Berg and Jamie Greene, a coach and therapist (see Chapter 3). A small and easy to carry case contains the recorded courses, a workbook with written exercises and self-assessments for users "who want to discover and reveal their hidden talents and abilities, who want to find long-term happiness and satisfaction and desire to know about how the system works." More broadly, sophisticated means have been developed to spread the teaching through distance learning. There is a "student support" by telephone in several languages and more than 150 publications, DVDs, audio and video lectures are sold online and in local branches. These products are part of the vast market of self-help, which allows the Kabbalah

Centre to gather financial resources from a mildly involved or consumerist public, whereas its door-to-door Zohar sales were abandoned. The Kabbalah Centre's latest project underlines its educational rebranding: through an on-line "University," students pay a monthly subscription for accessing online re-sources and courses. They can compose their "personal study plan" tailored to their needs and "learn as you go" (Kabbalah Centre 2012b). This is no different from Siddha Yoga's older "study tools," a home study course through monthly lessons. By and large, these religious movements draw on the long tradition of advice and self-help literature. The relation to this literature is particular, notes Illouz (2008, 75), because the appropriation of these "learning resources" is motivated by the intent to find "practical guidance," something to "carry away," which, in turn, encourages individual self-reliance. In this regard, the trans-mission of exotic religious teaching through this type of literature, courses and workshops sheds light on the pragmatic quest of their audience.

Synthesis

Religion has become an important locus for the psychologization of social life. It is a field of expansion and diversification of therapeutic discourses and prac-tices, where norms about the self are expressed, developed, and reinforced. Undoubtedly, therapy culture was able to make inroads into the religious field because of the religious origins of modern Euroamerican narratives about the self. In other words, certain modern Protestant interpretations of salvation as a personal spiritual journey may have been determinants in the formation of ideas about personhood and the meaning of life, which have become pervasive in the therapy culture. In addition, as we shall see later on, these narratives about the flexible, autonomous, and responsible self may resonate particularly well within neoliberal contexts. But perhaps the psychologization process is related to secularization as well. In secularizing contexts, religions tend to progressively abandon their eschatological and utopian perspectives, down-playing references to transcendence and developing mundane salvation goods for the here and now. Religions' this-worldliness is encouraged by the fact that, as institutions, they have lost their monopoly and social control function. Accordingly, they are ever more competing against each other, leading some to adapt to, and reflect, their audience's inner-worldly needs (Dobbelaere 1999, 235; Hervieu-Léger 2001, 81, 92). As social life is increasingly psychologized, self-help tools for personal growth constitute one of these needs.

Thus, the psychologization of religion is one of the fundamental processes that have transformed Western esotericism into contemporary spiritual and

New Age milieus (Champion 2004; Hanegraaff 1998). Dobbelaere (1999, 235) also observes that the majority of contemporary NRMs are this-worldly. They focus on the immediate everyday life and "offer their members esoteric means of attaining immediate and automatic success, recovery, heightened spiritual powers, assertiveness, and a clearer mind." But the psychologization process affects mainstream religions as well. Fader (2008), for example, describes how a synagogue in New York has become popular by taking a "spiritual turn"; now using a therapeutic language, it emphasizes self-realization, personal transcendence, healing, and well-being. Similarly, Sargeant (2000) studied the emergence in Protestant evangelicalism of "seeker churches," which are not characterized by a particular theological orientation but by the adaptation of their activities to those who are not regular church attendees and distrust "organized religions." Pastors of these seeker churches heavily draw on marketing methods and use modern media to create uplifting services. They focus on delivering "practical," "take-homeable" messages that are relevant to members' daily lives and congruent with values of personal choice and experience. More significant, these messages are therapy-oriented. Drawing on self-help and popular psychology, these pastors reshape Christian principles into the mold of self-realization. Sargeant argues that by insisting on the inner-worldly "benefits" of faith, as well as on the effectiveness of the practical methods they provide, they deliver a form of "applied religion." Further, the significant growth of seeker churches in the United States incites traditional institutions to change their outreach strategies and thus represents an increasingly important trend of religious life in advanced industrial societies.

However, it may well be that exotic religious resources are particularly affected by the psychologization of religion. Indeed, a similar process of psychologization affects other neo-Hindu movements, such as Sahaja Yoga and the Sri Chinmoy Centre. Drawing on participant observation, I have described elsewhere the recent popularization of a neo-Hindu movement that introduces its teaching in a setting shaped like group therapy (Altglas 1997; 2000). Scholars underline the psychologization of transnational Japanese religious movements such as Reiyukai (Hourmant 1995), as well as of Buddhism in Europe and North America (Lenoir 1999, 335; Sharf 1993, 39). In fact, Buddhism is often understood as a means of empowering, and freeing the self from suffering. New interpretations of Buddhist principles emphasize self-improvement, willpower, freedom of choice, and individual responsibility (Carrette and King 2005, 104, 106; Clarke 1997, 149–164). One of the characteristics of "Western Buddhism" is the tremendous importance of meditation and meditation retreats, even in Tibetan Buddhist groups that traditionally emphasize ceremonies and rituals (Coleman 2001, 14). Similarly, Hermansen

(2004, 8) describes American Sufism's emphasis on individual healing and personal growth. Drawing on Jungian and transpersonal psychology, some American Sufis become psychotherapists and organize events on "Sufi psychology." Philippon (2014) also notes that the Sufi Order International, founded in a Euroamerican context to cater to the needs of Westerners, aims to provide them with a program of "spiritual training" focused on well-being, through courses, retreats, and camps. In her *Primitive Passions,* Torgovnick (1997, 184) describes the identification with traditional Native American culture and the imitations of certain rituals among American New Age groups to "live a spiritual and harmonious life"; shamanic practices then become healing practices. Shamanism has overall become "therapeutized" (Hamayon 1995); it is explored in the format of workshops and courses that focus on personal growth (Lindquist 1997; Vazeilles 2008). Books, workshops, and websites refer to Tantra as source of knowledge for sex therapies (Urban 1999; 2000). It is equally significant that "exotic" traditional medicines are substantially psychologized. While in South Asia Ayurveda was adapted to scientific paradigms, in Britain it has shifted from curative medicine to "a focus on self-knowledge and self-empowerment as a path to 'holistic healing' (understood to address mental and spiritual, not just physical, wellbeing)" (Warrier 2008, 423). Barnes (2000) showed that the popularization of Chinese healing medicine in the United States entailed its psychologization. Westerners introduced new issues in these techniques relating to "the emotional life of the individual," and some practitioners of acupuncture, for instance, redefine their practice as a form of psychotherapy. Similarly, "Tibetan medicine in the West emerges as a form of enlightened self-care, in which pursuit of techniques to maintain health merges with Western ideas about Eastern spirituality" (Janes 2002, 286). The link between yoga and health was elaborated in Euroamerican societies; its use for psychological well-being is also specific to these social environments (Hoyez 2012). With these examples, I want to show that, however diverse they may be, knowledge and practices rooted in other cultures are primarily sought to fulfill emotional needs linked to advanced industrial societies' therapy culture.

The psychologization of salvation goods is particularly acute for "exotic" religious resources, maybe because they are already de-contextualized and therefore more prone to change. We can also assume that the successful exotic religions are those that have been able to adapt to the new expectations and have responded to the necessity to render exotic religious resources less foreign and less religious. Their adaptation to the therapy culture ethos and practices is therefore a core element of the domestication of religious exotic resources. By addressing the quest for personal growth and efficient self-help methods, neo-Hindu and Kabbalistic teachings become more familiar and desirable for individuals who have, more often than not, experienced several alternative therapies and personal growth-oriented religions. In other words, neo-Hinduism, Kabbalah, Buddhism, and Sufism in Euroamerican societies provide an appealing system of meaning by combining the therapy culture ethos with exoticism—the promises of true, ancient, and potent techniques for the development of the self that are believed to be lacking in Western culture.

This psychologization de-contextualizes and domesticates exotic religious resources. As self-help methods taught in the recognizable setting of group therapy and personal growth seminars, they become more familiar. This is, in essence, what makes them appealing for their audience: "exotic" religious resources embrace the therapy culture ethos and at the same time promise timeless, authentic, ancient, and powerful practices for the realization of the self that are believed to be lacking in the West. Thus, the teachings of the Kabbalah Centre, a wide range of neo-Hindu movements, and probably many other contemporary religious movements are structured by the narrative of the personal spiritual journey toward the self-realization. This journey involves self- examination and control of thoughts and emotions and the building of self-confidence, self-reliance, and adaptive skills. To achieve this goal, religious teachings are presented as efficient techniques one can learn and carry over from workshops, seminars, books, and audio and online sources. Thus, exotic religious resources tend to become relatively similar practical tools for personal growth, while in the quest of useful self-help carry-over, their respective religious particularism loses its significance. This homogenization (also observed in the mystic-esoteric nebula by Champion 2004) allows individuals to experiment and to combine many of these religious and therapeutic methods without being concerned with potential contradictions between them. It is therefore not surprising that in their views, all "share the same energy" and transcend cultural and religious differences. Nor it is surprising that, for example, newcomers to the Kabbalah Centre first thought that "it felt like home," as some explained to me. Non-committal and plural involvements are also encouraged by the fact that exotic religious resources are presented and appropriated as methods that are paid for, on the understanding that "it works." This encourages the very instrumental relation to exotic religions that we have previously described among their practitioners.

6

Bricolage and the Social Significance of Self-Realization

STUDENTS OF THE Kabbalah Centre, Siddha Yoga, and the Sivananda Centres are motivated by a desire of life transformation which, they believe, through the process of self-improvement will lead toward more resilient, autonomous, and adaptable selves. By and large, individuals appropriate and combine religious resources that are perceived as inner-worldly promises of self-realization. They attend classes and retreats to learn easy and "powerful" techniques that they can apply on their own in order to enhance personal skills and develop life outcomes. Exotic resources play a significant part in this bricolage: in the context of the psychologization of social life, they have been cast into the role of authentic, ageless, and mystical sources of knowledge and techniques of the self in order to fulfill new expectations.

The quest for self-realization therefore constitutes the drive of bricolage. Yet there have been scarce attempts within the sociology of religion to analyze the significance of self-realization itself. This loophole may well be the result of the fact that scholars take for granted the desirability of self-realization and therefore do not see the need to address it. Hence, the sociology of religion has "explained away" the significance of self-realization by looking at it as an evidence of this-worldliness and individualism. Luckmann (1990, 127) is probably the pioneer of such analysis, which can be summarized as such:

Modern social constructions of religious significance shifted away from the "great" other-worldly transcendences to the "intermediate" (political) and also to the minimal transcendences of modern solipsism whose main themes ("self-realization," personal autonomy, and self-expression) tend to bestow a sacred status upon the individual.

This modern shift from the social to the individual has become paradigmatic within the sociology of religion (Wood 2009). The works of Hervieu-Léger (1999, 2000, 2001, 2010) similarly emphasize individualism and subjectivism as major features of modern religious life. According to this view, because religious traditions have lost their regulatory functions, social actors cease to conform to shared norms. They develop instead pick and mix attitudes to beliefs and practices, in accordance to personally felt needs and experiences. With these religious resources that they voluntary choose, these autonomous individuals seek inner-worldly salvation goods such as personal growth, well-being, beauty, or vitality, and elaborate their personal identity "beyond any inherited or prescribed identity" (Hervieu-Léger 1999, 163, 65). In extreme cases, such as in New Age Milieus, Hervieu-Léger (1999, 180) believes that "self-validation of belief" occurs, when individuals exclusively refer to their subjective experience to authenticate religious teachings. In other words, religious individualism allegedly explains practices of bricolage as well as its aim, the realization of the self.

A more radical version of this explanatory framework is Heelas and Woodhead's (2005) "subjectivization thesis." Referring to philosopher Charles Taylor, the two authors describe a "subjective turn" (2005: 2), defined as "a turn away from life lived in terms of external or 'objective' roles, duties and obligations, and a turn towards life lived by reference to one's own subjective experiences." Hence a growing "subjective well-being culture" centered on individual self-expression and fulfillment, which, in turn, would lead to a "spiritual revolution"—a claim largely unsubstantiated by Heelas and Woodhead's own data as well as sociology of religion's main findings (Voas and Bruce 2007; Wood 2009). In his studies of New Age and "self religions," Heelas (1996a; 1996b) had already insisted on the growing significance of a radical de-traditionalization process and the resulting self-authority. Heelas (1996b, 67) contends that in New Age milieus, individuals free themselves from institutions and collective beliefs in favor of a truth to be found "within," so that "authority lies with the self, or more broadly, the *natural*" (my emphasis). In other words "self-authority" implies a clear opposition between the individual self, and the social.

By and large, the figure of the autonomous believer who freely chooses religious resources for his or her self-fulfillment has been embedded in a dual representation of religion in contemporary Euroamerican societies. A distinction between "inherited" and "chosen" religions (Fath 2010)— the latter growing at the expense at the former—had gained popularity within the sociology of religion. Hervieu-Léger (1999), for instance, contrasts the ideal-types of the "observant" and the "pilgrim": the observant is territorialized, stable, and suggests compulsory practices regulated by institutions, while the pilgrim is characterized by fluidity of belief and practice, autonomy, and mobility. Hervieu-Léger's typology is similar to Wuthnow's (1998) distinction between the stable "dwellers" whose beliefs and practices are rooted in religious institutions and the growing, itinerant "seekers" whose volatile spiritual journey is the result of personal and active choice according to one's subjectivity. All these perspectives tend to suggest that a chosen, volatile, and eclectic religious life grows at the expense of the inherited one, precisely because it seeks to respond to personal quests for self-realization and fulfillment.

This chapter provides another understanding of self-realization, the pursuit of which motivates individuals to engage in practices of bricolage with various religious resources. It shows that such a pursuit does not provide evidence for liberation from social norms and values. On the contrary, the realization of the self is an imperative in conformity with wider social constraints. It also suggests that the self has become the locus of discipline and conformity to collective norms. Realizing the self entails improving oneself; evaluating and controlling one's thoughts, emotions, and behaviors; learning appropriate techniques (yoga, meditation, etc.) to do so; and cultivating moral virtues. In fact, "spirituality," as a quest for self-realization, presents itself as a process through which individuals become the active and autonomous agents of their own regulation. Ultimately, the realization of the self (and what kind of self is desired to be realized) is not "natural" or even unique to each individual's subjectivity; rather, it reflects the political and economic structures of contemporary Euroamerican societies.

Assessing "Self-Authority"

This section addresses the assumption that social actors make religious choices such as those involved in bricolage, based on a unique subjective experience and independently from collective norms and values. Religious individualism is, in fact, a collective discursive practice. Besides, students of neo-Hindu movements and the Kabbalah Centre all share the idea that the self-realization they highly desire solely depends on them undertaking self-improvement. Accordingly, freedom as a value actually involves a tremendous sense of individual responsibility and duty. Ultimately, the normative dimension of self-realization is outlined by leaders and teachers: they present "spirituality" as a "discipline" demanding dedication, commitment, and rigor for those who want to realize and fulfill themselves.

Religious Individualism is Not "Individual"

I guess I have this sense of [Catholicism] as being external whereas I see yoga and Eastern philosophies as being internal, and about how you act and about how all the things that you do for yourself will then sort of play out and that you have to sort of take care of yourself first, and be a good person just yourself, and be happy with yourself and then everything else will fall into place. That's the contrast I see and that's what I rejected about Catholicism, that it was not about me as a person, and mind development, spirituality, and philosophy of life. It was about fitting into an external framework and how things should be done, it was not about my own personal growth. I found that oppressive.... I think the reason why Eastern religions or philosophies or ways of looking at life appeal to me was I always felt that all of this should come from within, that it should not be: "you should do this and you should do that," but that you should learn how to find it within yourself as opposed to relying on somebody external to tell you what you should do and shouldn't do, that it's about intent as much as it's about the end result. Catholicism just focuses on the end result really. It doesn't really matter how you are on the inside as a person as long as you're not acting on it.

This interview with an American yoga practitioner from Boston, whom I met in the London Sivananda Centre, captures a pervasive discourse among users of exotic religious resources. They repeatedly criticize their religious background, which they described as "imposed from the outside," normative, "out of touch with life," morally corrupted, inauthentic, rigid, and doctrinal. By contrast, the "spiritual" is believed to "come from within," it is experienced, and chosen for being genuine, meaningful, and oriented toward self-fulfillment. We have suggested in Chapter 2 of this book that these representations are core to the appeal of religious exotic resources, perceived as sources of a free and authentic "spirituality."

Discourses of rejection of obligations, rules, and constraints are pervasive among students of yoga, meditation, and Kabbalah. "I only do things that my guts instinct tells me are right," asserts Megan from the Sivananda Centre in London. "It has to come from me" says Hortense, a French disciple of Siddha Yoga, "I'm not going to read a book and think, 'this is written.'"

If you're looking for God, anything that can be called spirituality, you must look inside. It is not outside that you must look again. It's inside. And it has to come from your own experience. It's not important whether or not you follow some certain religious rules or certain religious ideology. It has to be an experience in you that confers what...is true. If that experience is not there, it might be very beautiful, it might tell you very beautiful things, but it has to be an inner experience, *and it has to be an inner change.* (Flavio, Siddha Yoga, London)

Overall, the belief that the teaching one has chosen is not coercive (by contrast with religion) is part of the appeal. Meir started to study Kabbalah at the Tel Aviv Centre nine years ago; he explains that he liked the fact that it was "not mixed with religion, it was not strict nor compulsory." Amira, also a student in the Tel Aviv Centre, liked the fact that the movement keeps the "idea behind" the principles of the Jewish tradition, while

> giving everybody the choice. You don't have to do it. It's if you want to do it. And sometimes in religion it's a feeling that you have to do it. But in Kabbalah and spirituality you don't have to do anything.

At first sight, these interviewees' expression of radical religious individualism seems to confirm the sociological approach of modern religion that emphasizes free individual choice. Yet my first contention is precisely that sociology of religion's paradigm of radical religious individualism seems to be merely variations of interviewees' discourse on religion and spirituality. Interviewees' claims of religious freedom are very significant for understanding modern religiosity in general, and the quest for self-realization in particular. But precisely for this reason, they need to be sociologically interpreted.

For a start, claims of self-determination in religious matters are not "individual." This is evidenced by the extreme banality of these assertions heard by every sociologist of religion, which explains how it has become a central component of theories of modern religious life. But these claims do not spring from a mosaic of individual subjectivities also because they are clearly formulated by leaders and founders of religious movements as well as the loosest spiritual networks (Champion 1990). As early as the nineteenth century, through their encounter with European culture, neo-Hindu leaders associated Hinduism with "spirituality," personal experience, and realization, in order to contrast their tradition with the doctrinal and theoretical character of religion, implicitly Christianity (Halbfass 1988, 380–381, 395–398). In this regard, Vivekananda's (1965, 16) address at the World Parliament of Religions in Chicago is illustrative: "While some people devote their whole lives to their idol of a church and never rise higher, because with them religion means an intellectual assent to certain doctrines and doing good to their fellows, the whole religion of Hindu is centered in realization." Consider, below, this more recent definition of yoga by the then leader of the Divine Life Society founded by Sivananda:

> Yoga is the practical aspect of the inner side of man's religion. The outer side of religion in its institutionalized and organized social aspect is its traditional form, made up of the periodical common or collective worship, be it in church, synagogue, mosque, temple or prayer house; its sacraments, ceremonial, ritual, etc. Whereas the inner side of religion in its deeply personal aspect of the individual's effort to spiritually progress towards God and obtain vital religious experience is termed yoga. (Chidananda 2000)

Muktananda defined the experience of the divine Self within as the "true religion" beyond all rituals and dogmas, this by contrast with "formal" or "orthodox" religion (1978, 157; 1998, 188). This common rhetoric of modern gurus has undoubtedly contributed to Euroamericans' belief that exotic practices such as yoga or meditation were "different" from the religious life they have been socialized to. Expressed in the collective settings of services and courses, these ideas are shared and reinforced collectively: I observed a "master of ceremony" during a satsang explaining to the audience that religion has no importance since, in Siddha Yoga, the goal is to find the divine Self within—a very common assertion in the movement. In other words, the authority of the self is an ideal that is paradoxically taught by religious authorities. There is therefore nothing "natural" in the authority of the self (if it existed). It is a social discourse, like the primacy of personal subjective experience, for instance. Indeed, religious leaders also teach the value of personal experience, as well as *what kind* of experience one is supposed to have. As an example, Siddha Yoga developed an entire literature addressing the visualization of the "blue pearl," a manifestation of the divine Self and a prelude to its realization, hence a desirable sign of a high consciousness. The "experience" of the blue pearl is addressed collectively in courses especially devoted to this theme.

Neo-Hindu gurus and teachers are not the only religious authorities who explicitly identify their teaching with "spirituality" as an individual, inner experience free from religious norms and doctrines. It may well be a general feature of many NRMs, New Age milieus, and what Champion (1990) called the post–New Age "mystic-esoteric nebula."[1] The Kabbalah Centre's leaders persistently assert a distinction between religion and spirituality as well, in order to shape the movement's identity. Their courses, commentaries of the scriptures and writings, and teachers' interviews all associate religion with dogma, constraint, obedience, "mindless ritual," lack of consciousness, and lack of fulfillment. By contrast, Kabbalah is defined as spiritual—"spirituality" being "mindful," "a standard that you hold yourself in order to create more awareness and consciousness," "with reason and purpose," and generating personal growth (Kabbalah Centre 2007a, booklet p. 37). Thus, Kabbalah is "not about rote behavior. It's not about doing things just because someone—even the Creator— wants you to do them" (M. Berg 2001, 206); one therefore needs to understand the "whys" of observance, rather than focusing on the "hows." It is assumed that once individuals appreciate the benefits they will find in practices and festivals (as efficient means to connect with the Light), they will want to observe them of their own free will. Indeed, "a principle of Kabbalah states: there can be no coercion in spirituality" (p. 47). Through this discourse, Kabbalah Centre teachers seek to distinguish themselves from mainstream Judaism, suggesting that Orthodox Jews observe rituals out of fear and obedience to tradition.

Kabbalah students are heavily familiarized with this rhetoric. "We are not here for a nice tradition, we're here for our spiritual connection," say teachers endlessly to the audience during festivals and Shabbat services. By and large, all holidays and religious practices are relentlessly explained as an efficient means to connect with the Light. In fact, being a participant observer allowed me to realize the importance of students' socialization to this way of thinking. On many occasions, like them I was taught to understand the "reason behind" religious norms—and hence to accept them voluntarily. Not long after having started my fieldwork in the movement, I was helping to set dinner tables for Shabbat at the London Centre. A *chevre* came toward me and asked me whether I had added water in the wine bottles, as I was asked to. I replied that I did so. Then she asked me whether I knew why I had to do this; no, I said. She then joked at my expense and answered, laughing, in the direction of other volunteers who were present, "because we are religious." A few minutes later, she came back and explained that, precisely, the Kabbalah Centre is not religious and that there is a good reason to add water in wine, from which followed an explanation about the circulation of energy in water and wine. "That's it," she resumed, "so that now you don't do things robotically," and she assured me that in the future, when I did not know why we have to do certain things, I should feel free to ask her. This was part of my learning to "freely" choose to observe certain rules of the Kabbalah Centre.

Thus, the example of the Kabbalah Centre actually shows that not only is religious individualism as a value a socially constructed discourse, but it is also a norm that can contribute to legitimate religious observance. In other words, it does not make sociological sense to oppose individualism to collective values and norms, as some sociologists of religion tend to do. The reference to "free will" among students and teachers of the Kabbalah Centre is in this regard illustrative. Indeed, they express a clear rejection of observance as obligation, but not of observance as such. They associate Kabbalah with practice "with consciousness," that is to say, the "understanding" of *why* one needs to observe certain practices and commandments. One of the first ideas students are introduced to is that the universe is governed by "spiritual laws." It is defined as an inescapable principle of "cause and effect," as karmic law is sometimes called (Vishnu-Devananda 1978, 6). Living in accordance with these laws maintains or intensifies a connection with the Light of the Creator, which, in turn, improves people's lives and contributes to remove chaos from the world. Compared with gravity and electricity, the works of these spiritual laws suggest that they should be observed for practical, but not for moral reasons: God does not command, reward, or chastise, just as no one is punished by electricity when electrocuted by putting their fingers in the socket, students are told. Consequently, through their understanding of these laws, one is believed to accept, of their free will, to respect these higher principles, as explained by Amira, a student from Tel Aviv:

> You need to learn why and then you will want to do it...because if you don't do it there is cause and effect on something. But not because something is punishing you, because there's just you know...if you put your hand in the fire you will burn your hand, it's just cause and effect.

Similarly, another student, Yitzhak, explains that "mitzvah" has wrongly been translated as "commandment"; it is rather a "recommendation," like avoiding "jumping off the roof":

> There is no law against jumping off the roof. But you know what happens for physical reasons if you jump off the roof....The same thing about mitzvot. You'd better follow them because sooner or later you're going to face the consequences of not following them.

This rationalization of religious rules does not conceal the fact that like gravity, or electricity, these spiritual laws are phenomena perceived as transcending individuals, over which they have no control and which, accordingly, they must respect to avoid adverse consequences. This remark applies to the reference to karmic law in neo-Hindu movements, and in both cases the use of the term "law" is highly significant in regard to the authoritative nature of these principles.

Having internalized these religious norms, students of the Kabbalah Centre nevertheless overwhelmingly insist on their free will and free choice to observe Jewish commandments and festivals because they "understand" the energy they can tap into by doing so, and therefore "because it's good for you and for the Universe." Observance is therefore a duty one has toward the "universe" as well. Accordingly, there may be free choice, but there is a "right choice" predefined by leaders and teachers as well, which is opting for all the attitudes and practices that, according to teachers, help connect with the Light. David and Thérèse, two French students originally from Tunisia, became fairly observant since they began to follow Berg's teaching. During their interview, their insisted many times on the difference between free spirituality and normative religion, giving several examples of how not being expected to be observant in the Kabbalah Centre had represented a real incentive for them to start practicing Shabbat and festivals. When I asked them about their practice, David explained they do "everything that is necessary." In fact, David continues, every *mitzvah* is an opportunity (implicitly, to connect with the Light) and that in "Judaism, we must do everything." He recognizes that they do not do so themselves, "but we should do everything, *everything should suit us*, everything should benefit us." His wife, Thérèse, objects: "we have to feel it, David." He replied, "of course *we have to feel it, but we should do it.*" This discursive combination of religious individualism and internalization of religious norms is not specific to the Kabbalah Centre. Patrick, a French student of the Parisian Sivananda Centres, makes a similar reasoning about the "moral" character that he perceives in yoga; "you should do this, you should not do that..." Yet, Patrick observes there are "profound reasons" to follow yoga rules, which are not moral: they enable one to become more skillful and happy in life. Again, like the students of the Kabbalah Centre, self-fulfillment is believed here to be attained only by respecting higher principles. In other words, "we are free to choose, but freedom does not mean that we can do whatever we like to do," says Swami Durgananda (2008, 13), a direct student of Vishnu-Devananda and founder of some of the first centers in Europe, before explaining how life in the ashram teaches visitors the lifestyle necessary for the successful practice of yoga.

Claims about self-determination in religious matters have therefore to be understood as a discursive mode. They represent an interpretation that social actors make of their religious life, nevertheless, as Wood and Bunn (2009, 289) outlined in their criticisms of the academic study of New Age Milieus, they are not to be taken as empirical evidence that people "do actually act in terms of their own authority rather than others' authorities." Indeed, claims of religious freedom do not preclude shared beliefs, observance, or acceptance of higher authorities, such as the universe's "spiritual laws." The fact that individuals claim to observe these religious rules and practices of their own will is actually secondary. Otero (2003, 29), in his critique of the sociology of individualism, summarizes the issue perfectly with an example: it does not matter whether a driver fastens his seatbelt because he feels compelled to respect the law, or "by himself" because he considers himself to be a responsible person actively involved in the preventive management of his security. What matters is that he *does* fasten his seatbelt. Similarly, what matters in the religious sphere is what "free" spiritual seekers actually do, and although few of them become observant, the majority do attend classes, read a certain literature, and embrace certain practices, even for a short-term period.

Duty and Responsibility of Improving Oneself

By taking for granted social actors' claims of self-determination, one tends to overlook discourses about "duty, obedience, and submittance" (Wood 2010, 272). And there is clear evidence that students of neo-Hindu movements and the Kabbalah Centre have all internalized an imperative of self-actualization, as well as what they are supposed to do in order to reach this goal. Peter, full-time staff at the London Sivananda Centre, motivates his practice of yoga by its positive effects on his life *and* the need for him to learn and change:

> I am happier and can manage my life much better. So I just think it speaks for itself, there's a purpose for me to be here; and *that it's necessary for me to learn* certain things for me just for a change.... Most people want to change, and *if you're not here to change, there's no point to be here....* I still feel that *I need to change to really find true happiness,* that's why *I need to change.* It's been a process going up for five, six, seven, eight years, whatever. But it's still *necessary.*

By and large, I found that this approach of learning and changing oneself is overwhelming among all individuals involved with yoga, meditation, or Kabbalah. "It is a necessity. I cannot but undertake a process of knowing myself," explains Patrick from the Paris Sivananda Centre, even if it is hard and compels him to practice yoga "when he does not want to," he explains. Susan, who practices yoga at the London Sivananda Centre, says she feels "as a duty to progress on my spiritual path whatever what may be in my lifetime and I look forward to being wiser that I am." The importance and necessity of such a task is recurrently expressed by the idea of "working on oneself," with a sense of effort and difficulty—"we *must* work on ourselves again and again," "really work hard," "really, sincerely and constantly"; "it demands a constant effort" and it is an "everyday struggle." One would wonder why, if people only embrace beliefs and practices according to their desires, free from social constraints, they would opt for such a strenuous process and use the vocabulary of work and duty to describe it. I will come back to this shortly, after having underlined expressions of guilt among interviewees that clearly show that an imperative of "working" on oneself has been internalized.

Daniel felt that some classes of the Kabbalah Centre often made him feel bad because he was confronted with expectations of life transformation that seemed unreachable: "I wouldn't feel up to what they were trying to get me to become," he said. While some are happy to have acquired "self-discipline," others deplore their intermittent and irregular practice. They regret not meditating enough, not practicing yoga enough—hence the need for courses, retreats, and workshops, which they describe as a means to revitalize a solitary practice. Note in passing, this shows the importance of collective activities for these religious individualists. "I'm now struggling again to, like with my practice, like I'm out of stage" says Mike about yoga and meditation, as well as his lifestyle: "Oh man! This is so hard work, I'm like, you know I am having beer again, I'm like, I'm having beer as much and, and feeling desperate to rejoin to that space where I found that calm." "I've been terrible this year," laments Eileen from Siddha Yoga in London,

> I've been through to another sort of turmoil this year but, yes for the last couple of years yes, I did practice everyday meditation and for a while I even chanted Guru Gita everyday....That was very beautiful the time I did do that, I was getting up very early and I meditated, I did Guru Gita and it does make a difference to your day actually when you do that, really, I must say.

Lise, from the Parisian Sivananda Centre, considers that she does not meditate enough: "If I were meditating everyday, it would go much better." Guilt, in the cases of Mike, Eileen, and Lise, but also Peter above, is linked to the belief that these practices, as part of their self-improvement, are prerequisites for their well-being. Indeed, self-fulfillment and realization are believed to depend exclusively on personal initiative and dedication—hence the imperativeness of the work on oneself and the resulting culpability when not fully matching the ideal representation of this work offered by teachers.

In fact, individual responsibility is a core element of religious individualism and the quest for self-realization, which goes well beyond our case-studies, as shown, for instance, by Champion's (1990) study of spiritual and New Age milieus. This, in addition, explains the search for practical and efficient tools one can learn and use by themselves. "If I have problems, I know now that it's me who create[s] them, who create[s] happiness, it is me who creates suffering and sadness," says Lydia, a full-time volunteer of the Parisian Sivananda Centre. While she acknowledges that she does not always find solutions "in" herself, Lydia refuses to blame others since "it comes from" her: "it is only up to me to be happy in each thing I do," she asserts. Similarly, Kabbalah Centre students refuse to have a "victim consciousness" and to blame external factors for their difficulties: "whatever YOU do, whatever you decide to do, you create your destiny. You can change it," explains one of them. For Meir, one must accept his responsibility to change in the Kabbalah Centre, because "if you don't want to change your life, it's not your place."

This sense of responsibility for one's self-fulfillment is clearly encouraged by religious leaders. In the previous chapter, I mentioned the ways in which the law of karma and *tikkun* have been interpreted in the explanatory framework of personal growth. These notions are thus presented as transcendent mechanisms, according to which present difficulties result from past lives and actions. As a result, every misfortune and difficulty are inescapable as well as deserved, and everyone has a karma or a *tikkun* to work on—problems can only be overcome if individuals learn from them and change. "You are responsible for your well-being or otherwise, through your own Karma or action" (Sivananda 1999 [1946]); "A person reaps the fruit of his own actions, no one else's. You are the cause of your own pleasure and pain. You have to bear the consequences of your past actions" writes Muktananda (1978, 67). "You are responsible for literally everything in your life" (Kabbalah Centre 2007a, booklet p. 217). *Tikkun* or karma, it is up to individuals to sort themselves out through work on the self, through "spirituality."

During courses and services and through the literature, students are constantly presented with "choices." "We can transform *proactively*, by nurturing the desire to share that is our bond with the Creator. Or we can stand apart from the Creator by building our lives around the desire to receive for the self alone" (M. Berg 2001, 66–67). "The choice is up to us" is often said to students who are invited to ask themselves: "Do I want to transform? Do I want to become a better version of myself?" (Kabbalah Centre 2007a, booklet p. 7). Because moral value is clearly put on these choices (in particular, the "choice" to accept to improve oneself), freedom of choice becomes a normative rhetorical device used to regulate behaviors, by calling upon the responsibility of each individual. Reiterated by Kabbalah students, this rhetoric about individual responsibility and determination often unveiled its normative dimension. During her interview, Corinne, a student from Tel Aviv, explained that the teachers' duty is to provide tools, but,

> after this it's up to you to do whatever you want with them. They are not behind you to check what you do, it's you, it's your work with yourself, and God, that's all. Either you know how to use them or you don't.

I had met Corinne at one of my first Shabbats in Tel Aviv: when I asked for her phone number, she told me to "be quick because it's Shabbat and they're not very paper-pen," referring to the prohibition of working (hence writing) on Shabbat. As I was writing down her number, she was covering my bag and notebook with her shirt, looking around, hoping no one would notice. This example shows that collective and internalized norms, on the one hand, and individual autonomy, on the other hand, are not necessarily mutually exclusive. Precisely, individual responsibility entails great emphasis on the individual's voluntary acceptance of norms that they have certainly not elaborated individually. Self-realization, as we shall see in this chapter, is such a norm.

Spirituality as Discipline

Moreover, while their discourse encourages individual autonomy and choice, presenting their teaching as simple and flexible, religious leaders and teachers are at the same time very prescriptive about the dedication and seriousness required by the quest for the realization of the self. In a fascinating lecture of the learning package "Living Kabbalah System" (Kabbalah Centre 2007a, CD3) that does not seek to conceal its normative nature, Yehuda Berg condescendingly rejects lack of commitment in spirituality:

> CD3 uses tools that give some structure and not be in a state of mind that a lot of people have when it comes to spirituality called free thinker mentality: "oh, you know what, I'm a spiritual person, I'm into freedom, I do what I want, when I want it, that's so spiritual." People think that spirituality is going to yoga class when you feel like it, you buy an occasional crystal and you wear it, or you put it by your TV, "oh you're so spiritual." That's not necessarily spiritual. The idea is, if we don't apply a strong structure and a discipline to our journey, we're never gonna get anywhere. Are you willing to buckle down, and say "I'm gonna commit

to these tools, these techniques..." and say, "I want to see specific results in my life?"

Spirituality *is* hard work that one *must* undertake. Similarly, a shaman teacher observed by Lindquist (1997, 85) warns: "one should never journey for the fun of it." For Muktananda, "strict religious discipline is essential for spiritual growth" because "if you dilute the discipline, realization is also diluted." Like Yehuda Berg seems to do implicitly, Muktananda (1978, 163) criticizes the attitude of some of his disciples:

> You can make certain external aspects easier, but as far as the inner truth of religion is concerned, you can't do anything about it. It is what it is. Ironically, you find young people all over the world wanting religious discipline made very, very easy, while their worldly life is becoming more and more complex.

To a disciple explaining his difficulty to find time to practice meditation, Muktananda (1994, 5) answered, "If you don't make time to work for your spiritual growth, what is the point of your human birth?" Similarly, Vishnu-Devananda (1978, 209) warns that "cessation of practice is a grave mistake; sadhana, spiritual practice, should never been given up under any circumstances." Sadhana, often understood as "spiritual path," is interestingly translated as "self discipline" by the Sivananda Centres (London Sivananda Centre n.d.). This is congruent with Vishnu-Devananda's (1978, 210) definition of yoga as "self-discipline," the term suggesting the development of self-regulating individuals:

> The practice of meditation *must* be continued, but without any expectations. Growth comes, but it is gradual. Sincerity, regularity and patience will ensure eventual advancement.... Real peace comes *only to those* who can control the body and mind with proper *self-discipline*. (My emphasis)

The idea of dedication, effort, and determination is pervasive: "Real change takes place internally and for this to happen perseverance is required" (Durgananda 2008, 14). The student on his sadhana must be an active and volunteer agent of his or her self-improvement. When evoking the different purification practices of yoga, Durgananda (2006, 24) notes that "many people may find this process austere." Yet, she underlines "austerities are individual, and depend solely on what we are used to. The nature of austerity is self-imposition."

The student of Kabbalah is also told about the difficulty, yet the necessity, of undertaking "spiritual work" within a "strong structure and discipline" (Kabbalah Centre 2007a, booklet p. 35). When Karen Berg gave a public talk in Rio de Janeiro in 2008, she stated that it is not a simple thing to become spiritual. Spirituality means work, so stop complaining and start working, she says, there reiterating a discourse I pervasively heard in the Kabbalah Centre. "No pain, no gain," repeat the teachers, who indicate that results will be proportional to effort and commitment. The Kabbalah Centre's teaching insists on the attitudes demanded by this spiritual work: perseverance, courage, determination, patience and willingness to stretch out of one's comfort zone. A proactive, voluntaristic and autonomous self is required since "spirituality is fundamentally an internally motivated experience" (M. Berg 2001, 207). At the same time, imperative injunctions overflow the movement's literature, such as: "it is important that we learn and internalize the power of Shabbat" (Kabbalah Centre 2004f); "it's important to realize that "study" in Kabbalistic terms has a special meaning" (Kabbalah Centre 2004g); about Kippur, "it must be understood that this tremendous gift... given to us on this day... we must completely immerse ourselves" (Kabbalah Centre 2004b); "people who study spirituality should take responsibility" (Y. Berg in *USAToday.com* 2004). "Remember," "beware," "be giving," "engage," "you have to"...

Overall, interviewees' descriptions of the work they undertake on themselves as an imperative mirror religious leaders' presentation of this work as a necessary and arduous discipline. It is therefore clear to me that, when their students explain that they adhere to the teaching because the teaching "felt right," "resonates with their heart," or because they "felt home," it is less a "self-validation of belief" than an implicit recognition, in the neo-Hindu or Kabbalistic teaching, of values and norms they have already, at least in part, accepted—hence the claim to "choose" to follow these teachings according to one's free will and subjective experience: sharing common values makes? adhesion seem "natural" to social actors. And it is surprising that sociologists did not see the normative aspects of "spirituality," since these "spiritual seekers" certainly do. As a yoga student at the Sivananda Centre put it: "we always talk about spirituality, yeah, that's convenient, you're made to swallow lots of bitter pills with it." During interviews, "resistance" and "doubts" are evoked, for example, about devotion toward gurus, or rituals that are by definition fixed, ruled series of symbolic actions. By and large, many interviews show individuals' awareness of contradictions between encouragements of individual freedom and norms, rules, exertion of power, and authority within the group. Tina questions the fact that "there are lots of things you shouldn't do and are disrespectful" in Siddha Yoga. She understands this attitude as a way "to have little customs to control people and keep people polite" and relates it to religion. However, "that's fine" for her: "I'm happy to do it because I love what I get from Siddha Yoga and I'm not going to go and just break the rules." One of the reasons that individuals like Tina accept these rules is that they do agree with the necessity for them to find efficient tools to undertake this "self-regulated" discipline. Indeed, like freedom, self-sufficiency is a discursive mode; it is an interpretation rather than a "reality." Their involvement may be short-term and superficial, but it is evidence of their need of religious resources in their quest of self-realization.

Self-Realization, Disciplining the Self

We now start to have another perspective about what self-realization means: the personal responsibility for being realized and fulfilled, through "choices." These choices are normative: they are pre-defined as right or wrong by religious authorities in relation to transcendent "laws," collectively shared by the group members, and internalized by individuals as imperatives. This section explores the ways in which "spiritual" teachings involve a constant observation, assessment, and regulation of the self. Thus, to become fully realized, students of the Sivananda Centres, Siddha Yoga, and the Kabbalah Centre must learn to monitor and assess their emotions, behaviors, and thoughts, control or eliminate "negative" attitudes, and finally adopt "positive" ones instead. The pursuit of self-realization, therefore, involves a collectively shared (and accepted) normative code of conduct, which transcends specific groups and networks through the value of self-control, the acceptance of responsibility for one's life conditions, and the cultivation of moral virtues. It entails a "self-discipline" through which individuals are encouraged to become the active and autonomous agents of their regulation.

The Self-Control of Emotions, Thoughts, and Behaviors

We now turn to what is, in substance, this work on the self. It essentially involves the control of the self, as evidenced by teachings that tend to focus on disciplining behaviors, attitude, and emotions. In this regard, I believe my case studies are far from being exceptional. By making yoga and meditation the core of their teaching, contemporary gurus give a tremendous importance to the control of the mind. The endless activities of the mind veil the divine Self and thus generate suffering; they are forms of "bondage" (Muktananda

1994: 115; Sivananda 1998 [1940]), from which one must liberate oneself in order to realize the Self but also to reach fulfillment. Accordingly, individual control of the mind is the key of one's pain or happiness: "our destiny is in our thought," writes Durgananda (2006: 24), clearly emphasizing individual responsibility. This control of the mind is undertaken by the practice of yoga, mantra repetition, and especially meditation, the latter being often described as a way to become a "witness" to one's thoughts. It is therefore a means to develop self-awareness and self-control.

> The challenge...is to *gain control of the internal world*. The mind is constantly conversing with itself, replaying past events, rearranging them in a better drama, planning for the future, discussing the pros and cons of this and that. By methodologically slowing down its conscious ramblings, the internal dialogue, and focusing on *positive* and uplifting objects, it is possible to begin to understand the mechanics of the psyche and bring about a more effective life. But the mind is an elusive *animal to tame* (Vishnu-Devananda 1978, 2, my emphasis).

Note the idea of wildness within that needs to be tamed and kept under control—controlling this wildness within is also present in discourses on the "ego," as we shall see further on. Also, the idea of positive or negative thinking suggests that there exist good and bad attitudes. Durgananda (2006, 23) evokes "thoughts which involve I-ness and My-ness" as particularly negative, reminding us that the sense of "I" in the Vedantic philosophy prevents one from realizing that he or she is a manifestation of the Divine Self. Yet, as she contrasts these negative thoughts with sharing, Durgananda gives a moral stance to this description. Ultimately, yoga and meditation are practices that are meant to be a form of temporary "pause" from actions and interactions in the world. As such, they embody an ideal of detachment from one's surroundings, reflected in students' willingness not to be affected by external events as well as by their own emotions and thoughts. As mentioned in the previous chapters, disciples of Siddha Yoga and the Sivananda Centres believe that they find in these teachings the means to take a distance from upsetting interactions with others, or worrying situations. They explain how they try to detach themselves from difficulties and the emotions they generate, how they reflect on the adequate way to respond to challenging situations and interactions. In other words, the control of thoughts, reactions, and emotions through detachment and "constant observation of the mind" (Vishnu-Devananda 1978, 1) relates to students' ideal of resilience.

Not reacting to the external world and not being overpowered by one's emotions has become a central principle of the Kabbalah Centre's teaching, through the normative distinction between "reactive" and "proactive" behaviors. Being reactive is rooted in the desire to receive for the self alone. It is "the reflex of anger. The impulse to hate. The immediate urge to take. The initial desire to grab. The pressure to get even. The need to outdo and one-up. The itch to bitch. The whim of whine. The compulsion to complain" (Kabbalah Centre 2007a, booklet p. 226). Many other "reactive" behaviors are identified in the teaching, such as anger, impatience, over-confidence, low self-esteem, vindictiveness, animosity, greed, selfishness, and self-indulgence. In other words, being reactive is associated with unrestrained and undesirable attitudes. It can be identified because it "requires no effort, discipline, or stretching to get out of our comfort zone" (Y. Berg 2008b, 129), and will lead to pain and chaos. Thus, teachers encourage their students to "apply resistance": to resist impulses and instead to let go, pause, and think about what to do in a given situation. This is being "proactive." In other words, it is about willingly and actively controlling attitudes considered to be "negative" in this moralistic framework: "Proactivity is the opposite [of being reactive]. It's a choice we make. It is an exercise of our free will. It's asking: *how am I going to handle this situation? Why is this happening? Is it serving me to act this way?*" (Y. Berg 2008b, 161). This, in turn, is said to draw more Light and hence bring happiness. Having the "right" attitude in every instance is therefore crucial and demands self-examination.

> Look back at the past month. Write down all the negative things that were in your consciousness (thoughts, actions, feelings). Ask yourself, with all this negativity in my life, do I really deserve to be fulfilled? (Kabbalah Centre 2007a, booklet p. 48)

Again, here, "free will" has to be understood, not as liberation from norms and values, but as individual responsibility. Students are expected to become the active and autonomous agents of their "self-discipline." They are encouraged develop self-awareness and examination in order to regulate themselves; this, in accordance to a set of moral values defining "positive" and "negative" attitudes and the works of a transcendent authority (the spiritual laws about the Light of the Creator), which generate rewards and penalties. Besides, in practice, no doubt the teaching on reactive and proactive behaviors is used to assess the behaviors of others as well: a group of students were waiting and chatting before the start of the Friday Shabbat service at the Rio de Janeiro Centre. Women were interacting with the children present and asked them about school. One of the children explained that he found school boring, in particular mathematics. Then a female student reprimanded him gently: "You have to be proactive. You know what it is to be proactive?" The child nodded. "You have to apply resistance."

The disciplining of the self through increasing self-control and examination is nowhere more obvious than in discourses on the "ego"—and these discourses are far from pertaining to neo-Hindu movements and the Kabbalah Centre only. They are pervasive in New Age milieus (Heelas 1996a, 206) and may find their roots in the 1960s post-psychoanalytic therapies that interpreted the ego as "what we think we are," the feeling of selfhood that is source of ambition, aggressiveness, and separation from others (Pelletier 1996, 446). It is again impulsiveness and selfishness that are judged as morally wrong and detrimental for personal growth. The teachings of the Sivananda Centres, Siddha Yoga, and the Kabbalah Centre convey the idea that the self is the exclusive source of problems and solutions for individuals and the world itself, and that individuals are responsible for regulating their thoughts, emotions, and behaviors through "self-discipline."

Neo-Hindu teachings present the ultimate goal of life as the realization of the divine Self, although this goal is often understood as a deification of the self and a quest of inner-worldly personal fulfillment. In the Vedanta, *ahamkara*, the sense of individuality, is seen as illusory, it is also a source of pain and ignorance that prevents one from realizing the Self. Interestingly, contemporary gurus tend to translate *ahamkara* as "ego," leading them to describe the ego as the individual's worst enemy. Accordingly, the subject as individuality becomes the source of his or her difficulties and pain: he or she can only overcome them by annihilating the "ego"—through yoga, meditation, devotion, and virtuous, selfless attitudes. In the Kabbalah Centre, the ego is invariably described as one's biggest enemy as well. Here, the ego is embedded in a reinterpretation of Satan: also called "the opponent," Satan is the ego, or in other versions of the teaching, Satan created the ego. Satan is the "unseen source of chaos in the world" (Y. Berg 2008b, *passim*) by stimulating envy, jealousy, greed, reactive behaviors in general, receiving for the self alone, negativities, rage, anger, judgment, pride, depression, desire to control, being inconsiderate, disconnection, and the "rash impulse" (Kabbalah Centre 2007a, booklet p. 93, 226). Associated with conflict, confrontation, and selfishness, the ego is contrasted with Light and unity; it generates "reactive" behaviors" and therefore prevents self-realization. Ego as Satan therefore places the source of evil within the individual. Fighting it entails taming a part of oneself with all the Kabbalistic tools on offer—it includes Shabbat and festivals that are presented as opportunities to "leave behind our ego."

Interviewees are sometimes puzzled by these teachings that focus on the realization of the S/self, on the one hand, and, on the other hand, demand the breaking of the ego. However, they share the idea that there is a wild element within themselves that needs to be tamed. They understand the ego as the source of personal difficulties and as an obstacle to their fulfillment. In accordance to the teachings described above, interviewees see the ego manifesting itself in "personal wants," a "kind of gimme gimme gimme" attitude, selfishness, and vanity, but also overpowering emotions. Indeed, the ego is also "everything that is impulsive," the "primal reaction" and, strikingly, "what has not been worked on." The need of self-control and discipline is again central in this description of the ego as the unrestrained and uncivilized part of oneself. Some interviewees indeed described the ego as an untamed animal, a lion, or "a very cunning beast." And, one more time, the discourses on the ego epitomize the full individual responsibility for self-fulfillment, since only taming the ego will allow one to reach self-realization. Thus, "[t]he responsible one is ALWAYS us, our worst enemy is not our neighbor, the brother, the sister, uncle, aunty whoever, it's not them, it is WE," explained Rebecca, a French student of the Kabbalah Centre.

In short, the quest for self-realization entails a clear set of collective norms and values regarding the regulation of individual behaviors, thoughts, and emotions. Religious discourses on the ego underline that the self, in other words, is the object of normative discourses that encourage its constant observation and regulation. One more time, individual subjectivity is significantly shaped by social discourses and norms, the representations of the ego being a case in point.

Self-Realization Requires Virtues

"Negative" and "positive" thinking, "reactive" and "proactive" behaviors—all these terms suggest indeed the existence of a moral code that is fully integrated in the "spiritual discipline." This reminds us that the practical reasons evoked by interviewees to justify practices and observance are merely a discursive mode. The teachings of the Sivananda Centres, Siddha Yoga, and the Kabbalah Centre are permeated by moral values, but as Champion (1990, 48) outlines, even spiritual and holistic loose networks do provide a moral framework (she notes the centrality of sincerity and a loving attitude), which aims to guide individuals in the transformation of their behavior. In other words, I believe there are strong moral assumptions in the representations of the realization of the self in environments calling themselves "spiritual." The "science of seven cultures" elaborated by Sivananda for his disciples, now used as a *vade mecum* for the spiritual life in the centers that bear his name, has a strong ethical dimension. Its "ethical" and "heart" cultures invite disciples to,

Speak the TRUTH.... Do not injure anyone in thought, word or deed. Be kind to all.... Be sincere, straightforward and open-hearted in your talks and dealings.... Be honest.... Develop nobility and integrity.... Control fits of anger by serenity, patience, love, mercy and tolerance. Forget and forgive. Adapt yourself to men and events.... Doing good to others is the highest religion. Do some selfless service for a few hours every week, without egoism or expectation of reward. Do your worldly duties in the same spirit. Work is worship. Dedicate it to God.... Share what you have with others. Let the world be your family. Remove selfishness.... Be humble and prostrate yourself to all beings mentally. Feel the Divine Presence everywhere. Give up vanity, pride and hypocrisy.... Do not hate anyone. (Divine Life Society 2011)

Gurumayi (1994) has particularly insisted on cultivating virtues, such as fearlessness, humility, selfless service, compassion, humility, respect, purity, and "freedom from anger." The opening and purity of the heart has become a core theme of Siddha Yoga under her leadership, as reflected by her books, talks, and messages on the theme of the "sadhana of the heart" (a "collection of talks on spiritual life"): "believe in love" (message for the year 2000), and *My Lord Loves a Pure Heart* (Gurumayi 1994). "Love thy neighbor" is one of the Kabbalah Centre's fundamental principles, as well as sharing the Light rather than receiving it for the self alone. Its teaching opposes selfishness, judgment, anger, and hatred to love, altruism, and mercy; it also emphasizes humility, repentance, trust in the Light, and pure intentions (M. Berg 2001). Like neo-Hindu movements, the Kabbalah Centre's teaching embeds moral values in the spiritual discipline advocated in its most practical courses. Indeed, sharing is presented as a powerful tool that can bring happiness and fulfillment into people's lives. By contrast, "negative" actions or intentions allow chaos and darkness to enter. Thus, one needs to adopt a moral attitude for one's sake, not "by tradition" or obligation.

Interviewees are particularly sensitive and receptive to the moral character of Hindu-based and Kabbalah teachings. In fact, the ideas of purity and rectitude, of loving and harmonious relationship with others, are core elements of their representations of spirituality and self-realization. Several students of Kabbalah cited "Love thy neighbor" as one of the most important Kabbalistic principles. The idea of love in particular resonates with interviewees' Jewish-Christian background. When I asked Timothy why he thought Christianity and Siddha Yoga were similar, he referred to Gurumayi's emphasis on love: "Jesus says 'love thy neighbor as you love yourself,' which is very similar.... His message was basically love, which is what Siddha Yoga is."

Claire, 53, discovered Siddha Yoga 12 years ago and is fairly involved in the Parisian Centre. Claire had received a Catholic education and she had a lot of interrogations about "love,"

> The teaching I received was, I mean what struck me was: God is love. And my question was: but concretely, how do we love? Is love to please? Is love about feeling love and when we don't feel love, can we love? Is it doing our duty? So my quest was also: at the end of the day, is non-violence a response in a way to love people?

These doubts about how to love others led her to read about Martin Luther King, Lanza Del Vasto,[2] Gandhi, and, through an association promoting the teaching of Lanza Del Vasto, she started to practice yoga. She also participated in personal growth trainings and practiced reiki, shiatsu, and tai chi before discovering Siddha Yoga, where she felt at home. Yet Claire would want to make alternative medicines her main occupation. Siddha Yoga has been for her the opportunity to renew her interest in Catholicism, although she regrets the lack of joy and "maturity" of the latter. We observe one more time that the socialization to religious values and norms plays a role in the discovery of exotic religious resources, so that, in part, social actors return to the same rather than adopting a completely new set of beliefs and ethics.

Overall, the moral dimension of social actors' "spiritual discipline" is reflected in the ways in which they define spirituality, a question I chose to ask disciples of neo-Hindu movements. The moral purity of attitudes and behaviors was systematically referred to in order to qualify as "spiritual people." For instance, one thinks that people who meditate are "more generous, warmer and perhaps more open." Another one believes that a "spiritual seeker" will be "more prone to tolerance and kindness," less judgmental and less prone to anger. By and large, "spirituality" was associated with purity, sincerity, and openness. I had not included a similar question in my interview guide for students of Kabbalah. But when I inquired about their practice of the teaching (and was expecting to hear about festivals, prayers, or Zohar scanning), they often responded by evoking a moral attitude. This question about the teaching as practiced prompted this answer from Francis: "It's made me a little bit more patient." I insisted:

> *So what is it that you DO, some bits of your practice you could expand?*
> I listen more to people.... And I have always been compassionate but I am more compassionate and I am stronger. In other words, people

may think that I'm compassionate and that I am going to be more caring and they can take me for a ride but I am more, I practice, I practice this feeling and I practice not to make value judgments. . . . I try not to work against the energies, I try to work with the forces as much as I can. So that's the practice I talk about.

Interestingly, Francis mentions that he was already compassionate before studying Kabbalah. Similarly, when I interviewed disciples of neo-Hindu movements about them adopting a new code of ethics, they consistently rectified my question: they explained that rather than revealing new values, the Sivananda Centres and Siddha Yoga teachings "strengthened" those they already had. Accordingly, Jean, a French disciple of Siddha Yoga, explains how this teaching helps him in "expressing" his values rather than reinforcing them. Yet he stresses that he doesn't "force" himself. According to him, values have to be "lived," "as a result of what is felt inside"; "I do it with pleasure, with an open heart, which is different from 'I'm straight, I respect the law.'" In other words, when interviewees claim that they only follow what comes from "within" themselves and not from an external source of authority, it suggests a resonance between norms they had already internalized (like Claire and "love") and those collectively held in one of these movements.

Ultimately, the respect of a moral code of ethics is encouraged by the belief that virtues participate in the work on the self, which, in turn, leads to fulfillment. For example, Daren's approach of self-realization puts considerable weight on his responsibility to have the appropriate attitude:

The way you behave will determine what comes back to you. So you think more carefully about the consequences of your actions and your behavior. And you learn that the more sharing you are, the more considerate you are, the better you treat people, the better your life will be. And it's also about the more you give of yourself, the more you can see how to get to the next level. It's a, it's a constant, constant 24/7 process. You can take a break whenever you like, but for me, if I take a break then I'm losing out, because if you're not moving forward, you're moving backwards, so what it means tragically is that the quality of my job, how much I enjoy it, how much money I make, the quality of my relationship with my wife, my daughter, my home, my friends, the health and prosperity of my family, everything is interlinked, and *everything depends 100% on me. On how I behave.*

Gender and the Relational Dimension of Self-Realization

The social and normative construction of selfhood is also evidenced by the fact that, probably more often than not, "spirituality" entails the elaboration of gendered selves. In some cases, "spiritual discipline" legitimates traditional gender roles and behaviors. In fact, gender is important for the study of the popularization of exotic religious resources because they attract more women than men. The satsangs of neo-Hindu movements were attended by one man for every three or four women. Staff and yoga teachers, as well as swamis, were more often women in the Sivananda Centres and Siddha Yoga. Similarly, the Kabbalah Centre's classes attract a majority of women—although, for reasons explained below, Shabbat services and festivals are equally attended by men and women, and maybe slightly more by the former. These gender gaps are not exceptional. Holistic and New Age milieus in Western Europe and North America are significantly composed of women (Rocchi 1999, 76; Trzebiatowska and Bruce 2012, 65). Interestingly, Campiche's (1997, 346) quantitative research shows that women are predominant in the group of young urban individuals who recompose religious beliefs from diverse sources. Overall, in advanced industrial societies, women tend to be more religious than men. They express greater interest in religion, are more involved, and have higher levels of practice and attendance, regardless of the religious organization or creed (Campiche 1997, 345; Miller and Hoffmann 1995, 63).

The appeal that religion and its alternative or exotic expressions exert on women leads us to again engage with the issues of self-realization and empowerment in "spirituality." Indeed, several scholars explain women's participation in religion by claiming that through female network and solidarity, women find in religion a form of empowerment, even in the most conservative groups (e.g., Brasher 1998; Griffith 1997; Masken 2009). Some would even go as far as claiming that there are common grounds between feminists and evangelical women (Griffith 1997). "Holistic spiritualities" in particular are said to "legitimate and subvert traditional practices and discourses of femininity": by encouraging women to nurture themselves rather than others, they would represent a "symbol of women's rebellion against their 'essential' roles of care" (Sointu and Woodhead 2008, 268, 273). Emphasizing the difficulties for contemporary women who strive to accommodate the demands of both work and family, Woodhead (2008, 191) explains that

> [w]here religion does attract female commitment it is likely to do so because it manages to *assist in one way or another* in helping women deal with their double dose of commitments. (My emphasis)

According to Woodhead (p. 191), this is the case of "alternative spiritualities" in particular, which "make use of a range of body and emotion-focused techniques to assist women in the difficult and novel task of constructing autonomous forms of selfhood."

The first problem with this argument is its lack of empirical evidence. Rather, quantitative sociology has consistently shown that in various regions of the modern world, women who are inactive are the most religious (partly because the religious woman is rather an older woman), with some studies showing that the gap in terms of religiosity between active and inactive women is greater than between genders (Azzi and Ehrenberg 1975; Bréchon 1997; Campiche 1997; de Vaus and McAllister 1987; Gee 1991). Accordingly, it is not women who have to juggle family and professional duties who are religious; on the contrary. Besides, the presence of children at home tends to increase the religiosity of both men and women (Cornwall 1989, 119). The second issue is once again about the empowerment and realization of the self. Little evidence is provided about what religion or "spirituality" empowers women to do exactly, how it would do so, and why it would not assist men equally. If, as Woodhead suggests, empowerment is about enabling women to meet the demands of professional and family life, it is difficult to see how that makes them subversive. In fact, "spiritual" teachings oriented toward self-realization can elaborate traditional, gendered views of the self: "spiritual" "work" would therefore contribute to encourage traditional roles and attitudes for men and women. Undoubtedly, religions offer a wide range of different perspectives on gender and gender relations (Palmer 1994). Siddha Yoga promotes leadership by women; the roles among the Sivananda Centres are very undifferentiated, with a high proportion of female leaders. However, the Kabbalah Centre is an illustration of how a gendered definition of selfhood encourages female members to adopt a traditional feminine role—this in the name of their "spiritual" development and personal fulfillment, which makes the elaboration of this gendered self desirable for female students.

The Kabbalah Centre, despite an eclectic dimension in its teaching, excludes women from the performance of rituals: they are not part of the minyan, they are not called to read the Torah or carry the scrolls. Sat separately during the liturgy, women are spectators of men performing rituals, leading songs and prayers. Using Orthodox Judaism's rhetoric (Myers 2010, 275), the members of the Kabbalah Centre explain that women "don't have to" perform rituals, for they are more advanced spiritually than men. Women are therefore more compassionate and intuitive. In her speech in Rio de Janeiro, Karen Berg reiterated women's specificities: born more spiritual, they are the nourishers of the world, they are stronger and can multitask, while men are more pragmatically involved in the world and more successful in it. In other words, the teaching insists on the caring role and abilities of women, hence their duties in this regard; the Kabbalah Centre's teaching stipulates that being more spiritual grants women the responsibility to help men working on their own *tikkun*. This is not a reciprocal duty, notes Myers (2010, 275) in her study of the movement's teaching on marital and sexual behaviors. She also underscores, in its specific courses for women, the reiteration of traditional stereotypes regarding gender roles. Men are described as breadwinners while women are believed to be in charge of the household and the respect of Kabbalistic values in the family, which requires a positive and loving attitude on their part. This conservative complementarity is reflected in the division of religious duties: while men draw and channel the Light through rituals, women are vessels who receive and manifest it. In the Kabbalah Centre's daily life, female volunteers, for instance, undertake meal preparation and watch children during services, while it seems that male volunteers are more involved with student support. A majority of teachers are men, female teachers often giving women-only classes about family and relationships.

When I discussed asymmetric gender roles with members of the Kabbalah Centre, some women justified them by expressing a desire for a clear distinction between men and women. I strikingly had similar answers when interviewing female members of Sahaja Yoga, a neo-Hindu movement which also emphasizes traditional gendered roles. Overall, similar observations have been made in various conservative religions (Davidman 1991, 42). During Shabbat services, Dahlia "feel[s] like the guys are having a great time and you feel like you're missing out." However, she appreciates the Kabbalah Centre's

> observation of the differences between men and women, which you know there's a lot in our society where women are supposed to be more masculine, and men have to get in touch with their feminine side. I like the fact that you do sort of tend to connect with the general feminine consciousness, and you do feel this charge going which I think is a good thing.[3]

Nathalie, at first, felt "very prickly" about the different gender roles in the Kabbalah Centre, which resonated with her Jewish upbringing. She thought, "ah this is just like a synagogue, anti-feminists, like, no!" But she was satisfied by the explanations she was given:

> It completely made sense and I think that, I feel there is a different energy in women than in a man and there are definitely different roles,

otherwise men could have children so, in my logic there are definitely different roles. So *if a woman's role is about having children I don't find it difficult to accept that a man needs to take on a different responsibility* and part of that responsibility is for prayer. It is not that I am excluded from it, but it is that they have a different role and the other thing that makes sense to me, and this is very controversial, but fits with my sense of the truth, is that I find women more spiritually evolved.

Nathalie here illustrates a common framework among female students of the Kabbalah Centre: the intertwining between biological differences between sexes, "spiritual" differences, and different, but complementary gender roles. I was often told that men's and women's spiritual specificities "make perfect sense," that men and women have different "roles" or "jobs," in reference to rituals but also to childbearing, child care, and relationships. Even if men have more to do on a ritual sphere, says Tamara,

> women are also hard working to *make the relationship work,* and to do the hard work, and to *make the family work.* So *this is part of our connection,* you know? And [men] daily need more time to do the rituals, the prayers and these things to be connected. We are *naturally* more connected and we manifest this more through our work that we have *with them, with the children, with the family.*

Thus, the Kabbalah Centre and its female members make a connection between women's specific spiritual nature and their nurturing roles. Therefore, "spirituality" has to do with undertaking nurturing functions. The Kabbalah Centre is not exceptional in this regard. Its approach to gender illustrates the fact that selfhood is not something that one does elaborate "freely" and individually—a criticism to Beck's (1992) and Giddens's (1991) theories that sociologists have made precisely in relation to gender, but also regarding ethnicity and class. In the Kabbalah Centre, being a woman entails being the enabler of her husband, a receiver rather than a channel of the Light, a sharing, nurturing being who has limited access to important roles and practices in the movement but predominates in subaltern tasks. Here, the gendered definition of selfhood entails a re-traditionalization of roles and status.

In addition, the consecration of women's inherent spiritual nature, rather than being an empowering celebration of womanhood in a de-traditionalized society, is very Victorian in kind. In the nineteenth century, Catholicism in France and Evangelicalism in Britain and the United States strategically started to focus on women's religiosity. They sacralized femininity and femininized religion in such a way that piety and womanhood became inextricably inter-twined (Brown 2001: 59; Gibson 1993). It is at that time that women started to be more religious than men in Europe and North America (Brown 2001; Fouilloux 1995; Langlois 2001). Women were made the guarantors of the sanc-tity of the family. The "angel in the house" was to "reign over the moral weak-ness and innate temptations of masculinity" and to ensure the transmission of moral values to children; as such, women were pillars of the rejuvenation of the nation. In addition, capitalism's gender division of labor meant that women became increasingly responsible for their children's moral education and welfare. Responsible for the morality of others, women's purity was piv-otal, and therefore the gravity of their faults was incommensurable—hence the necessity to subject them to more control and scrutiny (Brown 2001, *passim*).

In other words, and as shown by the teaching of the Kabbalah Centre, with women's spiritual "nature" come duties and expectations that have locked them in subordinate social roles. Women are indeed, at least in part, religious "on behalf of others" (Trzebiatowska and Bruce 2012, 146). Their duty of care helps to explain their higher level of religiosity, but also the fact that gender is the main factor explaining attitudes related to health as well. Women dis-play greater concern for health, greater involvement in healthy lifestyle and behaviors, and more frequent use of medical facilities (p. 76). There are also more women among alternative and holistic therapists and users (Flesch 2007, 2010), yoga students (Hasselle-Newcombe 2002, 42; Devinat 1992) and psychotherapies' patients (Briffault and Lamboy 2008,108). We have already noted that social actors attracted by exotic religious resources are often in-volved with alternative and holistic therapies, either as consumers or as therapists. In a nutshell, the use of these various practices, including exotic religious resources, is in part motivated by a similar concern about care, har-monious relationships and family life, which in the perspective of women can be perceived as part of their self-realization. The criticisms of ego-behaviors that entail selfishness and narcissism, the importance of developing sharing and loving attitudes in social actors' "spiritual life" converge with this argu-ment. In her study of motherhood, Smyth (2012) underscores the expectations for mothers to be active agents in a role characterized by conflicting and com-peting norms. I expect the Kabbalah Centre's normative advices and guidance to echo women's sense of uncertainty, as they need to respond to imperatives of self-sacrifice, caregiving, and self-fulfillment at the same time.

Indeed, female interviewees evoke, more than male interviewees, the ways in which their "spiritual path" helps them in their marital and family life. Christine, practicing and teaching yoga at the Sivananda Centres, evokes the work on herself as her duty she has to achieve in this world, and this includes something very important to her, which was to communicate with her parents.

Jane explained how the Kabbalah helped her to understand the need for "tough love" with her children, to allow them to encounter and overcome difficulties. Another explained how, while she wanted to leave her husband, teachers were constantly available to advise her and discouraged her from divorce. In other words, the "assistance" that women find in "spirituality" may well be, in some cases, guidance and incentives to perform traditional gendered roles and to conform to social ideals about womanhood. This includes "holistic" practices as well. Ceccomori's (1995) thorough history of yoga in France showed that yoga was popularized in the postwar period through women's magazines, advertised as an activity allowing women to remain young, beautiful, and re-laxed. Otero (2003, 245) makes the same remark about post-psychoanalytic therapies, whose clients are predominantly women, aiming to enable them to achieve their "natural" duties—hence the focus on children, marital harmony, and more broadly, the emotional sphere. The therapeutic sphere's focus on women is pragmatic, underscores Otero: children's health and well-being de-pend on them. Making the home a happy place and making the relationship with her partner "work" is still incumbent upon women. That is to say, the ful-fillment and realization of women is not an individual issue, because they are likely to envisage these goals as entailing harmonious relationships to their partner, children, and relatives. As far as women are concerned, there is no self-care that is not, in part, care for others. In fact, gender gives additional sig-nificance to self-improvement as duty. Thus, explaining "Kabbalah *for* women" (my emphasis), Karen Berg (2005, 162–163) encourages them to adjust to their partner's needs:

> When you know that your husband has returned from a business meeting and he's upset, take your ego out of the situation and let him express himself. Don't bombard him with your needs immediately....If an argument is brewing, say to yourself, "Okay, you know what? I can be generous here. I'm just going to listen and not disagree immedi-ately. I'll give Sam the space to vent emotionally. Later we can look at the situation from other viewpoints."

Karen Berg (p. 170) emphasizes the development of self-control, empathy, of "practicing the art of listening" and addressing issues "in a loving way." Women also have to accept that their partner's criticisms are "rarely arbitrary" while they are recommended to "refrain from criticizing others" themselves (p. 169). Self-improvement is desirable, but it is also an imperative in conformity with social norms: "spiritual" resources are indeed used to perform gendered roles and duties that are far from being always subversive.

Courses and the Internalization of Norms
about the Self

We are now able to understand better the significance of courses, workshops, and seminars that are used to transmit neo-Hindu and Kabbalistic teachings. Because these events are "spiritual services" that are paid for, sociologists of religion have associated them with consumerism, in order to contrast this superficial relationship to religious resources with other forms of religious commitment such as belonging and conversion (Carrette and King 2005, 79; Hervieu-Léger 2001, 148–151; Lau 2000, 13). Yet consumption does not only involve purchasing goods and services. It implies, for instance, that the object of consumption is invested of value. Contrary to what Heelas (2008) seems to believe in his defense against a "reduction" of "spirituality" to consumerist practices, consumption is not devoid of meaning, but full of it. Thus, social actors' motivations and expectations in spending time and money to attend "spiritual" courses outline a pragmatic relationship to exotic religious resources; nonetheless, they also shed light on the importance of acquiring efficient "tools" to enhance self-actualization, believed to be a necessary task one is answerable for. In other words, individuals may (and tend to) attend a wide range of courses and retreats, though the goal (to satisfy the imperative of self-improvement) remains relatively unchanged; it preexists the act of consumption itself and is not defined by "consumers" from their own self-authority, outside a framework of social norms about the self.

Moreover, the fact that this "learning environment" is consumed does not prevent it from being a locus of socialization to norms and values. Classes and workshops are indeed designed to socialize participants to particular religious ideas and practices that are presented as efficient means for personal growth (Lindquist 1997 makes a similar analysis regarding shamanic practices). For example, the Sivananda Centres organizes a weekend course that I attended on "tools to increase your will power and concentration." It covered willpower as the key of success in everything, the keys to positive changes and techniques to increase concentration in daily life—hence desirable skills to realize the self. Thus, the course unavoidably reinforced the importance of self-improvement. It also linked this objective with the practice of yoga and meditation. The swami presented the mind's mechanisms according to the Hindu scriptures, warned the attendants against its incessant manifestations, and stressed the need to control thoughts and desires that agitate and weaken the self. Presented as powerful means to control the mind, yoga and meditation classes were included in this two-day program. Other disciplining attitudes and virtues were advised: fasting, appropriate use of time, having a spiritual journal recording progress, patience, perseverance, being in the here and now, and dealing with affective bonds that undermine willpower.

Interactions with authorities such as teachers in the settings of workshops and classes considerably contribute to the socialization of students to new ideas and practices. In the Kabbalah Centre's cycle of 10 courses, Kabbalah One, participants are introduced to the spiritual laws of the universe, the necessity to transform themselves, and how to do so by resisting to reactive impulses, being proactive, and sharing. As in other classes I attended in the Kabbalah Centre, the transformation of the self is an imperative rather than an offer: those who think everything is going well in their life are in a very bad situation, asserted my teacher for Kabbalah One. This imperative was repeatedly reasserted by the teacher's demand for students to "share" "transformation stories" that occurred since the previous session. Observing our own behaviors, changing them according to learned Kabbalistic principles, and noting their positive outcomes in our life constituted the weekly "coursework" we had to complete. These transformation stories were then discussed with the group of students sitting around the same table, or told in front of all the attendants and then commented upon by the teacher. In addition, during moments of questions and answers, students would tell about a recent difficulty they encountered, a conflicting interaction with someone else, for instance; they would explain how they responded to the situation and ask the teacher whether he thought their behavior was reactive or proactive. Other students told how, in applying the newly taught principles, they were rewarded by positive outcomes, thus encouraging others to follow their example. By and large, in various courses of the Kabbalah Centre, I observed students asking the teacher why they have such and such uncontrolled behaviors, why a particular event occurred in their life, and the teacher would provide an interpretation relating to the works of the Light, these students' *tikkun*, and their need to make a "correction" of themselves by being more proactive.

In all these different forms of interactions, personal stories and experiences are given a new meaning according to the course content. In one of the Kabbalah One sessions, a woman explained that she had always been a giving person who had made a lot of sacrifices for others. She asked the teacher whether, by doing so, she had received from the Light, despite not knowing about it at the time. "What do you think, in your opinion?" the teacher asked her. "Yes I did," she said. "You think you have changed, that you are a better person through these sacrifices? "Yes," she replied. Then the teacher explained that she was wrong: she could have received much more by thinking about the Light, but instead she must have had a hidden interest in sharing. She replied she did not, but the teacher insisted she did. Visibly upset, she said she would think about it.

Interactions between students during courses, services, and satsangs also contribute to learning or reinforcing ideas and values, for instance the practice of "sharing" experiences and feelings. In Siddha Yoga, "sharing" occurs in every satsang: to enlighten an aspect of the teaching for the audience, the "master of ceremony (MC)" (the person leading the satsang) refers to his or her personal experience. An MC in Paris once evoked a course on miracles she attended in South Fallsburg. She told the audience that at first she felt disappointed by not having experienced miracles; but the very last day of the course, as she was walking around the ashram's lake, she felt a presence; stones around her had an incredible relief, she said, and she felt all along her walk that she really tasted the bliss that the Siddhas, the perfect ones, experience. As she came back from her walk, she was told by other disciples that her face was full of light (note the mutual validation of personal experience). Even if personal experience is given a tremendous significance, making sense of the teaching is therefore a collective, not an individual, process. In her study of the mystical-esoteric nebulae in France, Champion (1990) indeed stressed the fact that the fragmentation of beliefs and individuation are limited, precisely because those participating in "spiritual" courses and workshops highly value the sharing of their subjective experiences as a way of authenticating them, as my fieldwork examples show as well. Her experience, the MC explained, was a miracle. During a Shabbat service in the London Kabbalah Centre, I was invited to "share" with another student an example of moments when I feel "reactive." After I provided her with my example, the student responded that she felt exactly the same; she also added that when it happens to her, she tries to see the reason why the Light "sends" her this particular situation. It must be, she said, that it is a challenge sent by the Light and that she can overcome situations that are much more difficult. She therefore encouraged me to reconsider what occurs in my life and, instead of responding to events impulsively, to interpret them as challenges intended for me to improve.

Undoubtedly, norms are not followed simply because they are expressed and discussed. Dahlia explained her interest in Kabbalah by referring to "blockages" in her sentimental and professional life (see Chapter 5). Similarly, Daren explains why he was willing to follow a friend to the Kabbalah Centre:

> I was in a place, where I had a very big lack in my life. All my friends were getting married, that I socialized with since I was a kid, you know, I'd seen them fifty times a week, and I wasn't seeing them any more. And I had to sort myself out. And I thought, I have to do something to change myself somehow. And it was at that point that I met this person

who started it. So I had the craving to take responsibility to deal with my dire situation.

Daren illustrates the fact that, in the three case studies, there is a significant proportion of single individuals. While men rarely evoked the issue with me (they may have been uncomfortable with a female interviewer to do so), many female interviewees expressed the wish to meet someone, the anxiety of not having children. "Spiritual" milieus are hoped to be places where one could find a partner—Daren in fact met his wife in the Kabbalah Centre. Meredith, in her late thirties, and single after a long relationship with a married man, has not found love in Siddha Yoga. She thinks about leaving the group, and wonders whether the reason is that she feels disappointed because she has not met someone, as she hoped. Desires and hopes from single individuals like Dahlia, Daren and Meredith make them receptive to the teachings' encouragement to work on oneself, in being open and loving, controlling emotions such as feelings of low self-esteem or selfishness, and so forth. In short, students' expectations (here about love and relationship) make them receptive to certain norms and values. The following chapter will further this idea by focusing on other social and professional expectations.

Re-contextualizing Religion

By emphasizing the normative dimension of "spirituality," my aim is not to assert that religions have maintained a regularity power on individuals and hence to refute the secularization thesis. Indeed, I have stressed the superficial and short-term involvement that characterize the relationships with exotic religious resources, this from secularizing individuals. What I want to underline is the fact that the quest for self-realization entails the conformity to a set of norms and values, which in fact transcends specific religious teachings and reveals wider constraints exerted on individuals in advanced industrial societies. The last section of this chapter explores the psychologization of social life in political, economic, and cultural context in order to understand the social, economic and political dimensions of self-realization.[4]

The Political and Economic Dimensions of Self-Realization

The previous chapter underscored that an increasing number of issues and problems are today interpreted in a psychological language and hence "demand" psychological interventions (Ehrenberg 1995, 23); this, among other things, has blurred the boundaries between the religious and the therapeutic. Overall, social scientists relate the cultural and social success of psychology as a framework to its congruence with neoliberalism's political and economic mechanisms of privatization. Adopting a foucauldian approach, Rose (1989, 1998, 1999) analyzes the psychologization of social life as a particular way to exert political power. In particular, it fits with the neoliberal mode of governing populations; based on the moral principle of freedom, neoliberalism intends to regulate individuals, conceived as subjects of freedom. Thus, operating on subjectivity, the neoliberal state has become dependent upon knowledge of the self. Hence the central role of psychology, which makes selfhood intelligible and provides techniques to shape individual capacities and specificities for the good functioning of education, the family, the workplace, health care, law and order, and so forth. Experts such as counselors, therapists, or coaches are burgeoning, but psychology has also renewed the practice of professionals exerting authority over others (social workers, nurses, teachers, managers, prison officers, etc.). It provides them with the knowledge and techniques, with the legitimacy of science, to guide individuals toward the appropriate attitudes.

Other analyses of the psychologization of social life underline the economic dimension of neoliberalism's value of individual freedom. For Harvey (2007, 2),

> [n]eoliberalism is in the first instance a theory of political economic practices that proposes that human well-being can best be advanced by liberating individual entrepreneurial freedoms and skills within an institutional framework characterized by strong private property rights, free markets, and free trade.

In this perspective, the regulating role of the state is limited to the creation and protection of such a framework. This—neoliberalism's call for personal responsibility and self-reliance and the reduction in welfare state provision (Lemke 2001, 203)—constitutes the context of the psychologization of social life. Neoliberal politics attempt to reduce the state's role to fulfill social needs for health, well-being, security, and order. Conversely, individuals, "communities," families, charities, or religious organizations have been increasingly perceived as the "empowered" partners of the state, now in charge of their own well-being. The American and British New Right, in particular, developed policies (privatization, welfare cuts) that promote individuals' and civil society's initiatives, on the assumption that the moral and economic regeneration of the nation requires the destruction of a dependency culture and its replacement by a culture of enterprise (Du Gay 1995, 64).

On the one hand, individuals voluntarily seek the techniques to become this autonomous and realized self, believed to be the source of every success if actualized, in the "psychotherapies of normality." These include counseling, therapies, self-help and personal growth, and coaching, but the data presented in this book clearly suggest that religious and holistic milieus also contribute to these therapies of normality. On the other hand, as the welfare state has been increasingly undermined in Euroamerican societies since the mid-1970s, there is conversely an increasing popularity and legitimacy of psychotherapeutic modes of intervention to regulate social problems that are precisely generated by this new context of social inequality and vulnerability. Learning issues, drug use, unemployment, illness, sick leave, and lack of efficiency at work are increasingly identified as problems of selfhood, and hence addressed by psychological interventions in order to generate "adapted," desirable behaviors from "self-regulated" individuals (Otero 2003, 3). In other words, the subjectivization of social life can be seen as a contemporary form of "risk management" (Castel 1981b). It contrasts with the postwar "assistentialist" welfare practice, as well as forms of repression and punishment, in that it represents a flexible way to regulate populations, which values and extends individual responsibility. The social problems it aims to address are nonetheless probably not that different from the past (Otero 2003, 45).

Once we start to consider the regulating role of psychological discourses and techniques, their significance in the workplace is rather unsurprising. They provide means to think, assess, and reform the "personal dimension of work" and thus transform the relations of production toward increased competitiveness and efficiency (Castel 1981b, 210; Rose and Miller 1995). By focusing on the control of behaviors and emotions, they are integrated in management techniques to address organizational problems, interpersonal communication, cooperation, and decision making, as well as workers' motivation. Indeed, managerial methods have increasingly valued aspirations for personal fulfillment and achievement (especially for white-collar professions), on the assumption that they have a positive impact on performance, and hence on corporate success. Mayo's research in the 1920s and his Human Relations Movement profoundly transformed managerial theory by introducing personality factors, individual needs, and emotions (Illouz 2008). The 1960s post-psychoanalytic Human Potential milieu has substantially permeated managerial practices in the private sector. Influenced by Maslow's theory of self-actualization as people's highest need, this post-psychoanalytic movement focuses on self-awareness; it assumes the existence of an unexplored human potential which, once unleashed, would allow individuals to control their emotional states and experience fulfillment, but also, according to some methods, to reunite with the cosmos. In other words, it provides workers with techniques for self-fulfillment *and* for a more efficient organization of work (Stone 1982). In continuity with Human Potential therapies, a burgeoning sector of "religious-styled management development workshops and seminars" focuses on spiritual growth as the way forward to corporate success (Bell and Taylor 2003, 330).

In other words, by encouraging workers' autonomy and emotional self-awareness and by stimulating internal competitiveness and individual entrepreneurship, industrial psychologists, consultants, and coaches aim to establish an "alignment" between workers' aspirations in terms of self-realization and the corporate goals of quality, innovation, efficiency and productivity (Rose and Miller 1990; 1995)—hence the growing significance of the discourse of "excellence," which resonates with aspirations of self-improvement on the individual level, and responds to needs of competitiveness on the corporate level, suggesting that "everybody can and will benefit from cultivating some enterprising spirit and aspiring to excellence" (Du Gay 1995, 68). The psychologization of the workplace is therefore desirable for workers: it presents selfhood as the key to accomplishment and success, encourages self-knowledge and fulfillment through work, and offers practical techniques that facilitate communication, cooperation and management. Thus, an educated middle class actively seeks techniques of the self through personal growth literature and workshops, therapies, and coaching, as well as the "spiritual" (this will be described in the next chapter). However, it is not about changing the workplace's rules and structures, but rather adapting workers' attitudes to its needs (Castel (1981a, 124).

Self-realization is not a given. Interpreting life in the psychological framework of adaptability, self-actualization, and fulfillment (Rose 1998, 77) is not something that individuals pursue naturally or spontaneously, once "liberated" from social norms. The fact that self-realization is desired and voluntarily pursued by social actors does not exclude the fact that it is a socially constructed incentive which in fact has an increasing political and economic significance. For the same reasons that Otero (2003, 2) asserts that "demands" of therapy are rooted in a specific social and institutional framework, I contend that the exploration of yoga, meditation, or Kabbalah as a means to enhance the self epitomize the imperatives and constraints that are exerted on individuals in Euroamerican societies today—to be "enterprising selves" who have understood that only "working" on themselves will enable them to be realized and fulfilled.

Entrepreneurial Selfhood

It follows from this that "selfhood is more an aim or a norm than a natural given" (Rose 1998, 4) and it "is a category that does not pre-exist the discourses that constitute it" (Skeggs 2004, 19). In other words, we are not what we make of ourselves. There is, in fact, a convergence between, on the one hand, the "ideal" self (flexible, resilient, and autonomous) of the students of the Kabbalah Centre, Sivananda Centres, and Siddha Yoga, and defined as such by the therapeutic framework, and, on the other hand, the human model required in a neoliberal context, an "entrepreneurial self."

Contemporary Euroamerican economy is characterized by "flexible accumulation" (Harvey 1990, 141). Intense technological innovation, sharp competition, unprecedented mobility of capital, volatile markets, and patterns of consumption, all entailed the restructuration of labor market and processes toward flexibility: "reduced size, flatter hierarchies, smaller "just-in-time" inventories, a capacity to move materials and products quickly, reliance on global accessibility, and a fluid labor force at all levels" (Urciuoli 2008, 219). This economic context entails a high level of insecurity for workers: an increasing turnover, the decline of fixed employment, and the growth of casual and part-time work, the "rapid destruction and reconstruction of skills, modest (if any) gains in the real wage," high levels of structural unemployment, and weakened trade unions (Harvey 1990, 150). Ultimately, their vulnerability is aggravated by the fact that they are less protected by collective bargaining agreements, state regulations, and welfare provision. All of these are different aspects of what Castel (1995) called the "new social question"—the ways in which social actors increasingly experience instability and precariousness as a condition of existence.

The self is expected to be adaptive and proactively seeking self-actualization. In a flexible accumulation economy, individuals are less defined by their position or skills they have acquired, but by their capacity to develop new dispositions in order to adapt to tomorrow's challenges. In other words, students of Kabbalah, yoga, or meditation are not mistaken when they describe self-improvement as an imperative. The "language of 'change'—invariably the sort that challenges—is a constitutive element of contemporary managerial discourse" (Du Gay 1996, 153). Perpetual re-training and re-skilling have become normalized since the 1970s in order "to make every person capable of becoming an agent of change, capable that is of an improved understanding of the technical, cultural and social world that surrounds him, and of acting upon and changing the structures within which he lives" (Donzelot 1991, 273). The point, says Donzelot, is to change people's attitudes toward change, in order to modify their attitude toward society and public power. In other words, individuals are responsible for their good adaptation to their environment, rather than demanding compensations from public power for being ill adapted.

Responsibility has become a crucial feature of the contemporary individual (Ehrenberg 1995, 14). Individualized work contracts, performance-related pay, relentless and individualized appraisals, internal competition: all these managerial techniques (increasingly used in the public sector in Britain) "offer involvement" to workers perceived as "enterprising selves." But by doing so, it makes them responsible for the outcomes of their labor (Du Gay 1996, 158). Accordingly "individuals are more exposed to the cost of engaging in any activity and more dependent on their own resources for successfully carrying it out" writes Du Gay (1995, 183), pondering on the costs of the "empowering" promotion of autonomy and self-fulfillment in the workplace.

Selfhood thus becomes a project and "potential" on which social actors are encouraged to capitalize (Ehrenberg 1995, 126; Rose 1998, 154), without this project being unconstrained. Indeed, efforts are expected to accept criticisms, to work on resistance and blockages, to cultivate harmonious relationships with colleagues, to resist stress, to accept what cannot be changed and have instead a "positive" (that is, adaptive) attitude (Otero 2003:273). In other words, the project of the self has to be congruent with its environmental needs. In this regard, the emphasis on "soft skills" such as friendliness, sociability, taming anger and frustration, communication, and optimism (which are taught by this book's case studies) is not unrelated to the fact that the post-Fordist development of the service sector requires less technical than interpersonal skills (Urciuoli 2008, 212).

Thus, through various workshops, the services of coaches and other experts, and personal growth literature, an educated middle class actively seek to fulfill this imperative of self-management and actualization. They look for techniques that would allow them to control their emotions, have a "positive attitude," be flexible and resilient, manage stress, communicate with others efficiently, and be proactive and autonomous. Chapter 7 will explore the ways in which individuals activate these techniques of the self in particular social and professional contexts. It is the desire to acquire these "skills" that animate the students of Siddha Yoga, the Sivananda Centres, and the Kabbalah Centre; this ideal of selfhood preexists their "choice" for these particular religious resources. Interpreting their lives as a project of self-realization that requires an active "work" of self-improvement on their part, they explore religious resources and alternative therapies as sources of techniques of the self. And as I have pointed out, religious teachings offer an inner-worldly quest of fulfillment, which requires individual autonomy: by taking responsibility for one's fate and accepting change, disciples are encouraged to control their emotions and thoughts, to be proactive instead of reactive, to be sharing, open, "positive," and so on. In this regard, the "spiritual" fully converges with the wide range of existing therapeutic methods, in their aim of enabling individuals to be in charge of their professional success, their family life, their health, and so forth (Otero 2003, 56–58; Rose 1998, 79). In short, the desire of so-called spiritual seekers to become self-sufficient, resilient, and flexible is not elaborated through their "self-authority." The project of self-realization that they believe they undertake freely does not demonstrate reflexivity or individual appropriations of one's identity, but their conformity to social imperatives for them to be adaptable, to control their emotions, and to cultivate moral dispositions.

Freedom and Social Regulation in Neoliberal Societies

Finally, this discussion forces us to rethink the issue of freedom in the religious field—a freedom that is supposed to generate eclectic forms of bricolage. Many sociological analyses underline the increasing significance of autonomy *as a norm* (Ehrenberg 1995, 19). That is to say, in contemporary Euroamerican societies, individuals may be "free" to a certain extent, yet they "are *obliged* to be free, to construe their existence as the outcome of choices that they make among a plurality of alternatives" (Rose 1998, 78–79). This is the reason that Cronin (2000) talks about a "compulsory individuality": subjects have to be oneself or find their "true" self through voluntaristic choices. In addition, these "choices" are already pre-defined through norms that constitute the desirable and undesirable qualities of the self: "spiritual seekers" are free to study Kabbalah or practice yoga or both, yet they are pressed to accept the need to improve themselves, undertake work on themselves to become proactive, practice yoga regularly, control reactive behaviors, or annihilate the ego. The fact that they find this aim personally desirable and that they claim to engage with it on their free will does not alter its normative dimension, as Otero's metaphor of the driver fastening his seatbelt underlined. On the contrary, their claim of freedom and responsibility for their spiritual commitment is consistent with mainstream injunctions for individuals to take care of themselves. Therefore, the opposition made by some sociologists of religion between social constraints and individual freedom makes little sense since, as Foucault demonstrated, "power...works through, and not against, subjectivity" (Rose 1998, 151). Therapy and "spirituality" precisely make of the self the locus of discipline and of conformity to collective norms.

Indeed, the more individuals are deemed responsible, the more they become dependent on experts (Castel et al. 1979, 298; Ehrenberg 1995, 252). "In
striving to live our autonomous lives, to discover who we really are, to realize
our potentials and shape our lifestyles, we become tied to the project of our
own identity and bound in new ways into the pedagogies of expertise" (Rose
1999, 93). Counselors, therapists, and coaches, as well as "spiritual" leaders
and teachers, address the realization of the self. They provide a rationale to do
so which, Otero underlines, stresses personal responsibility and adaptation
to one's environment. They also offer a language and techniques to develop
self-inspection, to evaluate and manage thoughts, emotions, and attitudes
(Rose n.d.). This, for the making of individuals regulating themselves in accordance to political and economic structures. Overall, it is doubtful that this
psychologization of religion reflects the empowerment of individuals in regard
to structure, or their ability to invent their self-identities. Indeed, the normative and regulating function of the psychologization of social life is outlined by
the sanctions applied to those who do not display the desired attitudes. Nolan
(1998, 292–297) gives various examples in the workplace, educational institutions, prisons and medical institutions of what he calls "therapeutic coercion,"
that is to say, situations in which individuals are made to accept psychological
interpretations of themselves and of society, or face sanctions for not doing so.

Rather, the issue of social power today becomes subtler because it subjec-
tivizes and privatizes social issues. "Those who have failed to link their personal fulfillment to social reform are lumped together as 'social problems,' are
diagnosed as 'lacking self-esteem' and are charged with 'antisocial behavior,' "
notes Cruikshank (1993, 330). This is the reason that Castel (1981a) sees the
psychological apparatus as a means to conceal, and hence a contribution to,
the distribution of social power. Castel's argument actually resonates with the
discourse of Christine, who regularly practices yoga in the Parisian Sivananda
Centre and was a union activist when she was younger. She thinks that what
she did for workers at the time may have been helpful on a short-term basis,
but believes she now helps others much more by giving yoga courses. In fact,
Christine considers her past union activities useless and a waste of energy
because "they [workers] were making no effort, we were not helping them
to work on themselves." Such emphasis on individual responsibility seems
to dissolve the possibility of collective action or political alternative. Rather,
the combination of autonomy and vulnerability creates a paradoxical situation in which, on a private level, individuals seem to have a relatively important margin for maneuver, when on a social and economic level they seem to
have lost control of their destiny. Thus, "nothing is really forbidden, and yet
nothing is really possible" (Otero 2003, 1).

Ultimately, the psychologization of social life seems to reflect the fact that social actors feel increasingly less capable to influence their social environment as social and economic structures have become highly complex and impersonal. Post-Fordist capitalism has a dominant class without a face (Castel 2001, 151); it is characterized by the growing de-personalization of capital ownership. Large-scale corporate bodies become the major stock providers and owners, giant corporations rise, economic concentration intensifies; all these trends make it more difficult to identify the exertion of power and control (Abercrombie et al. 1986, 132–137). If we follow Berger (1965), psychology may find a particular significance as a way to understand the world and human experience in this context. For Berger (p. 39), the psychological idea of the unconscious, of something invisible, mysterious, and unruly expresses the impossibility today to perceive society as a whole, due to its complexity and opacity. Because "the individual, in modern society is typically acting and being acted upon in situations the motor forces of which are incomprehensible to him,"

> [s]ociety confronts the individual as mysterious power, or in other words, the individual is unconscious of the fundamental forces that shape his life. One's own and the others' motives, meanings and identities, insofar as they are comprehensible, appear as a narrow foreground of translucency, the background of which is provided by the massive structures of a social world that is opaque, immensely powerful, and potentially sinister.

Berger's article, written in 1965, finds a striking resonance in neoliberal Euroamerican societies today. I do not see that "the more societies are modernized, the more agents (subjects) acquire the ability to reflect on the social conditions of their existence and to change them in that way" (Beck 1994, 174), not the least because the psychologization of social life hinders, rather than facilitates, reflexivity. The belief system of students of yoga, Kabbalah, and meditation mirrors the contemporary model of human beings, subjected to strong social forces but nonetheless considered to be responsible for their fate. The cosmic laws of the universe, the Light, or the energy are highly impersonal; their effects seem as rational and inescapable as those of electricity or gravitation. The acknowledgment of these transcendent principles prompt individuals to "choose" to act accordingly: the rewards, framed in terms of self-realization and fulfillment, depend on their active commitment to take responsibility, accept every difficulty as an opportunity to improve themselves, stretch out of their comfort zone, and adapt to, rather than resist, their current situation.

Synthesis

> Sociology's misfortune is that it discovers the arbitrary and the
> contingent where we like to see necessity, or nature... and that
> it discovers necessity, social constraints, where we would like to
> see choice and free will. The habitus is that unchosen principle
> of so many choices that drives our humanists to such despair.
> It would be easy to establish... that the choice of this philoso-
> phy of free choice isn't randomly distributed... the sociologist
> discovers the necessity, the social constraints of social condi-
> tions and conditionings, right in the very heart of the 'subject,'
> in the form of what I have called the habitus.... It is through
> the illusion of freedom from social determinants (an illusion
> which I have said a hundred times is the specific determina-
> tion of intellectuals) that social determinations win the free-
> dom to exercise their full power. (Bourdieu 1990, 14–15)

This chapter provided an interpretation of the incentive of the psychologized
use of exotic religious resources. They are undoubtedly instrumentalized for
an inner-worldly and individualistic quest of self-realization; however, I disagree with the interpretation of religious individualism that is given by many
sociologists of religion. "Spiritual seekers" insist on their freedom of choice
as guiding their quest, yet there is a wealth of empirical evidence underlining,
in this quest, the acceptance of transcendent authorities, shared beliefs and
norms, and processes of socialization in which interactions with teachers and
other members are very significant. Moreover, rather than the possibility to be
whoever one wants to be, "freedom" proved to be the individual responsibility
to be as one *should* be: an autonomous and self-managed person, constantly
striving for improving oneself. Self-realization is certainly the object of strong
individual aspirations, yet it is also thought of as an imperative and a duty,
which in fact sheds light on merciless social, political, and economic pressures exerted on individuals in contemporary Euroamerican societies. In this
regard, the fact that "spiritual seekers" claim to "work" on themselves of their
own free will does not matter. Besides, they have not defined the terms of this
self-realization, nor of the "work" on themselves they have to undertake. They
depend on the sheer number of experts of the soul who provide the techniques
to develop the desirable selfhood—that is to say, an adaptive and responsible
person: these techniques to scrutinize, monitor, and manage the self converge
toward individuals' adaptation to their social environment. Considering the
standardization of these techniques, the fact that individuals "choose" among

a diversity of them is therefore relatively secondary. In short, bricolage and its aim, self-realization, do not entail a move away from conformity to social norms. On the contrary: they reflect a new way of regulating social actors, through individual responsibility and self-discipline.

Beyond the simple discussion of the use of exotic religious resources, this chapter has shed light on important methodological and epistemological problems of the sociology of religion. The first of these problems is the uncritical approach taken by sociologists when they take for granted interviewees' claims of religious freedom. This has often led sociologists of religion to fail to see the existence of norms and constraints, or the role of socialization and authorities in the religious field. The theoretical distinctions between society and the individual, the external and the internal, the objective and the subjective, are also highly problematic on an epistemological level. This is a weakness that, by and large, affects the sociology of individualism represented by Giddens, Beck, Sennett, Lash, and Lipovetsky and which, as such, has been debated by sociologists of mental health such as Rose, Castel, Otero, and Ehrenberg. The research of the latter emphasize that "it's not because human life seems more personal today that it is less social, less political and less institutional. It is so, in another way," (Ehrenberg 2010, 15, my translation). More important, the individual *is* social in essence and could not be otherwise; without a world of meanings, norms, and values, the self, emotions, or subjective experiences could not be thought or understood. Besides, not only is individualism a type of social organization, but it also fundamentally needs interdependence among individuals (Ehrenberg 2010, 344). In fact, the belief in freedom simply results from the plurality and complexity of the contemporary social actor's socialization, which makes it difficult to have a sense of the existing social determinism (Lahire 2011, 207). Responding to those who seem to think that determinism equates passivity, Lahire (p. 206) reminds that, on the contrary, social determinism necessarily entails an active and personal involvement from individuals: "To be resolutely *determined* to commit this or that action is a common way of feeling and living the social determinisms of which we are the product." The next chapter illustrates Lahire's claim by investigating the active appropriation of exotic religious resources in relation to individuals' social positions and trajectories.

7

Religious Exoticism and the "New Petite Bourgeoisie"

THE PRECEDING CHAPTERS emphasized that exotic religious resources are popularized as authentic and efficient means to manage emotions and attitudes, in relation to an increasingly pervasive ideal of self-realization. This ideal, while desired by social actors, also reflects increasingly strong demands of autonomy and flexibility made upon them. Thus, exotic religious resources, along with other religious and therapeutic techniques, contribute to the wider trend of the psychologization of contemporary social life. This last chapter of the book discusses *who* actually uses exotic religious teachings and the role they play in specific social and professional trajectories. I draw on Bourdieu's (1987) assumption that salvation goods tend to express the temporal interests and concerns of the specific social categories of individuals that a religious movement targets, the conditions of its success being harmony between these interests and its message. It already has been suggested that exotic religious resources may be used to perform gender roles; this chapter presents social class as a determinant of patterns of bricolage. Like other religious and therapeutic resources, exotic ones are appropriated as techniques enhancing middle-class emotional competence. Yet the exotic character of religious resources such as yoga, meditation, or Kabbalah finds its significance in relation to the cultural competence of the new petite bourgeoisie.

Exotic Religious Resources, "Spirituality" and a "Dream of Social Flying"

This section describes the ways in which the teachings of neo-Hindu movements and the Kabbalah Centre resonate with their members' social and professional aspirations. The critical stance toward a materialistic and meaningless society, and strong aspirations of self-fulfillment and freedom are discourses that express a desire for emancipation from the social constraints that characterize the lives of an educated yet dominated fringe of the middle class, unable to reach the position of the upper class and anxious to distinguish itself from strata below.

Self-Realization, Fortune, and Fame

First and foremost, it is necessary to recognize the variations in the ways in which individuals make use of exotic resources for their self-realization, in part because they follow religious teachings that envisage differently the material benefits implied by self-realization. For instance, while this-worldliness affects all religious traditions in secularizing societies, neo-Hinduism is slightly ambivalent regarding prosperity and socio-professional success. To be sure, some movements, such as Transcendental Meditation, developed management courses and seminars in order to outreach to professionals. It was also noted that the discourses of Maharishi Mahesh Yogi and Rajneesh are in tune with capitalist societies through their emphasis on individual freedom and responsibility (Prashad 2000, 62; Urban 1996). Deepak Chopra, author of bestsellers such as *Creating Affluence* (1993) and *Seven Spiritual Laws of Success* (1997), offers programs that teach how to maximize one's potential and develop leadership skills, alongside other Indian-born management thinkers who refer to Hindu concepts and scriptures in the American corporate world. This is what Engardio (2006) calls "karma capitalism." Yet, even Deepak Chopra (cited in Zimmerman 2009) warns against fortune and fame as ultimate goals: more important is "the ability to love and have compassion," "be in touch with the creative source inside you," and "ultimately move from success to significance." By and large, neo-Hinduism draws on Advaita Vedanta, which is originally other-worldly; it treats the world as an illusion (*maya*), which one needs to renounce in order to realize the divine absolute. This ambivalence is illustrated by Sivananda's (1950) book, *How to Become Rich*, which addresses

> the development of certain virtues which will enable one to increase his earning capacity and to become a self-made man. Some qualities of one's character that will help him to win friends, to develop his power of observation, some suggestions to start business, the role of agriculture and industry in the business-life and the ways of making best use of money are also explained.

Yet Sivananda warns that the book "does not exclusively relate to material prosperity. For, if it does so, there can be no permanent value to it—not at all worthy of aspiration to a really intelligent person." In fact, Sivananda explicitly presents wealth and professional success as preliminary and secondary effects of religious practice, which "prepares [the reader] for a life of absolute self-restraint and complete renunciation or a life entirely devoted to the attainment of the supreme goal, Self-realization." Overall, the psychologization of the teachings of Siddha Yoga and the Sivananda Centres instigated an emphasis on personal fulfillment in this world; at the same time, however, an other-worldly asceticism is embodied by the monastic life in the ashram, the value of selfless and volunteer work from all students, and a religious elite (gurus and swamis) who renounce family life and material possessions. It is probably fair to say that Buddhism, through its approach to desire and attachment as the roots of suffering, similarly limits the importance of wealth, fortune, and fame for the realization of the self.

By contrast, the Kabbalah Centre belongs to those movements that have little inhibition in relation to professional and financial success. On the contrary: "spirituality" does entail very inner-worldly benefits:

> Realize that wealth does not need to be less spiritual than prayer, meditation, or any other tool that we've given you. A spiritual person can also be wealthy. A spiritual person can have physical things. A spiritual person doesn't have to be a person who is homeless or with no material possession. (Kabbalah Centre 2007a, CD20)

The Kabbalah Centre places no value on having an ascetic lifestyle. Money is desirable: it is seen as "energy" given by the Creator. The desire for money is, in fact, believed to be a desire to receive Light. Students are therefore invited to "recognize the spiritual potential of money." Some of the movement's courses aim to teach how to "harness this force and profit from it in our world"[1] by applying Kabbalistic tools. The "spiritual" value placed on material and professional achievements in the Kabbalah Centre is well illustrated by the London branch's network called Business Gym Global Foundation. The aim of this network is to teach Kabbalah to "members at any business level" through "monthly seminars, transformational courses, and interactive workshops," so that they can "learn, exchange ideas and forge new business relationships" (London Kabbalah Centre 2011). Thus, in these special courses that reflect the Kabbalah Centre's endeavor to attract successful individuals and meet their expectations, teachers insist on the fact that one can only maximize wealth and sustainability by respecting the "spiritual laws of the universe."

Spirituality and a Dominated Fraction of the Middle Class

This short preliminary explains why members of neo-Hindu movements tend to understand "spirituality" as the opposite to materialism, while students of the Kabbalah Centre generally tend not to (although the latter would agree with the idea that the material world is transcended by higher values and principles). As a consequence, we find in neo-Hindu movements individuals who see self-realization as a form of emancipation from the pursuit of material wealth and careerism. The worldview of these individuals underlines that discourses on "spirituality" and self-realization have to do with social positioning. "If you got involved in *yoga* I think it would make you see the pointlessness of just wanting to make more and more and more money," says Barbara, a teacher of English. Colin, 45, worked as a nautical engineer, which he learned on the job, after a degree in philosophy from Oxford University. More attracted by the artistic milieu, Colin now composes music and lives off private music lessons. Colin explained how he believes his involvement in Siddha Yoga changed the way he envisaged his future and his ambitions in life:

> It kind of undermined it. It just made me question more and more, investigate more and more deeply what is it based on what is the foundation, that is a notion or a concept you have about yourself, what is the foundation for it. I would see other people quite happily pursuing, money or careers, or getting on with making their life better, but from the perspective of what I had been shown it all seemed to me to be kind of ridiculous. Not that it is really ridiculous, it's quite natural, but it seemed from...that perspective, it seemed meaningless. They live very conventional lives with careers and houses and families and mortgages.

Several neo-Hindu disciples express a rejection of consumerism, professional ambitions, competition, mass production, and standardization encouraged by capitalism. These are perceived by them as corrupt, illusory, and as constituting a recipe for enslavement. The derogatory references to driving a "big flashy car" or having a mortgage were persistent among these interviewees: "I don't believe in owning a car," says a member of Siddha Yoga. Christophe, also from Siddha Yoga, criticizes materialist individuals' desire to "have a bimbo as wife, a beautiful car, dough and so on."

Instead, these interviewees give precedence to a quest for aesthetics, authenticity, freedom, peace, and loving interpersonal relations. This is where orientalism becomes highly significant: the Mystical East embodies a form of nostalgia for an authentic and spiritual world, which is contrasted with consumerist and capitalistic societies. Others express a form of romanticism, celebrating nature and traditional societies. Éric, 31, is an IT technician practicing yoga at the Sivananda Centre in Paris. With the industrial revolution, science, and materialism, Éric believes contemporary society threw out the baby with the bath water, abandoning folklore and religion. The result is, for Éric, an absence of ethics, a society in which lying, killing, or manipulating others is accepted to reach one's ends—a society epitomized by *American Psycho* (Bret Easton Ellis's novel). Thus, Éric explains that he meditates to improve himself but also to emancipate himself from "cravings that do not come from me but from outside: you have to study, you have to have a good job, you have to have a good salary etc. All of this." "And if we meditate or have other practices that are a sort of cocoon out of all this," continues Éric, "it enables you to have a sort of inner strength in the end…which I think allows you to be much more resistant to social pressure." We now grasp another aspect of the opposition that is made between spirituality, inner self, and authenticity, on the one hand, and institutions, norms, illusion, and modernity, on the other hand: for some, this opposition expresses a resistance toward social expectations that were described in the preceding chapter.

Moreover, the opposition between "spirituality" and a rejected "materialism" among these neo-Hindus captures something about their social positioning. This is suggested by, first, the fact that this opposition implicitly involves a self-identification with "spirituality" and the association of "others" with the meaningless car and mortgage; and second, by the expression of feelings of being "different," slightly isolated, or "not fitting," suggesting the position of individuals who are *déclassés*. Françoise, 26, studied economics. She has not been able to complete her studies for health reasons; she suffered from depression because she was unsuccessful in the milieu of the theater. She joined Sahaja Yoga after trying Tibetan Buddhism for a few weeks. She now works for the French tax office, which she sees as a boring but also alienating occupation, as illustrated by her description of a training session she attended in her workplace:

> They made us play with a giant monopoly game with accountings. One does not need to be Einstein to understand accounting. That being said, then, as I was watching the others do, there was something which for me was completely meaningless. It was something very spiritual, whereas the others were really involved in this game…Then I thought, really you're not like them! For me it's totally meaningless, and really

I think we're very different.... I always have been branded as being eccentric, ok. So of course I watched as a spectator and I have not always understood... I have no sense of money, but really none. None.

Françoise then refers to people she knows who "changed" and became ruthlessly ambitious, whereas she said she "studied to experience unemployment," suggesting in her case a perception of distinct socio-professional trajectories. In other words, the emphasis on different values (ethics and spirituality versus ambitions and greed), used to differentiate oneself from "others," denotes a discourse about social positioning.

Aspirations of emancipation from social constraints and pressures are also found among those who seem to have more successful careers. Andrew is a manager in the banking sector who practices yoga in the London Sivananda Centre:

I work for an investment bank, which is obviously an environment entirely and utterly dominated by the pursuit of money. By the pursuit of material things, and when I first joined there... I was telling myself "I love it," but could I really have loved it, when I was getting so much stress and disappointment?... Career, yeah! It's something, once again, it's told to you from the day you're born, isn't it. This is the most important thing, the career, you've got to have a career, you've got to support your family, you've got to have money for your old days, you've got to do this, and you've got to do that, and it's told to you by your parents, by your teachers, by your friends, by television, by radio, by everything. You walk in the streets, and you see a billboard that says, "drive this car," "brush your teeth with this toothpaste," everything, it's all built around these material aspects, and it's what keeps society moving.... And so it's discouraged to, you're actually discouraged to look inside of yourself.

Andrew's discourse may seem relatively banal, but what is highly significant is, first, the ways in which exotic religious resources are used here to claim alternative values that oppose mainstream ones; and second, the fact that some individuals make new choices of lifestyle and profession in relation to their religious practice and values. This is a crucial issue that the chapter will explore in detail. During the interview, Andrew was thinking about leaving his current job to create a "yoga bar" or an ashram for yoga retreats and courses. A year after the interview, he indeed left for India to practice yoga in depth.

Theses discourse express a general desire for social emancipation by neo-Hindu disciples, despite having different socio-professional trajectories. Jean clearly expresses this desire of "social flying," as Bourdieu (1984, 370) put it, to describe countercultural practices, when I asked what self-realization meant to him: "not being subjected to the rules of material life for a start," he responded, through "an understanding that goes beyond the everyday life." In other words, the "spiritual" is perceived as a means to transcend the social constraints of this world. Jean, a manager in the private sector and an active member of the Siddha Yoga Parisian branch, explains being torn between a desire of "spiritual renunciation" and strong professional ambitions. Lionel, also a French Siddha Yoga member and a manager, considers that his "spiritual involvement" was something fundamental he could draw on, giving him courage and discernment about what he wanted to do or not in his professional life. Lionel describes choices he made in relation to values "which were not driven by material interest," "dictated by external references," or influenced by social representations of success, power, or money. This led him, Lionel explains, to renounce posts with high-level responsibilities. The trajectory of Elena is different, yet she shares with Jean, Lionel, and the other interviewees cited in this section this desire of social emancipation. Involved in Siddha Yoga, Elena is 35; she is Brazilian and has lived in London for 10 years. Previously a swimming teacher, she took massage courses to become a therapist. Currently unable to live off this activity, she works as a cashier in an organic shop. For her, the realization of the self is about accepting not having fulfilled professional ambitions.

> Something in me relaxed a bit more, in terms of expectations from life. My priority now, is not to succeed in whatever. I've never been ambitious, anyway, but, it just helped my mind to, to ease off a bit, not to worry so much about the things that I used to before....It hasn't changed my professional plans or projects, no. But it made me more peaceful, regarding them. I've not been so hard on myself, like I used to be before, and also accepting my own person more....It made me realize that all those years that I felt lost, and *not fitting*, it was okay, because, the answer's here and now. So I can breathe, and go on....It's not that I'm...not working or anything. I'm doing my job and doing my work as usual, but it's not my priority. I want to do it the best I can, but I'm saving my energy in this [spiritual] search.

A common approach among these interviewees is to express a distance from working life, professional ambitions, and material comfort as unfulfilling and alienating. They contrast these aims with self-realization, happiness, finding one's true self, and the "spiritual." In the light of these discourses of acceptance and renunciation, one could wonder whether, in some cases, it is *because* social and professional expectations were unfulfilled that these individuals, who are usually highly educated, turned to alternative priorities. It is a thorny issue, since the language of choice (i.e., I *decided* not to devote myself to a career) conceals potential structural constraints. Yet the sociology of work can help us to grasp this identification with a "spiritual" life-style detached from professional and material ambitions. For instance, Dubar (2000, 243–257) sees the de-valorization of one's occupation, the rejection of professional identity, combined with personal dedication to eclectic types of training and extra-professional projects, as an indicator of downward mobility. In short, such social actors may seek to realize an identity perceived as true and authentic, uprooted from the usual social and professional markers. This understanding sheds new light on what Christophe, for instance, a French disciple of Siddha Yoga, expresses when he discusses "materiality":

> A mystical person, who is a little bit detached from materiality and so on...knows that his appearance, his social position, having a beautiful car, beautiful children and to do well is secondary. It's not that important...he knows perfectly well that he is not this situation, this car etc. you see, that he should not identify with that. Because all of this is ephemeral, and there are things that are more essential than that and which are, precisely, eternal.

Christophe, 28, currently works as a shop assistant; he completed a master's degree in philosophy. A year after being interviewed, he enrolled for a research degree, despite what he regarded as academia's "puerile intellectualism," which he contrasted with spirituality's ability to change the self day after day. In other words, we could understand his involvement in Siddha Yoga as a refusal to identify with social markers of success—the car, the nuclear family, the career that he does not have access to, despite his high educational capital. The reference to mysticism, to "real" personal change through "spiritual" practice and to what is "eternal" thus encapsulates Christophe's desire to transcend these social markers which pinned him down in a mildly satisfying trajectory at the time of the interview. Religious values indeed seem to play an important part in ways of thinking about one's social position. "For two years, I was unemployed since I was in Sahaja Yoga; qualifications, the working life, having a profession, all of this was becoming secondary" explained Monique. As I asked her whether, before this, having a career was important, Monique replied that social achievement and recognition through her professional life and social relations were crucial, but "this spiritual revelation totally modified...Completely reversed my values," she added.

Thus, these individuals' detachment from their professional and material ambitions is hardly an expression of rejection of the world;[2] in fact, very few of students of yoga and meditation choose to devote themselves completely to these teachings and live in an ashram. Rather, it seems to reflect the social positioning of individuals who are "déclassés," that is to say, those having a high cultural and educational capital that is not translated in their material achievements. They accordingly express a desire to raise themselves "above" an unfulfilling position. Indeed, as we shall see, many of them wish to have more creative and vocational occupations, thereby expressing a desire of upward mobility. Socio-professional trajectories are nonetheless diverse: the cultural and financial capitals of some of these educated middle-class individuals suggest that, as we shall see further on, they modify their lifestyle and sometimes renounce material comfort to pursue what they see as higher goals, precisely because they can afford to do so. This chapter will also show that in many cases, individuals use exotic religious resources with the aim of optimizing their working life.

This section underlines that, overall, the realization of the self is not a desire unrelated to issues of social positioning. And this is far from being an emancipation from the social, as the paradigm of spirituality suggests. On the contrary, it is precisely a discourse about social position and mobility, a desire of "social flying" shared by neo-Hindu and Kabbalistic students alike. I was deeply struck by Patrick's response regarding yoga's Hindu origins: dismissive, he explained that he "took whatever means" he found (before yoga, Patrick was involved in the Rosicrucian movement, the Sri Chinmoy Centre, and Zen Buddhism). Patrick summarized the logic of his explorations as such: "whatever ladder, as long as it goes up, is good for me." In other words, it is less the nature of the means than the end—an ascension—that matters. "Climbing the ladder of yoga" was also an expression used by an interviewee from London, underscoring the notion of ascension implied by personal "growth" and "development," learning, "actualization" or "realization" of the self. This is one of the reasons that the quest of exotic religious resources and, more generally, "spiritual techniques" for the realization of the self resonate with the expectations of middle-class individuals, whose self is characterized by mobility and improvability (Skeggs 2004).

Indeed, the middle classes are highly sensitive to anticipatory or retrospective socialization. Their members act less in accordance with their present situation than with the one to which they aspire to belong or with the one they came from and to which they would like to return (Touraine 2005). Most of the interviewees in the neo-Hindu movements and the Kabbalah Centre are from the urban middle classes; artisans, farmers, and manual workers are absent, with the exception of Catherine, a case we will explore in depth further on. A majority have been to university; a third of neo-Hindu disciples have a master's degree. More than half of disciples of neo-Hindu movements, in France and England, work in liberal professions (communication and advertising, design, entertainment) and management, while others are often self-employed, mainly in artistic activities or in the field of alternative therapies. The profiles of the Kabbalah Centre students are similar. Those who refuse to identify with their current professions and material conditions often have technical and administrative occupations (IT and engineering, secretarial jobs, and accounting). They thus aspire to pursue more vocational, creative, or meaningful activities in the artistic domain but also, significantly, as providers of post-psychoanalytic and holistic therapies. These activities often involve working as freelancers in competitive fields, and rarely provide material wealth and security. To survive in such avant-garde and unregulated milieus, individuals need to constantly renew their skills and reinvent themselves— hence the significance of an endless "work" to actualize oneself. In other words, the users of exotic religious resources tend to belong to an educated but dominated fraction of the middle classes (it would be rare to meet a lawyer or a surgeon in these movements, for instance). Some strive to remain in this fraction, while others aspire to reach it; they then disinvest their current occupation to identify with their "spiritual" practice, which, in some cases, involves a new lifestyle (living in an ashram or in the Kabbalah Centre; trying to live off alternative therapy). In other words, "spirituality" *talks* of social mobility. The remainder of this chapter looks at how this quest for mobility through exotic religious resources is concretized in various trajectories.

Long-Term and Short-Term Breaks

This exploration of various socio-professional trajectories starts with those whose desire for "social flying" leads them to become full-time members of new religious movements (swamis, teachers, and "staffs"), thereby renouncing professional activity. This is clearly the most radical detachment of the social game, which represents a minority of individuals using exotic religious resources. Most full-time volunteers joined Siddha Yoga, the Sivananda Centres, and the Kabbalah Centre as young adults, either before entering the labor market or shortly after, in what they describe as a period of transition. After studying engineering and specializing in renewable energies, Lydia realized that she did not want to work in this domain and dreamed of going to India, influenced by the travel stories of some of her friends. It is there that she discovered the Sivananda Centres' ashram, where she stayed three months. Six months later, Lydia left France again to live in this Indian ashram for a year and a half. She is now a brahmacharya (those preparing to become swamis) in the Paris Sivananda Centre and "works on people's energy" instead, because "big French companies, no, that was not for me," she says. Guillaume also joined the Sri Chinmoy Parisian centre as a full-time member after his studies:

> I had absolutely nothing in my life anymore, I mean I was seeking a job [as sales representative] normally but a month and a half before [joining the Sri Chinmoy Centre] I had stopped to look for work because I really felt that something was not right. I felt that I had to give up, I had to let things go, so I had nothing else in my life...I looked for work but I really felt that really it was not right, people I met found me interesting but they were feeling I was not made for that....On 10 interviews for a job none invited me for a second interview...There was really a gap. No, I didn't want to.

Like Lydia and Guillaume, other highly committed members shared feelings of inadequacy or evoked unfulfilled expectations (a breakup with a partner is sometimes also evoked as part of this transitional phase). Teachers and *chevre* of the Kabbalah Centre follow a similar pattern. Most were in their twenties when they became full-time volunteers; they had completed higher education courses (a significant number studied computing or engineering) but did not work or did so for a relatively short period of time. In Israel, the completion of military service is a crucial turning point, after which some volunteers joined the Kabbalah Centre:

> For me it was during my BA studies. I studied social behavior and communication and I was working in a research institute but I felt like I was missing something you know? Like I'm there at the moment working, studying, I had my plans to go to do my Master....So I had this plan but I didn't feel attached to it you know? It was only on paper you know. And here in Israel it's like you finish the army and go do your trip somewhere like in the Far East, I decided to go to the United States, you study and then you go to work, you marry and have kids, that's about the...So I had a plan [laughs] but it didn't feel like it was coming

from the deepest you know, my deepest desires or that my soul was really there. (Noa, full-time volunteer of the Tel Aviv Kabbalah Centre)

The cases of full-time members are the most radical and least representative of all interviewees' trajectories. Less extreme, a good number of interviewees chose to undertake long travels, for several months or even years, expressing a similar desire to emancipate themselves from a social and professional context, which they describe as meaningless or alienating. For neo-Hindus, India is the favorite destination, not the least because ashrams facilitate long stays. Because of its transnational branches, the Kabbalah Centre offers a similar possibility for its full-time volunteers and teachers. An IT Engineer, Léonard took a sabbatical year to travel, in order to take some distance from his professional life, which dissatisfied him, and to find meaning in his life.

(I felt) that what we were doing had no meaning, work itself, running after buying stuff, even buying a house, all this . . . So I needed to make a break because I couldn't feel, I couldn't see where I was going. . . . It's not the material level which fulfills me.

Léonard spent five months in India; there he became interested in meditation, and visited Aurobindo's ashram. Back in France, he changed his lifestyle, described as not overworking, but to enjoy life more despite a dissatisfying job, and therefore try to "be more detached" in relation to it. Léonard explains that yoga and meditation, which he practices several times a week at the Sivananda Centre, help him to relax and to be more detached in relation to his working life. Eileen was working in computing before making a year-long world tour, including nine months in Asia, accompanied by readings on "Eastern philosophies." This was when she started thinking about giving up her occupation: "the traveling was important because certainly my perspectives on the world were changing and then perhaps that made me a little bit more open when I came back." On her return to Britain, she gave up computing and trained in energetic massages, which she currently provides in a psychiatric hospital. It is also in this period that she discovered Siddha Yoga. Thus, Eileen's trajectory typically combines interest in Asian religions and the pursuit of self-fulfillment through a career shift, from a technical domain to alternative therapies. Helen's case is similar in this regard. Helen practices yoga at the London Sivananda Centre. Having a post of high responsibility in a public relations company, she decided to leave her job to live in Kenya, a desire she discovered as she was meditating.

I thought, "I'm going to go to Kenya and live in Kenya, I'm going to give up my job." It all just fitted into place so brilliantly and that's how I know you can have in life whatever you want.... I had a very good job, I suppose and clients had to be told and it was all terribly dramatic and everybody thought I was mad to do it, some told me and some didn't, but I was going to do this, I had to do it. And to this day I have no regrets on doing it. It was a real goal and it was what I wanted to do and everything fell in to place like a jigsaw.... I rented this flat out, it was the income from this flat that I lived on, but it was never quite enough, I'd been used to the good life, I had lunch with clients every day of the week, very successful person but it wasn't what I wanted to do.

When Helen came back to Britain after living in Kenya, she did not attempt to go back to her previous career. She prefers to have a part-time job that pays the rent and "gets by until things change":

I think I realized I could do what I wanted to do and not what was ex-pected of me, that it was up to me what I do and I don't have to worry about what the neighbors think or making waves—all the things I'd been brought up with.... I didn't want to do that job again. I didn't want a high powered job and I don't think I would get a high powered job and I'm completely out of touch for those sort of jobs so that's fine. I know the responsibilities that go with those sorts of jobs and I don't want that. Very stressful, been there, done that, seen the video, worn the t-shirt!

Traveling allowed Eileen and Helen to initiate changes in their professional life according to new priorities. Helen's example suggests that it is not neces-sarily people who have no professional future who seek social emancipation; they rather sacrifice technical or technocratic occupations as well as material comfort for a life that is hoped to be more meaningful and fulfilling. Yet risks are limited: they also have the financial and cultural capitals to do so. Helen has probably a large social network that can help her find a job and she also owns her own apartment, which limits her income needs. Similarly, Eileen's world tour and retraining in a new field implies the ownership of resources (we can assume that Léonard's frustration resulted from his current inability to make similar changes). In short, these middle-class trajectories of eman-cipation entail potential sacrifices, yet without the risk of being excluded or marginalized. These individuals seem to deliberately choose instability and to nurture a "withdrawal from economic necessity" (Bourdieu 1984, 54), a characteristic of the bourgeoisie who have the financial and cultural means to make this sort of choice.

Professional Reorientations as Projects of the Self

The desire of social emancipation, as Eileen's case above suggested, is often translated in professional reorientations. Again, it is important to stress that it is not the constrained change of profession that is often the fate of unskilled workers. Interviewees often express the desire to leave technical, managerial, commercial, or technocratic jobs for activities in the artistic and alternative milieus (holistic therapies, personal growth, coaching). And many have done so. While we cannot be sure that the commitment to specific religious teachings was the turning point for such career changes, interviewees significantly draw on the values and practices of the Sivananda Centres, Siddha Yoga, and the Kabbalah Centre to justify and accompany these reorientations in less secure and less profitable occupations. Patrick started yoga for health reasons before he discovered yoga's "spiritual" side after three or four years of practice. Practicing (and teaching) yoga five times a week, he now defines his "profound motivation" as "spirituality, the spiritual and concrete benefits of asanas [yoga postures]" for his "personal development," which is about his new occupation. Patrick evokes his past professional ambitions, his desire to "become someone," yet having occupied important posts did not make him happy; Patrick has now become an artist and storyteller. Colin, who left nautical engineering to become a composer, draws on neo-Hinduism's asceticism to deal with his lack of material comfort and security.

> I live on a boat, I keep my life simple in that sense. But there is a sacrifice involved. Because I look at my friends and they have got long term careers and plans and financial commitment, but the security they imagine they've got I don't think is real anyway.... I know there is no real security in that, so I tend not to look for it so much. So in that sense I've seen people pursue those goals and those aims and in the end it doesn't work. Things happen, life can be quite ruthless.

Similarly, Pierre, a musician and composer, worked with some of the most famous filmmakers and acquired substantial wealth. However, he decided to stop doing so in order to write music for himself. Pierre says yoga helped him in this decision. Talking about his impressive Parisian loft in which the interview took place, like Colin he evokes the sacrifice of prosperity in the pursuit of self-fulfillment, the reality of such goals contrasting with the illusory nature of material comfort:

I don't have work at all, see I have to sell my beautiful house. But it's true that yoga teaches me to accept to renounce a commodity which is plaster, stone, metal and, as beautiful as it is, it will never make me as happy as the freedom that it can give me because I will be able to sell it for a very high price and, somehow, be free. But I have to renounce it you see.... For now I don't have an impressive audience, but whatever, I mean I create a belief for myself; I go in a direction that seems to me to be right for me.

For several interviewees, the artistic milieu represents an ideal of creativity, a personal quest of self, and the transcendence of economic and institutional constraints. Virginie, who practices yoga in Paris, explains that she chose to work as a freelance filmmaker, by refusal of constraints and the impossibility for her "to go to work everyday." Practices such as yoga and meditation accompany a renouncement of career and material comfort for an ideal of freedom and self-realization (yet again, let's not forget that Pierre's, Colin's, and Virginia's career changes presuppose financial, social, and cultural capitals). As we will see further on, the Kabbalah Centre's success-oriented teaching does not support renouncement and sacrifices; it is nevertheless used by individuals who, similarly, look for fulfillment in their professional life. Thus, for many interviewees, self-realization finds its meaning through more vocational and creative professions. Elisa believes that yoga involved a radical change of lifestyle for her. She spent six weeks in India practicing yoga and visiting ashrams, a period during which she decided to stop working in the entertainment industry in public relations (a "superficial milieu" which she found frustrating). Now teaching dance, Elisa says: "my activity is only dance and yoga, in other words what I've always dreamed of." The use of exotic religious tools is particularly relevant: their emphasis on personal fulfillment encourages and legitimates the quest for professional careers that become "projects of the self."

Accordingly, freedom, as Colin's and Pierre's examples suggest, entails a more independent but also less secure activity. The relative indeterminacy of these professional activities therefore suggests that freedom is for them a subjective value rather than an objective situation, since these providers of cultural goods and services depend on the demands of a rather unpredictable market that requires constant newness. In other words, we need to be cautious of social actors' discourse about their professional activities. Claims of freedom do not entail objective liberation from social and economic constraints. The research conducted by Korbe (forthcoming) on individuals who become full-time teachers of yoga in France and Estonia underscores the pressures exerted on these self-employed workers in a competitive market. She also observes that yoga teachers who created their own studio had often been professionals, and therefore were able to draw on their previous professional network and skills (in communication, management, finance) to create their new activity, which for some becomes a new business venture. In other words, discourses of professional breaks should not be taken for granted either.

A significant number of interviewees undertake a quest of emancipation and self-realization in the milieus of holistic therapies and personal growth. I met Martine at a Kabbalah Centre course in Paris. She was a secretary before working in sales and training. Martine believes that it is when she joined the Rosicrucian movement that she realized her desire to have a more fulfilling professional activity. It is while meditating that the word "sophrology" came up: Martine decided to undertake such training, 15 years ago. At 52, she now works full-time as a therapist in Paris, practicing sophrology, massage, rebirth. and reiki. She had to keep her previous job on a part-time basis for a while—this is quite common among alternative therapists, due to the difficulty of making a living from this activity. Martine indeed describes the development of this new activity as a struggle. Yet, she emphasizes her refusal to remain in her previous professional activity, which entails renouncing material comfort:

I don't want to work in this society, I really don't feel like it....I see people who are suffering from depression, either they are overworked, or they are subjected to more abuse, I mean, this is despicable. I find this society despicable. We don't treat people like humans anymore. So I don't want that. I'd rather look after those who are not going well. Even if I don't roll on money, I don't roll on money but that's not important, it is enough for me. I prefer this than entering a system that really sucks.

Similarly, Warrier's (2008, 5) study of British students of Ayurveda indicates that those who decide to work in alternative therapies express "frustration with stressful experiences at work and the desire for a change of profession, the search for alternative lifestyles, the desire to become healers."

More than a quarter of students of the Kabbalah Centre, Sivananda Centre, and Siddha Yoga whom I have interviewed in Britain and France are trained in alternative therapeutic techniques, which they provide as a full-time or part-time activity. This is not surprising: I outlined that these religious movements share with these practices a very similar ethos around the realization of the self (Chapter 5), which explains that many students of yoga, meditation, and Kabbalah have explored alternative forms of therapies and personal growth (Chapter 2). Besides, as we will see further on, for some individuals

the exploration of a wide range of techniques for the realization of the self contributes to the development of highly transferable skills between "spiritual"
and "professional" activities, boundaries of which become blurred. When
Lucy, a disciple of Siddha Yoga in London, discovered yoga, she decided to
change radically her lifestyle and profession. A hairdresser, she became an
aromatherapist and she practices massage, reflexology, and reiki on clients. In
such a competitive, diverse, and unregulated field, one might need to diversify
(and renew) skills to sustain activities, like Martine and Lucy.

Professional reorientations in the teaching of yoga, holistic therapies, and
personal growth predominantly concern female students of neo-Hindu movements and the Kabbalah Centre. This reflects the fact that by and large, the
professionals in these alternative milieus and in health care in general are
mostly women, usually well-educated individuals (Ceccomori 1995; Nissen
2011; Wootton and Sparber 2001). For a start, women's involvement in these
activities can be explained by their particular relationships with care and the
management of emotions (Hochschild 1983: 163). Indeed, female interviewees insist on the importance of developing loving and nurturing attitudes
as part of their self-realization (which is encouraged by the Kabbalistic and
neo-Hindu teachings they are involved with): becoming a therapist is a way for
some to achieve this aim. Flesch (2010, 21) notes that students and teachers of
complementary alternative therapies tend to perceive women as "innate healers," while "female students consistently noted the caring, nurturing nature
of CAM [complementary and alternative medicine] as the reason it appealed to
women." Ironically, this reminds us that women do not enter the labor market
on the same terms as their male counterparts since their gendered, natural-
ized, identity and attitudes are often part of the work they perform (Adkins
2000; Adkins and Lury 1999; Hochschild 1983). Indeed, "in many senses the
role of therapist, healer or counselor is a continuation of the carer role that
many women will have performed in their private and their working lives"
(Trzebiatowska and Bruce 2012, 74).

Women's investment in alternative therapies also relates to their particular
position in the labor market. Engaged in multiple and simultaneous tasks
and responsibilities, women are often disadvantaged in their career, for they
cannot always match men's commitment to paid employment. Thus "the
ways in which women attempt to negotiate the clock time of work with domestic labour, is evident in the higher proportion of women opting for flexible working arrangements" (Odih 2007, 182). Alternative therapies require
a short and accessible training, and allow a flexible (sometimes home-based)
activity that one can exercise part-time to reconcile domestic work and child
care. It may constitute a modest, complementary source of income in the

household (Flesch 2010; Nissen 2011). Cécile, a 64-year-old housewife, follows the Kabbalah Centre's teaching in London but also practiced yoga in the London Sivananda Centres. She started to use the Alexander technique when she was 43 because of personal health issues. She then trained in this technique, and started to teach it in a center for yoga and alternative therapies. When I asked why she started at that period in her life, she mentioned that at the time her "children were raised" and at school, leaving her spare time. Other female interviewees explained that they started to teach yoga when their children began to go to school, emphasizing that they wanted to be able to share quality time with them.

Alternative therapies may also be sought by women as a way to attempt to gain autonomy and social status. Ceccomori (1995, 937) notes, for example, that in France the majority of yoga teachers are women without professions. This is similar to the religious field to a certain extent. Obadia (1999, 193) explains the feminization of Buddhism, or women's important role and responsibilities in French Buddhist centers, as resulting from their marginalization in the professional sphere; they would therefore seek other sources of fulfillment and recognition in civil society. Women's quest for status in informal or peripheral social spaces is not new, as shown by various nineteenth-century examples: the important number of female mediums (Edelman 1995); the remarkable role of working-class women as Methodist preachers in Britain and of middle-class women in the Genevan revival in Switzerland (Campiche 1997, 332); lay women's active involvement in philanthropic activities under the patronage of religious institutions (Brown 2001, 59); and the extraordinary growth of female congregations in nineteenth-century France and their involvement with children, the sick, and the poor (Fouilloux 1995, 321). However, alternative therapies or the teaching of yoga are not necessarily "empowering," as claimed by Sointu and Woodhead (2008) and Nissen (2011). To begin,

> women choose careers in CAM because of financial and biological constraints not necessarily experienced by their male counterparts, and remain constrained in their educational choices by the lack of financial resources and societal support to pursue more extensive medical training, particularly in Western medicine. (Flesch 2010, 24)

Furthermore, as suggested above, by their emphasis on care, they represent one more way to fulfill gender roles rather than confronting them. Because it is difficult to fully live off alternative therapies, they also potentially reinforce women's dependence on male income. Finally, these career choices maintain women in peripheral health care professions, not only in relation to the male-dominated profession of doctors (Miles 1991, 121). Indeed, research on alternative therapies suggests that women predominate in the holistic therapies that are more marginal (e.g., herbal medicine, reiki), by contrast with those that are more legitimate, science-oriented, and full-time, such as chiropractic and osteopathy, which draw a higher number of men (Nissen 2011, 191). The increasing alignment of alternative practices with Western medical models of education, practice, and research has the effect of marginalizing women on the fringes of already peripheral holistic techniques. Thus, perhaps in continuity with women's traditional relation to folk medicine, "the very qualities of CAM that make it an alternative to conventional medicine are, paradoxically, the same qualities that lock women into caring roles devalued by society and by the medical profession, and which render them glorified auxiliaries to their biomedical physician counterparts" (Flesch 2007, 170).

Exotic Religious Resources, Emotional Competence, and the Middle Classes

The quest for self-realization denotes an aspiration of social emancipation through non-conventional types of lifestyle and occupations that escape the usual social classifications. Exotic religious resources' emphasis on self-realization represents an incentive to make those choices. They are also appropriated as knowledge and skills that are transferable from the "spiritual" domain to professional life—hence the emphasis on the applicability of these "tools" (Chapter 5). Unsurprisingly, interviewees evoke the ways in which yoga, meditation, or Kabbalah enhance their emotional and relational skills, which, in turn, contribute positively to their working life. As we shall see further on, these soft skills are more relevant to middle-class professionals. This section also explores cases in which the transferability of skills and knowledge is so direct that the professional and the "spiritual" are in symbiosis in individuals' lives. It concerns those who work in the field of personal growth, post-psychoanalytic and holistic therapies, and who in fact represent a significant number of students of neo-Hindu movements and the Kabbalah Centre. Thus, their participation in a wide range of course and events should not be considered as a "journey," but rather a continuous re-skilling of individuals who are often freelancers in competitive and unregulated markets of cultural and symbolic resources.

Self-Improvement as Enhancement of
Professional Skills

As suggested in the two preceding chapters, the use of exotic religious resources contributes to the endeavor to develop personal resilience, autonomy, and flexibility. I insisted on how the incentive of realizing the self was seen as beneficial to the organization of work and society. This can only occur because social actors find this aim of self-actualization desirable: interviewees evoke an ability to deal with the pressures and difficulties in the workplace which, in their view, is linked to the application of the teachings of Siddha Yoga, the Sivananda Centres, and the Kabbalah Centre. Patrick, for example, explains that thanks to yoga, he was always serene when working in companies characterized by tensions and conflicts. Now a storyteller, Patrick believes this practice helps him to deal with the constant judgments and criticisms in the milieu of theater. This is for Patrick a definite advantage in a competitive field: "I've seen a lot of people who gave up because of criticisms and as far as I'm concerned it has never hurt me, or even touched me, thanks to this distance." Tina, 29, has been involved in Siddha Yoga for two years after exploring various healing practices and personal growth techniques. She is an actress and has just completed a contract for the Royal Shakespeare Company, yet she would like to work in alternative therapies.

> I would like to have harmony around me. And that job actually had quite a lot of disharmony in terms of the people, even in like my dressing room, there were four of us in there and there was one girl, one woman who we just didn't get on at all, and it was quite hard to be in each other's space a lot of the time. Yes I think Siddha Yoga did help me a lot to stay in my own love, and go, "well there's not that much love out here, but that's fine because I'm in here!" [pointing to herself], whereas I identified a lot more in the past with the outside world and would be thrown more by the ups and downs.

Tina's example suggests that, as underlined previously, individuals try to cope in difficult professional situations by managing their own emotions and adapting to their environment. Feeling good in a competitive, stressful, and uncertain professional environment is shared by many other interviewees. Valérie is involved in Siddha Yoga in Paris. She has worked in a dietetic shop for several years and is very interested in alternative therapies. She practices massage, and trained in neuro-linguistic programming and energetic therapy. She would like to become a therapist herself but currently works as a telemarketing agent to pay the rent. Valérie evokes resilience and acceptation as the benefits of her "spiritual practice" in her current job.

> At work, when I'm precisely confronted to things, that I don't like to do and this is exactly what I'll be given to do.... It wouldn't have happened, I wouldn't have reacted like that before, I would have been shattered, it would have upset me...And now well I say to myself "ok, listen, do it, since"...

Valerie's interview reminds us that what is seen as helpful for social actors (finding ways to accept situations and problems) is also desirable for organizations. Other interviewees explain how they find, in exotic religious resources, a way to deal with the uncertainties of keeping a job or even finding one. One of the founders of the Sri Chinmoy Centre in Paris, who works freelance in advertising, explains that her approach to life makes her confident that she would get work: "the fact of having this path, I have such a distance in relation to this kind of things, I'm so detached, I couldn't care less, I don't feel up against the wall, I have some distance and because of this distance, I'm much more free." Timothy, a disciple of Siddha Yoga in London, works as a broker in a financial firm that has merged twice over the last two years:

> I'm over fifty, now, and I would be the first to go. But I survived the first merges. But this time, I thought, "it doesn't matter, what Gurumayi wants, it's going to happen," and they've taken me on. And all those young people are losing their jobs, lots of people have gone, and there, I'm still there! It's amazing! So obviously Gurumayi wants me to carry on for a year or so, but we'll just see what happens now...

Timothy's case emphasizes that, paradoxically, resilience and coping skills may involve drawing on higher authorities or principles, such as the guru's power and intention. In the Kabbalah Centre, the Light, the power of which is materialized in the Zohar, plays a similar role for some students: they explain keeping the book with them at all times, in particular at work, in difficult moments. Now retired, Rebecca was the secretary of important senior officers in the French civil service. She describes her past work environment as plagued with hatred and jealousy from co-workers, envying each other's positions. She also had, at some point, a very conflicted relationship with her manager. Rebecca says she found help in the teaching of the Kabbalah Centre, first because it encouraged her to see her difficulties as an opportunity to improve herself. She also remembered taking and opening her Zohar book at

work because "there was such negativity" and she "needed to protect myself"
by scanning the letters.

Overall, interviewees describe the enhancement of their emotional skills
through Kabbalah, yoga, or meditation and the resulting improvement of
interpersonal relations in the workplace. Daniel, 28, is French and lives in
London. He practices yoga and meditation at the Sivananda Centres and
works part-time as a steward for Eurostar to dedicate himself to yoga and to
save money to do the Teaching Training Course in India. I would learn, a year
after the interview, that he achieved this project. Daniel links his "spiritual"
practices with his ability to be happy and generate harmonious relations in his
job, when everybody else in the company is "fed up."

> And me I feel real good. And I feel fine, and my contract has been ex-
> tended; I've heard the managers and all that, "I heard about you, you
> get along with everybody"... See, there is a harmony, it's everywhere,
> it's me, it's what I do.

By and large, as mentioned in the previous chapter, emotional and soft
skills have become crucial in a wide range of workplaces. Nonetheless, we
can expect the development of such skills to be particularly relevant for
middle-class occupations. Claire from Siddha Yoga has sought ways of loving
others in "spiritual" teachings (Chapter 6). Working in information technology (IT), she would like to become a reiki therapist. Claire describes difficult
relationships at work. The teaching of Siddha Yoga helps her to remember
that "God is within each of us." The movement's emphasis on selfless service
and devotion also guides her in her interpersonal relations: Claire now understands that conflicts with colleagues may "just" be the game of the ego. "From
the moment I re-center myself in my heart, and I'm in relation to the heart of
the other person, it changes everything," she explains. Rather than participating in conflicts, Claire tries to focus on humility, love, and understanding to
attenuate them. It is often female interviewees who emphasize the development of nurturing and caring attitudes through neo-Hindu and Kabbalistic
teachings, not least because women's occupations often entail the extension
of these gendered attitudes and roles. For instance, two female students of the
Sivananda Centres mentioned how yoga helped them as teachers by encouraging them to be more patient with children. They also explain having developed an understanding of "how the mind works in terms of concentration
and relaxation," and now better consider children's needs in terms of calm
and feelings of safety. Martine is certain that her personal "spiritual" path is
fully mobilized in her professional practice; as a therapist, she tries to comfort

her patients by providing them with "another vision of life which helps them to feel better."

Male interviewees describe the development of similar caring attitudes toward others, yet perhaps more as a way to enhance their managerial skills through less antagonistic behaviors. Jonathan, a sales manager in London and involved in Siddha Yoga, explains how "spiritual teachings" enable him to do so:

> Ten years ago, I was terrible. I knew of only one way of managing, and that was by fear! Getting a life out of them and getting them to work for you. I'm trying to change that....I'm trying to take that competitive edge out of myself, or not the competitiveness, but the aggressiveness with it. I'm trying to be a little bit more understanding, in effect. I mean, I've recently had a problem at work, with someone at work. A person who thinks she is not very good at her job. But I can't expect her to change that. I've got to change, and I've got to change my attitude, in order for us to be able to work together which we have to do! And I'm slowly trying to turn that round, so that I'm not going back to the same attitude towards her....I accept the fact that it's not my place to change that person, anyway. It's up to me to deal with it and to accept who they are as much as I expect them to accept me for who I am.

Similarly, Daren has held highly responsible posts in the banking sector and believes the Kabbalah Centre's teaching encourages him to "appreciate the people around" him more:

> I stood out very judgmental, I still am very judgmental, but to a lesser degree. I had a very low opinion of a lot of my colleagues who I used to work with, but in time I learned to appreciate them more and see that they're actually really nice people, because, I just learned to see things differently.

Both Jonathan and Daren emphasize that they changed their own attitudes at work through religious teachings, rather than trying to change others' attitudes.

Those who work in the service sector in particular consider that they found in exotic religious resources a useful means to manage their emotions and hence to improve their dealings with customers. Arthur is an estate agent in London. He follows the Kabbalah Centre's teaching and insists on the need to apply it:

That kind of application in an everyday situation, in everyday life, is challenging, especially when you have got somebody screaming down the phone at you tearing your diary up, or they are complaining in the other ear about how inefficient you are or, you know, suddenly you have to take 20 minutes or half an hour off, to come to a new perspective, you have to come back to dealing with it but that's what it's all about.... If someone shouts at you, do you shout back? Are you able to control yourself? Are you able to understand why they are shouting at you? Can you treat it with understanding and can you treat it in a way that *that person feels you have helped that person?* Do you react or are you going to be, not reactive, you're going to be proactive?

Here Arthur clearly refers to the Kabbalah Centre's emphasis on developing "proactive" behaviors to manage difficult situations. Corinne works in a tourist agency in Tel Aviv. She underlines the importance of emotional skills in her professional activity: she defines her job as "95 percent" a discussion with clients; less than half of the discussion really relates to the actual work and the rest, she says, "I'm simply a psychologist." To make me understand the ways in which the Kabbalistic techniques she learned are useful for her working life, Corinne gives an example about customers' anger as well. A client was very angry and insulting her in the agency, "and me, very calm, thanks to the tools we were taught at the Centre, I was very calm, he didn't succeed to affect me. It's like I had a shield in front of me," she says. Thus, "instead of playing his game," Corinne suggested to the angry client that he get a coffee and come back ten minutes later once he was calmer. When the customer came back, he apologized and conceded she was right; Corinne was then able to work through his demand. Overall, Corinne uses the prayer Ana Bekoach every day on her way to work, but also when she feels clients become "hysterical" and she is going to talk back. She also insists on the personal skills she developed through Kabbalah: "people feel they can speak to me, and they speak to me, they ask me advice."

The control of behaviors and emotions encouraged by neo-Hindu movements and the Kabbalah Centre are transferable skills, in particular in middle-class professions. Because of their ambiguous in-between position in the organization of work, educated middle-class individuals are expected to exhibit efficiency, responsibility, initiative, flexibility, and a willingness to permanently update their skills; unsurprisingly, they are therefore particularly receptive to this encouragement to develop personal potential. Illouz (2008, 198) underscores that the middle classes "achieve economic security at the price of constraining and constricting their emotions, impulses, and desires"—hence interviewees' sense of empowerment as they described to me their abilities to cope with professional situations. But this empowerment is certainly not a form of liberation from social pressures and constraints: it is rather an endeavor to generate class distinction. Illouz notes that in his time Freud had already observed that this social strata "treat their emotions as an economic asset" while the working classes seemed to be "less stifled by emotional constraints"—something that fits with Elias's (2000) analysis of the "civilizing process." In other words, "emotional life is not only stratified but stratifying as well" (Illouz 2008, 200). Thus, as she analyzes therapies and personal growth as a means for the middle classes to enhance their "emotional capital," we could equally argue that exotic religious resources also contribute to social stratification by helping those involved in collaborative work, service, and caring occupations to develop particular attitudes which, in turn, can be converted into career advancement or material comfort. Bricolage is therefore structured by a quest for emotional capital.

The contribution of therapeutic and "spiritual" techniques to the formation of the middle-class habitus is also evidenced by the fact that several interviewees say they felt encouraged to be more ambitious and entrepreneurial by following neo-Hindu or Kabbalistic teachings. They indeed encourage individual responsibility, to see challenges as opportunities, to be self-confident and proactive, and to realize oneself in one's job. When asked about whether Kabbalah benefits her professional life, Ranit explained that she opened her own design company in Israel. Kabbalah, she explains, helps her to understand that even if such a venture is difficult, it is down to her will, strength, and patience to be successful. Ranit also says it allows her to be "positive": she can focus on her creative activity rather than worry about the current economic context. The transferability of emotional competence or entrepreneurial skills, explored in individual socio-trajectories, confirms the argument advanced in the previous chapter: the realization of the self is both a social requirement and a desirable individual quest. The following section will nonetheless emphasize why it is more beneficial to middle-class individuals.

Before that, it is worth noting that the quest of students of the Sivananda Centres, Siddha Yoga, and the Kabbalah Centre for transferable skills to enhance their working life is evidenced by these movements' teaching and learning environment (see Chapter 5). The transmission of these religious teachings indeed reflects the world of universities, academies. and professional training, with which the middle class is familiar (Beckford 1984). Not only are "workshops," "training courses," and "intensives" part of their educational and professional experience, but it is also through them that the middle class typically gains social mobility. By and large, knowledge and skills transferred by educational institutions have been essential to the rise of this stratum, because its members are generally not defined by owning production means but by their organizational and skills assets. Hence the desire, among interviewees, to participate in extra-professional activities that "add up" or benefit to their knowledge, which resembles the learning and training experience that is part of their socialization.

> I didn't want to consume only, to watch, but to do something, to learn something. I wanted at all cost, I had this desire to learn... and to take notes, and to attend classes. So I saw yoga courses, I chose one. (Éric, Sivananda Centres, Paris)

We now fully understand the significance of the ways in which Siddha Yoga, the Sivananda Centres, and the Kabbalah Centre transmit their teachings in the framework of "courses," thereby trying to respond to "a particular category of needs proper to determinate social groups by a determinate type of practice or discourse" (Bourdieu 1987, 119). Overall, I noted interviewees' eagerness and enthusiasm for learning: about the various "spiritual" courses and events they attend, many say they "really love learning" or "studying things." We can also further the understanding of consumerism in religion: social actors pay for "spiritual" classes and events, but they do so in the hope that what is acquired will contribute to cultural and emotional forms of capital, which in turn, is convertible into career prospect and wealth, as suggested in *Distinction* (Bourdieu 1984).

The Light, Its Gifts, and Social Stratification

The comparison below of the socio-professional trajectories of Daren and Catherine, two followers of the Kabbalah Centre, sheds light on the fact that learning to control emotions, accept responsibility for one's destiny, or become an entrepreneurial self are skills that have a different significance, in relation to individuals' already owned financial, cultural, and social capitals. These two examples also show how the relation with a religious teaching varies with followers' social positions.

Daren is 38 and had been involved in the Kabbalah Centre for four and half years. When we discussed the possible effects of the movement's teaching on his professional life, Daren evoked having developed a more accepting attitude toward his colleagues. But he also changed his career: working as a financial analyst in the banking sector, he decided to work for a hedge fund two years prior to the interview, something he says he enjoys "a thousand times more, and there's much more responsibility, much more opportunity, much more flexible working hours, it's literally chalk and cheese." This career change was encouraged by the teaching of the Kabbalah Centre, believes Daren.

> [Kabbalah] taught me to understand what, how can I add value in the workplace. When I identified what I could do best, the Light gave me the opportunity that matched it. I'd kept pushing in the wrong direction and not even realizing it, and when I understood, this is what I should be doing, then the opportunity came, and it enabled me to do that.

In other words, Daren explains that Kabbalah helped him to identify his skills and to undertake self-appraisal. Therefore, "Kabbalistic tools" seem to have enabled him to activate his social predispositions, resulting from the cultural capital that he owned as a middle-class professional. This is an important point because scholars tend to take for granted that therapeutic or "spiritual" techniques *do something*, as research participants claim. But the latter may at least in part attribute to these teachings and practices the bonuses of their social capital. That is to say, Daren may have changed career anyway, the same way that other interviewees would have tried in any case to control their emotions and have harmonious relations with their clients and co-workers. Daren sees the "opportunity" for professional reorientation as a gift from the Light: from a sociological perspective, there is little doubt that such opportunity is made possible by Daren's knowledge of the banking sector, his social and professional networks in this domain, and his ownership of skills and experience without which such career change would not be possible. In other words, Daren attributes to the mysterious doings of transcendent forces the effects of his social and cultural capital, which is, for social actors, no less invisible and impenetrable. Logically, trusting the Light is about gaining confidence in one's ability to take professional risks and achieve success—a crucial asset and typical disposition of the middle classes. And indeed, Daren explains he was "tapping into something bigger than us, and getting support from that" in order to change career:

> What Kabbalah does, is it teaches you how to deal with the challenges in your workplace far more effectively. It teaches you how to...not eliminate, but manage stress. How to get more out of working with other people, how to manifest results more quickly, and how to get help and assistance for example (from) what's far bigger than us, and therefore...to be more effective in what you do. So it teaches to tap into something bigger than ourselves, and life becomes much easier

[silence]. Otherwise my job would be literally impossible. How can anyone possibly understand what's going on in the whole world and then…, it's just impossible.

Note the emphasis on stress management, collaborative skills, effectiveness, and confidence; these are essential in Daren's professional life, without which it would be "impossible." In his current job, he advises clients on financial investment on a very short-term basis, from five minutes to a month, "although on average it's probably nearly always short term," he explains. Daren finds very exciting these activities that are "moving super fast," but they require him to be swift as well. When I asked whether his job is about finding the good opportunity today, he responded:

> You're right, *which is why I couldn't possibly do it without asking for help from something bigger than me.* Yeah. I often, many times at work, I just do not have a clue, how to do this. Literally, every day, there's a point where I haven't got a clue what's going on or how to do this, and I'll ask for help. And invariably, *if I'm in the right place, things will happen.* So for example, I need to work out a specific problem and I haven't got a clue on how to do it, and I'll sit back and I'll ask for help, and I'll get an email with a piece of research that exactly answers this question for me. So that's how *the universe can help you. It sends people and situations that give you what you need to know.*

There is undoubtedly an element of hazard and uncertainty in financial speculations, yet Daren attributes to the Light what is granted by his social positioning: self-confidence and the ability to research, find, and understand relevant information, and knowledge of relevant people who can pass on the relevant information. In other words, he is objectively already "in the right place" to benefit from the Light, which seems to give him confidence in decision making—probably a crucial skill in his professional sector. It is therefore natural for Daren to associate the teaching of the Kabbalah Centre with success and fulfillment. He also met his wife at the London branch, which gathers an important number of (often single) young middle-class professionals like him—one more miraculous effect of social habitus:

> My work's been transformed, my private life's been transformed, my social life's been transformed, and then my…in terms of prosperity, financially, again, I've had blessing after blessing.… *It just comes.* You

see that's the thing. When you pursue this path you're *just overwhelmed with the amazing things that happen to you.*

Catherine also puts her trust in the Light of the Creator, but its miracles are more uncertain. Catherine is 53; she is a divorcee with three adult children. She discovered the Kabbalah Centre through Rebecca, whom she met in a synagogue in the Parisian suburbs where they both live. Catherine embraced the Jewish tradition when she married a Jew, but did not convert because she has to work on Saturdays. Yet she wishes to remain close to Judaism's values and sociability (see Chapter 2). Accordingly, she is hardly a typical bricoleur. Catherine has a working-class background, which is unusual for the Kabbalah Centre's students. As a child, she experienced extreme poverty. Her parents had six other children; the family was evicted for not paying their rent, lived in squats, and was supported by Catholic charities. Catherine left school before gaining any qualifications, trained as a seamstress, and married very young. Catherine explained that she would have done anything not to endure her parent's life and worked very hard to have her house on her own with her husband. She started by sewing curtains, subcontracted by someone owning a little clothes repair shop in a shopping mall. Then she became a partner and helped manage this shop, before having a clothes repair shop herself in the same mall. Until I met her, this had been the activity she had developed through hard work and the entrepreneurial skills of artisans and little shopkeepers. Yet, Catherine's clothes repair shop is not profitable anymore and she works in supermarkets as a demonstrator to make both ends meet. She currently lives in the basement of her boutique to save on rent and to support financially her daughter who is in higher education.

During the interview, Catherine said she would like the Kabbalah Centre to reopen in Paris because she "needs to learn" and would like to attend introductory classes again. When I asked her why, she spontaneously told me that she decided to change direction in her professional life—in other words, she needs the study of Kabbalah to undertake this change. She has just taken a short training in permanent makeup and would like to become a mobile makeup artist. Like Daren, she insists on the importance of trusting the Light. However, in explaining how Kabbalah helps her to gain confidence, her discourse evoke the "doubts," "fears," and "negativities" she wants to keep at bay, contrasting with Daren's solid confidence. At several points during the interview she reprimands herself for having expressed such feelings, reiterating for herself her urge to have "certainty," to practice more and "be positive."

I mean I'm not afraid anymore but there are times when, when I lost my mummy, I felt back in doubt, and the worries, the worries you know, it's not easy, there are moments when we are destabilized, in addition to be alone, to do something again, to re-create a professional activity, I've been unemployed for 2 years and a half to go to L. to see often my mummy, so...and hum...But you see miracles, it comes back. You feel confident again and you should go often to the Kabbalah Centre to be always confident, and practice. If you practice, there's no worries. And that's why you have to scan the Zohar, it's here the Zohar [she shows hers to me]. We can heal, but you need to have certainty, you have to be confident. Yes.

Catherine's discourse expresses more an aspiration of confidence than confidence in life itself. She also takes responsibility for un-received miracles, resulting from her fears and lack of practice that "blocks" the Light. For instance, she would like to have a home, "but I need to wait because, that's the way it is, because I need to study [Kabbalah] more and for sure it would go faster if I was studying it more, so the doors would open more"—note here the feelings of deference and of being subjected to a higher authority that reflect her dominated social position. Hence the repetition of the need for her to "correct" her attitudes, and stop making similar "mistakes" in her life, to stop being negative, and to be positive instead. Like Daren, Catherine's discourse reflects her social position: one could say it is indeed her, through her lack of social, cultural, and economic capital, that prevents certain gifts of life to be sent to her.

When Catherine feels worried or desires to "unblock" a situation, she intensifies her reading and scanning of the Zohar; she recites Ana Bekoach more. Catherine always has with her a copy of this prayer, as well as the miniature Zohar that she frequently covers with kisses. She uses a calendar from the Kabbalah Centre, pinned on the wall next to her bed, which indicates the positive, negative, or neutral days in relation to energy of the moment, in order to make important decisions. She also pays attention to the smallest principles taught at the centre, such as not leaving her handbag on the floor, which is supposed to be bad for prosperity. She would explain at length to me all the benefits of these Kabbalistic tools. All of this underscores her dependence on higher forces, her inability to harness them as Daren feels he does, and hence her lack of confidence, which in the end she believes is the cause of not receiving enough from the Light.

Catherine's relation with the teaching of the Kabbalah Centre contrasts with Daren's evocation of empowerment and fulfillment. Interestingly, Obadia

(1999, 191) found that middle-class Buddhists are prone to interpret their religious belonging in terms of self-realization, while the less privileged understand their relation to Buddhism as a form of psychological or social reform of themselves, in response to social and economic hardship. Being proactive and entrepreneurial involves much more risk for Catherine, due to her more limited financial, cultural, and social capitals. In this regard, it is not by chance that Catherine proved to be one of the very few students of the Kabbalah Centre looking for the solidarity and support of a community life in a synagogue outside the Kabbalah Centre (Chapter 2). The emotional skills offered by the use of "Kabbalistic tools" (being proactive, controlling the ego, and so forth) seem also of little help in Catherine's new professional project, and actually she did not mention them during the interview. The gifts that the Light can grant her seem less large than Daren's; the effects of such religious teachings (as legitimation and reinforcement of social, cultural, and financial forms of capital) rather resonate with middle-class habituses and trajectories.

When Exotic Religious Resources Are in Symbiosis with Work

Farrah was a teacher and "worked [her] way up the professional ladder" to deputy head, but she wanted to expand on the degree she had in psychology; "I wanted to do more than what I was doing," as she put it. She trained in counseling after seeing a counselor herself, following the death of her mother. She then thought she would like "to train in this to help other people." She has also been familiar with esotericism since her childhood (Chapter 2) and, discovering her own skills as a healer, Farrah started to learn a wide range of alternative healing techniques.

> As part of my training [in counseling], I got placed in a...well known drug centre where you're helping very serious addicts, and I was also helping with a women's refuge....And I began to realize that I needed more tools as a therapist to help these people in deep distress, so I trained in stress management, I became a stress management consultant. I also have just had very informal training as a healer with my father....I trained in reiki, and from reiki got involved with this government project in prison. As I say, from meeting that friend I then became a Feng Shui consultant, and then I added to that by training in America, and in India with Vaastu and learning all about sacred geometry and that earth healing. *So I've constantly been upping what I've been doing.*

To make both ends meet, Farrah still does "contract teaching" with special needs children "because [she's] been used to working on quite a deep level." Farrah insists on the value of her diversified skills, being "slightly unusual as a teacher. Because usually, people work with young people, or they work with the older ones. With me, I work across the board. And I also do special needs." She also mentions how teaching agency staff are impressed with her wide range of skills. Kabbalah became part of them; it was on her "to do list," as she "wanted to take that to another level":

> I feel that Kabbalah has added to what I do, I think it's strengthened me and made me more aware, it's heightened my awareness...and I think also it has helped me with my therapy work, and you know, *be-cause it's deepened the knowledge within me,* I feel I have, I mean I hope I have, I think I work on a different level with people than I was be-fore....I feel that the people who come to me are often in a transfor-mation, they are in a point in their lives where they want to find their true paths, and clear some blockages. And...yes, it's kind of, I feel now, because it has deepened me, *I am able to help them more, so that, it seems to happen quicker, with them, they clear things. Faster. Maybe my vibrations...within me.*

In this long abstract, Farrah clearly explains how she feels that her own self-realization (heightened awareness, deeper knowledge, vibrations within) make her a better therapist, thereby underlining the clear communication between her personal quest of self-realization and her professional skills, which is particularly the case of those working in alternative therapies. In these cases, self-realization as a potential for social success is most obvious. Unsurprisingly, Farrah finds Kabbalah interesting because "no matter in what job you are, you can kind of relate it to whatever you are doing. To improve what you are doing and the way you do it. And also, in that way being an ex-ample and help others." "Being an example" reminds us of the value of the self in the production of social distinction.

Farrah's example illustrates the fact that, overall, the ideas and practices explored in neo-Hindu movements and the Kabbalah Centre constitute highly transferable knowledge and skills for those working in the fields of alterna-tive medicines, coaching, personal growth, or post-psychoanalytic therapies. They can contribute to a diverse yet relatively coherent framework, a set of dis-courses and practices for self-management that individuals can use as coach, therapist, or even spiritual leader in competitive markets that value "things foreign" and new. Korbe (forthcoming) found that yoga teachers in France and

Estonia often offer a range of alternative therapies in the attempt to "stand out" with a unique and attractive combination of services (of course, this does not mean it *is* unique). Thus, social actors combine complementary and alternative medicines with yoga and other holistic practices such as energetic massages, reiki, or Ayurveda. Warrier (2008, 14) and Pordié (2008, 13) both found that individuals trained in Ayurveda therapists and Tibetan medicine, respectively, combine different alternative healing techniques as well as counseling. Martine, for instance, is attracted to Kabbalah because of the power of the Hebrew letters she had discovered when, after the death of a relative, she went to see a therapist who healed her by giving her a stone with a Hebrew letter. Interestingly, this healer was also present at the Kabbalah Centre's introductory course during which I met Martine, perhaps to complete his own skills or know what's around. A full-time therapist herself, Martine is aware of several people who use Hebrew letters in their therapy work and, she says, "this is by the way something I might do later; maybe, surely, I feel, I'll use the letters to help in therapy." Martine is determined: she "know[s] where to go" if she cannot get what she wants from the Kabbalah Centre's teaching. It is highly significant that it is precisely at this point in the interview that she insists on the non-Jewish, universal nature of Kabbalah (Chapter 2), to assert her legitimacy and desire to freely tap into these resources. In other words, it is also the desire to transform exotic religious resources into life skills and professional competence that requires their dissociation from their specific cultural or ethnic roots.

Two individual cases illustrate the ways in which exotic religious teachings can be in perfect symbiosis with professional success. Jane and Robin are both London students of the Kabbalah Centre and have created their own coaching companies. Like several other members of this movement, their training in post-psychoanalytic therapies, counseling, and personal growth techniques predisposes them to be interested in the recently psychologized version of Kabbalah that is offered by the Kabbalah Centre.

Jane is 48 and has been following the Kabbalah Centre's teaching in London for four and a half years. She left school at 16 when she met her husband and had two children. She is now divorced. She benefited from professional training while working in television production and, in the same period that she joined the Kabbalah Centre, she became a freelance consultant. She set up her own business two years ago to train people in managerial skills—"there is no way I would have ever dreamt of setting anything up my own business or anything without the Centre, absolutely no way would I have taken the risk and responsibility," Jane says. Jane regularly attends a wide range of courses and seminars; she studied personal growth and post-psychoanalytic methods such as transactional analysis, NLP, and psychometrics. Yet she finds these techniques "very scientific": "I don't find them, more how the brain works rather than spiritual." Indeed, some of the trainings she attends are led by religious figures; for instance, she refers to Big Mind, a technique that blends psychological techniques and Zen meditation. We can therefore understand how the Kabbalah Centre's teaching could be attractive to her, in combining a psychological framework with the "spiritual," which for Jane relates to an ethical perspective: "There is a very big difference as to why you do these things" she explains, referring to the fact that according to her, techniques such as NLP can be used to "manipulate" people, while "that isn't something Kabbalah would teach to do."

Jane defines the training she provides her clients as "about helping people to treat each other well, and to put some positive energy around." Thus, as a consultant she aims to

> share with them some really strong management principles embedded with ways of encouraging people to treat each other better at work and I think they're good practices to teach each other at work and the knock on effect has to be that they are... treating each other better after work, and all that. So, um, to be more proactive, to help people to be more proactive, I do what I do, that's what my business is about.

"To help people to be more proactive": this formulation suggests that Jane embeds the teaching of the Kabbalah Centre in the training she provides to her clients. This is something she acknowledges during the interview, although she does not refer to the movement explicitly, which could drive potential clients away. Yet, the discourses and vocabulary she uses to talk about her profession mirrors the Kabbalah Centre's rhetoric, underlining a transfer of knowledge. The Kabbalah Centre's teaching thus contributes to her skills as a consultant. But there is more than a transfer of skills: Jane insists on the ethical dimension of her training. Her company is, in fact, advertised as a training consultancy organization "with a big difference,"[3] referring to its emphasis on individuals' self-knowledge and "positive" attitudes toward others. Indeed, Jane believes that "business is just beginning to understand" the importance of such skills.

> For years I've been saying you have got to look at behaviors, you got to look at more values and belief systems than, and people will (go off) and I was not back on one contract only 2 years ago, but the same organization has now come back to me, asking for all the other things around what I was talking about then, just in 2 years. Organizations... understand

that it doesn't matter how skillful someone is, if they display behaviors and interactions with people, if they are not emotionally intelligent in their approach to things.

In other words, the Kabbalah Centre's moral principles about sharing and about controlling one's reactive and ego-driven attitudes constitute important add-ons to the managerial techniques Jane delivers—hence her emphasis on the positive energy she puts in her training. These principles that she learned in the Kabbalah Centre therefore contribute to her positioning in the consultancy field, giving her company a niche (consultancy "with a big difference") in a diverse and competitive market.

Turning to Robin, he is a consultant who set up his own coaching company in London. Robin is 52, married, with two children. He has followed the Kabbalah Centre's teaching for five years. Like Jane, Robin has not completed his education and found in personal growth an opportunity for professional success. Having learning difficulties and conflicting relationships with his family, Robin rebelled against his family and school; he left both and married in his teens. First working successfully in real estate, he underwent counseling after marital difficulties and became passionate about psychological techniques that he discovered in the United States a decade ago. "I went on every single course I could" says Robin, laughing, listing a large range of techniques; "and I just became like a sponge for psychology and, you know, parenting, business, negotiation, selling, leadership, everything I could get my hands on, that involved people." For Robin, it combines caring activities with personal success:

> I realized that actually inspiring other people was something that just made me feel fantastic and I was doing it for nothing, and then I thought, "well actually, I can find a way of making money doing that."

Robin now delivers in Britain an American program designed to "help lone parents in America get back into work," "a practical course that can be delivered to everyone, you know, unemployed people, people in recovery, people who are disabled, the offenders, you know all people who are failing." Yet Robin personalized his training, which also blends techniques such as NLP and cognitive behavioral therapy. "But actually, it is very Kabbalistic, very Kabbalistic," Robin says, although like Jane he does not mention Kabbalah in his work. Robin does not want to jeopardize his contracts with governmental agencies, due to what he perceives as the Kabbalah Centre's poor image. Nonetheless, the movement's emphasis on self-realization facilitates greatly the transfer of ideas and practices, from its religious setting to his professional practice. This is why Robin defines himself as a "channel for this wisdom."

> So the channel comes through me. I go to Kabbalah; I listen to the Torah, that gives me strength and courage; I listen to [the teacher], that gives me some wisdom. And I then teach it. And that then effects what I generate for the business. So for me, it is a very important source of wisdom and strength.

Robin's description of his coaching indeed resonates with the Kabbalah Centre's teaching:

> In essence, it is teaching people about taking responsibility, working on yourself, sharing, setting goals, having a big vision, you know, changing people's lives and getting people trained up to help other people to change their lives.... So that is the work I do, which is about building self-esteem, getting people to take responsibility, to stop blaming, to understand how their mind work, to overcome their ego, you know, to take control of their lives.

It is therefore unsurprising that Robin feels that the work he does "is an extension of the teachings of Kabbalah." This fluidity between Robin's professional activities and commitment to Kabbalah is also evidenced by the fact that he hired several Kabbalah students as coaches in his company. Conversely, some of his staff frequented the Kabbalah Centre after joining Robin's coaching company. Robin thus found in the Kabbalah Centre "people who want to make a difference and are genuine, whom I can trust 100 per cent and know that they are here, because they want to make a difference in people's lives."

By and large, cases such as Farrah, Jane, and Robin show that for those working in the fields of post-psychoanalytic and holistic therapies, there is potentially great fluidity, if not symbiosis, between professional skills and the extra-professional exploration of religious teachings focused on self-realization. "Spiritual" discipline, the work on oneself, then becomes a valuable asset for the professional life. Many people in these movements do not work in similar fields, yet they might also be building up the potential for doing so in the future. Andrew, who works in the banking sector, explained his motivation for undertaking the Sivananda Centre's Teacher's Training Course as such: "I don't know whether I want to make it my career, teaching yoga, but I want to be able to have that skill, to be able to do it if I wanted to." He also explains that he would like to open a "yoga bar" or an ashram one day. No doubt his current professional skills would constitute a tremendously important cultural capital for accomplishing such a project, as Korbe's (forthcoming) research shows.

These interviewees are both clients and professionals in a field that deals with very specific symbolic goods and services (alternative medicines, personal growth, etc.). This helps us to understand the circulation of individuals in a wide range of seminars, courses, and events without conversion or long-term commitment: it is for some a quest for new skills, which, combined together, provide an advantage in a competitive market, in which they are most of the time freelancers. Practices of bricolage are hardly devoid of social coherence and consistence; they are shaped by classed professional strategies.

Synthesis: Exoticism Comes Full Circle

Over the last three decades, social class and more largely issues of social positioning, social mobility, and professional life have been largely ignored in both French- and English-speaking sociology of religion. There is no doubt that in advanced industrial societies, class is difficult to define and processes of socialization are plural and complex. Nevertheless, this omission is clearly one more sign of the demise of the social within the sociology of religion, leading scholars to overlook crucial aspects of individuals' religious life. For instance, religious discourses "talk" about social positioning: the first part of this chapter underscored the ways in which references to Hindu asceticism in particular allow some social actors to express a desire of social emancipation; it significantly concerns the "executant" middle class (clerical workers, IT workers, and junior executives) who long for more meaningful or vocational occupations "above," in the artistic and therapeutic milieus in particular. On the whole, the pursuit of personal growth and self-realization encapsulates a desire for social mobility and achievement, as epitomized by the "ladder" metaphor in reference to yoga. Moreover, one could say that religious discourses and practices contribute to social stratification and hence to the social order, albeit in a modest way since, as Daren's example suggests, they in part reinforce or legitimize a form of capital already valued and partly possessed. Exotic religious resources nevertheless embody strong incentives to control emotions and to develop flexibility, responsibility, and proactive attitudes. As such, they represent skills that are particularly valuable and beneficial for middle-class professionals—the fact that the Sivananda Centres, Siddha Yoga, and the Kabbalah Centre socialize their members to such incentives, rather than freeing them from any social norms, as is often alleged by scholars of religion (Chapter 6), is therefore highly significant. Bricolage with proliferating "spiritual" and therapeutic techniques overall denotes the importance of a stratifying "emotional capital" in advanced industrial societies (Illouz 2008).

Finally, in this last section of the chapter, I would like to suggest that the exoticism of neo-Hindu movements and the Kabbalah Centre also plays a significant part in this class formation. Members of the Sivananda Centres, Siddha Yoga, and the Kabbalah Centre are characteristically members of the "new petite bourgeoisie" (Bourdieu 1984)—as shown by the early sections of this chapter, some *aspire* to belong to this social stratum, others refuse to play the social game. Some, like Catherine, represents exceptions in this religious milieu. The petite bourgeoisie comprises social groups located between the upper class and the proletariat. It is a fragmented stratum, divided between the declining petite bourgeoisie (artisans, shopkeepers), the rising, executant petite bourgeoisie (clerical workers, junior executives), and the "new petite bourgeoisie." The latter tend to exert "new or renovated professions," such as those "involving presentation and representation" (marketing, advertising, public relations, fashion and design) and the production of symbolic goods and services (medico-social professions, counselors and therapists, individuals working in media, craft workers and artists). In short, the new petite bourgeoisie plays the role of cultural intermediaries and tastemakers; the production and control of symbolic goods are therefore vital for its reproduction. The trajectories of the members of the new petite bourgeoisie are also particularly heterogeneous due to the indeterminacy of these professions (Accardo 2006, 367–368; Bourdieu 1984, 358–361).

The desire for social emancipation and countercultural lifestyle choices of yoga and Kabbalah students—from living in an ashram to becoming a therapist—reflect their social positioning as part of this social stratum. As intermediary group between the upper class and the proletariat, the middle class in general tends to be torn between contradictory influences and expectations on the political, ideological, or cultural level—hence an anxious quest of distinctive lifestyles and social practices that social actors rationalize as "choices" (Accardo 2006, 364; Bidou 2004, 120–121). This is illustrated, for instance, by interviewees' insistence on, and justification of, the sacrifice of professional ambitions and material comfort to a more meaningful and authentic way of life. In fact, the issue of distinction is particularly acute for the new petite bourgeoisie, since it is composed of either "petits bourgeois" lacking social capital to fully benefit from their high cultural capital, or individuals from the upper classes who did not acquire the necessary qualifications that would have allowed them to maintain themselves in the dominant class. The new petits bourgeois are therefore *déclassés*. They seek to escape identification with the working class while being unable to share the lifestyle of the upper class. Thus, they share an "anti-institutional temperament"—as epitomized by interviewees' discourse of rejection of a conventional car, mortgage, and married way of life—and they are characterized by a refusal of all forms of classification and competition:

> Their lifestyle and ethical and political positions are based on a rejection of everything in themselves that is finite, definite, final, in a word, petit bourgeois, that is, a refusal to be pinned down in a particular site in social space, a practical utopianism which was until then the privilege of intellectuals and which predisposes them to welcome every form of utopia. Classified, déclassé, aspiring to a higher class, they see themselves as unclassifiable, "excluded," "dropped out," "marginal," anything rather than categorized, assigned to a class, a determinate place in social space. (Bourdieu 1984: 370)

Despite their diversity, the social trajectories of research participants are well captured by this specific positioning of the new petite bourgeoisie described by Bourdieu: refusal to enter the labor market and instead living full-time in an ashram or a branch of the Kabbalah Centre, dropping one's job to travel abroad for a year or more, refusing to identify with one's professional activity, leaving it for a freelance occupation in alternative and avant-garde milieus.

Because of its ambivalent social positioning, the new petite bourgeoisie is attracted by all strategies of cultural subversion and heresy (Accardo 2006, 369)—hence the attraction for alternative therapies or exotic new religious teachings. Bourdieu (1984, 370) views individuals' involvement in Transcendental Meditation, yoga, Zen, martial arts, holistic and post-psychoanalytic therapies, as well as esotericism, as "an inventory of thinly disguised expressions of a sort of dream of social flying, a desperate effort to defy the gravity of the social field." Scholars of Buddhism also find that in Euroamerican societies Buddhism tends to attract middle-class and upper middle-class individuals, in particular "bohemian, intellectuals, and artists" (Coleman 2001, 20, 196). One could say that the rejection of the individualistic, materialistic, secular, and decadent West, which is contrasted with a quest for a cultural alternative (a "spiritual," that is altruistic, lifestyle referring to an ancient, mystical tradition) expresses this "dream of social flying." The lifestyles these discourses justify are deliberately opted for, and they do not relate to the working class' "resignation to the inevitable" (Bourdieu 1984, 372). Thus, the new petite bourgeoisie is predisposed to play a vanguard role in relation to lifestyle regarding, for example, values, consumption, family life, and intimacy. Aiming to distinguish itself both from the declining petite bourgeoisie's conservative values and the executant petite bourgeoisie's asceticism, the art of living of the new petite bourgeoisie promotes pleasure and fulfillment. It values body- and self-expression as well as harmonious relationships with others; it emphasizes personal experience and subjectivity, thereby psychologizing social relations. The new petit bourgeois are actually the users and professionals of alternative therapies and personal growth (Accardo 2006, 370; Bourdieu 1984, 367). This lifestyle may have recently expanded more widely among rising educated professionals, prone to treat their health and the enhancement of their self as valuable assets (Savage 1992, 113; Skeggs 2004, 75).

Because of the significance of culture and symbols for the new petite bourgeoisie, the "exotic" nature of the studied religious resources is of paramount importance: it allows the new petite bourgeoisie to display cultural competence and maintain their role in the game of cultural and symbolic struggle. Accessing and knowing other cultures, and displaying this knowledge, are crucial for these "cultural brokers," whose role is "to make visible what was previously hidden, thereby attributing new value to new visibilities" (Skeggs 2004, 149, 157)—hence, for example, the constant exploration of diverse events and courses, animated by the desire to discover new—yet authentic—religious teachings which may, in turn, dramatize foreign and mysterious origins (Kashmir Shaivism or Sephardic Kabbalah). Lindquist (1997, 285) makes similar observations about the shamanic life of her research participants: in some cases it "tends to be considered as an asset, making the person in question 'stranger, but exciting, interesting.'" Thus, bricolage contributes to a process of distinction through which emotional but also cultural forms of capital are potentially convertible into economic capital by cultural intermediaries whose job is to aestheticize everyday life (Featherstone 1991, 65). An obvious example is Martine, who wants to learn Kabbalah in order to include it in her therapeutic practice. I met in the Kabbalah Centre several individuals with their own therapeutic practice or having founded their own "spiritual" group. Following the movement's courses and events is, then, clearly a way to enhance and actualize a vital cultural capital. Overall, for individuals like Martine, Farrah, Jane, or Robin, it is critical to access and control forms of knowledge in alternative religious, "spiritual," and therapeutic fields: what is earned in the "spiritual" domain of their lives also benefits their professional and economic life.

Bricolage with exotic religious resources therefore contributes to the ways in which a fraction of the middle class reproduces itself by accessing, appropriating, and domesticating the cultures of others. By and large, "the relation of

ownership and entitlement for culture is central to understanding class differences" writes Skeggs (2004, 158), therefore devising the issue of *who can appropriate culture for self-making,* and *who can be appropriated.* Skeggs's main argument
is that while working-class identities are relatively ascribed and fixed, the middle
classes have ownership of their individuality and are able to optimize or "extend"
themselves by appropriating and consuming selected cultural resources. Class
formation, self-making, and culture are therefore strongly intertwined. This is
well captured by the concept of the "prosthetic self," emphasizing the ways in
which selfhood is generated and performed through experimentations, add-ons,
and detachment of cultural resources, which become "extensions" integral to
the individual (Lury 1997; Skeggs 2004; Strathern 2004). This entails access to,
and knowledge of, the "right" cultural resources, as well as the ability to choose
and "play" with them. The crucial role of culture for the formation of the middle
classes (and in particular for the traders of culture, the new petite bourgeoisie)
explains its predisposition to cosmopolitanism. Yet Skeggs (p. 158) suggests that
cosmopolitanism is less a capacity to engage with the other cultures than a way
to turn "them into objects of distanced contemplation for oneself." As exoticism,
cosmopolitanism is self-referential. In fact, Skeggs's understanding of cosmopolitanism (a competence through which otherness constitutes a resource for
self-enhancement) is entirely relevant to exoticism:

> whole bodies and cultures are not taken on in the construction of the
> aesthetic/prosthetic self, but rather the aspects that can be fetichized,
> which are seen to add value to the self who has entitlement and access
> to, and is powerful enough to appropriate, others/strangers. (p. 166)

This understanding of bricolage and cosmopolitanism prompts questions
about Srinivas's (2010) suggestion that Sai Baba devotees demonstrate an ability
to live in a pluralist and multicultural world—unless we take it as a "boutique
multiculturalism" through which, despite feeling attracted, individuals "stop
short of approving of other cultures at a point where some value at their center
generates an act that offends against the canons of civilized decency as they
have been either declared or assumed" (Fish 1999, 56). Interestingly, one of
Fish's examples relates to Native American rituals: they may exert a certain appeal and may be praised in discourses about religious freedom and pluralism,
until they involve animal sacrifice or consumption of peyote. This makes the
cosmopolitan middle class cringe; so does the Jewishness of Kabbalah and
its teachers, the devotional attitude required toward gurus, engagements with
rituals and languages in Hindi or Hebrew, the Kabbalah Centre's potential

identification with the state of Israel and its politics, and the nationalist claims made by some Indian gurus.

The exoticism of cultural and religious resources now comes full circle. Yoga, meditation, shamanism, Sufism and Kabbalah are "domesticated" by the middle class as resources to produce an emotionally and culturally competent self. This is what bricolage is about, and exoticism is central to this process of distinction.[4] We begin to grasp the sense of urgency in Kim's motto that opened this book: "whatever new things come up, I'm up for trying." One can look at this as a form of "empowerment," but must remember that it only concerns a relatively small fraction of the social world that seeks to detach itself both from the non-cosmopolitan working classes and the more conventional fractions of the bourgeoisie. Cosmopolitan identity, engrained with the making of the middle class, "is socially at least as restricted as any other strong ethnic identities" (Friedman 2005, 24). The claim in Chapter 1 is thus confirmed: exotic religious beliefs and practices are de-contextualized, constructed, disseminated, and appropriated in ways that reflect desires and expectations that were initially external to them. As a process of domestication of otherness for new purposes, religious exoticism indeed cannot be about conversion or the affirmation of an ethnic identity, as underscored in Chapter 2. The cultural traders of the petite bourgeoisie have no intention to claim a mono-religious or ethnic identity for themselves, which would involve moving away from the cultural vanguard they aim to be—this also helps to understand secularized, middle-class Jews' conflicting relations with visible and orthodox expressions of Judaism, which tend to attract less educated populations. Accordingly, they appropriate religious and cultural resources in practices of bricolage, on the condition that they can be de-contextualized, de-ethnicized, and psychologized. This is reflected in organizations' outreach strategies, involving a universalistic rhetoric, a renouncement of their initial identity-claims (Chapter 3) and a psychological reinterpretation of religious teachings. The new petite bourgeois nonetheless desire the existence of an authentic other (the guru, the Jewish Kabbalist, the shaman and the Sufi master) that they can absorb, yet without becoming this "other," proximity to which generates discomfort and resistance. Hence selective practices, superficial, short-term involvement, and, overall, limited prospects for the popularization of exotic beliefs and practices (Chapters 2 and 3): exoticism entails a pragmatic relationship with fetishized religious and cultural resources. This is why otherness needs to be deliberately ignored, at the same time as it is desired and fantasized.

Conclusion

THIS BOOK STARTED with a historical overview of the dissemination of neo-Hindu and Kabbalistic teachings in Euroamerican societies. It described the counter-mission undertaken by Hindu leaders in response to India's colonization, explored the formation of a Christian Kabbalah as part of Western esotericism, and finally presented the 1960s counterculture as a pivotal moment for the popularization of Asian religions and Kabbalah. Of the conclusions borne out by this historical perspective, foremost was that exotic religious resources in Euroamerican societies have been largely shaped by the concerns and expectations of their host societies. They have been represented as primordial and mystical sources of wisdom; as such, they were expected to regenerate their polar opposite—an individualistic, materialistic, secular, and decadent West. Yet, Hinduism, Kabbalah, Buddhism, Tantrism, or Sufism arouse fascination as much as they provoke distaste; their popularization has entailed their universalization and partial abstraction from their original cultural and religious systems.

The second and third chapters reinforced this observation. Looking at the students of yoga, meditation, and Kabbalah, Chapter 2 demonstrated that they do not seek to become Hindu or Jewish. Indeed, the confrontation with these religious traditions' languages and liturgies clearly generates feelings of discomfort and transgression. These deeply ambivalent attitudes, balanced between fascination and repulsion, partly explain why an overwhelming number of individuals adopt only a selection of doctrines and practices, remain superficially and temporarily involved, and may continue to explore other religious teachings and alternative therapies. The success of exotic religious resources is therefore both triggered *and* limited by their foreignness (even in a receptive and porous religious landscape such as Brazil). The ambivalent nature of religious exoticism also demands a "domestication" of the appropriated religious resources so that they appear safe and familiar: students of yoga, meditation, or Kabbalah view these teachings as non-religious, universal forms of "spirituality"—that is to say, a pool of available resources they can freely tap into according to their personal expectations and needs.

Chapter 3 investigated the doctrines and discourses of the studied movements and also confirmed that the popularization of exotic religious resources entails a partial detachment from their specific cultural and religious roots. This detachment takes the shape of a universalistic rhetoric: in order to reassure their audience, modern gurus and leaders of the Kabbalah Centre present Vedanta and Kabbalah, respectively, as universal wisdoms that transcend religious, cultural, and national differences. Accordingly, these religious figures had to reinterpret the core tenets that bind religion with a territory and a people and that make traditional Hinduism and Judaism ethnic religions. They also downplayed or modified the significance of liturgy; and they emphasized and introduced new practices. These changes regarding collective identity, doctrines, and practices are not without challenges, as shown by the recent evolution of the Kabbalah Centre. Furthermore, such a process of de-ethnicization is unavoidably affected by constraints and opportunities encountered by transnational movements on the local level. Chapter 4 showed the importance of national responses to religious diversity and of the physiognomy of national religious landscapes for understanding religious movements' adaptive strategies (why, for instance, some neo-Hindu movements claim to be universal in some places, but Hindu in others) and the effect of these strategies (why, when the Kabbalah Centre started to present itself as a "universal wisdom," some local branches declined while others expanded). It underscores again the fact that the availability of exotic religious resources depends, in part, on specific social environments.

The last three chapters focused on the social significance of exotic religious teachings in advanced industrial societies. The dissemination of exotic religious resources was analyzed in the context of the "psychologization of social life" in such societies, which grants to selfhood and its transformation an unprecedented and tremendous importance. Members of neo-Hindu movements and the Kabbalah Centre have no intention to practice Judaism and Hinduism as such, but instead appropriate Kabbalah and "Eastern spiritualities" as, in their view, timeless and authentic sources of wisdom that hold promises of personal growth and self-realization. This form of appropriation—exotic religious resources as a means of realizing the self—plays a central role in the domestication of exotic religious resources. It is encouraged, if not enabled, by the fact that teachers of Kabbalah, yoga, and meditation present an inner-worldly path of self-improvement; they offer their teaching as a set of easy, "take-homeable," and effective techniques of self-realization; and they transmit these techniques in courses and workshops along the model of personal growth and group therapies. The pragmatism characterizing the relationship with these religious teachings is thus hardly surprising (Chapter 5).

The desire for self-realization is central to the dissemination of exotic religious resources; it reflects the strong demands for autonomy and flexibility made upon individuals in advanced industrial societies. This argument goes against the dominant sociological paradigm that understands self-realization as the expression of a free and voluntary individual choice, which liberates individuals from social roles and duties. By contrast, Chapter 6 demonstrates that the claims of religious freedom made by "spiritual seekers" are in conformity with a collective discourse, which is encouraged and shaped by their teachers. Besides, these claims of emancipating freedom also express personal responsibility to make the "right" choices. The pervasive discourses on the necessity of "working" on oneself clearly show that self-realization is an imperative that in fact encourages the normalization of individuals' conducts—hence the focus on controlling the ego, eliminating "negative" emotions, and cultivating moral virtues. The self is actually the locus of discipline: through norms and practices learned in "spiritual" settings, individuals become the active and autonomous agents of their own regulation. Finally, the quest of self-realization cannot be understood outside its political and economic context. A "flexible" economy, combined with the undermining of state welfare provision, requires proactive, self-reliant, flexible, and endlessly actualizing individuals. Here lie the roots of the psychologization of social life: individual transformation becomes the solution for everything, from personal troubles to social problems. Experts, professionals, and therapeutic methods have thus proliferated to answer these social needs. Through techniques of self-realization, social actors try to find ways to gain control over their lives, as their increasingly opaque and complex social environments offer smaller safety nets and less collective protections.

Which individuals are prone to use exotic religious teachings for this purpose and what role these teachings play in their socio-professional trajectories were the questions addressed in the last chapter. Chapter 7 described how religious discourses and values allow some individuals to express anxieties about their social positioning as well as desires of social emancipation, which are reflected in their unconventional lifestyles and occupations. Self-realization, as enhancement of emotional and cultural competence, is ultimately about social positioning and mobility. Indeed, it is typically middle-class individuals who practice yoga, meditation, or Kabbalah as a means of managing their behaviors and emotions, thereby meeting the specific requirements of middle-class professional and social lives. Gender matters as well: the previous chapter noted that the predominantly female students seem to find emotional skills in yoga, meditation, or Kabbalah, enabling them to perform gendered roles. Gender and class overlap: exotic religious resources fully and directly become professional skills for those who work in the fields of personal growth, post-psychoanalytic, and holistic therapies, and these individuals are often women who find in these professions a continuation of their role as caregiver and nurturer. These particular social trajectories underscore the potential transferability of skills between the religious, professional, and domestic realms, which is implicitly encapsulated in the pursuit of self-realization. Ultimately, it is in relation to the cultural competence sought by the middle class that religious exoticism per se takes its full significance. Students of exotic religious teachings typically (but not exclusively) belong to the "new petite bourgeoisie." They therefore tend to be society's cultural brokers for whom access to, production, and control of cultural resources are of paramount importance—hence their predisposition to cosmopolitanism, whereby the cultures of others are appropriated as resources of self-making, distinction, and assets in their professional fields (design, entertainment, therapy, etc.). Such use of yoga or Kabbalah by traders of culture and tastemakers explains the pursuit of fetishized forms of otherness, but also the absence of conversion, the rejection of ethnic identities, and discomfort toward values and practices that are not in tune with those of the urban middle class.

The notion of religious exoticism allowed us to describe a particular relationship with religious traditions. Religious exoticism does not concern *all* forms of interaction with religions, and on the micro-level it can simply represent a phase of commitment in the trajectory of individuals who may later have a different involvement with the Hindu or Jewish tradition. Yet I contend that it captures a relatively common form of relationship with religious resources and plays a central part in the worldwide popularization of Hindu, Buddhist, Kabbalistic, Sufi, or shamanic teachings. This relationship implies the idealization of religious traditions as being primordial, mystical, and authentic; it aims at dramatizing an opposition to one's own culture and religious background in order to reflect on, criticize, and reclaim the latter through a cultural detour. Religious exoticism is pragmatic and, paradoxically, self-referential. Thus, exotic religious resources are constructed and disseminated on the terms of those who appropriate them. Behind aesthetics and pleasure, religious exoticism implies implicit power relations and prompts questions about who can appropriate symbolic resources, who can be appropriated, and who defines the terms of appropriation—even if religious leaders

have proved to be active agents of this process of appropriation. Religious exoticism is fundamentally ambivalent: fascination coexists with discomfort, resistance, and dismissive attitudes. This ambivalence has direct implications
for the nature of members' commitment and identity, and for the possible
expansion of religious movements offering Hindu, Kabbalistic, Buddhist, shamanic, or Sufi teachings.

Religious exoticism's ambivalence and pragmatism entail a translation
of cultural and religious resources that renders them safe, comprehensible,
and therefore available for appropriation. While exoticism dramatizes and
fetishizes differences, paradoxically their domestication involves the neutralization of these differences. Indeed, neo-Hindu movements or the Kabbalah
Centre may "exoticize" their teachings by referring to Kashmir Shaivism or
Moroccan Kabbalah, for example, but the dissemination of their teachings
primarily means their detachment from their original religious and cultural
frameworks, their universalization, and their presentation as non-prescriptive
"spiritualities." This explains why on the macro-level the popularization of
exotic religious resources primarily takes the shape of the diversification of
fragmented teachings that are de-contextualized—hence religious exoticism's
inherent link to bricolage. Yet, this process of domestication also generates a
process of homogenization of religion: the doctrines, practices, and modes of
transmission of Kabbalah, Hinduism, Sufism, Buddhism, and so forth have
been significantly shaped by Euroamerican therapy culture. They are more
often than not consumed as practical and efficient techniques of management
of emotions and attitudes. This consumption contributes to the self-making
of the middle classes of advanced industrial societies, who seek to acquire the
emotional and cultural capital that is necessary for their formation.

Religious exoticism sheds new light on bricolage. Sociologists of religion
have viewed bricolage as one of the main features of religiosity in advanced
industrial societies. By this term they have often implied that, as a result of
the privatization of religion, social actors freely pick and mix, and consume,
a variety of religious resources, thereby making personal combinations of
their own (Hervieu-Léger 2001; Luckmann 1990). To describe these practices, Mary (1994) prefers to use the notion of "collage," which, contrary to
the Levi-Straussian notion of bricolage, is neither limited by a restricted range
of available symbolic resources, nor constrained by the original meaning
of these resources. According to Mary, postmodern individuals engage in
self-conscious practices of cutting and pasting, celebrating the fragmentary
and the liberation from grand narratives. Working on a similar field to mine,
Srinivas (2010) insists on the free usage of religious resources in the so-called
postmodern world: she argues that Sathya Sai Baba devotees "craft" a personal

religious system and identity according to their own subjective authority. Bricolage is, in Srinivas's view, empowering for the *bricoleurs,* demonstrating their agency and ability to live in a multicultural environment.

These approaches to bricolage (or "collage") in advanced industrial societies thus assume that social actors engage with otherness in a free, unproblematic, and playful manner. This book shows that this is inaccurate: relationships with exotic religious resources are often ambivalent. As such, they raise feelings of discomfort and provoke attitudes of rejection. Individuals' superficial involvement with exotic religious resources does not demonstrate their freedom, but rather the difficulty of engaging with foreign religious beliefs and practices. And I contend that this is precisely what limits the transnational expansion of, for instance, neo-Hindu and Kabbalistic teachings. Accordingly, while Mary (1994) rightfully suggests that collages partially break with original systems of meaning, the de-contextualization of exotic religious resources is not a result of indifference to meaning. Quite the contrary: the popularization of exotic religious resources is conditioned, to a certain extent, by a process of neutralization of differences and particularisms. Hinduism and Judaism need to appear less Hindu and less Jewish respectively (in terms of language, liturgy, doctrine, and identity of the movements, leadership, and members), to be popularized. In fact, organizational strategies, transformations of leadership and membership, and hazardous symbolic transformations constitute the backstage of bricolage. Furthermore, these complex and conflicted processes of negotiations and reinterpretations also respond to the management of religious diversity and the religious landscape at the national level. Therefore, in all sorts of ways, otherness matters in contemporary bricolage. The ignorance of Hinduism or Judaism as lived and practiced is not indifference, but a necessary and functional feature of the domestication of otherness. In other words, contemporary practices of bricolage are more constrained than Mary presumes, although he rightfully underlines the fact that they fundamentally differ from those undertaken in colonial contexts: in its contemporary form, bricolage presupposes ambivalence toward otherness and a sense of entitlement, both allowing reinterpretations that are truly freer than in the syncretisms of colonized cultures.

We cannot consider that individuals pick and mix components of various religious traditions unproblematically, because their practice of bricolage presupposes interpretations and transformations that made these components familiar and safe. This book has shown that through a long historical process, neo-Hinduism and Kabbalah have gradually been constructed as ancient, authentic, mysterious, and vibrant alternatives to the disenchantment of the modern West. Exotic religious resources are in fact all the more "easily" appropriated because they have been shaped by their new audience's expectations. Neo-Hinduism and Kabbalah are desired to be universal, malleable, and tolerant "spiritualities" that one can freely draw on to find techniques for the realization of the self. This self-referential and pragmatic usage of exotic religious resources certainly prompts questions about Srinivas's claim that through their practice of bricolage, western disciples of Sathya Sai Baba display an ability to engage with pluralism. Cultural competence is indeed what this bricolage wants to generate and express, but the author fails to recognize the process of distinction that is at play in bricolage. In this regard, it is striking that Srinivas (2010, 249) does not ponder on these multicultural skills when evoking tensions between the Indian and overseas branches of the Sathya Sai Baba movement. Nor does she reflect on the nationalistic dimension of the guru's teaching, and how this relates to the alleged pluralistic mindset of his disciples. By emphasizing the freedom and playfulness of individuals engaged in practices of bricolage, scholars overlook issues of power and politics that are at play in bricolage. Bricolage in advanced industrial societies does not involve *any* religious tradition, but draws on specific cultural encounters. The asymmetrical nature of these encounters (European imperialism in Asia and the Christian West's relationship with Judaism) reminds us that bricolage is far from being simply a "personal" matter; it also explains its ambivalent nature, as well as the sense of entitlement that it presupposes in fetishizing, constructing, appropriating, and consuming otherness.

    Sociological approaches to bricolage often overestimate agency and, by assuming that individuals craft personal patchworks of religious resources, they inflate the eclecticism of bricolage. They thus do not investigate fully the limits, logics, and coherence of contemporary practices of bricolage, which are nonetheless indicated by Campiche (2003) and Champion (2004). In recent writings, Hervieu-Léger (2005) has acknowledged that individual practices of bricolage are restricted by the availability of resources in a given social environment (yet we have underlined that they are not "available" but are made available) and by social actors' unequal access to these resources encountered by social actors. But Skeggs (2004) showed that, rather than an issue of "access," the appropriation of symbolic resources is a class-based, stratifying predisposition. Despite noting these limits of bricolage, Hervieu-Léger (2005, 30) still believes in the eclectic nature of bricolage.

    Bricolage is not as eclectic as one might think, precisely because of the process of domestication and de-contextualization this book describes. As they spread transnationally, neo-Hindu movements and the Kabbalah Centre presented their teaching as "universal" and downplayed references to Hindu or Jewish doctrines. Increasingly drawing on ideas and methods from popular psychology, they provided standardized methods for self-realization. In fact, there is considerable coherence within bricolage, whose central narrative is the inner-worldly realization of the self. Despite their different cultural roots and provenance, exotic religious teachings tend to offer similar methods for assessing, improving, and normalizing the self toward more resilience, autonomy, and adaptability. This coherence around a central narrative and the standardization of religious teachings through their psychologization explain the facility with which social actors use many of them, successively or simultaneously. They consistently explain that they do not see any contradiction between them. This may suggest that they are indifferent to differences in terms of doctrines, but also that these differences are actually not that outstanding. Their biographical discourses are standardized and emphasize the desire to realize one's self, a perception of life as a process of self-improvement, the emphasis on autonomy and resilience, a sense of individual responsibility and voluntarism in the process of self-improvement, and an accepting attitude. Self-realization is what drives practices of bricolage. Through exotic religious resources, individuals consistently seek practical methods for personal growth in "lifelong religious learning." The participation in a wide range of course and events also ensures the continuous re-skilling of alternative therapists, coaches, and "spiritual" teachers; for these freelancers in competitive and unregulated professions, knowledge and control of such religious resources are vital. Accordingly, despite an apparent eclecticism, religious incursions in yoga, meditation, or Kabbalah contribute to a quest that is far from being volatile, inconsistent, or truly eclectic.

Bricolage is not as individual as one would think, either. Mary (2005) views the significance of individualism to be a norm that structures what he calls postmodern collages, but without considering the extent to which individualism considerably limits the individual and eclectic nature of these collages. By and large, contemporary sociology of religion is often prone to misinterpreting individualism, as discussed in Chapter 6 of this book. It is sometimes assumed that, nowadays, empowered individuals free themselves from collective norms, roles, and duties, self-consciously choose beliefs and practices in accordance with personally felt needs and experiences, and, by doing so, craft identities and even religions of their own. I will not further discuss the unsociological nature of these assumptions (see Chapter 6). Bricolage is, in fact, structured by social norms and pressures that are exerted upon individuals in advanced industrial societies, in particular the personal responsibility for realizing one's self through their active participation. This involves learning to become the active and autonomous agent of one's own regulation—recognizing and managing emotions, behaviors, and thoughts, eliminating "negative" attitudes, being proactive, taking responsibilities, and cultivating moral virtues. Assuming the empowering nature of self-realization reveals a profound misunderstanding: individualism does not entail emancipation from, but the internalization of, social norms. In addition, one could argue that, through individuals' engagement with a diversity of books, retreats, courses, and rituals, practices of bricolage reinforce the learning of a normative code of conduct that transcends specific religious teachings and therapeutic techniques. Neoliberalism, as flexible economy and political agenda, requires individuals to be increasingly responsible for their well-being. It rewards entrepreneurial individuals who are willing to actualize and manage themselves, to adapt to their environment rather than seeking to modify it. Unsurprisingly, middle-class individuals are better equipped in this regard.

The idea of free individual choice in bricolage has been also suggested by the emphasis on consumerism. Yet the consumption of religious goods and services does not preclude the adoption of norms and values: in fact, classes and workshops that are paid for are important contexts of teaching, learning and internalizing norms. Besides, the reader of Marx's *Das Kapital* is aware that capitalism is fundamentally about value, which is enshrined in the object of consumption and drives its circulation on the market. Accordingly, what matters in the fact that social actors pay for "spiritual" services is not the monetary transaction, but the issue of *value* granted to techniques for the enhancement of the self. It is through this enhancement that one hopes to "change" and hence find a partner, have a harmonious family life, develop new professional skills and ventures, and so forth. As shown by Bourdieu (1984), consumption is a matter of social distinction and social positioning. The consumption of exotic religious teachings contributes to the acquisition of emotional and cultural forms of capital that are of paramount importance for women and the middle class. This gendered and class-based process of distinction is therefore not an individual strategy transcending social norms and values, not the least because the transmission of religious teachings in workshops and courses strongly reflects the habitus of their participants.

Finally, bricolage does not generate personal and eclectic religious patchworks because its practice is gender- and class-based. Bricoleurs are predominantly female (Campiche 1997). The emphasis of exotic religious teachings (like many others) on managing emotions and developing loving and caring attitudes resonates with women's quest of harmony in the private sphere, as well as with the requirements of the professions they often occupy in the medical, therapeutic, and educational sectors. Bricoleurs are also predominantly middle class: the ability to manage emotions is indeed constitutive of the reproduction of this social stratum (Illouz 2008) and explains the appeal of techniques of the self. Furthermore, it is typically the members of the "new petite bourgeoisie" who "talk" about their social positioning through the exploration and appropriation of foreign religious resources. Some of their discourses and distinctive countercultural life-styles express a desire for emancipation from the social constraints that characterize the lives of this educated yet dominated fringe of the middle class. *Déclassés*, the members of the "new petite bourgeoisie" refuse social forms of classification and are attracted by cultural subversion and heresy. As such, they are predisposed to play a vanguard role in relation to cul-ture and lifestyle. Practices of bricolage with mysterious and distinctive symbolic resources thus allow these cultural intermediaries to display cultural competence and maintain their role in the game of cultural and symbolic struggle. This entails access to, and knowledge of, cultural re-sources: knowing what is worthy of interest and how cultural resources can be "played" with. Ironically, it is as a stratifying social practice that one could say bricolage is empowering, for those who have the abilities and en-titlement to undertake it.

This book was written with the aim of contributing to a better under-standing of practices of bricolage with foreign religious traditions. I believe that the framework of religious exoticism allows the book to accomplish this aim. Beyond the study of this particular issue, the study presented here also has sought to address important weaknesses of today's sociology of religion. The isolation of this subfield from mainstream social theory, as well as its overestimation of subjectivity and agency through the excessive consideration given to discourses and representations, is taking its toll. There is an urgent need to reintegrate issues of power, class formation, social interactions, and practice, and to renew the understanding of individualism in religious life, if we do not want to see sociology becoming (or re-becoming?) theology's ancil-lary discipline.

Notes

INTRODUCTION

1. The names of research participants have been changed to protect their anonymity.
2. By "spirituality," this book refers to research participants' use of the term, hence my use of quotation marks. For reasons explained in Chapter 6, I do not believe that "spirituality" is a useful sociological concept, especially when contrasted with "religion."
3. A pejorative term first used by Native Americans, referring to those trying to pass as traditional Native American healers.
4. Interviews have been conducted in French, English, and Brazilian Portuguese in accordance with interviewees' mother tongues. I used French and English to conduct my interviews in Israel; English has significantly spread among the Israeli population, and the Kabbalah Centre's audience tend to be educated, middle-class Israeli who usually have a good command of English. Many also have Sephardic origins and French is their mother tongue. Not speaking Hebrew was not a hindrance in participant observation either; it prompted students to engage with me intensively, by explaining rituals and prayers and by translating teachers' commentaries. The interviews cited in this book have been translated into English by myself when originally in French or Portuguese.
5. Post-doctoral fellowship funded by the British Economic and Social Research Council (PTA-026-27-0864).
6. In France: the president of the MIVILUDES, the persons in charge of the Office of religious organizations (Bureau des Cultes), and the spokesperson of the CAP, an organization which in the name of NRMs and their members sued the main anti-cult organization. In England: representatives of the Inner Cities

Religious Council, the Cohesion and Faith Unit, the Charity Commission, and INFORM, a charity based in the London School of Economics whose aims are to collect and diffuse information on NRMs to the public. A quick interview was conducted by phone with the chair of the Cult Information Centre.

7. Funded by a research grant from the British Economic and Social Research Council (RES-063-27-0041).

CHAPTER 1

1. "All Oriental religions, without exception, were being asphyxiated to death by the poisonous gas of Western official science, through the medium of the educational agencies of European administrations and missionary propagandists, and...the natives graduates and undergraduates of India, Ceylon and Japan had largely turned agnostics and revilers of the old religions" (Blavatsky 1951, 113–114).

2. King (1999, 107) criticized the use of "neo-Hinduism" since this concept implies the existence of a clear-cut, definite, and unambiguous category "Hinduism" from which "neo-Hindu" movements departed. However, this concept, used by Hacker (in Halbfass 1995), presents some advantages: it insists on the inclusion of Western values and religious revitalization, encapsulated in an affirmation of Hindu identity.

3. Vivekananda's emphasis on this particular Hindu doctrine is not independent from the fact that European orientalists and philosophers had been fascinated by Vedanta, through which they "discovered" a universal and monistic metaphysical principle, believed to be the central component of Hinduism itself and the source of Western philosophy. With the Orientalists and the Theosophical society, Vivekananda would largely contribute to furthering the generalization of a particular Vedantic school, the Advaita Vedanta of Shankara (circa 800 C.E.), as the essence of Hinduism and as a universal religion—despite the fact that, before its translation into English and modern Indian languages in the nineteenth century, little was known about Advaita Vedanta by Hindus themselves (King 1999, 118–142; Killingley 1993, 92; Kopf 1969, 38; Schwab 1950, 447).

4. Interview with a representative of Liberal Judaism, London, November 19, 2008.

5. The following section has greatly benefited from the thorough history of the Kabbalah Centre written by Myers (2007). It is completed by data collected through the interviews of teachers and students who have been in the Centre for many years and have witnessed its evolution.

6. Certificate of incorporation of National Institute for Research in Kabbalah, July 14, 1965, New York.

7. This even applies to accusation of black magic and occult practices against Jews, sometimes made in relation to Kabbalah.

8. "The term 'protestant Buddhism' in my usage has two meanings. (a) [...] many of its norms and organizational forms are historical derivatives from Protestant Christianity. (b) More importantly, from the contemporary point of view, it is a protest *against* Christianity and its associated Western political dominance prior to independence" (Obeyesekere 1970, 46–47).

CHAPTER 2

1. Marranos were Jews of the Iberic Peninsula who, forced to convert in the fifteenth century, secretly continued to observe Judaism.

2. I have purposely interviewed individuals who do not only come to the Sivananda Centres for yoga classes, because I expect that they would not necessarily have a particular attraction for Hinduism as religious resources. It is striking that those I have interviewed, that is to say, who come to the weekly satsangs, give yoga courses in or outside the Centre, volunteer more or less regularly to help the Centre, or even live full-time in the ashram, express such resistance regarding the Centre's Hindu-ness.

3. In Siddha Yoga the audience faces the pictures of Gurumayi, Muktananda, and his own guru, Nityananda. A large armchair (either occupied by Gurumayi or symbolizing her presence) also faces the followers.

4. This is by no means a characteristic of these two case studies. About Sathya Sai Baba's followers, Bowen (1988, 55) writes that "amongst the problems encountered by non-Indian devotees in the United Kingdom [...] is their concern to be associated with Sathya Sai Baba's devotional and mystical way without having to become 'English Hindus' and to 'engage in ritualistic worship.'"

5. On responsibility and empowerment, see Chapter 6.

6. A student told Myers (2007, 191) that, years ago, the Kabbalah Centre had a program of conversion. Like Siddha Yoga swamis, people's short-term commitment made the Kabbalah Centre drop this initiative.

7. Like "spiritual India," exoticism is easy to observe in interviewees' evocation of their trips to Israel, which is less about the current Israeli society than diving in its mythical references and having "experiences." For instance, Farrah, whose travels of the last decade have all been "spiritual trips," described an "amazing energy experience" along Jerusalem's wailing wall, at Masada and Safed, thereby exclusively referring to Israel's ancient history. By and large, there is a whole market for "spiritual tourism" in Israel, as in India. Thus it is possible to get the "Safed Kabbalah experience," sponsored by the Jewish Federation of Palm Beach County. This "Kabbalah-Tour" package includes classes, workshops, excursions, and "a variety of exciting activities, guaranteed

to make the visitors want to extend their stay and deepen their experience" (Safed Kabbalah World Center n.d.). "Mystical Tours of Israel" with spiritual leaders "open hearts and minds by giving a fresh perspective on the holiest of Chasidic and Kabbalistic sites in Eretz Yisrael" (Hachesed n.d.). Finally, the Lubavitch movement organizes Shabbat weekends in Safed (Ascent of Safed n.d.). The Kabbalah Centre, too, organizes "Kabbalistic Energy Tours" to "sacred" places such as Safed, the Dead Sea, and Jerusalem (Kabbalah Centre 2012a).

8. Similarly, Romy "loved Israel" at the same time she is dismissive of it: Israel "just feels really like home. But the climate is bad and the Israelis are rude, and I don't want to live here but . . . [laughs] . . . Tel Aviv as such is a mess. Dusty, dirty, hot, sticky, you know. What's good in Tel Aviv? But it has Bnei Baruch. And the whole area feels absolutely amazing."

9. One of the Kabbalah Centre teachers told me that he was confronted with anti-Semitism once, when teaching Kabbalah in Poland. A student asked him whether he was Jewish and once he told him he was, the student replied he did not look like a Jew. "Why?" the teacher asked, "Is it a compliment or an insult?" The student replied that a Jew was someone who does not take his breakfast before having taken advantage of someone else. The teacher explained he did not take it personally and did not stop teaching the student because he was an anti-Semite, but because he was constantly contradicting and questioning his legitimacy. One could wonder whether these are two different reasons.

10. Fixed on the doorway, a mezuzah contains a parchment with Torah verses.

11. I would like to thank Patricia Birman, Michel Gherman, Emerson Giumbelli, David Lehmann, and Bila Sorj for their comments and discussion on ideas developed in this section.

12. Spiritism became fashionable among the Brazilian elite when Kardecism was imported from France in the nineteenth century; today it attracts primarily the middle classes (Brown 1994, 16). Pentecostal churches have attracted the poorer sections of Brazilian society, although they now seem to develop among middle classes, too (Oro 2000).

13. Umbanda appeared in the 1920s and refers to a range of diverse beliefs and practices drawing on Kardecism and Afro-Brazilian religions. Umbanda shares with these two religious traditions "a belief in the active intervention of spiritual entities in the lives of humankind, and the practices of spirit possessions as the central means by which these entities communicate with and help or hinder humans" (Brown 1994, 2).

14. Tony Robbins (1960–) is an American self-help expert. NLP stands for neuro-linguistic programming, a post-psychoanalytic therapy created in the American countercultural context.

15. A few nonetheless explain being uncomfortable when non-Jewish men hold the Torah scrolls during Shabbat and festivals.

CHAPTER 3

1. See, for example, Naam Yoga n.d.; Universal Kabbalah Network 2007.
2. This former teacher considers that Israeli students are religious in some ways, even when they identified themselves as secular and express defiance toward religious institutions and their authority.
3. According to the Talmud, God gave seven laws to Noah for all humanity. They prohibit idolatry, murder, theft, immoral sexual practices, blasphemy, and the consumption of a living animal. The seventh principle is that just laws and a court of justice are also required to enforce these six principles.
4. *Dasanami* refers to the 10 ancient monastic orders founded by Shankara, probably the most respected in India.
5. Most of them have retracted their approbations since then.
6. Ninette was interviewed in French, her mother tongue.
7. At the same time, Israeli students do not reject entirely the movement's cosmopolitan approach. A former teacher recalls that in the 2000s the Tel Aviv branch was very successful in bringing a "universal touch by creating, let's say, an Indian Shabbat. So Indian Shabbat was on a Friday night and we had sitting with us at the head of the table the Indian Ambassador and his wife and somebody was a specialist in Hindu religions, teaching people about the basics of Hinduism and how it's connected to Kabbalah [...] we had a Georgian Shabbat, we had a Moroccan Shabbat, we had also, we had a Druze Shabbat that involved Druzes [...] to talk about their beliefs, what they are allowed to talk about. So we brought a whole busload of the leaders of the Druze community. So every Friday night like this was six hundred people [...] *people did not feel it's nationalism, people were kind of more lefty* [...] *people loved it.*"
8. Before founding his ashram in Pondicherry in 1910, Aurobindo (1872–1950) was an activist for the Independence of India and was arrested for terrorism by the British police. For him, "[n]ationalism is not a mere political programme," but "a religion that has come from God"; "If you are going to be a nationalist, if you are going to assent to this religion of nationalism, you must do it in the religious spirit" (cited in Bhatt 2001, 38).
9. This form of divide is even found in India: Hoyez (2012, 103–106) found that Rishikesh's ashrams are characterized by a "socio-spatial segregation" between those primarily welcoming foreigners (often the guru lived in Europe or North America and is bilingual), and those focused on the observance of Hinduism. Targeting an Indian audience, the latter may even deny entry to foreigners.
10. ISKCON has also a distinctive trajectory as a result of South Asian migration to Britain and North America in the 1960s and 1970s (Chapter 4). It would be interesting to see whether the popularization of Buddhism in Euroamerican societies was facilitated by similar membership characteristics—for instance,

Coleman (2001, 20) observes that in what he calls "Western Buddhism," members are overwhelmingly "white."

11. The Sufi Order International described by Philippon (2014) might operate in a similar fashion: while in Euroamerican context the movement celebrates Sufism as being above all religions and dogma (which allows and involves bricolage), in Pakistan it contributes to a re-islamization of its members and therefore its teaching aims to be faithful to Islam in some ways.

12. Bnei Baruch now disseminates Kabbalah to non-Jews, too. It maintains traditional Kabbalah's distinctions between Jews and non-Jews and the idea that the Jewish people will initiate the repair of the world. Religious observance is advised for Jewish students only (Myers 2011). Throughout my fieldwork, I found that Bnei Baruch attracts disappointed students of the Kabbalah Centre.

CHAPTER 4

1. I use the word "community" between quotes precisely to signify that I do not assume the factual existence of "communities" and want to emphasize the political meaning of the term. In the British political context, "communities" are social constructions enforced by a particular type of relation between institutions and specific collective actors, identified as ethnic or religious minorities.

2. The controversy over the Bhaktivedanta manor thoroughly investigated by Nye (1996a, 1996b, 1997, 1998, 2001) reinforced ISKCON's bonds with other Hindu organizations and raised its profile as a legitimate Hindu movement. Festivals in the manor are extremely popular and gather up to 25,000 participants, but posed problems for residents in the surrounding area in terms of traffic, noise, and parking space. In the 1980s, local planning authorities initially attempted to limit the numbers of visitors. They argued that the manor was registered as a theological college and as such could not welcome participants for worship activities, which are in fact inappropriate activities in the protected area where the manor is located. ISKCON fought several legal battles at the national and European levels to allow public worship at the manor, before its right to do so was granted in 1996. The limitation of the manor's activities was successfully presented by ISKCON as epitomizing a Christian hegemony against the Hindu minority in Britain and as an offense against religious freedom. ISKCON received the support of many stakeholders, such as the VHP, Hindu Council of the UK, and the NCHT, insisting on the importance of the manor for the Hindu "community" in Britain. This successful campaign projected "Hindus as a recognizable community within the logic of multicultural Britain, a community with 'rights' based on their religious practices that were legitimately defendable in public contexts" (Zavos 2008, 329).

3. The word is used by social actors and in official documents.

4. This results, first of all, from Hinduism's internal diversity. Hinduism is traditionally not seen as a unitary religion but as a diversity of schools, sects, and gurus' teachings; religious practices are also diversified by ethnic and caste divisions and, unlike some other religions, Hinduism does not have one unified and regulating structure. Accordingly, this diversity is unavoidably reflected in British Hinduism. Second, in Britain, migration trends are culturally diverse—from South Asia, East Africa, Fiji, and Caribbean islands. Third, patterns of local settlement generated a mosaic of various local Hindu "communities" (Bowen 1987; Knott 1987, 1989, 2009).

5. A fixed term advisory body set up within the Department of Communities and Local Government in order to explore good practices around cultural and religious diversity and social cohesion on the local level.

6. Information collected during an informal discussion with a UNADFI volunteer.

7. In comparison, British charity status facilitates a hierarchical organization. British charities decide how many trustees manage the branch and the length of their mandate; these trustees are not necessarily elected but can be co-opted by their peers according to criteria they have decided upon. In this context, trustees make organizational decisions and do not need a majority vote from the members. Thus, in Britain, nothing in Siddha Yoga formalizes membership. This structure facilitates a top-down organization through communication from the guru and the headquarters to the British trustees, who then apply decisions without the agreement of other followers, which elicited certain criticisms about the lack of consultation and transparency from some British interviewees.

8. Ironically, this underlines the fact that while the 1905 law stipulates that the Republic does not recognize any religion, this founding principle tends to be contradicted by the normative usage of 1905 and 1901 laws.

9. By comparison, there were at the same time up to 700 weekly students at the London Sivananda Centre.

10. Interview with civil servants from the Interior Ministry's office of religion.

11. An earlier version of this section has been published in Altglas (2011).

12. This is actually not an exceptional view in ultra-Orthodox Judaism; other religious figures, such as Ashlag, linked the neglect of Kabbalah with the Holocaust, and felt that from now on the dissemination of Kabbalah was imperatively needed (Garb 2008, 31).

13. Sophie Favier: a television animator who started her career in nude magazines and unsuccessfully tried to further her career as a singer and an actress, and writer Paul-Loup Sulitzer, whose best-sellers, perceived as commodities written by a team, are rejected by the literary milieu. In the 2000s he was involved in an important case of arms trafficking in Angola and subsequently was condemned for fraud.

14. The media's frequent references to academics have the same effect, since there also has been a normative debate among scholars of Jewish studies regarding the Kabbalah Centre. Renowned expert on Kabbalah, Joseph Dan (2002, 285 n.56), commented on Berg's enterprise: "it was heartbreaking to observe how this authentic enterprise deteriorated into New Age mishmash of nonsense." Some refused to see it as a proper teaching of Jewish mysticism rather than a commercial venture (Garb 2006) or a cult (Ludwig 2006, 118–122). Referring to the Kabbalah Centre's bottles of Kabbalah water, red string, and scanned Zohar, Rose (2005, 27) also contended that "these are not the kabbalistic practices we need to perpetuate." In response, other academics questioned the legitimacy of these "guardians" of the tradition (Huss 2007b) to evaluate the authenticity of religious teachings. They have underlined that some aspects of the Kabbalah Centre that are today criticized have precedents and can also be understood in the context of modern expressions of Judaism (Goldish 2005; Mopsik 2004; Myers 2007). Thus, Huss (2005, 623) contends that the Kabbalah Centre "is a significant contemporary cultural phenomenon; it deserves to be studied rather than sneered at" (see also Huss 2007a; 2007b; forthcoming).

15. For example, Jacob Immanuel Schochet, a Lubavitch rabbi and scholar in Canada who has written many books, including one on Kabbalah's concepts and doctrines. In the beginning of the 1990s, the Kabbalah Centre attempted to sue him for libel and slander after he criticized it in a conference in South Africa.

16. My translation. References cannot be given to protect the interviewee's anonymity.

17. These reports simply mention the media's interest for the Kabbalah Centre; drawing on press articles, they present the movement as an example of the debasement of esotericism and of the instrumentalization of humanitarian assistance (MIVILUDES 2005a, 2005b).

18. Interviewed by the parliamentary commission on the influence of cults on children, the head of the Bureau des Cultes (the Interior Ministry body that registers "religious organizations" and "congregations") strongly criticized the MIVILUDES's interest in the Lubavitch. He deplored the MIVILUDES's normative judgments and the fact that its stigmatization of movements such as the Lubavitch could justify anti-Semitic and malevolent acts under the cover of a righteous combat against "cultic aberrations." Didier Leschi's public interview at the Parliamentary Commission on the influence of cults on children, Paris, October 17, 2006.

19. Statement written around 2004 and obtained directly from the United Synagogue.

20. My translation. References cannot be given to protect the interviewee's anonymity.

21. When they do so, 60 percent are affiliated to a mainstream Orthodox synagogue, yet more than 27 percent are affiliated to one of the Progressive sectors (Gidley and Khan-Harris 2010, 1; Institute for Jewish Policy Research 1996, 16 and 2000, 11).

22. Israel uses the Millet system inherited from the Turkish law, hence only recognizing certain religious groups that are entitled to government financial support—Druze, Orthodox Judaism, Islam, and the historical Christian denominations (Beit-Hallahmi 1991, 206).

23. The most important of Israeli anti-cult movements is Yad Laahim, an anti-missionary movement supported by the state, Orthodox, and ultra-Orthodox organizations. Yad Laahim is at war against what conflicts with Orthodox values, from abortion to mixed marriages with Israeli Arabs (Beit-Hallahmi 1991, 210); its combat against "cults" aims to draw their members back into the fold of Orthodox Judaism (Cavaglion 2008, 88).

24. France has the biggest Jewish population in Europe with 500,000 individuals, while there are 267,000 Jews in Britain (data from the UK National Statistics, *Census 2001: National Report for England and Wales*; Erik Cohen 2004).

25. This intellectual interest in Kabbalah finds its roots in the École d'Orsay of Jewish studies with Léon Ashkénazi (1922–1996) and Emmanuel Lévinas (1906–1995). These philosophers have been fundamental in developing modern Jewish thought in the postwar period. They have often referred to Kabbalah but were primarily interested in its philosophical implications (Mopsik 2007).

CHAPTER 5

1. For example, informed by a Jungian framework, the American 12-step programs such as Alcoholic Anonymous, created in the 1930s, already drew on the assumption that addiction results from unfulfilled spiritual needs. Therefore the cure involves accepting to surrender to a higher force; it encourages prayer and meditation in order to reach a healing spiritual awakening (Rice 1994).

2. I'm grateful to Nicola Carr for pointing out this effect of self-improvement to me.

3. Cf. Chopra (1997). Deepak Chopra's 10 key steps to happiness emphasize the existence of a higher reality beyond the physical world, self-examination and control of thoughts and emotions, building of self-confidence, replacing "fear-motivated" behaviors with "love-motivated" ones, and taking responsibility rather than blaming others (cited in Carrette and King 2005, 100).

4. In his research on American "seeker churches," Sargeant (2000, 5) evokes a special version of the Bible sold by a Baptist reverend called "Kwickscan": presenting essential passages in bolder type, it allows one to "scan words" for speed Bible reading.

5. London Kabbalah Centre (2008b).

CHAPTER 6

1. However, conservative religions do not necessarily involve a form of "coercion" distinct from the present case studies or New Age milieus. Berman's (2009, 75) study of Chabad in the United States outlines that as part of their outreach strategy, members tend to avoid "verbal persuasion" or open normative comments about transgression of commandments, appropriate clothing, texts to study: "some families, of course, used more verbal persuasion than others. Nonetheless, I never heard an individual directly asked to change anything about his or her beliefs or lifestyle."

2. Lanza Del Vasto (1901–1981) was one of the French personalities who popularized Hinduism before the countercultural period. Influenced by Romain Rolland's books on Gandhi, Lanza del Vasto traveled to India in 1936 to meet the Indian sage. Lanza del Vasto considered Gandhi to be his spiritual guide and endeavored to popularize the Gandhian principle of nonviolence in Europe. At the end of the 1950s, he founded the "Order of Gandhians in the West," also called the Ark, which would become one of the first rural communities of postwar France. This avant-garde community became influential in the context of May 1968.

3. Men can also express this desire of differentiated roles, as Avi illustrates: "in post-modern society it's really... fading but I really connect to that, I feel like, I want to be a man and I want my woman to be a woman. And I'm not a chauvinist or something." After leaving the Kabbalah Centre, Avi joined a more traditional synagogue in Tel Aviv.

4. This section draws on sociological research conducted in European and North American societies and is therefore most relevant for the case studies we have explored in France and the United Kingdom. Nevertheless, this general overview does not want to dismiss the importance of local variations. While Brazilian and Israeli societies certainly share some economic, social, and political features with Euroamerican societies, the limits of my expertise as well as the scarcity of the available literature on the subject do not allow me to claim that the social trends described in this section apply to these societies, irrespective of their specificities. I refer the reader to Dawson (2007) and Rocha (2006), who address the particular cultural, economic, and political factors that help to explain Brazilians' attraction for New Age milieus and Buddhism, respectively.

CHAPTER 7

1. Advertisement for a course at the London branch in 2010.

2. By and large, the "new religious consciousness" lost its radical edge since its emergence in the countercultural context of the 1960s; living a communitarian

utopia severed from a corrupt society is not what most individuals today are involved in or what NRMs aspire to.

3. The ethical dimension of Jane's training is emphasized by the name of her company, which cannot be indicated here for anonymity purposes.

4. Similarly, in Brazil, it is the urban middle class that is attracted by Buddhism: it allows them to differentiate themselves from the rest of the Brazilian population, and identify with the overseas cosmopolitan elites and their exclusive subculture (Rocha 2006, 149–150). In Pakistan and Morocco, westernized forms of Sufism attract a fraction of the urban, westernized, educated. and liberal bourgeoisie, repelled by popular or politicized Sufisms (Haenni and Voix 2006; Philippon 2014).

References

Abercrombie, Nicholas, Bryan S. Turner, and Stephen Hill. 1986. *Sovereign Individuals of Capitalism*. London: Allen & Unwin.

Accardo, Alain. 2006. *Introduction à une sociologie critique: lire Pierre Bourdieu*. Marseille: Agone.

Adkins, Lisa. 2000. "Objects of Innovation: Post-Occupational Reflexivity and Re-traditionalizations of Gender." In *Transformations: Thinking Through Feminism*, edited by Sara Ahmed, Jane Kilby, Celia Lury, Maureen McNeil, and Beverley Skeggs, 259–272. London: Routledge.

Adkins, Lisa, and Celia Lury. 1999. "The Labour of Identity: Performing Identities, Performing Economies." *Economy and Society* 28(4): 598–614.

Atkinson, Will. 2007. "Beck, Individualization and the Death of Class: A Critique." *British Journal of Sociology* 58(3): 349–366.

Adveeff, Alexis. 2010. "The Art of Living: Un mouvement indien au-delà des clivages religieux?" *Archives de Sciences Sociales des Religions* 149: 169–187.

Alderman, Geoffrey. 1992. *Modern British Jewry*. Oxford: Oxford University Press.

Allen, Chris. 2005. "From Race to Religion: The New Face of Discrimination." In *Muslim Britain: Communities under Pressure*, edited by Tahir Abbas, 49–65. London: Zed Books.

Altglas, Véronique. 2012. "La religion comme symptôme." In *Penser le religieux: le théologique et le social avec Pierre Gisel*, edited by Philippe Gonzalez and Christophe Monnot, 33–46. Geneva: Labor et Fidès.

———. 2011. "The Challenges of Universalizing Religions: The Kabbalah Centre in France and Britain." *Nova Religio* 15(1): 22–43.

———. 2010. "Laïcité Is What Laïcité Does: Rethinking the French Cult Controversy." *Current Sociology* 58(3): 1–22.

———. 2008. "French Cult Controversy at the Turn of the New Millennium: Escalation, Dissensions, and New Forms of Mobilisations across the Battlefield." In *The Centrality of Religion in Social Life: Essays in Honour of James A. Beckford*, edited by Eileen Barker, 55–68. London: Ashgate.

——. 2005. *Le nouvel hindouisme occidental*. Paris: CNRS.

——. 2000. "Living in Harmony: le pranayama à des fins thérapeutiques." *Ethnologie Française* 30 (4): 545–553.

——. 1998. *La diffusion de l'hindouisme en France à travers les divers mouvements religieux et pratiques se référant à l'hindouisme*, Sciences des religions et des systèmes de pensée, Postgraduate diss., École Pratique des Hautes Études.

——. 1997. *L'implantation des nouveaux mouvements religieux néo-hindous en France. Deux cas d'études: le Centre Sri Chinmoy et Sahaja Yoga*. Master diss., Université Paris X-Nanterre.

Appadurai, Arjun. 1986. *The Social Life of Things: Commodities in Cultural Perspective*. Cambridge: Cambridge University Press.

Arac, Jonathan, and Harriet Ritvo. 1991. "Introduction." In *Macropolitics of Nineteenth-Century Literature: Nationalism, Exoticism, Imperialism*, edited by Jonathan Arac and Harriet Ritvo, 1–11. Philadelphia: University of Pennsylvania Press.

Ariel, Yaakov. 2011. "From Neo-Hasidism to Outreach Yeshivot: The Origins of the Movements of Renewal and Return to Tradition." In *Kabbalah and Contemporary Spiritual Revival*, edited by Boaz Huss, 17–37. Beer-Sheva: Ben-Gurion University of the Negev Press.

——. 2003. "Hasidism in the Age of Aquarius: The House of Love and Prayer in San Francisco, 1967–1977." *Religion and American Culture* 13(2): 139–165.

——. 1999. *Evangelizing the Chosen People: Missions to the Jews in America, 1880–2000*. Chapel Hill: University of North Carolina Press.

Arriada Lorea, Roberto. 2009. "Brazilian Secularity and Minorities in the Biggest Catholic Nation in the World." *Archives de Sciences Sociales des Religions* 146: 81–97.

Asad, Talal. 1990. "Multiculturalism and British Identity in the Wake of the Rushdie Affair." *Politics and Society* 18: 455–480.

Asprem, Egil. 2007. "Kabbalah Recreata: Reception and Adaptation of Kabbalah in Modern Occultism." *The Pomegranate International Journal for Pagan Studies* 9(2): 132–153.

Atkinson, Jane M. 1992. "Shamanism Today." *Annual Review of Anthropology* 21: 307–330.

Atkinson, Will. 2007. "Beck, Individualization and the Death of Class: A Critique." *British Journal of Sociology* 58(3): 349–366.

Azzi, Corry, and Ronald Ehrenberg. 1975. "Household Allocation of Time and Church Attendance." *Journal of Political Economy* 83: 27–56.

Babb, Lawrence A. 1986. *Redemptive Encounters: Three Modern Styles in the Hindu Tradition*. Berkeley: University of California Press.

Bainbridge, William S. 1997. *The Sociology of Religious Movements*. New York: Routledge.

Bainbridge, William S., and Daniel H. Jackson. 1981. "The Rise and Decline of Transcendental Meditation." In *The Social Impact of New Religious Movements*, edited by Bryan R. Wilson, 135–158. New York: The Rose of Sharon Press.

Banerjee, Sikata, and Harold Coward. 2009. "Hindus in Canada: Negotiating Identity in a 'Different' Homeland." In *Religion and Ethnicity in Canada*, edited by David Seljak and Paul Bramadat, 30–51. Toronto: University of Toronto Press.

Barnes, Linda 2000. "The Psychologising of Chinese Healing Practices in the United States." *The European Journal of Oriental Medicine* 3(4). Accessed August 22, 2013. http://www.ejom.co.uk/vol-3-no-4/featured-article/the-psychologising-of-chinese-healing-practices-in-the-united-states.html.

Bastide, Roger. 1970. "Mémoire collective et sociologie du bricolage." *L'Année Sociologique* 21: 65–108.

Baumann, Martin. 2001. "Global Buddhism: Developmental Periods, Regional Histories, and a New Analytical Perspective." *Journal of Global Buddhism* 2: 1–43.

Bauman, Zygmunt. 1993. *Modernity and Ambivalence.* Cambridge: Polity Press.

Beaman, Lori G. 2013. "The Will to Religion: Obligatory Religious Citizenship." *Critical Research on Religion* 1: 141–157.

Beck, Ulrich, 1994. "Replies and Critiques: Self-Dissolution and Self-Endangerment of Industrial Society: What Does This Mean?" In *Reflexive Modernisation*, edited by Anthony Giddens, Ulrich Beck, and Scott Lash, 174–183. Cambridge: Polity Press.

——. 1992. *Risk Society: Towards a New Modernity.* London: Sage.

Beck, Ulrich, and Elisabeth Beck-Gernsheim. 2002. *Individualization.* London: Sage.

——. 1996. "Individualization and 'Precarious Freedom': Perspectives and Controversies of a Subject-Oriented Sociology." In *Detraditionalization, Critical Reflections on Authority and Identity*, edited by Scott Lash, Paul Morris, and Paul Heelas, 23–48. Oxford: Blackwell.

Beckerlegge, Gwilym. 2000. *The Ramakrishna Mission: The Making of a Modern Hindu Movement.* Delhi: Oxford University Press.

——. 1998. "Swami Vivekananda and Seva: Taking 'Social Service' Seriously." In *Swami Vivekananda and the Modernization of Hinduism*, edited by William Radice, 158–193. Delhi; New York: Oxford University Press.

Beckford, James A. 2012. "Public Religions and the Postsecular: Critical Reflections." *Journal for the Scientific Study of Religion* 51(1): 1–19.

——. 2004. "'Laicité', 'Dystopia,' and the Reaction to New Religious Movements in France." In *Regulating Religion, Cases Studies from Around the Globe*, edited by James T. Richardson, 27–52. New York: Kluwer Academic/Plenum Publishers.

——. 1989. *Religion and Advanced Industrial Society.* London: Routledge.

——. 1984. "Holistic Imagery and Ethics in New Religious and Healing Movements." *Social Compass* 31: 259–272.

——. 1983. "The Public Response to New Religious Movements in Britain." *Social Compass* 30(1): 49–62.

Beckford, James, Richard Gale, David Owen, Ceri Peach, and Paul Weller. 2006. *Review of the Evidence Base on Faith Communities*. London: Office of the Deputy Prime Minister.

Beit-Hallahmi, Benjamin. 1992. *Despair and Deliverance: Private Salvation in Contemporary Israel*. Albany: State University of New York Press.

——. 1991. "Judaism and the New Religions in Israel: 1970–1990." In *Tradition, Innovation, Conflict: Jewishness and Judaism in Contemporary Israel*, edited by Benjamin Beit-Hallahmi and Zvi Sobel, 203–224. Albany: State University of New York Press.

Bell, Emma, and Scott Taylor. 2003. "The Elevation of Work: Pastoral Power and the New Age Work Ethic." *Organization* 10(2): 329–349.

Bellah, Robert N. Richard Madsen, William M. Sullivan, Ann Swidler, and Steven M. Tipton. 1985. *Habits of the Heart*. Berkeley: University of California Press.

Ben-Ari, Eyal, and Yoram Bilu. 1997. "Saints' Sanctuaries in Israeli Development Towns: On a Mechanism of Urban Transformation." In *Grasping Land: Space and Place in Contemporary Israeli Discourse and Experience*, edited by Eyal Ben-Ari and Yoram Bilu, 61–83. New York: State University of New York Press.

Ben Rafael, Eliezer. 2005. "From Religion to Nationalism: the Transformation of the Jewish Identity." In *Comparing Modernities: Pluralism versus Homogenity*, edited by Eliezer Ben Rafael and Yitzhak Sternberg, 365–394. Leiden: Brill.

——. 1998. "Quasi-Sectarian Religiosity, Cultural Ethnicity and National Identity: Convergence and Divergence among *Hamamei Yisrael*." In *Jewish Survival: The Identity Problem at the Close of the Twentieth Century*, edited by Ernest Krausz and Gitta Tulea, 33–63. New Brunswick: Transaction Publishers.

——. 1982. *The Emergence of Ethnicity: Cultural Groups and Social Conflict in Israel*. Westport: Greenwood Press.

Ben Rafael, Eliezer, and Stephen Sharot. 1991. *Ethnicity, Religion and Class in Israeli Society*. Cambridge: Cambridge University Press.

Benayound, Chantal. 1990. "La question d'une politique juive aujourd'hui." In *Histoire Politique des Juifs de France*, edited by Pierre Birnbaum, 258–277. Paris: Fondation Nationale des Sciences Politiques.

Bender, Courtney, Wendy Cadge, Peggy Levitt, and David Smilde. 2013. *Religion on the Edge: De-Centering and Re-Centering the Sociology of Religion*. New York: Oxford University Press.

Benveniste, Arthur. 1997. "Finding Our Lost Brothers and Sisters: The Crypto Jews of Brazil." *Western States Jewish History* 29(3): 103–109.

Berger, Peter. 1965. "Towards a Sociological Understanding of Psychoanalysis." *Social Research* 32(1): 26–41.

Berman, Elise. 2009. "Voices of Outreach: The Construction of Identity and Maintenance of Social Ties among Chabad-Lubavitch Emissaries." *Journal for the Scientific Study of Religion* 48(1): 69–85.

Bevir, Mark. 2000. "Theosophy as a Political Movement." In *Gurus and Their Followers: New Religious Reform Movements in Colonial India*, edited by Anthony Copley, 159–179. New Delhi: Oxford University Press.

Bharati, Agehananda. 1970. "The Hindu Renaissance and its Apologetic Patterns." *The Journal of Asian Studies* 242: 267–287.

Bhatt, Chetan. 2001. *Hindu Nationalism: Origins, Ideologies and Modern Myths.* Oxford: Berg.

Bhatt, Chetan, and Parita Mukta. 2000. "*Hindutva* in the West: Mapping the Antinomies of Nationalism." *Ethnic and Racial Studies* 23(3): 401–406.

Bidou, Catherine. 2004. "Les classes moyennes: définitions, travaux et controverses." *Education et sociétés* (14): 119–134.

Bilu, Yoram. 1991. "Personal Motivation and Social Meaning in the Revival of Hagiolatric Traditions among Moroccan Jews in Israel." In *Tradition, Innovation, Conflict: Jewishness and Judaism in Contemporary Israel*, edited by Benjamin Beit-Hallahmi and Zvi Sobel, 47–69. Albany: State University of New York Press.

Birman, Patricia, and David Lehmann. 1999. "Religion and the Media in a Battle for Ideological Hegemony: The Universal Church of the Kingdom of God and TV Globo in Brazil." *Bulletin of Latin American Research* 18(2): 145–164.

Blain, Jenny. 2002. *Nine Worlds of Seid-Magic: Ecstasy and Neo-Shamanism in North European Paganism.* London: Routledge.

Blau, Joseph Leon. 1965. *The Christian Interpretation of the Cabala in the Renaissance.* New York: Kennikat Press.

Bongie, Chris. 1991. *Exotic Memories: Literature, Colonialism, and the Fin de Siècle.* Stanford: Stanford University Press.

Bourdieu, Pierre. 2013. "In Praise of Sociology: Acceptance Speech for the Gold Medal of the CNRS." *Sociology* 47(1): 7–14.

———. 2010 [1987]. "Sociologists of Belief and Beliefs of Sociologists." *Nordic Journal of Religion and Society* 23(1): 1–7.

———. 1990. *In Other Words: Essays in Reflexive Sociology.* Cambridge: Polity.

———. 1987. "Legitimation and Structural Interests in Weber's Sociology of Religion." In *Max Weber: Rationality and Modernity*, edited by Scott Lash and Sam Whimster, 119–137. London: Allen and Unwin.

———. 1984. *Distinction: A Social Critique of the Judgement of Taste.* London: Routledge & Kegan Paul.

Bowen, David. 1988. *The Sathia Sai Baba Community in Bradford: Its Origins and Development, Religious Beliefs and Practices.* Leeds: University of Leeds.

———. 1987. "The Evolution of Gurajati Hindu Organizations in Bradford." In *Hinduism in Great Britain: The Perpetuation of Religion in a Cultural Milieu*, edited by Richard Burghart, 15–31. London: Tavistock Press.

Boyer, Alain. 2001. "Congrégations et associations cultuelles." *Projet* 267. Accessed August 22, 2013. http://www.ceras-projet.org/index.php?id=1920.

References

Brasher, Brenda. 1998. *Godly Women: Fundamentalism and Female Power*. New Jersey: Routledge.

Brannen, Julia, and Ann Nilsen. 2005. "Individualisation, Choice and Structure: A Discussion of Current Trends in Sociological Analysis." *Sociological Review* 53: 412–428.

Bréchon, Pierre. 2001. "L'évolution du religieux." *Futuribles* 260: 39–48.

———. 2000. "Les attitudes religieuses en France: quelles recompositions en cours?" *Archives de Sciences Sociales des Religions* 109: 11–30.

———. 1997. "Le Mystère des identités religieuses masculines et féminines." In *Ni Ève ni Marie: luttes et incertitudes des héritières de la Bible*, edited by Françoise Lautman, 307–328. Geneva: Labor et Fides.

Brekke, Torkel. 1999. "The Conceptual Foundation of Missionary Hinduism." *The Journal of Religious History* 23(2): 203–214.

Breslauer, S. Daniel 1995. "Hasidism and its Effects on Alternative Jewish Movements in America." In *America's Alternative Religions*, edited by Timothy Miller, 109–117. Albany: State University of New York Press.

Briffault, Xavier, and Françoise Champion. 2008. "L'expérience sociale de la psychothérapie." In *Psychothérapie et Société*, edited by Françoise Champion, 122–139. Paris: Armand Colin.

Briffault, Xavier, and Béatrice Lamboy. 2008. "Les psychothérapies en France. Données quantitatives." In *Psychothérapie et Société*, edited by Françoise Champion, 101–121. Paris: Armand Colin.

Brown, Callum. 2001. *The Death of Christian Britain: Understanding Secularisation 1800–2000*. London: Routledge.

Brown, Diane. 1994. *Umbanda Religion and Politics in Urban Brazil*. New York: Columbia Universita Press.

Brzezinski, Jan. 1998. "What Was Srila Prabhupada's Position: The Hare Krishna Movement and Hinduism." *ISKCON Communications Journal* 6(2). Accessed August 22, 2013. http://content.iskcon.org/icj/6_2/62jagat.html.

Burmistrov, Konstantin. 2010. "Kabbalah and Secret Societies in Russia (Eighteenth to Twentieth Centuries)." In *Kabbalah and Modernity: Interpretations, Transformations, Adaptations*, edited by Boaz Huss, Marco Pasi, and Kocku Von Stuckrad, 77–106. Leiden: Brill.

Caldwell, Sarah. 2001. "The Heart of the Secret: A Personal and Scholarly Encounter with Shakta Tantrism in Siddha Yoga." *Nova Religio* 5(1): 9–51.

Campbell, Colin. 2007. *The Easternization of the West*. Boulder: Paradigm Publisher.

Campiche, Roland. 2004. *Les deux visages de la religion: fascination et désenchantement* Geneva: Labor et Fides.

———. 2003. "L'individualisation constitue-t-elle encore le paradigme de la religion en modernité tardive?" *Social Compass* 50(3): 297–309.

———. 1997. "Femmes et religion: identité spécifique ou identité construite?" In *Ni Ève ni Marie: luttes et incertitudes des héritières de la Bible*, edited by Françoise Lautman, 329–350. Geneva: Labor et Fides.

———. 1993. "Invention du croire et recomposition de la religion." *Archives de Sciences Sociales des Religions* 81: 117–131.

Carrette, Jeremy, and Richard King. 2005. *Selling Spirituality: The Silent Takeover of Religion*. London: Routledge.

Carey, Sean. 1987. "The Indianization of the Hare Krishna Movement in Britain." In *Hinduism in Great Britain: The Perpetuation of Religion in a Cultural Milieu*, edited by Richard Burghart, 81–99. London: Tavistock Press.

Carpenter, Robert T. 2004. "The Mainstreaming of Alternative Spirituality in Brazil." In *New Religious Movements in the 21st century: Legal, Political, and Social Challenges in Global Perspective*, edited by Phillip Lucas and Thomas Robbins, 213–229. London: Routledge.

Carter, Lewis F. 1990. *Charisma and Control in Rajneeshpuram: The Role of Social Values in the Creation of a Community*. Cambridge: Cambridge University Press.

Carvalho, Francisco Moreno 2001. "Entre o messias do Brooklin e o zen-judaismo: um renascimento judaico no Brazil?" *Cadernos de Língua e Literatura Hebraica* 3. Accessed December 19, 2012. http://www.editorahumanitas.com.br/downloads/Hebraican3Capitulo7.zip.

Carvalho, José Jorge. 2000. "An Enchanted Public Space: Religious Plurality and Modernity in Brazil." In *Through the Kaleidoscope: The Experience of Modernity in Latin America*, edited by Vivian Schelling, 275–296. London: Verso.

Castel, Françoise, Robert Castel, and Anne Lovell. 1979. *La société psychiatrique avancée: le modèle américain*. Paris: Grasset.

Castel, Robert. 2001. *Propriété privée, propriété sociale, propriété de soi: entretiens sur la construction de l'individu moderne*. Paris: Fayard.

———. 1995. *Les métamorphoses de la question sociale*. Fayard: Paris.

———. 1982. "L'homo Psychologicus." In *Thérapies de l'âme: l'inflation du psychologisme*, edited by Daniel Friedmann and Edwige Lambert, 132–142. Paris: Autrement.

———. 1981a. *Le psychanalysme: l'ordre psychanalytique et le pouvoir*. Paris: Flammarion.

———. 1981b. *La gestion des risques: de l'anti-psychiatrie à l'après-psychanalyse*. Paris: Éditions de Minuit.

Cavaglion, Gabriel. 2008. "The Theoretical Framing of a Social Problem: The Case of Societal Reaction to Cults in Israel." *Israel Affairs* 14(1): 84–102.

Ceccomori, Silvia. 2001. *Cent ans de Yoga en France*. Paris: Edidit.

———. 1995. *Cent ans de yoga en France: étude socio-culturelle des modalités de réception des doctrines et techniques de yoga de 1895 à 1995*. Paris: Université Paris 3, Doctoral thesis, 5 vol.

Cenkner, William. 2001. *A Tradition of Teachers: Sankara and the Jagadgurus Today*. Delhi: Motilal Banarsidass.

Champion, Françoise. 2013. "La nouvelle présence du religieux dans la psychiatrie contemporaine. L'exemple anglais" *Archives de Sciences Sociales des Religions* 163: 17–38.

———. 2004. "Logique des bricolages: retours sur la nébuleuse mystique-ésotérique et au-delà." *Recherches sociologiques* XXXV: 59–77.

——. 1993. "Religieux flottant, éclectismes et syncrétismes dans les sociétés con-temporaines." In *Le fait religieux dans le monde d'aujourd'hui*, edited by Jean Delumeau, 741–772. Paris: Fayard.

——. 1990. "La nébuleuse mystique-ésotérique: orientations psycho religieuses des courants mystiques et ésotériques contemporains." In *De l'émotion en religion*, edited by Françoise Champion and Danièle Hervieu-Léger, 17–69. Paris: Centurion.

Chor Maio, Marcos, and Carlos Eduardo Calaça. 2001. "New Christians and Jews in Brazil: Migrations and Antisemitism." *Shofar: An Interdisciplinary Journal of Jewish Studies* 19(3): 73–85.

Cimino, Richard. 2008. "USA: Growing Indian Membership leads to Conflict in Vedanta Movement." *Religioscope*. Accessed August 22, 2013. http://religion. info/english/articles/article_390.shtml.

Clarke, John J. 2000. *The Tao of the West*. London: Routledge.

——. 1997. *Oriental Enlightenment: The Encounter Between Asian and Western Thought*. London: Routledge.

Clémentin-Ojha, Catherine, and Jean-Luc Chambard. 1994. *Bibliographie de l'hindouisme et de l'anthropologie religieuse en Inde*. Paris: Librairie de l'Inde.

Cohen, Erik. 2004. "Une communauté inscrite dans la socialité: valeurs et identités des Juifs de France." *Observatoire du Monde Juif* (10–11): 7–14.

Cohen, Martine. 2000 "Les Juifs de France: modernité et identité." *Vingtième Siècle* 66: 91–106.

Cohen, Steven M. 1983. *American Modernity and Jewish Identity*. London: Tavistock.

Cohen, Steven M., and Arnold M. Eisen. 2000. *The Jew Within: Self, Family, and Community in America*. Bloomington: Indiana University Press.

Cohen, Stephen M., and Ari Y. Kelman. 2007. *The Continuity of Discontinuity: How Young Jews are Connecting, Creating and Organizing Their Own Jewish Lives*. The Andrea and Charles Bronfman Philanthropies. Accessed August 22, 2013. http:// www.bjpa.org/Publications/details.cfm?PublicationID=327.

Coleman, John. 2001. *The New Buddhism: The Western transformation of an Ancient Tradition*. New York: Oxford University Press.

Coney, Judith. 1999. *Sahaja Yoga: Socializing Processes in a South Asian New Religious Movement*. Richmond: Curzon Press.

——. 1995. "'Belonging to a Global Religion': The Sociological Dimensions of International Elements in Sahaja Yoga." *Journal of Contemporary Religion* 10(2): 109–119.

Cornille, Catherine. 2000. "New Japanese Religions in the West: Between Nationalism and Universalism." In *Japanese New Religions in Global Perspective*, edited by Peter B. Clarke, 10–34. London: Routledge.

Cornwall, Marie. 1989. "Faith Development of Men and Women over the Life Span." In *Aging and the Family*, edited Stephen J. Bahr and Evan T. Peterson, 115–139. Lexington: Lexington Books.

Corten, André. 1995. *Le pentecôtisme au Brésil: émotion du pauvre et romantisme théologique*. Paris: Karthala.

Coward, Harold. 2000. "Hinduism in Canada." In *The South Asian Religious Diaspora in Britain, Canada and the United States*, edited by Harold C. Coward, John R. Hinnells, and Raymond Brady Williams, 151–172. New York: State University of New York Press.

Cronin, Anne M. 2000. "Consumerism and Compulsory Individuality." In *Transformations: Thinking Through Feminism*, edited by S. Ahmed et al., 273–287. London: Routledge.

Cruikshank, Barbara. 1993. "Revolutions Within: Self-Government and Self-Esteem." *Economy and Society* 22 (3):327–344.

Dan, Joseph. 2007. *Kabbalah: A Very Short Introduction*. New York: Oxford University Press.

——. 2005. "Jewish influences III: 'Christian Kabbalah' in the Renaissance." In *Dictionary of Gnosis & Western Esotericism*, edited by Wouter J. Hanegraaff, 638–642. Leiden: Brill.

——. 2002. *The Heart and the Fountain: An Anthology of Jewish Mystical Literature*. Oxford: Oxford University Press.

——. 1998. "Christian Kabbalah: From Mysticism to Esotericism." In *Western Esotericism and the Science of Religion*, edited by Antoine Faivre and Wounter Hanegraaff, 117–130. Leuven: Peeters.

Danzger, Herbert. 1989. *Returning to Tradition: The Contemporary Revival of Orthodox Judaism*. New Haven: Yale University Press.

Davidman, Lynn. 1991. *Tradition in a Rootless World: Women Turn to Orthodox Judaism*. Berkeley: University of California Press.

Dawson, Andrew. 2007. *New Era, New Religions: Religious Transformation in Contemporary Brazil*. Aldershot: Ashgate.

Decol, Rene Daniel. 2001. "Judeus no Brasil: explorando os dados censitários." *Revista Brasileira de Ciências Sociais* 46(16): 147–160.

De Michelis, Elisabeth. 2004. *A History of Modern Yoga: Patanjali and Western Esotericism*. London: Continuum.

De Vaus, David A., and Ian McAllister. 1987. "Gender Differences in Religion: A Test of the Structural Location Theory." *American Sociological Review* 52: 472–481.

Devinat, François. 1992. "Le yoga se diffuse dans le corps social." *Libération*, June 1.

Dobbelaere, Karel. 1999. "Towards an Integrated Perspective of the Processes Related to the Descriptive Concept of Secularization." *Sociology of Religion* 60(3): 229–247.

Donzelot, Jacques. 1991. "Pleasure in Work." In *The Foucault Effect: Studies in Governmentality*, edited by Graham Burchell, Colin Gordon, and Peter Miller, 251–280. Chicago: University of Chicago Press.

Du Gay, Paul. 1996. "Organizing Identity: Entrepreneurial Governance and Public Management." In *Questions of Cultural Identity*, edited by Paul du Gay and Stuart Hall, 151–169. London: Sage.

———. 1995. *Consumption and Identity at Work*. London: Sage.

Dubar, Claude. 2000. *La socialisation: construction des identités sociales et profession-nelles*. Paris: A. Colin

Durkheim, Émile. 1971 [1915]. *The Elementary Forms of the Religious Life*, London: Allen and Unwin.

Dyczkowski, Mark S. G. 1987. *The Doctrine of Vibration: An Analysis of the Doctrines and Practices of Kashmir Shaivism*. Albany: State University of New York Press.

Edelman, Nicole. 1995. *Voyantes, guérisseuses et visionnaires en France 1785–1914*. Paris: Albin Michel.

Ehrenberg, Alain. 2010. *La société du malaise*. Paris: Odile Jacob.

———. 2008. "La quête du *self* idéal: psychothérapies, narcissisme et individualisme aux États-Unis." In *Psychothérapie et Société*, edited by Françoise Champion, 289–315. Paris: Armand Colin.

———. 1995. *L'individu incertain*. Paris: Calman-Levy.

Eisen, Robert. 1999. "The Revival of Jewish Mysticism and its Implications for the Future of Jewish Faith." In *Creating the Jewish Future*, edited by Michael Brown and Bernard Lightman, 27–44. Walnut Creek: Altamira Press.

Eisenberg, Gary D. 1988. *Smashing the Idols: A Jewish Inquiry into the Cult Phenomenon*. New Jersey: Jason Aronson.

Eisenstadt, Shmuel Noah. 1992. *Jewish Civilization: The Jewish Historical Experience in a Comparative Perspective*. Albany: SUNY Press.

Elias, Nobert. 2000. *The Civilizing Process: Sociogenetic and Psychogenetic Investigations*. Oxford: Blackwell.

Esnoul, Anne-Marie. 1952. "La Bhakti." In *L'Inde classique: manuel des études indiennes* vol. 1, edited by Louis Renou and Jean Filliozat, 661–667. Hanoi, Paris: École Française d'Extrême-Orient.

Fader, Ayala. 2008. "Jewish Spirituality and Late Capitalism." In *New Age Judaism*, edited by Celia Rothenberg and Anne Vallely, 34–51. London; Portland: Vallentine Mitchell.

Faivre, Antoine. 1996. *Accès de l'ésotérisme occidental*. Paris: Gallimard.

Fath, Sébastien. 2010. "Héritage/Choix." In *Dictionnaire des Faits Religieux*, edited by Régine Azria et Danièle Hervieu-Léger, 476–480. Paris: Presses Universitaires de France.

Faure, Bernard. 1995. "The Kyoto School and Reverse Orientalism." In *Japan in Traditional and Postmodern Perspectives*, edited by Charles Wei-Hsun Fu and Steven Heine, 245–281. Albany: State University of New York Press.

Featherstone, Mike. 1991. *Consumer Culture and Postmodernism*. London: Sage

Feher, Shoshanah. 1994. "Maintaining the Faith: the Jewish Anti-cult and Counter-missionary Movement." In *Anti-cult Movements in Cross-cultural Perspective*, edited by David G. Bromley and Anson D. Shupe, 33–48. New York: Garland.

Fenton, Paul. 1994. "La Cabale et l'académie: l'étude historique de l'ésotérisme juif en France." *Pardès* (19–20): 216–237.

Ferziger, Adam S. 2008. "Religion for the Secular: The New Israeli Rabbinate." *Journal of Modern Jewish Studies* 7(1): 67–90.

Figueira, Dorothy Matilda. 1994. *The Exotic: A Decadent Quest.* New York: State University of New York Press.

Fine, Robert. 2012. "The Dialectics of Universality: The Jewish Question." Paper presented at the mid-term conference of European Sociological Association, RN31, Thessaloniki, August 31.

Fish, Stanley. 1997. "Boutique Multiculturalism, or Why Liberals Are Incapable of Thinking about Hate Speech." *Critical Inquiry* 23(2): 378–395.

Flesch, Hannah. 2010. "Balancing Act: Women and the Study of Complementary and Alternative Medicine." *Complementary Therapies in Clinical Practice* 16(1): 20–25.

———. 2007. "Silent Voices: Women, Complementary Medicine, and the Co-option of Change." *Complementary Therapies in Clinical Practice* 13(3): 166–173.

Foster, Stephen William. 1982. "The Exotic as a Symbolic System." *Dialectical Anthropology* 7(1): 21–30.

Fouilloux, Étienne. 1995. "Femmes et Catholicisme dans la France Contemporaine." *CLIO: Histoires, Femmes, Sociétés* 2: 319–329.

French, Harold W. 1974. *The Swan's Wide Waters: Ramakrishna and Western Culture.* New York: Kennikat Press.

Friedman, Jonathan. 2005. "The Relocation of the Social and the Retrenchment of the Elites." In *The Retreat of the Social: The Rise and Rise of Reductionism*, edited by Bruce Kapferer, 19–29. Oxford: Berghahn.

Friedman, Menachem. 1994. "Habad as Messianic Fundamentalism: From Local Particularism to Universal Jewish Mission." In *Accounting for Fundamentalism*, edited by Martin E. Marty and R. Scott Appleby, 328–360. Chicago: Chicago University Press.

Frykenberg, Robert E. 1997. "The Emergence of Modern Hinduism as a Concept and as an Institution: a Reappraisal with Special Reference to South India." In *Hinduism Reconsidered*, edited by Gunther Sontheimer and Hermann Kulke, 82–107. Delhi: Manohar.

Furedi, Frank. 2004. *Therapy Culture: Cultivating Vulnerability in an Uncertain Age.* London: Routledge.

Garb, Jonathan. 2011. "Towards the Study of the Spiritual-Mystical Renaissance in the Contemporary Ashkenazi Haredi World in Israel." In *Kabbalah and Contemporary Spiritual Revival*, edited by Boaz Huss, 117–140. Beer-Sheva: Ben-Gurion University of the Negev Press.

———. 2008. *The Chosen Will Become Herds: Studies in Twentieth Century Kabbalah.* New Haven: Yale University Press.

———. 2007. "Twentieth Century Kabbalah." Lecture at the École des Hautes Études en Sciences Sociales, Paris, March 20.

———. 2006. "The Power and the Glory: A Critique of "New Age" Kabbalah." *ZEEK*. Accessed August 22, 2013. http://www.zeek.net/604garb/.

Garnoussi, Nadia. 2011. "Le Mindfulness ou la méditation pour la guérison et la croissance personnelle: des bricolages psychospirituels dans la médecine mentale." *Sociologie* 3(2): 259–275.

———. 2008. "Les offres de psychothérapies sur le marché du mieux-vivre au miroir de *Psychologies magazine*." In *Psychothérapie et Société*, edited by Françoise Champion, 267–285. Paris: Armand Colin.

Gee, Ellen M. 1991. "Gender Differences in Church Attendance in Canada." *Review of Religious Research* 32: 267–272.

Gibson, Ralph. 1993. "Le Catholicisme et les femmes en France au XIXe siècle." *Revue de l'Histoire de l'Eglise de France* LXXIX: 63–93.

Giddens, Anthony. 1991. *Modernity and Self-Identity: Self and Society in the Late Modern Age*. Stanford: Stanford University Press.

Gidley, Ben, and Keith Kahn-Harris. 2010. *Turbulent Times: The British Jewish Community Today*. London: Continuum.

Giles, Clare. n.d. "The Changing Shape of Vedanta Societies in America." *The Pluralism Project at Harvard University*. Accessed August 22, 2013. http://pluralism.org/affiliates/student/giles/index.php.

Gilliat-Ray, Sophie. 2004. "The Trouble with 'Inclusion': A Case Study of the Faith Zone at the Millennium Dome." *The Sociological Review* 52(4): 459–477.

Giumbelli, Emerson. 2002. *O fim da religião: dilemas da liberdade religiosa no Brasil e na França*. São Paulo: Attar.

Goel, Urmila. 2008. "People Marked as 'South Asians' in France." Accessed August 22, 2013. http://www.urmila.de/DesisinD/Europa/france.html.

Goldish, Matt. 2005. "Kabbalah, Academia, and Authenticity." *Tikkun* 20: 63–67.

Gombrich, Richard F., and Gananath Obeyesekere. 1988. *Buddhism Transformed: Religious Change in Sri Lanka*. Princeton: Princeton University Press.

Goodrick-Clarke, Nicholas. 2008. *The Western Esoteric Traditions: A Historical Introduction*. New York: Oxford University Press.

Goreau-Ponceaud, Anthony. 2009. "La diaspora tamoule en France: entre visibilité et politisation." *EchoGéo*. Accessed August 22, 2013. http://echogeo.revues.org/11157.

Greenberg, Anna. 2007. *Grand Soy Vanilla Latte with Cinnamon, No Foam: Jewish Identity and Community in a Time of Unlimited Choices*. Accessed August 22, 2013. www.acbp.net/About/PDF/Latte%20Report%202006.pdf

Griffith, R. Marie. 1997. *God's Daughters: Evangelical Women and the Power of Submission*. Berkeley: University of California Press.

Grin, Mônica. 2005. "Judaísmo no Brasil. Entrevista com Mônica Grin." *Revista do Instituto Humanitas Unisinos Online* 169: 49. Accessed August 22, 2013. http://www.ihuonline.unisinos.br/media/pdf/IHUOnlineEdicao169.pdf

Guerriero, Silas. 2003. "A Diversidade Religiosa no Brasil: A Nebulosa do Esoterismo e da Nova Era." *Revista Electrônica Correlatio* 3. Accessed August 22, 2013. http://www.metodista.br/ppc/correlatio/correlatio03/a-diversidade-religiosa-no-brasil-a-nebulosa-do-esoterismo-e-da-nova-era/.

———. 2000. "L'ISKCON au Brésil: la transformation occidentale d'une religion védique et l'incorporation de ses caractéristiques culturelles à la société locale." *Social Compass* 47(2): 241–251.

Haenni, Patrick, and Raphaël Voix. 2006. "God by All Means: Eclectic Faith and Sufi Resurgence among the Moroccan Bourgeoisie." In *Sufism and the 'Modern' in Islam,* edited by Martin van Bruinessen and Julia Day Howell, 241–256. London: Tauris.

Halbfass, Wilhelm. 1995. *Philology and Confrontation: Paul Hacker on Traditional and Modern Vedanta.* Albany: State University of New York Press.

———. 1988. *India and Europe: An Essay in Understanding.* Albany: State University of New York Press.

Hamayon, Roberte. 1995. "Pour en finir avec la "transe" et l'"extase" dans l'étude du chamanisme." *Études Mongoles et Sibériennes* 26: 155–190.

Hanegraaff, Wouter J. 2010. "The Beginnings of Occultist Kabbalah: Adolphe Franck and Eliphas Lévi." In *Kabbalah and Modernity: Interpretations, Transformations, Adaptations,* edited by Boaz Huss, Marco Pasi, and Kocku Von Stuckrad, 107–128. Leiden: Brill.

———. 1998. *New Age Religion and Western Culture.* Albany: State University of New York Press.

Harvey, David. 2007. *A Brief History of Neoliberalism.* Oxford: Oxford University Press.

———. 1990. *The Condition of Postmodernity: An Enquiry into the Origins of Cultural Change.* Oxford: Blackwell.

Hasselle-Newcombe, Suzanne. 2002. *Yoga in Contemporary Britain: A Preliminary Sociological Exploration.* Master diss., London School of Economics and Political Science.

Healy, John Paul. 2010. *Yearning to Belong: Discovering a New Religious Movement.* Farnham: Ashgate.

Heelas, Paul. 2008. *Spiritualities of Life: New Age Romanticism and Consumptive Capitalism.* Oxford: Blackwell.

———. 1996a. *The New Age Movement: The Celebration of the Self and the Sacralization of Modernity.* Oxford: Blackwell.

———. 1996b. "De-traditionalisation of Religion and Self: The New Age and Postmodernity." In *Postmodernity, Sociology and Religion,* edited by Peter C. Jupp and Kieran Flanagan, 64–82. London: Macmillan.

Heelas, Paul, and Linda Woodhead. 2005. *The Spiritual Revolution: Why Religion Is Giving Way to Spirituality.* London: Blackwell.

Herberg, Will. 1960. *Protestant-Catholic-Jew: An Essay in American Religious Sociology.* New York: Anchor Books.

Hermansen, Marcis. 2004. "What's American about American Sufi movements?" In *Sufism in Europe and North America*, edited by David Westerlund, 36–64. London: Routledge.

Hervieu-Léger, Danièle. 2010. "Le partage du croire religieux dans des sociétés d'individus." *L'Année Sociologique* 60(1): 41–62.

———. 2005. "Bricolage vaut-il dissémination? Quelques réflexions sur l'opérationnalité sociologique d'une métaphore problématique." *Social Compass* 52(3): 295–308.

———. 2001. *La religion en miettes ou la question des sectes*. Paris: Calmann-Lévy.

———. 2000. *Religion as a Chain of Memory*. Cambridge: Polity Press.

———. 1999. *Le pèlerin et le converti*. Paris: Flammarion.

Hochschild, Arlie Russell. 1983. *The Managed Heart: The Commercialization of Human Feeling*. Berkeley: University of California Press.

Hourmant, Louis. 1995. "Les nouveaux mouvement religieux japonais en France entre laïcisation et euphémisation du sacré." *Social Compass* 42(2): 207–220.

Hoyez, Anne-Cécile. 2012. *L'espace-monde du yoga: de la santé aux paysages thérapeutiques mondialisés*. Rennes: Presses Universitaires de Rennes.

Huggan, Graham. 2001. *The Postcolonial Exotic: Marketing the Margins*. London: Routledge.

Hulin, Michel. 2001. *Shankara et la non-dualité*, Paris: Bayard.

Humes, Cynthia Ann. 2005. "Maharishi Mahesh Yogi: Beyond the TM Technique." In *Gurus in America*, edited by Thomas A. Forsthoefel and Cynthia Ann Humes, 55–80. Albany: State University of New York Press.

Hummel, Reinhart 1988. *Les gourous*. Paris: Cerf.

Huss, Boaz. Forthcoming a. "Kabbalah and the Politics of In-authenticity: The Controversies over the Kabbalah Center." In *Religion and Identity Politics*, edited by Tim Jansen and Olav Hammer.

———. Forthcoming b. "Contemporary Forms of Kabbalah in the Late 20th and Early 21st Centuries." In *The Cambridge Companion to Kabbalah*, edited by Elliot R. Wolfson. Cambridge: Cambridge University Press.

———. 2010. "The 'Sufi Society from America': Theosophy and Kabbalah in Poona in the Late Nineteenth Century." In *Kabbalah and Modernity: Interpretations, Transformations, Adaptations*, edited by Boaz Huss, Marco Pasi, and Kocku Von Stuckrad, 167–194. Leiden: Brill.

———. 2007a. "The New Age of Kabbalah: Contemporary Kabbalah, The New Age and Postmodern Spirituality." *Journal of Modern Jewish Studies* 6(2):107–125.

———. 2007b. " 'Authorized Guardians': The Polemics of Academic Scholars of Jewish Mysticism against Kabbalah Practitioners." In *Western Esotericism and Polemics*, edited by Kocku von Stuckrad and Olav Hammer, 80–103. Leiden: Brill.

———. 2006. "Admiration and Disgust: The Ambivalent Re-Canonization of the Zohar in the Modern Period." In *Study and Knowledge in Jewish Thought*, edited by Howard Kreiesel, 203–237. Beer Sheva: Ben-Gurion University of the Negev Press.

——. 2005. "All You Need Is LAV: Madonna and Postmodern Kabbalah." *Jewish Quarterly Review* 95(4): 611–624.

Idel, Moshe. 1988. *Kabbalah: New Perspectives*. New Haven: Yale University Press.

Idel, Moshe, and Victor Malka. 2000. *Les chemins de la Kabbale*. Paris: Albin Michel.

Illouz, Eva. 2008. *Saving the Modern Soul: Therapy, Emotions, and the Culture of Self-Help*. Berkeley: University of California Press.

Imbarrato, Susan Clair. 1998. *Declarations of Independency in Eighteenth-Century American Autobiography*. Knoxville: University of Tennessee Press.

Inden, Ronald B. 1986. "Orientalist Contruction of India." *Modern Asian Studies* 20 (3): 401–446.

Institute for Jewish Policy Research, 2000. *A Community of Communities: Report of the Commission on Representation of the Interests of the British Jewish Community*. London: Institute for Jewish Policy Research.

——. 1996. *Social and Political Attitudes to British Jews: Some Key Findings of the JPR Survey*. London: Institute for Jewish Policy Research.

Ireland, Rowan. 1991. *Kingdoms Come: Religion and Politics in Brazil*. Pittsburgh: University of Pittsburgh Press.

Jackson, Carl T. 1994. *Vedanta for the West: The Ramakrishna Movement in the United States*. Bloomington: Indiana University Press.

Jaffrelot, Christophe. 1994. "La Vishva Hindu Parishad: structures et stratégies." *Purusartha* 17: 183–217.

——. 1993. *Les nationalistes hindous*. Paris: Presse de la Fondation Nationale des Sciences Politiques.

——. 1992. "Le syncrétisme stratégique et la construction de l'identité nationaliste hindoue. L'identité comme produit de synthèse." *Revue Française de Science Politique* 42(4): 594–617.

Janes, Craig R. 2002. "Buddhism, Science, and Market: The Globalisation of Tibetan Medicine." *Anthropology & Medecine* 9(3): 267–289.

Jencks, Charles 1992. "The Post-Modern Agenda." In *The Post-Modern Reader*, edited by Charles Jencks, 10–39. New York: St. Martin's Press.

Jilek, Wolfgang G. 2003. "La métamorphose du chamane dans la perception occidentale." In *Chamanismes*, edited by Roberte Hamayon, 209–237. Paris: Quadrige/PUF.

Johnson, Paul Christopher. 2001. *Secret, Gossip and Gods: The Transformation of Brazilian Candomblé*. Oxford: Oxford University Press.

Jones, Kenneth. 1989. *Socio-religious Reform Movements in British India*. Cambridge: Cambridge University Press.

Jordens, Joseph. 1978. *Dayananda Sarasvati: His Life and Ideas*. New Delhi: Oxford University Press.

Kalmar, Ivan Davidson and Derek J. Penslar. 2005. "Orientalism and the Jews: An Introduction." In *Orientalism and the Jews*, edited by Ivan Davidson Kalmar and Derek J. Penslar, xiii–xl. Waltham: Brandeis University Press.

Kalra, Virinder S., and John Hutnyk. 1998. "Brimful of Agitation, Authenticity and Appropriation: Madonna's 'Asian Kool.'" *Postcolonial Studies* 1(3): 339–355.

Kamarás, István. 2000. "Conscience de Krishna: interprétation hongroise." *Social Compass* 47(2): 221–239.

Kamerkar, Mani. 1978. "The Theosophy Movement in India, with Special Reference to Maharashtra." In *Social Contents of Indian Religious Reform Movements*, edited by Siba Pada Sen, 399–410. Calcutta: Institute of Historical Studies.

Kapferer, Bruce. 2005. "Introduction: The Social Construction of Reductionist Thought and Practice." In *The Retreat of the Social: The Rise and Rise of Reductionism*, edited by Bruce Kapferer, 1–18. Oxford: Berghahn.

Kehoe, Alice B. 2000. *Shamans and Religion*. Long Grove: Waveland Press.

Kelly, Aidan A. 1990. *Cults and the Jewish community: Representative Works of Jewish Anti-cult literature*. New York: Garland.

Kellner, Douglas. 1990. "The Postmodern Turn: Problems, Positions and Prospects." In *Frontiers of Social Theory*, edited by George Ritzer, 255–286. New York: Columbia University Press.

Kent, Alexandra. 2000. "Creating Divine Unity: Chinese Recruitment in the Sathya Sai Baba Movement of Malaysia." *Journal of Contemporary Religion* 15(1): 5–27.

Kepp, Michael. 2006. "Synagogue Offers Alternative to Orthodox Judaism in Brazil." *Jewish Telegraphic Agency*, January 9.

Kilcher, Andreas B. 2005. "Jewish Influences IV: Enlightenment/Romanticism." In *Dictionary of Gnosis & Western Esotericism*, edited by Wouter Hanegraaff, 642–644. Leiden: Brill.

Killingley, Dermot. 1999. "Vivekananda's Western message from the East." In *Swami Vivekananda and the Modernisation of Hinduism*, edited by William Radice, 138–157. New Delhi: Oxford University Press.

———. 1993. *Rammohun Roy in Hindu and Christian Tradition*. Newcastle upon Tyne: Grevatt & Grevatt.

King, Richard. 1999. *Orientalism and Religion: Postcolonial Theory, India and 'the Mystic East.'* London: Routledge.

King, Ursula. 1985. *Indian Spirituality and Western Materialism: An Image and its Function in the Reinterpretation of Modern Hinduism*. New Delhi: Indian Social Institute.

Klass, Morton. 1991. *Singing with Sai Baba: The Politics of Revitalization in Trinidad*. Prospect Heights: Waveland Press.

Klein, Micha. 2004. "'Afro-ashkenazim' e outras experiências com identidades." In *Experiência Cultural Judaica no Brasil. Recepção, inclusão e ambivalência*, edited by Mônica Grin and Nelson H. Vieira, 249–271. Rio de Janeiro: Topbooks.

Knott, Kim. 2009. "Becoming a 'Faith Community': British Hindus, Identity, and the Politics of Representation." *Journal of Religion in Europe* 2(2): 85–114.

———. 2000. "In Every Town and Village: Adaptive Strategies in the Communication of Krishna Consciousness in the UK, the First Thirty Years." *Social Compass* 47(2): 153–167.

———. 1989. "Hindu Communities in Britain." In *Religion, State and Society in Modern Britain*, edited by Paul Badham, 243–253. Lewiston: Edwin Meller Press.

———. 1987. "Hindu Temple Rituals in Britain: The Reinterpretation of Tradition." In *Hinduism in Great Britain: The Perpetuation of Religion in a Cultural Milieu*, edited by Richard Burghart, 157–179. London: Tavistock Press.

———. 1986. *My Sweet Lord: The Hare Krishna Movement*. Northampton: Aquarian Press.

Kopf, David. 1979. *The Brahmo Samaj and the Shaping of Modern India*. Princeton: Princeton University Press.

———. 1969. *British Orientalism and the Bengal Renaissance: The Dynamics of Indian Modernization, 1773–1835*. Berkeley: California University Press.

Korbe, Merit. Forthcoming. *De l'évasion à l'engagement: les Occidentaux à la recherche du lien social à travers la pratique du yoga*. PhD diss., Université Paris V-Descartes.

Kosmin, Barry, and Ariella Keysar. 2009. *American Religious Identification Survey 2008: Summary Report*. Hartford: Institute for the Study of Secularism in Society & Culture. Accessed August 22, 2013. http://commons.trincoll.edu/aris/publications/aris-2008-summary-report/.

Kurien, Prema. 2001. "Religion, Ethnicity, and Politics: Hindu and Muslim Indian Immigrants in the United States." *Ethnic and Racial Studies* 24(2): 263–229.

Lahire, Bernard. 2011. *The Plural Actor*. Cambridge: Polity Press.

Lakshmi Dassaradanayadou, Sophie. 2007. "Tamouls indiens: de Pondichéry à la France." *Hommes et Migrations* (1268–1269): 68–81.

Lambert, Yves. 2001. "La renaissance des croyances liées à l'après-mort: les évolutions en France et dans plusieurs pays européens." *Recherches Sociologiques* 2: 9–19.

Langlois, Claude. 2001. *Histoire de la France Religieuse*, vol. 3. Paris: Seuil.

Lapeyronnie, Didier, Marcun Frybes Kristin Couper and Danièle Joly. 1990. *L'intégration des minorités immigrées: étude comparative France-Grande-Bretagne*. Issy-les-Moulineaux: Agence pour le Développement des Relations Interculturelles.

Lappin, Elena. 2004 "The Thin Red Line." *The Guardian*, December 11.

Lau, Kimberly J. 2000. *New Age Capitalism: Making Money East of Eden*. Philadelphia: University of Pennsylvania Press.

Lemke, Thomas. 2001. "The Birth of 'Bio-Politics': Michel Foucault's Lecture at the Collège de France on Neo-Liberal Governmentality." *Economy & Society* 30(2): 190–207.

Lenoir, Frédéric 1999. *Le bouddhisme en France*. Paris Fayard.

Lerman, Antony. 2008. "Jewish Self-Hatred: Myth or Reality?" *Jewish Quarterly* 210. Accessed August 22, 2013. http://www.jewishquarterly.org/issuearchive/article2366.html?articleid=432.

Lesser, Jeffrey. 2004. "How the Jews Became Japanese and Other Stories of Nation and Ethnicity." *Jewish History* 18(1): 7–17.

Levi-Strauss, Claude. 1966. *The Savage Mind*. London: Weidenfeld & Nicolson.

Liebman, Charles S. 1990. *Religious and Secular: Conflict and Accommodation Between Jews in Israel*. Jerusalem: Keter.

Liebman, Arthur. 1979. *Jews and the Left*. New York; Chichester: Wiley.

Lindquist, Galina. 1997. *Shamanic Performances on the Urban Scene: Neo-Shamanism in Contemporary Sweden*. Stockholm: Gotab.

Linzer, Judith. 1996. *Torah and Dharma: Jewish Seekers in Eastern Religions*. New Jersey: Jason Aronson.

Loss, Joseph. 2010. "Buddha-Dhamma in Israel: Explicit Non-Religious and Implicit Non-Secular Localization of Religion." *Nova Religio* 13(4): 84–105.

Lowe, Scott. 2011. "Transcendental Meditation, Vedic Science and Science." *Nova Religio* 14(4): 54–76.

Losonczy, Anne-Marie, and Silvia Mesturini Cappo. 2011. "Pourquoi l'*ayahuasca*?" *Archives de Sciences Sociales des Religions* 153: 207–228.

Luckmann, Thomas. 1990. "Shrinking Transcendence, Expanding Religion?" *Sociological Analysis* 50: 127–138.

———. 1979. "The Structural Conditions of Religious Consciousness in Modern Societies." *Japanese Journal of Religious Studies* 6: 121–137.

Ludwig, Quentin. 2006. *Comprendre la Kabbale: de Rabbi Siméon bar Yochaï à Madonna*. Paris: Eyrolles.

Lury, Celia. 1997. *Prosthetic Culture: Photography, Memory and Identity*. London: Routledge.

Magid, Shaul. 2006. "Jewish Renewal: Toward a 'New' American Judaism." *Tikkun* 21: 57–60.

Magnani, José Guilherme Cantor. 1999. "O Xamanismo Urbano e a Religiosidade Contemporânea." *Religião e Sociedade* 20(2): 113–140.

Mann, Ted. 1993. "The Crazies—Who Follows Rajneeh and Why." In *The Rajneesh Papers: Studies in a New Religious Movement*, edited by Susan J. Palmer and Arvind Sharma, 17–45. Delhi: Shri Jainandra Press.

Mary, André. 2005. "Métissage and Bricolage in the Making of African Christian Identities." *Social Compass* 52(3): 281–294.

———. 2000. *Le bricolage africain des héros chrétiens*. Paris: Cerf.

———. 1995. "Religion de la tradition et religieux post-traditionnel." *Enquête* 2:121–142.

———. 1994. "Bricolage afro-brésilien et bris-collage moderne." In *Roger Bastide ou le « réjouissement de l'abîme »*, edited by Philippe Laburthe-Tolra, 85–98. Paris: L'Harmattan.

Maskens, Maïté. 2009. "Identités sexuelles pentecôtistes: féminités et masculinités dans les assemblées bruxelloises." *Autrepart* 49: 65–82.

Mayer, Jean-François. 1989. "L'introduction des mouvements religieux orientaux en Occident: l'exemple de la Suisse." *The Journal of Oriental Studies* 2: 20–25.

McKean, Lise. 1996. *Divine Enterprise: Gurus and the Hindu Nationalist Movement*. Chicago: University of Chicago Press.

Meilicke, Christine A. 2002. "Abulafianism among the Counterculture Kabbalists." *Jewish Studies Quarterly* 9: 71–101.

Meir, Jonathan. 2011. "The Boundaries of the Kabbalah: R. Yaakov Moshe Hillel and the Kabbalah in Jerusalem." In *Kabbalah and Contemporary Spiritual Revival*, edited by Boaz Huss, 163–180. Beer-Sheva: Ben-Gurion University of the Negev Press.

Mendes-Flohr, Paul. 1991. "Fin-de-siècle Orientalism, the Ostjuden, and the Aesthetics of Jewish Self-Affirmation." In *Divided Passions: Jewish Intellectuals and the Experience of Modernity*, 77–132. Detroit: Wayne State University Press.

Messner, Francis. 1997. "La législation culturelle des pays de l'Union européenne face aux groupes sectaires." In *Sectes et démocraties*, edited by Françoise Champion and Martine Cohen, 331–358. Paris: Seuil.

Michaël, Tara. 1995. *Yoga*. Paris: Point.

Miles, Agnes 1991. *Women, Health and Medicine*: Open University Press.

Miller, David M. 1989. "The Divine Life Society Movement." In *Religion in Modern India*, edited by Robert D. Baird, 81–112. Delhi: Manohar.

Miller, Alan S., and John P. Hoffmann. 1995. "Risk and Religion: An Explanation of Gender Differences in Religiosity." *Journal for the Scientific Study of Religion* 34(1): 63–75.

Mills, Charles Wright. 1959. *The Sociological Imagination*. New York: Oxford University Press.

Minor, Robert N. 1986. "In Defense of Karma and Rebirth: Evolutionary Karma." In *Karma and Rebirth: Post Classical Developments*, edited by Ronald W. Neufelt, 15–40. Albany: State University of New York Press.

Mittleman, Alan. 2010. "Judaism: Covenant, Pluralism, and Piety." In *The New Blackwell Companion to The Sociology of Religion*, edited by Bryan S. Turner, 340–363. Oxford: Wiley-Blackwell.

Modood, Tariq. 1994. "Establishment, Multiculturalism and British Citizenship." *Political Quarterly* 65(1): 53–73.

Monaghan, Karen. 2001. "Limitations and Opportunities: A Review of the Likely Domestic Impact of Article 14 ECHR." *European Human Rights Law Review* 2: 167–180.

Mopsik, Charles. 2007. "Les formes multiples de la cabale en France au XXe siècle." In *Réceptions de la cabale*, edited by Pierre Gisel and Lucie Kaennel, 255–282. Paris: l'Éclat.

———. 2004. *Chemins de la Cabale. Vingt-cinq essais sur la mystique juive*. Paris: l'Éclat.

———. 2003. *Cabale et cabalistes*. Paris: Albin Michel.

———. 1988. *La Cabale*. Paris: J. Grancher.

Morris, Brian. 2005. *Religion and Anthropology: A Critical Introduction*. Cambridge: Cambridge University Press.

Motta, Roberto. 2002. "L'expansion et la réinvention des religions afro-brésiliennes : réenchantement et décomposition." *Archives de Sciences Sociales des Religions* 117: 113–125.

——. 1988. "Indo-Afro-European Syncretic Cults in Brazil: Their Economic and Social Roots." *Cahiers du Brésil Contemporain* 5: 27–48.

Mukherjee, Amithaba. 1978a. "The Brahma Samaj Movement and its Social Challenge." In *Social Contents of Indian Religious Reform Movements*, edited by Siba Pada Sen, 269–294. Calcutta: Institute of Historical Studies.

——. 1978b. "Religious Reform Movements in Bengal in the Nineteenth Century." In *Social Contents of Indian Religious Reform Movements*, edited by Siba Pada Sen, 1–17. Calcutta: Institute of Historical Studies.

Mukta, Parita. 2000. "The Public Face of Hinduism." *Ethnic and Racial Studies* 23 (3): 442–466.

Myers, Jody. 2011. "Kabbalah for the Gentiles: Diverse Souls and Universalism in Contemporary Kabbalah." In *Kabbalah and Contemporary Spiritual Revival*, edited by Boaz Huss, 181–211. Beer-Sheva: Ben-Gurion University of the Negev Press.

——. 2010. "Marriage and Sexual Behaviour in the Teaching of the Kabbalah Centre." In *Kabbalah and Modernity: Interpretations, Transformations, Adaptations*, edited by Boaz Huss, Marco Pasi, and Kocku Von Stuckrad, 259–281. Leiden: Brill.

——. 2007. *Kabbalah and the Spiritual Quest: The Kabbalah Centre in America*. Westport: Praeger Publishers.

Nanda, Meer. 2009. "The Hour of the Saints." *The Telegraph (Calcutta, India)*, May 12. Accessed August 22, 2013. http://www.telegraphindia.com/1090512/jsp/opinion/story_10947801.jsp.

Narain, Priyanka P. 2008 "With Swamis' Help, BJP Looks to Reach Moderate Masses." *Mint*, August 5. Accessed August 22, 2013. http://www.livemint.com/2008/08/05000854/With-swamis8217-help-BJP-l.html.

Nissen, Nina 2011. "Challenging Perspectives: Women, Complementary and Alternative Medicine, and Social Change." *Interface* 3(2): 187–212.

Nolan, James L., Jr. 1998. *The Therapeutic State: Justifying Government at Century's End*. Albany: State University of New York Press.

Noll, Richard. 1997. *The Jung Cult: Origins of a Charismatic Movement*. New York: Free Press.

Nye, Malory. 2001. *Multiculturalism and Minority Religions in Britain: Krishna Consciousness, Religious Freedom, and the Politics of Location*. Richmond: Curzon.

——. 1998. "Minority Religious Groups and Religious Freedom in England: The ISKCON Temple at Bhaktivedanta Manor." *Journal of Church and State* 40: 411–436.

——. 1997. "ISKCON and Hindus in Britain: Some Thoughts on a Developing Relationship." *ISKCON Communications Journal* 5(2). Accessed August 22, 2013. http://content.iskcon.org/icj/5_2/5_2nye.html.

——. 1996a. "Hare Krishna and Sanatan Dharm in Britain: The Campaign for Bhaktivedanta Manor." *Journal of Contemporary Religion* 11(1): 37–56.

——. 1996b. "The Iskconisation of British Hinduisms." Paper presented at SOAS, London, November.

Obadia, Lionel. 1999. *Bouddhisme et Occident: la diffusion du bouddhisme tibétain en France*. Paris: L'Harmattan.

Obeyesekere, Gananath. 1970. "Religious Symbolism and Political Change in Ceylon." *Modern Ceylon Studies* 1(1): 43–63.

Oddie, Geoffrey Archdall. 1991. *Hindu and Christian in South-East India*. London: Curzon Press.

———. 1979. *Social Protest in India: British Protestant Missionaries and Social Reforms, 1850–1900*. New Delhi: Manohar.

Odih, Pamela. 2007. *Gender and Work in Capitalist Economies*. Open University Press. http://lib.myilibrary.com?ID=133098.

O'Flaherty, Wendy D. 1980. "Karma and Rebirth in the Vedas and Puranas." In *Karma and Rebirth in Classical Indian Traditions*, edited by Wendy D. O'Flaherty, 3–37. Berkeley: University of California Press.

Oro, Ari Pedro. 2000. "Religiões brasileiras transnacionais." In *Identidade e mudança na religiosidade latino-americana*, edited by Roberto Cipriani, Paula Eleta, and Arnaldo Nesti, 277–290. Petrópolis: Vozes.

Otero, Marcelo. 2003. *Les règles de l'individualité contemporaine: santé mentale et société*. Canada: Presses de l'Université Laval.

Palmer, Norris W. 2005. "Baba's World: A Global Guru and his Movement." In *Gurus in America*, edited by Thomas A. Forsthoefel and Cynthia Ann Humes, 97–112. Albany: State University of New York Press.

Palmer, Susan J. 1994. *Moon Sisters, Krishna Mothers, Rajneesh Lovers: Women's Roles in New Religions*. New York: Syracuse University Press.

———. 1992. "Therapy, Charisma and Social Control in the Rajneesh Movement." *Sociological Analysis* 53 (S): S71-S85.

Parfitt, Tudor, and Emanuela Trevisan Semi. 2002. *Judaising Movements: Studies in the Margins of Judaism*. London: Routledge Curzon.

Pasi, Marco. 2010. "Oriental Kabbalah and the Parting of East and West in the Early Theosophical Society." In *Kabbalah and Modernity: Interpretations, Transformations, Adaptations*, edited by Boaz Huss, Marco Pasi, and Kocku Von Stuckrad, 151–166. Leiden: Brill.

Peach, Ceri, and Richard T. Gale. 2003. "Muslims, Hindus and Sikhs in the New Religious Landscape of England." *The Geographical Review* 95(4): 469–490.

Pelletier, Pierre. 1996. *Les thérapies transpersonnelles*. Québec: Fides.

Percot, Marie, Andréa Tribess, and Gérard Robuchon. 1995. "Tamouls Sri-Lankais en France." *Migrations Etudes* 59: 1–8.

Philippon, Alix. 2014. "De l'occidentalisation du soufisme à la réislamisation du New Age? Sufi Order International et la globalisation du religieux." *Revue des mondes musulmans et de la Méditerranée* 135.

Pickering, William S. F. 1975 *Durkheim on Religion: A Selection of Readings with Bibliographies*. London: Routledge and Kegan Paul.

Pierucci, Antônio Flávio, and Reginaldo Prandi. 1996. *A Realidade social das Religiões no Brasil.* Sao Paulo: Hucitec.

Pordié, Laurent. 2008. "Tibetan medicine today. Neo-traditionalism as an analytical lens and a political tool." in *Tibetan Medicine in the Contemporary World. Global Politics of Medical Knowledge and Practice,* edited by Laurent Pordié, 3–32. London; New York Routledge.

Prandi, Reginaldo. 2004. "O Brasil com axé: candomblé e umbanda no mercado religioso." *Estudos Avançados USP* 18(52): 223–238.

Prashad, Vijay. 2000. *The Karma of Brown Folk.* Minneapolis: University of Minnesota Press.

Ramagem, Sonia Maria Bloomfield. 1997. "A Fênix de Abraão." In *Judaismo: Memória e Identidade,* edited by Helena Lewin, 750–785. Rio de Janeiro: Universidade do Estado do Rio de Janeiro.

Renou, Louis. 1993. *L'hindouisme.* Paris: Presses Universitaires de France.

———. 1952. "Les sectes." In *L'Inde classique: manuel des études indiennes* vol. 1, edited by Louis Renou and Jean Filliozat, 620–666. Paris: École Française d'Extrême-Orient.

Rice, Steadman John. 2002. "The Therapeutic School." *Society* 39(2): 19–28.

———. 1998. *A Disease of One's Own: Psychotherapy, Addiction, and the Emergence of Co-Dependency.* New Brunswick: Transaction Publishers.

———. 1994. "The Therapeutic God: Transcendence and Identity in Two Twelve-Step Quasi-religions." In *Between Sacred and Secular: Research and Theory on Quasi-religion,* edited by Arthur L. Greil and Thomas Robbins, 151–164. Greenwich: JAI Press.

Risseuw, Carla. 2000. "Thinking Culture Through Counter-culture: The Case of Theosophists in India and Ceylon and their Ideas on Race and Hierarchy (1875–1945)." In *Gurus and Their Followers: New Religious Reform Movements in Colonial India,* edited by Anthony Copley, 180–205. New Delhi: Oxford University Press.

Robilliard, St John A. 1984. *Religious Liberty and the Law: Religious Liberty in Modern English Law.* Manchester: Manchester University Press.

Rocchi, Valérie. 1999. *Du religieux au thérapeutique: étude sociologique des réseaux psycho-mystiques contemporains.* PhD diss., Université Paris V-Descartes.

Rocha, Christina. 2006. *Zen in Brazil: The Quest for Cosmopolitan Modernity.* Honolulu: University of Hawaii Press.

Rochford, Burke E. 2007. *Hare Krishna Transformed.* New York: New York University Press.

———. 1995. "Hare Krishna in America: Growth, Decline, and Accommodation." In *America's Alternative Religions,* edited by Timothy Miller, 215–222. Albany: State University of New York Press.

———. 1991. *Hare Krishna in America.* New Brunswick: Rutgers University Press.

Rogers, Matt. 2012. "Contextualizing Theories and Practices of Bricolage Research." *The Qualitative Report* 17: 1–17.

Root, Deborah. 1995. *Cannibal Culture: Art, Appropriation and the Commodification of Difference*. Boulder: Westview Press.

Roper, David. 2003. "The Turbulent Marriage of Ethnicity and Spirituality: Rabbi Theodore Falcon, Makom Ohr Shalom and Jewish Mysticism in the Western United States, 1969–1993." *Journal of Contemporary Religion* 18(2): 169–184.

Rose, Nikolas. 1999. *Powers of Freedom: Reframing Political Thought*. Cambridge: Cambridge University Press.

———. 1998. *Inventing Our Selves: Psychology, Power, and Personhood*. Cambridge: Cambridge University Press.

———. 1989. *Governing the Soul: The Shaping of the Private Self*. London: Routledge.

———. n.d. *Power and Subjectivity: Critical History and Psychology*. Accessed August 22, 2013. http://www.academyanalyticarts.org/rose1.htm.

Rose, Nikolas, and Peter Miller. 1995. "Production, Identity, and Democracy." *Theory and Society* 24: 427–467.

———.1990. "Governing economic life." *Economy and Society* 19(1): 1–31.

Rose, Or N. 2005. "Madonna's Challenge: Understanding Kabbalah Today." *Tikkun* 19: 24–27.

Rothenberg, Celia. 2006. "Jewish Yoga: Experiencing Flexible, Sacred, and Jewish Bodies." *Nova Religio* 10(2): 57–74.

Rothman, Stanley and Robert S. Lichter. 1982. *Roots of Radicalism: Jews, Christians, and the New Left*. New York: Oxford University Press.

Rudin, Marcia R. 1978. "The New Religious Cults and the Jewish Community." *Religious Education* 73(3): 350–360.

Said, Edward W. 1993. *Culture and Imperialism*. London: Chatto & Windus.

———. 1978. *Orientalism*. Harmondsworth: Penguin Books.

Salkin, Jeffrey K. 2000. "New Age Judaism." In *The Blackwell Companion to Judaism*, edited by Jacob Neusner and Alan J. Avery-Peck, 354–370. London: Blackwell.

Sanchis, Pierre. 2007. "The Brazilians' Religion." *Teoria & Sociedade* 3. Accessed August 22, 2013. http://socialsciences.scielo.org/scielo.php?pid=S1518-44712007000100001&script=sci_arttext.

Sargeant, Howland Kimon. 2000. *Promoting Traditional Religion in a Nontraditional Way*. New Brunswick: Rutgers University Press.

Savage, Mike. 2000. *Class Analysis and Social Transformation*. Milton Keynes: Open University Press.

———. 1992. *Property, Bureaucracy and Culture*. London: Routledge.

Scheifinger, Heinz. 1999. *Previous Research Concerning Hare Krishnas and Hindus*. Unpublished paper, University of Warwick.

Schnapper, Dominique, Chantal Bordes-Benayoun, and Freddy Raphaël. 2009. *La condition juive en France*. Paris: Presses Universitaires de France.

Scholem, Gershom. 1998. *La Kabbale*. Paris: Gallimard.

Schuster, Joshua. 1998. "Brazilian Rabbi Brings Practical Take on Kabbalah to S.F." *JWeekly*, October 23. Accessed August 22, 2013. http://www.jweekly.com/article/full/9320/brazilian-rabbi-brings-practical-take-on-Kabbalah-to-s-f/.

Schwab, Raymond. 1950. *La Renaissance orientale*. Paris: Payot.

Selengut, Charles. 1988. "American Jewish Converts to New Religious Movements." *The Jewish Journal of Sociology* 30(2): 95–109.

Sharf, Robert H. 1995. "The Zen of Japanese Nationalism." In *Curators of the Buddha: The Study of Buddhism under Colonialism*, edited by Jr. Donald S. Lopez, 107–160. Chicago: University of Chicago Press.

Sharma, Arvind. 1998. *The Concept of Universal Religion in Modern Hindu Thought*. Basingstoke: Macmillan.

——. 1993. "Rajneesh and the Guru Tradition in India." In *The Rajneesh Papers: Studies in a New Religious Movement*, edited by Susan Palmer and Arvind Sharma, 1–16. Delhi: Shri Jainandra press.

——. 1992. "Ancient Hinduism as a Missionary Religion." *Numen* 39(2): 175–192.

——. 1990. "The Concept of Universal Religion in Rammohun Roy." In *Political Thinkers of Modern India*, edited by Verinder Gorver, 195–213. New Delhi: Deep and Deep Publications.

——. 1985. "The Rajneesh Movement." In *Religious Movements: Genesis, Exodus, and Numbers*, edited by Rodney Stark, 115–128. New York: Paragon House.

Sharma, Sri Ram. 1978. "The Arya Samaj and Its Social Contents." In *Social Contents of Indian Religious Reform Movements*, edited by Siba Pada Sen, 320–339. Calcutta: Institute of Historical Studies.

Sharot, Stephen. 2007. "Judaism in Israel: Public Religion, Neo-traditionalism, Messianism, and Ethno-religious Conflict." In *The Sage Handbook of the Sociology of Religion*, edited by James A. Beckford and N. Jay Demerath, 671–792. London: Sage.

——. 2001. *A Comparative Sociology of World Religions: Virtuosi, Priests and Popular Religion*. New York: New York University Press.

——. 1996. "Traditional, Modern or Postmodern? Recent Developments among Jews in Israel." In *Postmodernity, Sociology and Religion*, edited by Peter C. Jupp and Kieran Flanagan, 118–133. Basingstoke: Macmillan.

——. 1991. "Judaism and the Secularization Debate." *Sociological Analysis* 52(3): 255–275.

——. 1990. "Israel: Sociological Analyses of Religion in the Jewish State." *Sociological Analysis*, 51: S63–S76.

Skeggs, Beverley. 2004. *Class, Self, Culture*. London: Routledge.

Smith, David. 2003. *Hinduism and Modernity*. Oxford: Blackwell.

Smyth, Lisa. 2012. *The Demands of Motherhood: Agents, Roles and Recognition*. Basingstoke: Palgrave Macmillan.

Sointu, Eeva, and Linda Woodhead. 2008. "Spirituality, Gender, and Expressive Selfhood." *Journal for the Scientific Study of Religion* 47(2): 259–276.

Sorj, Bila. 1997. "Conversões e casamentos 'mistos.'" In *Identidades judaicas no Brasil Contemporâneo*, edited by Bila Sorj, 67–86. Rio de Janeiro: Imago.

Srinivas, Tulasi. 2010. *Winged Faith: Rethinking Globalization and Religious Pluralism through the Sathya Sai Movement*. New York: Columbia University Press.

Stark, Rodney, and William S. Bainbridge. 1985. *The Future of Religion: Secularization, Revival and Cult Formation*. Berkeley: University of California Press.

Stone, Donald. 1982. "Les Oncles d'Amérique." In *Thérapies de l'âme: l'inflation du psychologisme*, edited by Daniel Friedmann and Edwige Lambert, 107–130. Paris: Autrement.

——. 1978. "New Religious Consciousness and Personal Religious Experience." *Sociological Analysis* 39(2): 123–134.

——. 1976. "The Human Potential Movement." In *The New Religious Consciousness*, edited by Charles Y. Glock and Robert N. Bellah, 93–115. Berkeley: University of California Press.

Strathern, Marylin. 2004. *Partial Connections*. Walnut Creek: AltaMira.

Stratton, Jon. 2008. *Jewish Identity in Western Pop Culture*. Basingstoke: Palgrave Macmillan.

——. 2000. *Coming Out Jewish. Constructing Ambivalent Identities*. London: Routledge.

Strauss, Sarah. 1997. *Re-orienting Yoga: Transnational Flows from an Indian Center*. PhD diss., University of Pennsylvania Press.

Tabory, Ephraim. 1991. "The Identity Dilemma of Non-Orthodox Religious Movements: Reform and Conservative Judaism in Israel." In *Tradition, Innovation, Conflict: Jewishness and Judaism in Contemporary Israel*, edited by Benjamin Beit-Hallahmi and Zvi Sobel, 135–152. Albany: State University of New York Press.

Taji-Farouki, Suha. 2007. *Beshara and Ibn 'Arabi: A Movement of Sufi Spirituality in the Modern World*. Oxford: Anqa.

Tapper, Aaron J. 2002. "The "Cult" of Aish HaTorah: Ba'alei Teshuva and the New Religious Movement Phenomenon." *Jewish Journal of Sociology* 44(1): 5–29.

Taylor, Donald. 1987. "Sathya Sai Baba Movement in Britain: Aims and Methods." In *The New Evangelists: Recruitment, Methods and Aims of New Religious Movements*, edited by Peter B. Clarke, 77–93. London: Ethnographica.

Thapar, Romila. 1997. "Syndicated Hinduism." In *Hinduism Reconsidered*, edited by Gunther Sontheimer and Hermann Kulke, 54–81. Delhi: Manohar.

Thompson, Judith, and Paul Heelas. 1986. *The Way of the Heart: the Rajneesh Movement*. Wellingborough: Aquarian.

Thursby, Gene R. 1986. "Kashmir Shaivism in Siddha Yoga." *Proceedings of the Eighth International Symposium on Asian Studies* 4: 1227–1238.

——. 1984. "Succession in the Siddha Yoga Movement." *Proceedings of the Sixth International Symposium on Asian Studies* 4: 1397–1411.

Tipton, Steven M. 1982. *Getting Saved from the Sixties: Moral Meaning in Conversion and Cultural Change*. Berkeley: University of California Press.

Todorov, Tzvetan. 1993. *On Human Diversity: Nationalism, Racism and Exoticism in French Thought.* Cambridge, Mass.: Harvard University Press.

Torgovnick, Marianna. 1997. *Primitive Passions: Men, Women and the Quest for Ecstasy.* New York: Alfred A. Knopf.

Topel, Marta Francisca. 2008. *Jerusalem and São Paulo: The New Jewish Orthodoxy in Focus.* Lanham: University Press of America.

———. 2005. "Judaísmo(s) brasileiro(s): uma incursão antropológica." *Revista da USP* 67: 186–197.

———. 2003. "O lugar da nova ortodoxia judaica paulistana no cenário do campo religioso brasileiro: algumas observações." *Revista de Estudos da Religião* 1: 110–117.

Touraine, Alain. 2005. "Classes moyennes." *Encyclopaedia Universalis.* [DVD].

Trzebiatowska, Marta, and Steve Bruce. 2012. *Why are Women More Religious than Men?* Oxford: Oxford University Press.

Turner, Brian S. 1991. *Religion and Social Theory.* London: Sage

Urban, Hugh B. 2003. "Avatar for Our Age: Sathya Sai Baba and the Cultural Contradictions of Late Capitalism." *Religion* 33: 73–93.

———. 2000. "The Cult of Ecstasy: Tantrism, the New Age, and the Spiritual Logic of Late Capitalism." *History of Religions* 3: 268–304.

———. 1999. "The Extreme Orient: The Construction of "Tantrism" as a Category in the Orientalist Imagination." *Religion* 29: 123–146.

———. 1996. "Zorba the Buddha: Capitalism, Charisma and the Cult of Bhagwan Shree Rajneesh." *Religion* 26(2): 161–182.

Urciuoli, Bonnie. 2008. "Skills and Selves in the New Workplace." *American Anthropologist* 35 (2): 211–228.

Vallely, Anne. 2008. "Jewish Redemption by Way of the Buddha: A Post-Modern Tale of Exile and Return." In *New Age Judaism,* edited by Celia Rothenberg and Anne Vallely, 19–33. London; Portland: Vallentine Mitchell.

Vande Berg, Travis, and Fred Kniss. 2008. "ISKCON and Immigrants: The Rise, Decline, and Rise Again of a New Religious Movement." *Sociological Quarterly* 49(1): 79–104.

Vásquez, Manuel A. 1998. *The Brazilian Popular Church and the Crisis of Modernity.* Cambridge: Cambridge University Press.

Vazeilles, Danièle. 2008. "Connexions entre le néo-chamanisme et le néo-druidisme contemporains. Étude en anthropologie/ethnologie comparée." *Cahiers d'Études du Religieux. Recherches interdisciplinaires* 3. Accessed August 22, 2013. http://cerri.revues.org/161.

Vertovec, Steven. 2000. *The Hindu Diaspora: Comparative Patterns.* London: Routledge.

———. 1997. "Les religions de l'Asie du Sud en Grande Bretagne: influences et développements." In *Histoire religieuse de la Grande-Bretagne: XIXème-XXème siècle,* edited by Hugh McLeod, Stuart Mews and Christiane d'Haussy, 251–260. Paris: Cerf.

Voas, David, and Steve Bruce. 2007. "The Spiritual Revolution: Another False Dawn for the Sacred." In *A Sociology of Spirituality*, edited by Kieran Flanagan and Peter Jupp, 43–61. Aldershot: Ashgate.

Von Stuckrad, Kocku. 2003. "Le chamanisme occidental moderne et la dialectique de la science rationnelle." In *Chamanismes*, edited by Roberte Hamayon, 281–301. Paris: Quadrige/PUF.

Wallis, Roy. 1984. *The Elementary Forms of New Religious Life*. London: Routledge.

Waingort Novinsky, Anita 2010. *Os "Marranos" de Campina Grande: Uma Experiência Inesquecível*. São Paulo: Hineni.

———. 2006. "The Myth of the Marrano Names." *Revue des Études Juives* 165(3–4): 445–456.

Warrier, Maya. 2008. "Seekership, Spirituality and Self-discovery: Ayurveda Students in Britain." *Asian Medicine: Tradition and Modernity* 4: 423–451.

———. 2003. "Processes of Secularization in Contemporary India: Guru Faith in the Mata Amritanandamayi Mission." *Modern Asian Studies* 37(1): 213–253.

Waterhouse, Helen, and Tony Walter. 1999. "A Very Private Belief: Reincarnation in Contemporary England." *Sociology of Religion* 60(2): 187–197.

Waxman, Chaim I. 2003. "Identity and Identification of Jewish Baby Boomers." In *Contemporary Jewries: Convergence and Divergence*, edited by Eliezer Ben Rafael, Yosef Gorny, and Yaacov Ro'i, 151–160. Leiden: Brill.

Weber, Max. 1996. *The Religion of India*. New Delhi: Munshiram Manoharlal Publishers.

Weissler, Chava. 2011. "Performing Kabbalah in the Jewish Renewal Movement." In *Kabbalah and Contemporary Spiritual Revival*, edited by Boaz Huss, 39–74. Beer-Sheva: Ben-Gurion University of the Negev Press.

———. 2006. "Meanings of Shekhinah in the 'Jewish Renewal' Movement." *Nashim: A Journal of Jewish Women's Studies & Gender Issues* 10: 53–83.

———. 1989. *Making Judaism Meaningful: Ambivalence and Tradition in a Havurah Community*. New York: AMS Press.

Werczberger, Rachel. 2011. "Self, Identity and Healing in the Ritual of Jewish Spiritual Renewal in Israel." In *Kabbalah and Contemporary Spiritual Revival*, edited by Boaz Huss, 75–100. Beer-Sheva: Ben-Gurion University of the Negev Press.

Wertheimer, Jack. 1992. *The Uses of Tradition: Jewish Continuity in the Modern Era*. New York: Jewish Theological Seminary of America; London: Harvard University Press

Westerlund, David. 2004. "The Contextualisation of Sufism in Europe." In *Sufism in Europe and North America*, edited by David Westerlund, 13–35. London: Routledge.

Wilkes, George. 2005. "Jewish Renewal." In *Modern Judaism*, edited by Nicholas De Lange and Miri Freud-Kandel, 114–125. Oxford: Oxford University Press.

Williams, Raymond Brady. 2001. *An Introduction to Swaminarayan Hinduism*. Cambridge: Cambridge University Press.

———. 1992. *A Sacred Thread: Modern Transmission of Hindu Tradition in India and Abroad*. Chambersburg: Anima publications.

——. 1984. *A New Face of Hinduism: The Swaminarayan Religion.* Cambridge: Cambridge University Press.

Wilson, Bryan R. 1976. "Aspects of Secularization in the West." *Japanese Journal of Religious Studies* (3/4): 259–276.

Wolffe, John. 1994. "And There's Another Country"...Religion, State and British Identities." In *The Growth of Religious Pluralism: Britain from 1945,* edited by Gerald Parsons, 85–121. London; New York: Routledge in association with The Open University.

Wood, Matthew. 2010. "The Sociology of Spirituality: Reflections on a Problematic Endeavor." In *The New Blackwell Companion to the Sociology of Religion,* edited by Bryan S. Turner, 267–285. Oxford: Blackwell.

——. 2009. "The Nonformative Elements of Religious Life: Questioning the 'Sociology of Spirituality' Paradigm." *Social Compass* 56 (2): 237–248.

Wood, Matthew, and Véronique Altglas. 2010. "Reflexivity, Scientificity and the Sociology of Religion: Pierre Bourdieu in Debate." *Nordic Journal of Religion and Society,* 23(1): 9–26.

Wood, Matthew, and Bunn, Christopher. 2009. "Strategy in a Religious Network: A Bourdieuian Critique of the Sociology of Spirituality." *Sociology* 43(2): 286–303.

Woodhead, Linda. 2008. "Gendering Secularization Theory." *Social Compass* 55(2): 187–193.

Wootton, Jacqueline C., and Andrew Sparber. 2001. "Surveys of Complementary and Alternative Medicine: Part I. General Trends and Demographic Groups." *The Journal of Alternative and Complementary Medicine* 7(2): 195–208.

Wuthnow, Robert. 1998. *After Heaven: Spirituality in America since the 1950s.* Berkeley: University of California Press.

Yates, Frances. 1979. *The Occult Philosophy in the Elizabethan Age.* London: Arks Paperbacks.

Yeo, Kenneth A. 1987. *Siddha Yoga in Britain: A Case-Study of a New Religious Movement.* PhD diss., Norwich University of East Anglia.

Zafrani, Haïm. 1996. *Kabbale, vie mystique et magie: judaïsme d'Occident musulman.* Paris: Maisonneuve et Larose.

Zaidman, Nurit. 2000. "The Integration of Indian Immigrants to Temples run by North Americans." *Social Compass* 47(2): 187–204.

——. 1997. "When the Deities are Asleep: Processes of Change in an American Hare Krishna Temple." *Journal of Contemporary Religion* 12(3): 335–352.

——. 1996. "The American ISKCON Temple as a Global Site: The Forms of Interaction of Western Converts with Indian Immigrants." *Eastern Anthropologist* 49(3/4): 373–396.

Zaidman-Dvir, Nurit, and Stephen Sharot. 1992. "The Response of Israeli Society to New Religious Movements: ISKCON and Teshuvah." *Journal for the Scientific Study of Religion* 31(3): 279–295.

Zavos, John. 2008. "Stamp It Out! Disciplining the Image of Hindus and Hinduism in a Multicultural Milieu." *Contemporary South Asia* 16(3): 323–337.

Zilbergeld, Bernie. 1983. *The Shrinking of America: Myths of Psychological Change.* Boston; Toronto: Little Brown and Company.

PRIMARY SOURCES

Anon. n.d. "The Larger Perspective, Leaving Siddha Yoga." Accessed January 25, 2004. http://www.leavingsiddhayoga.net/larger_perspective.htm.

Ascent of Safed. n.d. "Ascent Shabbat Experience." Accessed August 22, 2013. http://ascentofsafed.com/cgi-bin/ascent.cgi?name=shabbat.

Berg, Karen. 2005. *God Wears Lipstick: Kabbalah for Women.* Canada: Research Centre of Kabbalah.

Berg, Michael. 2005. "Kabbalah for Everyone. Interview by Rebecca Phillips." Accessed August 22, 2013. http://www.beliefnet.com/Faiths/Judaism/2005/01/Kabbalah-For-Everyone.aspx.

———. 2001. *The Way: Using the Wisdom of Kabbalah for Spiritual Transformation and Fulfillment.* Hoboken: John Wiley & Sons.

Berg, Philip. 2009. *The Kabbalah Connection.* New York: The Kabbalah Centre International.

———. 2000. *Education of a Kabbalist.* Canada: Research Centre of Kabbalah.

———. 1995. *Kabbalah for the Layman 1.* USA: Kabbalah Learning Center.

———. 1993. *Miracles, Mysteries, and Prayer 1.* USA: Research Centre of Kabbalah.

———. 1987a. *Kabbalah for the Layman 2.* USA: Kabbalah Learning Center.

———. 1987b. *Kabbalah for the Layman 3.* USA: Research Centre of Kabbalah.

———. 1983. *The Kabbalah Connection.* USA: Research Centre of Kabbalah.

Berg, Yehuda. 2008a. *Kabbalah on the Sabbath.* Canada: Kabbalah Centre International.

———. 2008b. *Living Kabbalah: A Practical System for Making the Power Work for You.* USA: Kabbalah Centre International.

———. 2003a. *Kabbalistic Bible: Genesis.* USA: Kabbalah Publishing.

———. 2003b. *The Power of Kabbalah: Technology for the Soul.* London: Hodder and Stoughton.

Besant, Annie. 1993. *La Sagesse antique: exposé général de l'enseignement théosophique.* Paris: Adyar.

Blavatsky, Helena. P. 1951. *The Theosophical Movement, 1875–1950.* Los Angeles: Cunningham Press.

Bonder, Nilton. 1992. *A Cabala da Inveja.* Rio de Janeiro: Imago.

———. 1991. *A Cabala do Dinheiro.* Rio de Janeiro: Imago.

———. 1989. *A Dieta do Rabino: A Cabala da Comida.* Rio de Janeiro: Imago.

Brent, Peter Ludwig. 1972. *Godmen of India.* London: Penguin.

British Prime Minister Office. 2010. "Government Launches Big Society Programme." Accessed August 22, 2013. http://www.number10.gov.uk/news/big-society/.

British Wheel of Yoga. n.d. "About the BWY." Accessed June 16, 2012. http://www.bwy.org.uk/information/2/About_the_BWY.htm.

Brooks, Douglas R., et al. 1997. *Meditation Revolution: A History and Theology of the Siddha Yoga lineage.* New York: Agama Press.

Bruckner, Pascal. 1982. "Les gourous du troisième type." *Le Point* 506, May 31.

Bureau des Cultes. 2003. "Congrégation non Catholiques légalement reconnues au 1er mai 2003." Unpublished document.

Burke, Marie-Louise. *Swami Vivekananda in the West.* Calcutta: Advaita Ashrama, 1983–1986.

Cashman, Greer Fay. 2012. "Kabbala Comes to Ramallah." *The Jerusalem Post,* May 10.

CCMM. 2005. "L'abécédaire: Méditation." Accessed June 16, 2003. http://www.ccmm.asso.fr/spip.php?page=404.

Centre de Yoga Sivananda. n.d. "Qui Sommes nous?" Accessed August 22, 2013. http://www.sivananda.org/paris/centre_sivananda.html.

Chidananda. 2000. "What Is Yoga?" Accessed August 22, 2013. http://www.dlshq.org/discourse/apr2000.htm.

Chopra, Deepak. 1997. *The Seven Spiritual Laws of Success.* London: Rider.

——. 1993. *Creating Affluence: Wealth Consciousness in the Field of All Possibilities.* San Rafael: New World Library.

Cohen, Benjamin. 2003. "The Mainstreaming of McMysticism." *Jewsweek,* October 31.

Cole, Richard J. 2007. "Forty Years of Chanting: A Study of the Hare Krishna Movement from its Foundation to the Present Day." In *The Hare Krishna Movement: Forty Years of Chant and Change,* edited by Graham Dwyer and Richard J. Cole, 26–53. London; New York: Tauris and Co.

Cushman, Anne, and Jerry Jones. 1998. *From Here to Nirvana: The Yoga Journal Guide to Spiritual India.* New York: Riverhead Books.

Department of the Environment, Transport and the Regions. 1997. *Involving Communities in Urban and Rural Regeneration: A Guide for Practitioners.* Great Britain: DETR.

Divine Life Society. 2011. *The Science of Seven Cultures by Sivananda.* Accessed June 22, 2013. http://www.sivanandaonline.org/public_html/?cmd=displaysection&section_id=1524.

Durgananda. 2010. "From Emotion to Devotion." *YOGALife* Winter: 14–15.

——. 2008. "Be Up and Doing: The Yoga of Action." *YOGALife* Summer: 13–16.

——. 2006. "Practice with Understanding." *YOGALife* Spring/Summer: 22–24.

Engardio, Pete. 2006. "Karma Capitalism." *Business Week,* October 30.

Eshman, Rob. 2007. "Maybe It's Not So Weird after All." *Jewish Journal,* December 6.

Fajnkuchen, Laurent. 1997. "Sarcelles se débarrasse de son Zohar." *Actualité Juive,* February 6.

GEMPPI. 2003. *Découvertes sur les Sectes et les Religions* 59, October.

Gest, Alain, and Jacques Guyard. 1996. *Les Sectes en France*. Paris: Assemblée Nationale.

Gilmore, Inigo. 2004. "Opponents United in Protest against 'Pilgrim' Madonna." *The Telegraph*, September 17.

Graham, Michael. 2001. *From Guru to God: The Experience of Ultimate Truth*. Australia: U-turn Press.

Greene, Jamie. 2010. "About Jamie Greene." Accessed August 22, 2013. http://jamiegreene.la/about/.

Gurumayi. 1994. *My Lord Loves a Pure Heart*. United States: SYDA Foundation.

Hachesed. n.d. "Your Once-In-A-Lifetime Mystical Tours of Israel." Accessed July 6, 2012. http://www.hachesed.com/mystical_tours.asp.

Harris, Lis. 1994. "O Guru, Guru, Guru." *The New Yorker*, November 14.

Hayes, Peter. 1988. *The Supreme Adventure: The Experience of Siddha Yoga*. New York: Aquarian.

Hazan, Jenny. 2003. "Israelis Distribute Mystical 'Zohar' to Palestinians." *The Jerusalem Post*, March 12.

Hindu Council of the UK. 2012. "Home." Accessed August 22, 2013. http://www.hinducounciluk.org/.

Home Office. 2004. *Working Together: Co-operation Between Government and Faith Communities*, London: Home Office.

Horn, Marcia L. 2005. "Kabbalah in Kansas City." *The Kansas City Jewish Chronicle*, January 15.

India Link International. 2004. "Sri Sri Ravi Shankar, Head of Art of Living Movement Speaks Out." Accessed August 22, 2013. http://www.indialink-online.com/index.php?id=98.

Jewish Community Relations Council of Greater Philadelphia. 1978. *The Challenge of the Cults: An Examination of the Cult Phenomenon and its Implications for the Jewish Community*. Philadelphia: Jewish Community Relations Council of Greater Philadelphia.

Kabbalah Centre. 2012a. *Zohar Scanning Chart 2012–2013*. Accessed August 22, 2013. cdn1.Kabbalah.com/files/scanchart12_13_eng.pdf.

———. 2012b. "Create a Personal Study Plan." Accessed August 22, 2013. http://www.Kabbalah.com/student-support.

———. 2011a. "In Depth with Karen Berg." *Sparks* 4, Fall/Rosh Hashanah.

———. 2011b. "Kabbalah and Christianity with Billy Phillips." Accessed August 22, 2013. http://www.Kabbalah.com/Kabbalah_tv/billy_phillips.webloc.

———. 2007a. *The Living Kabbalah System Level 2: Into the Light*. [Learning Package]. USA: Kabbalah Centre International.

———. 2007b. "Frequently Asked Questions." Accessed November 6, 2007. https://www.Kabbalah.com/03.php.

———. 2007c. "Relationships." Accessed November 6, 2007. http://www.Kabbalah.com/14.php.

———. 2006a. "About the Centre." Accessed November 6, 2007. https://www.72.com/lks/about_centre.php.

———. 2006b. *Discover Kabbalah: Timeless Principles for Achieving Fulfillment at its Core.* [DVD]. USA: Kabbalah Centre International.

———. 2004a. "Welcome to Kabbalah.com!" Accessed November 6, 2007. https://www.Kabbalah.com/k/index.php/p=about/welcome.

———. 2004b. "Yom Kippur." Accessed November 6, 2007. https://www.Kabbalah.com/k/index.php/p=life/holidays/yomkippur.

———. 2004c. "Rabbi Michael Berg." Accessed November 6, 2007. https://www.Kabbalah.com/k/index.php/p=about/masters/michael.

———. 2004d. "Rabbi Yehuda Berg." Accessed November 6, 2007. https://www.Kabbalah.com/k/index.php/p=about/masters/yehuda.

———. 2004e. "Rosh Hashanah." Accessed November 6, 2007. https://www.Kabbalah.com/k/index.php/p=life/holidays/roshhashanah.

———. 2004f "Shabbat." Accessed November 6, 2007. https://www.Kabbalah.com/k/index.php/p=life/tools/shabbat.

———. 2004g. "Studying the Zohar." Accessed November 6, 2007. https://www.Kabbalah.com/k/index.php/p=zohar/about/studying.

———. n.d.a. *The Kabbalah Centre: Everything You Always Wanted to Know...* Brochure collected in 2007–2008, London.

———. n.d.b. "Worldwide Zohar Projects." Accessed November 6, 2007. http://www.Kabbalah.com/k/index.php/p=zohar.

Krishna, Gopala. 1995. *The Yogi: Portrait of Swami Vishnu-Devananda.* Saint Paul Minnesota: Yes International Publishers.

Krishnafrance. 2006. "L'Iskcon et l'hindouisme." Accessed June 16, 2012. http://goloka.free.fr/Krishnafrance/mouvement-dans_le_monde-ofla.htm.

Kuczynski, Alex. 2001. "Spiritual Balm, at Only $23.95." Accessed October 21, 2008. http://www.rickross.com/reference/deepakchopra/deepakchopra17.html.

Le Parisien. 2011. "Les Hindous préparent l'anniversaire de Ganesh." August 27.

Lecadre, Renaud. 2003. "Kabbale business." *Libération*, November 18.

Lemle, Alfred. 1998. *O homem que gostava da gente.* Rio de Janeiro: Imago.

Lifschutz, Yisrael. 1975. "The Transformation of Philip Berg." *Jewish Look* 1(6): 16–17.

Living Kabbalah System. 2006a. "What Is Kabbalah?" Accessed February 2, 2012. https://www.72.com/lks/about_Kabbalah.php.

———. 2006b. "What Is Living Kabbalah System?" Accessed June 3, 2010. https://www.72.com/lks/about_lks.php.

Local Government Association. 2002. *Faith and Community: A Good Practice Guide for Local Authorities.* Great Britain: LGA.

London Kabbalah Centre. 2011. "Business Gym Network." Accessed August 24, 2011. http://www.Kabbalahcentre.co.uk/charitable-projects/business-gym-network/.

———. 2008a. *Pesach 2008.* Brochure, London.

———. 2008b. *Course Program September 2008–January 2009.* Brochure, London.

——. 2007a. *Course Program June–December 2007*. Brochure, London.

——. 2007b. *Course Program 23–29 March 2007*. Brochure, London.

London Sivananda Centre. n.d. *Certificate Courses*. Accessed March 11, 2013, from http://www.sivananda.org/london/residential_courses.html.

Magnet, Julia. 2004. "Who's that girl?" *Daily Telegraph*, June 18.

Manhattan Kabbalah Centre. 2010. "Creating Yourself #7." Accessed August 7, 2012. http://www.meetup.com/Kabbalahcentreny/events/12295522/.

Mann, Richard D. 1984. *The Light of Consciousness: Explorations in Transpersonal Psychology*. Albany: State University of New York Press.

MIVILUDES. 2005a. *Rapport au Premier Ministre*. Paris: La Documentation Française.

MIVILUDES. 2005b. *Le risque sectaire: année 2004*. Paris: La Documentation Française.

Muktananda. 1998. *Conversations with Swami Muktananda: The Early Years*. USA: SYDA Foundation.

——. 1996. *Bhagawan Nityananda of Ganeshpuri*. Ganeshpuri: Gurudev Siddha Peeth.

——. 1994. *From the Finite to the Infinite*. South Fallsburg: SYDA Foundation.

——. 1993. *The Self Is Already Attained*. South Fallsburg: SYDA Foundation.

——. 1981. *Where Are You Going?* USA: SYDA Foundation.

——. 1980. *Meditate*. Albany: State University of New York Press.

——. 1978. *In Company of a Siddha: Interviews and Conversations with Swami Muktananda*. Oakland: SYDA Foundation.

——. 1977. *Siddha Meditation: Commentaries on the Shivasutras and Other Sacred Texts*. Oakland: SYDA Foundation.

Naam Yoga. n.d. "Universal Kabbalah." Accessed August 22, 2013. http://www.naamyoga.com/universal-Kabbalah.html.

National Council of Hindu Temples. 2005. "Welcome to the Website of National Council of Hindu Temples UK." Accessed August 22, 2013. http://www.nchtuk.org/.

Pereira, Paula. 2003. "O poder da cabala." *Epoca*, July 11.

Reform Judaism. 2010. "Where Are Our Synagogues?" Accessed August 22, 2013. http://www.reformjudaism.org.uk/about-us/where-are-our-synagogues.html.

Rifkin, Ira. 2007. "Mysticism for All?" *Fort Worth Star-Telegram*, January 20.

Rothschild, Nathalie. 2007. "Kabbalah: Therapy with a dash of Mysticism." *Spiked*, July 4.

Rowan, David. 2004a. "Strings Attached: The Kabbalah Centre Exposed." *The Times*, April 3.

——. 2004b. "Chief Rabbi Sounds Alarm on Mystical Kabbalah group." *The Times*, April 3.

——. 2002. "The Kabbalah Centre Exposed: Investigation." *Evening Standard*, October 3.

Safed World Kabbalah Center, n.d. "Kabbalah Tour." Accessed August 22, 2013. http://www.tzfat-Kabbalah.org/minisite.asp.

Shelden, Michael. 2003. "We're Always There for Madonna." *Daily Telegraph*, August 12.

Siddha Yoga. 2003. "The Chanting." Accessed December 11, 2003. http://www.siddhayoga.org/practices/chanting/chanting.html.

Siddha Yoga Dham France. 2011. "Les Centres de Méditation Siddha Yoga Francophones." Accessed June 16, 2012. http://www.siddhayogafrance.org/siddhayoga-centers.htm.

———. 2005. "Cours sur le message 2004/2005." Accessed April 5, 2005. http://www.siddhayogafrance.org/cours-bruxelles.htm.

———. 1983. *Les Nouvelles du Siddha Yoga* 9.

———. 1982. *Les Nouvelles du Siddha Yoga* 6.

Sitruk, Joseph. 2006. *Le cours du Grand Rabbin de France*. [Audio]. Épinay-sur-Seine: Dvar Torah.

Sivananda, 2001 [1938]. *Practical Lessons in Yoga*. Accessed August 22, 2013. http://www.dlshq.org/download/practical.pdf.

———. 2000 [1958]. *Autobiography of Swami Sivananda*. Accessed August 22, 2013. http://www.dlshq.org/download/autobio.htm.

———. 1999 [1947]. *All about Hinduism*. Accessed August 22, 2013. http://www.dlshq.org/download/hinduismbk.htm.

———. 1999 [1946]. *What Becomes of the Soul after Death*. Accessed August 22, 2013. http://www.dlshq.org/download/afterdeath.htm.

———. 1998 [1947]. *Essence of Yoga*. Accessed August 22, 2013. http://www.dlshq.org/download/essence_yoga.htm.

———. 1998 [1940]. *Mind: Its Mysteries and Control*. Accessed August 22, 2013. http://www.dlshq.org/download/mind.htm.

———. 1950. *How to Become Rich, by . . . Swami Sivananda*, Rishikesh: Yoga Vedanta Forest University.

———. 1949. *Moksha Gita*. Accessed August 22, 2013. http://www.Swami-Krishnananda.org/moksh/moksh_06.html.

Sivananda Ashram Yoga Camp. n.d. "Teacher Training Course." Accessed August 22, 2013. http://www.sivananda.org/camp/?page_id=1040.

Sivananda Centres. 2012. "Our Ashrams in India." Accessed August 22, 2013. http://www.sivananda.org/india/default.htm.

———. 1998. "Memories of Swami Vishnu-Devananda." *YOGALife*, Spring.

———. 1994. "Years with the Master." *YOGALife*, Spring.

———. n.d.a. "Executive Board." Accessed August 22, 2013. http://www.sivananda.org/about/ebm.html.

———. n.d.b. "Teachings." Accessed August 22, 2013. http://www.sivananda.org/teachings/.

———. n.d.c. "The Four Paths of Yoga." Accessed August 22, 2013. http://www.sivananda.org/teachings/fourpaths.html#jnana.

Sivananda Yoga Vedanta Dhanwantari Ashram. n.d. "Special programs." Accessed October 27, 2003. http://www.sivananda.org/neyyardam/special.html.

Sri Chinmoy. n.d. "Un entretien avec Sri Chinmoy." Brochure, Centre Sri Chinmoy, Paris.

Sri Sri Ravi Shankar. n.d. "Official website." Accessed August 22, 2013. http://srisri-ravishankar.org/.

The Jewish Chronicle. 2011. "The Rebranding of Kabbalah." March 4.

Tucker, Karen Iris. 2011. "Sandra Bernhard Shows Her Softer Side: Acerbic Comedian Settles Down at Home and in Shul." *The Jewish Daily Forward*, December 20.

Tugend, Tom. 2008. "Kabbalah Centre Sues Former Directors." *The Jewish Chronicle*, October 17.

UK National Statistics. 2001. *Census 2001: National Report for England and Wales.* Accessed June 19, 2003. http://www.statistics.gov.uk/StatBase/Product.asp?vlnk =10441&Pos=&ColRank=1&Rank=422.

U.S. Census Bureau. 2009. "Table 74. Religious Composition of U.S. Population: 2007." *The Statistical Abstract 2009.* Accessed February 2, 2012. http://www.census.gov/ compendia/statab/2009/cats/population.html.

UNADFI. 2005. "Da Kabbalah Code." *Bulles* 85. Accessed August 22, 2013. http:// www.unadfi.org/IMG/pdf/Da_Kabbalah_Code.pdf.

———. 2002. "Paysage sectaire lié à la rencontre Orient Occident." *Bulles* 76. Accessed August 22, 2013. http://www.unadfi.org/paysage-sectaire-lie-a-la.html.

———. 1990a. "L'Orient dévoyé (1). Vrais et faux Gourous." *Bulles* 25. Accessed August 22, 2013. http://www.prevensectes.com/orient1.htm.

———. 1990b "L'Orient dévoyé (2). La Méditation comme Instrument de Dépendance." *Bulles* 26. Accessed August 22, 2013. http://www.prevensectes.com/orient2.htm.

United Synagogue. 2010. *Welcome to the United Synagogue.* Accessed August 22, 2013. http://www.theus.org.uk/the_united_synagogue/about_the_us/welcome.

Universal Kabbalah Network. 2007. "Universal Kabbalah in Contrast to Jewish Kabbalah." Accessed August 22, 2013. http://www.universalKabbalah.net/ vs_jewish_Kabbalah.

USAToday.com. 2004. "Kabbalah Expert: Yehuda Berg." May 25, 2004. Accessed August 22, 2013. http://cgi1.usatoday.com/mchat/20040526006/tscript.htm.

Vishnu-Devananda. 1995. "Swami Vishnu-Devananda Speaks on Samadhi, Rebirth & World Karma." *YogaLife, Fall.*

———. 1988 [1960]. *The Complete Illustrated Book of Yoga.* New York: Harmony Books.

———. 1985. "Lettre Ouverte: l'enseignement du Yoga." *Revue de Yoga Sivananda* 8: 12–14.

———. 1978. *Meditation and Mantras.* New York: OM Lotus Publishing Company.

Vishwa Samvad Kendra. 2011. "RSS Pays Shraddhanjali to Sri Sathya Sai Baba." Accessed August 22, 2013. http://samvada.org/2011/news/ rss-pays-tribute-to-sri-sathya-sai-baba/.

Vivekananda. 1985. *The Nationalistic and Religious Lectures of Swami Vivekananda.* Madras: Sri Ramakrishna Math.

——. 1968. *The Complete Works of Swami Vivekananda,* Vol. 2. Calcutta: Advaita Ashrama.

——. 1965. *The Complete Works of Swami Vivekananda,* Vol. 1. Calcutta: Advaita Ashrama.

——. 1964. *The Complete Works of Swami Vivekananda,* Vol. 3. Calcutta: Advaita Ashrama.

Weizman, Steve. 2007. "Madonna: I'm an 'Ambassador for Judaism.'" *The Huffington Post,* September 16.

Zimmerman, Mike. 2009. "Deepak Chopra: A Life of Fulfillment. On Moving from Success to Significance." *Success,* November 2.

Index